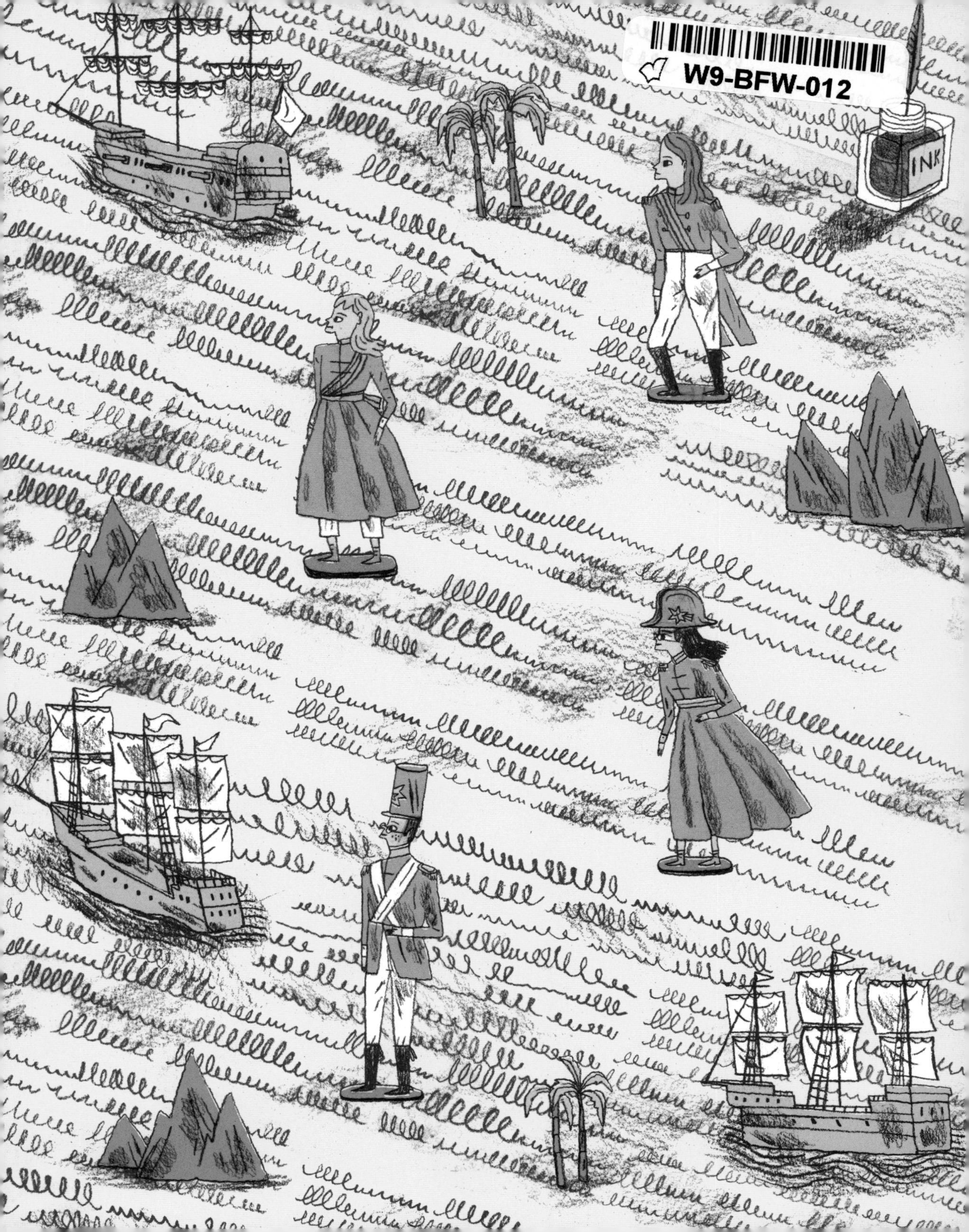
INK

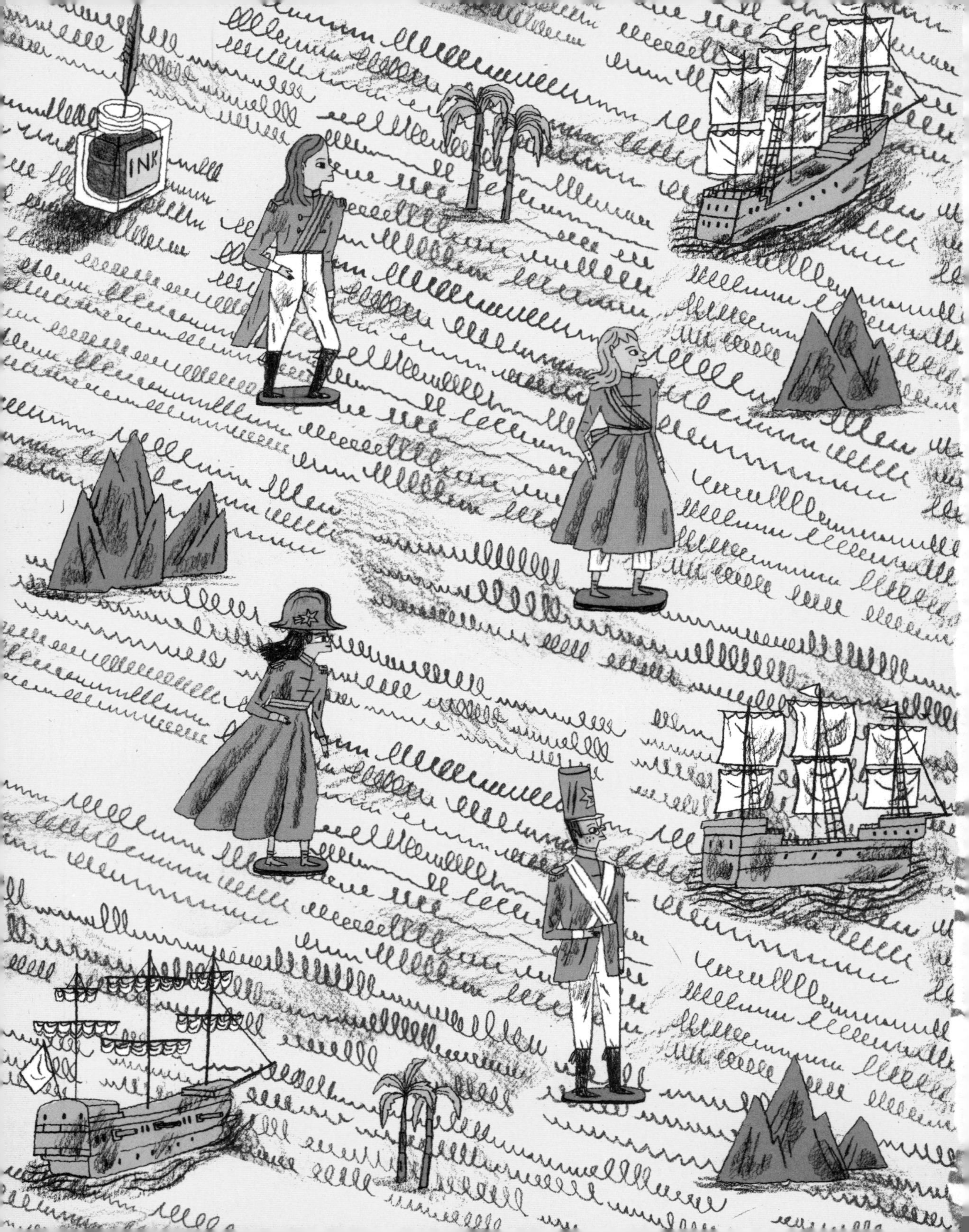
INK

Glass Town

Glass Town

ISABEL GREENBERG

ABRAMS COMICARTS, NEW YORK

Note to Reader

The following book is a work of historical fiction. Whilst some of the biographical details of the life of Charlotte Brontë and her siblings are accurate, I have, especially in the Glass Town sections of the book, embroidered, embellished, and indulged in a great deal of supposing.

What is indisputably true is that the Brontë siblings, throughout their childhood and teens, wrote vast amounts of poetry and stories set in the imaginary worlds of Angria and Gondal. All the characters you will meet, and many of the plot details, have been lifted directly from their juvenilia. But this is assuredly my Glass Town, so please expect inaccuracy and anachronisms and many flights of fancy, and enjoy this book as a work of fiction.

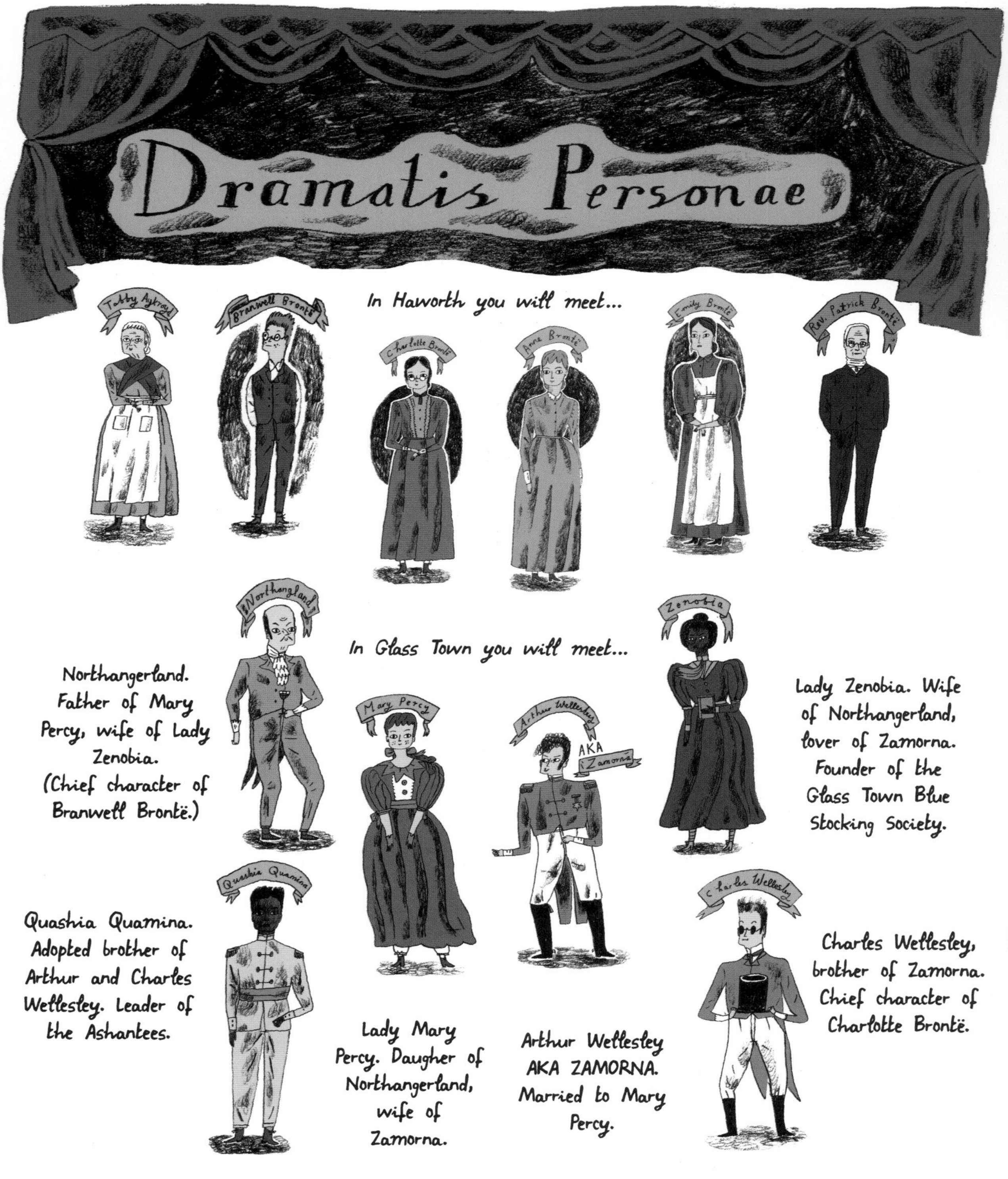
Dramatis Personae
In Haworth you will meet...
Tabby Aykroyd
Branwell Brontë
Charlotte Brontë
Anne Brontë
Emily Brontë
Rev. Patrick Brontë
In Glass Town you will meet...
Northangland
Northangerland. Father of Mary Percy, wife of Lady Zenobia. (Chief character of Branwell Brontë.)
Zenobia
Lady Zenobia. Wife of Northangerland, lover of Zamorna. Founder of the Glass Town Blue Stocking Society.
Mary Percy
Arthur Wellesley
AKA Zamorna
Quashia Quamina
Quashia Quamina. Adopted brother of Arthur and Charles Wellesley. Leader of the Ashantees.
Lady Mary Percy. Daugher of Northangerland, wife of Zamorna.
Arthur Wellesley AKA ZAMORNA. Married to Mary Percy.
Charles Wellesley
Charles Wellesley, brother of Zamorna. Chief character of Charlotte Brontë.

PROLOGUE

July 1849

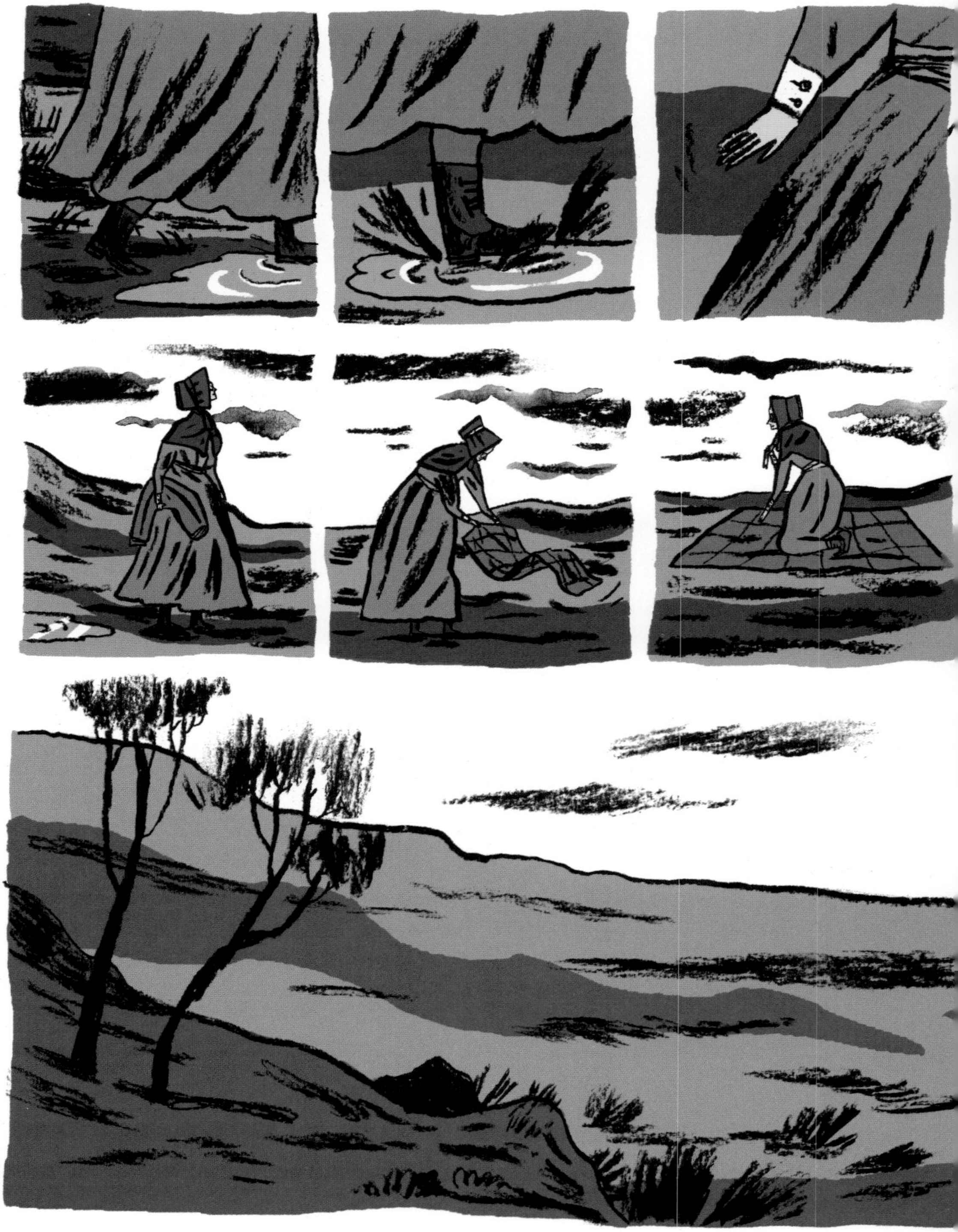

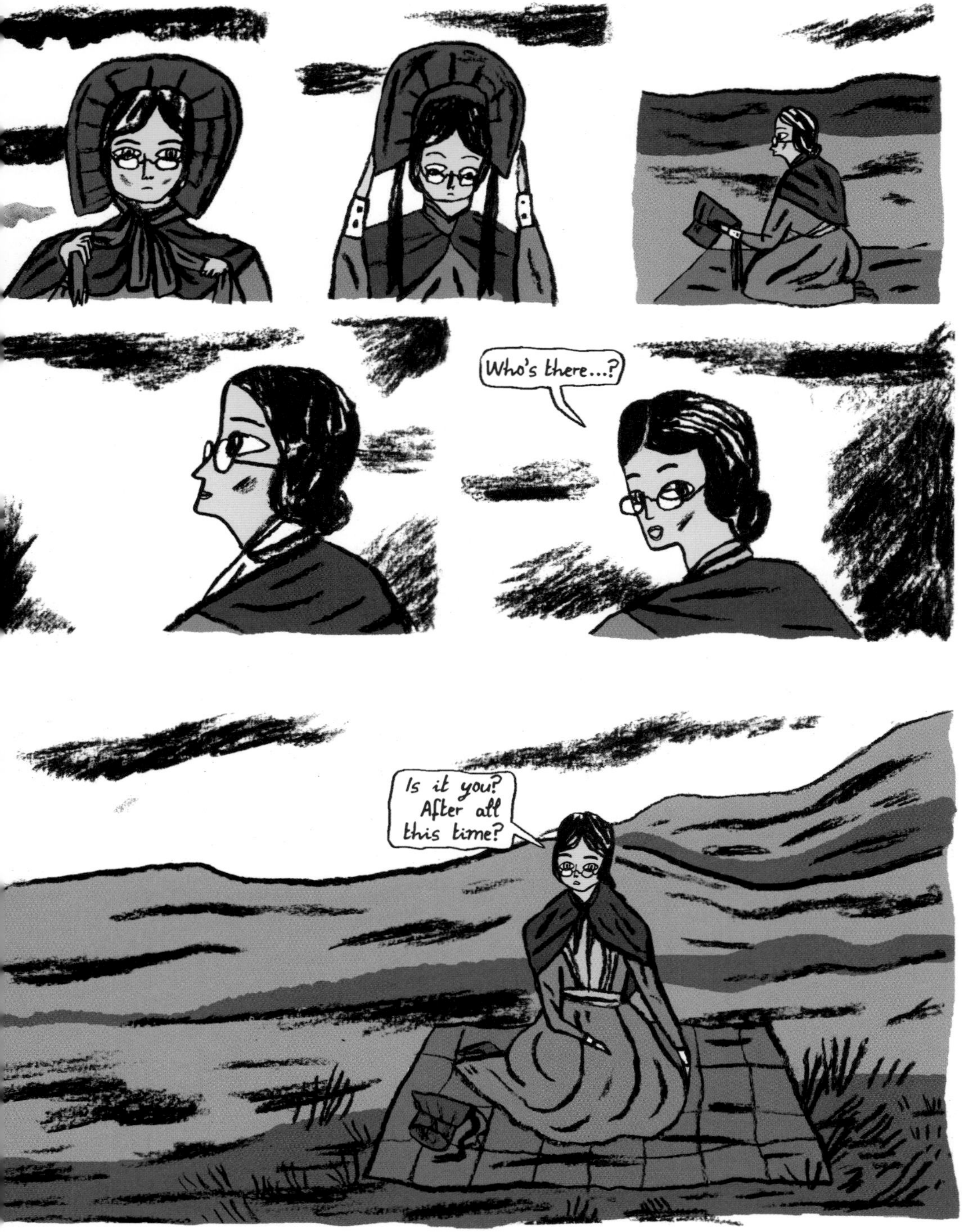
Who's there...?
Is it you? After all this time?

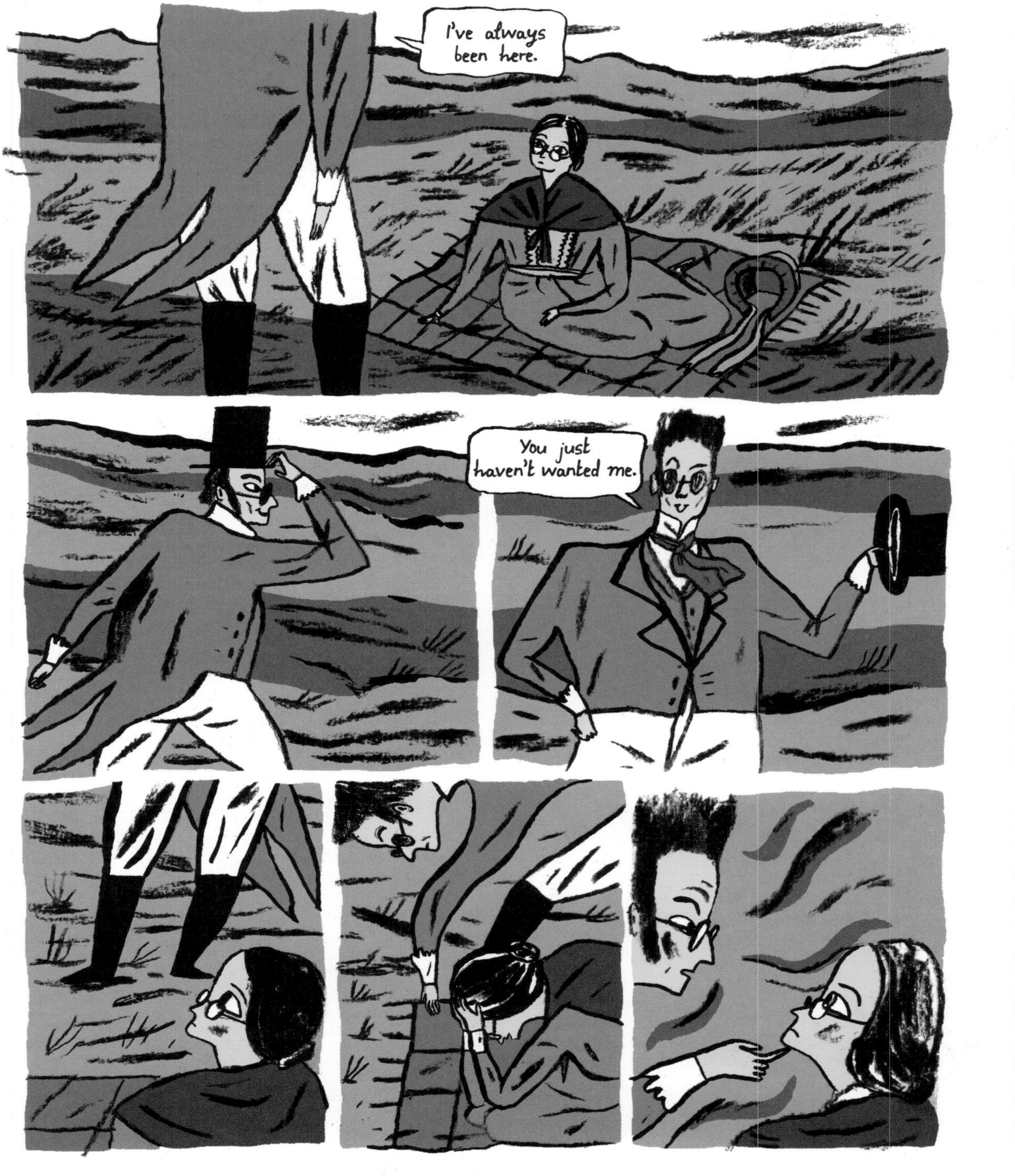
I've always been here.
You just haven't wanted me.

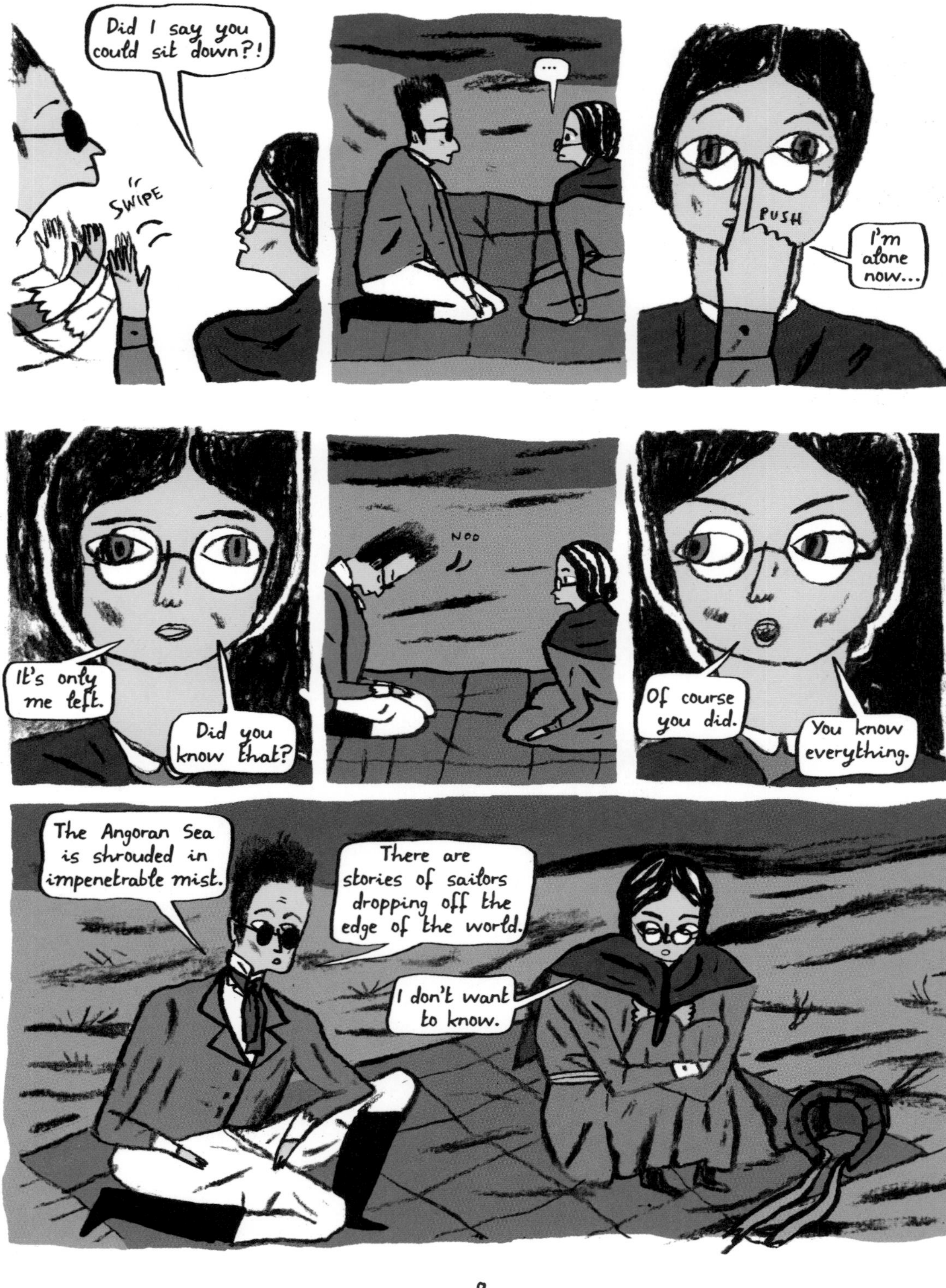
Did I say you could sit down?!
SWIPE
...
PUSH
I'm alone now...
It's only me left.
Did you know that?
NOD
Of course you did.
You know everything.
The Angoran Sea is shrouded in impenetrable mist.
There are stories of sailors dropping off the edge of the world.
I don't want to know.

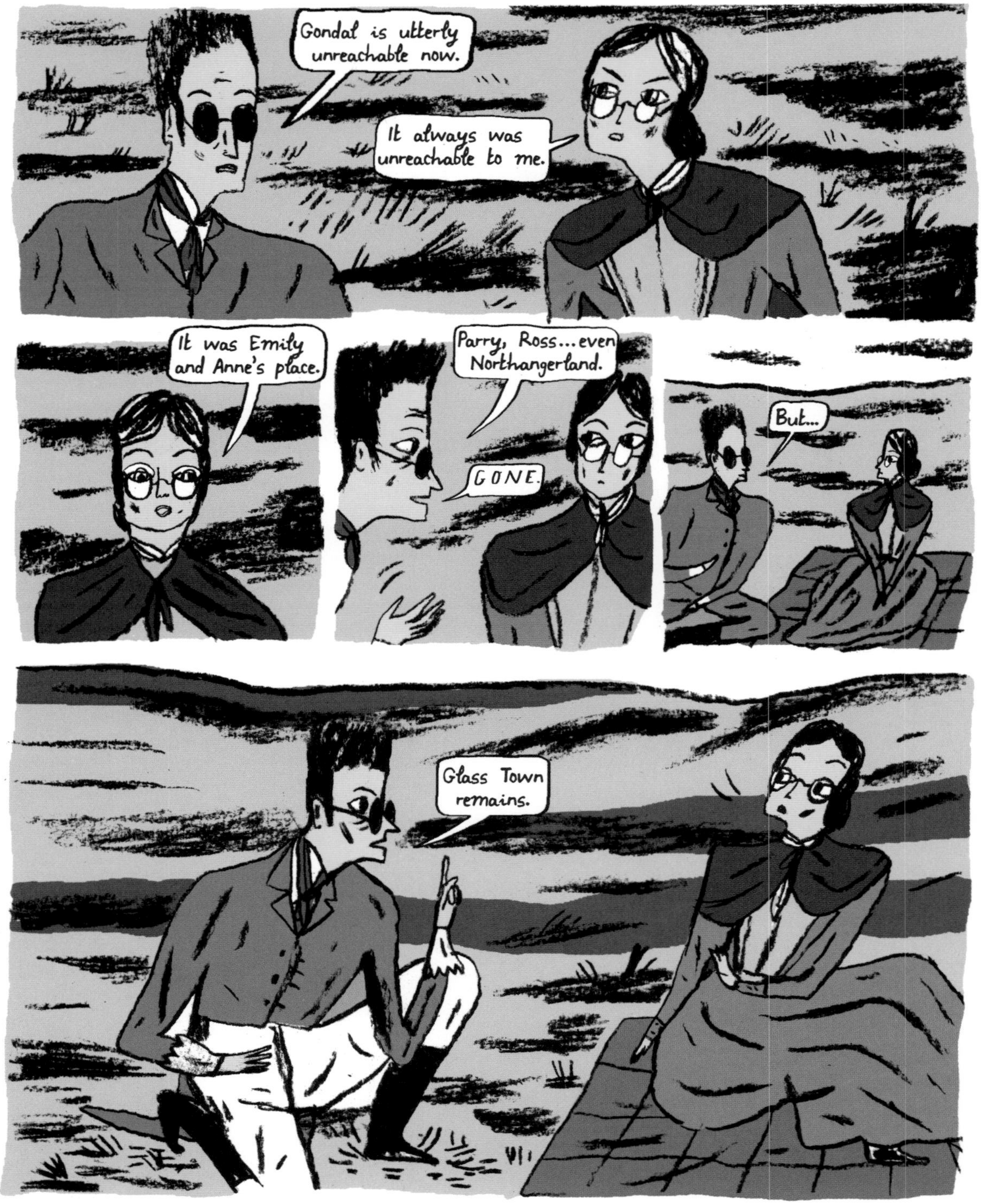
Gondal is utterly unreachable now.
It always was unreachable to me.
It was Emily and Anne's place.
Parry, Ross...even Northangerland.
GONE.
But...
Glass Town remains.

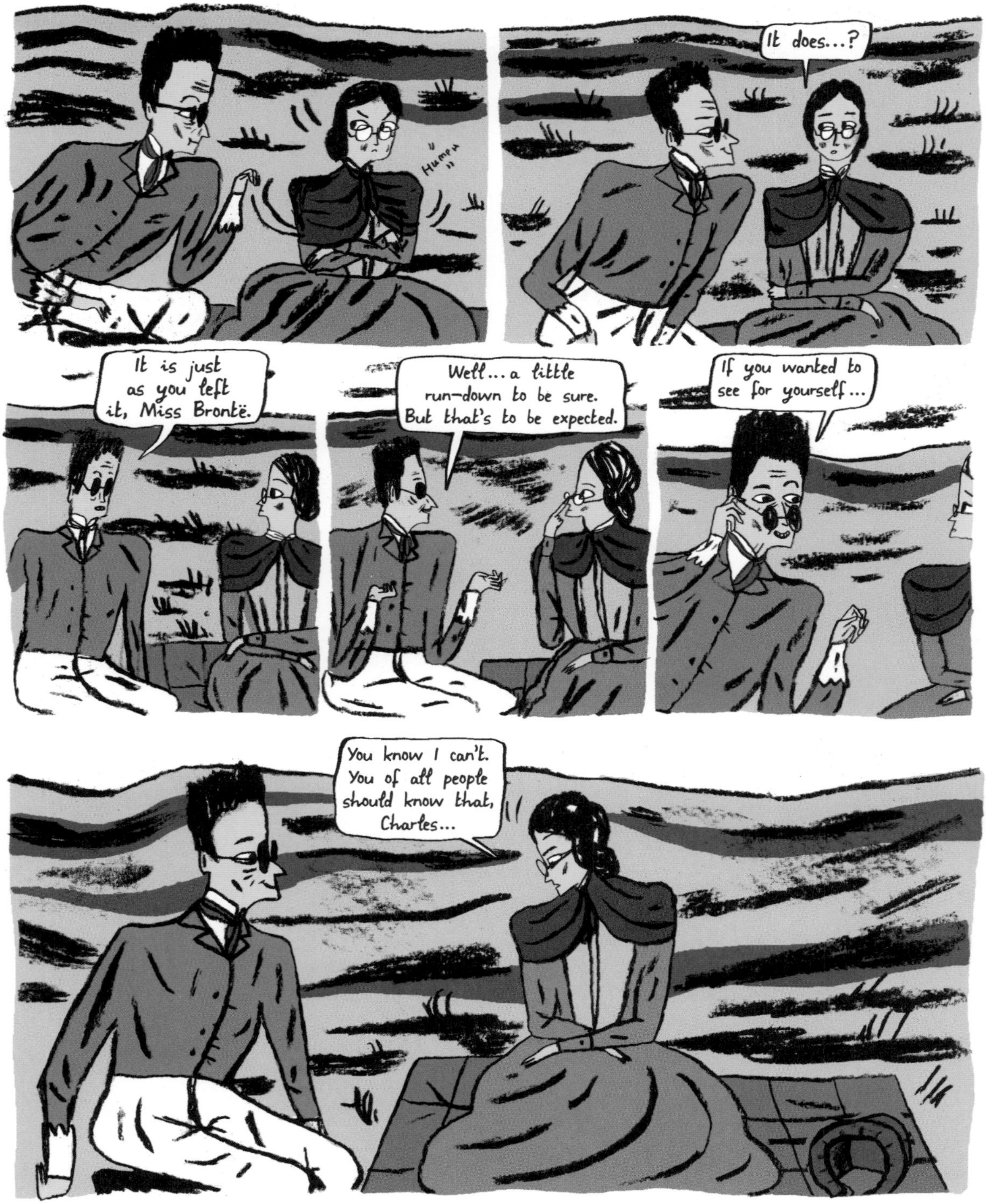
"Humph"
It does...?
It is just as you left it, Miss Brontë.
Well... a little run-down to be sure. But that's to be expected.
If you wanted to see for yourself...
You know I can't. You of all people should know that, Charles...

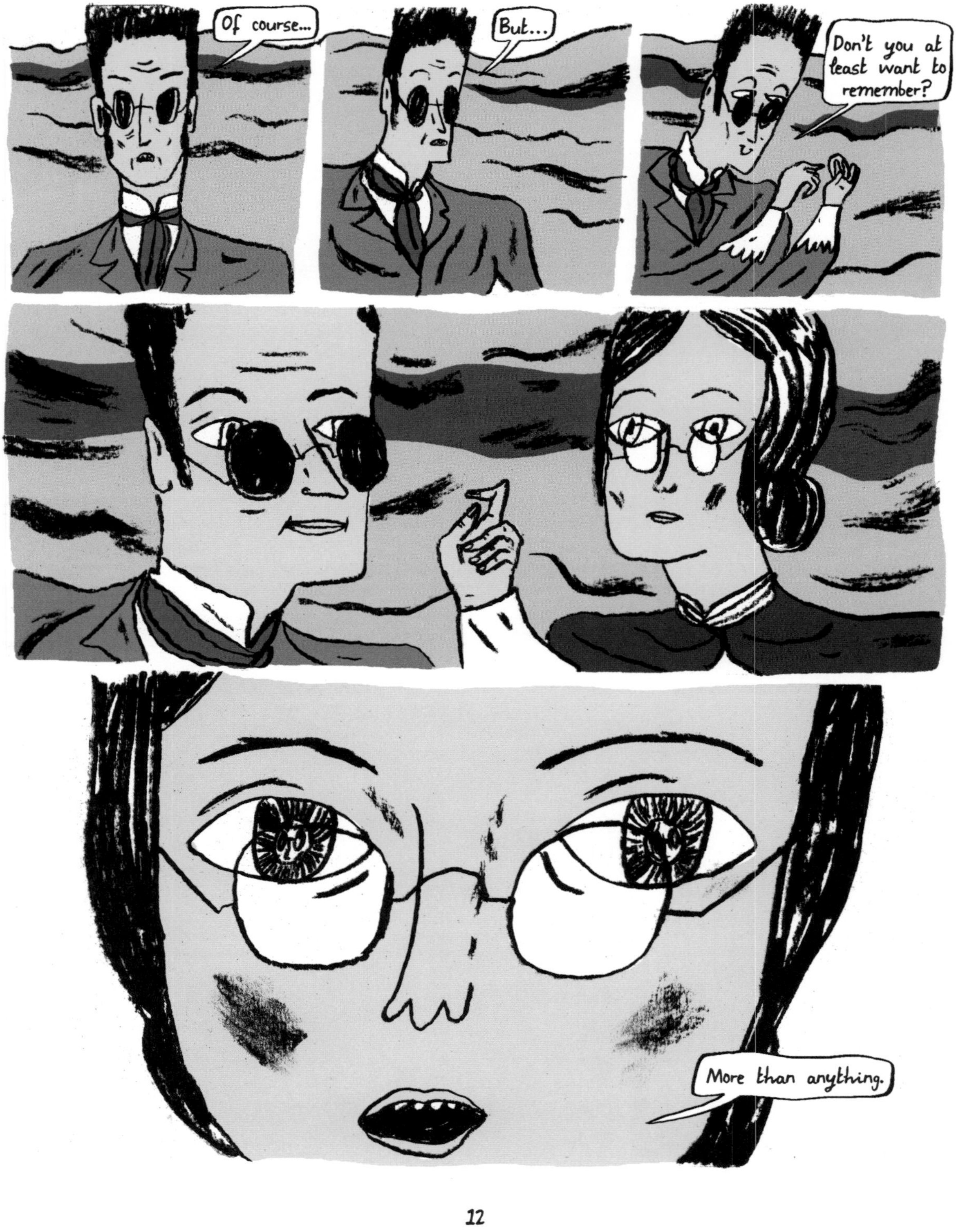
Of course...
But...
Don't you at least want to remember?
More than anything.

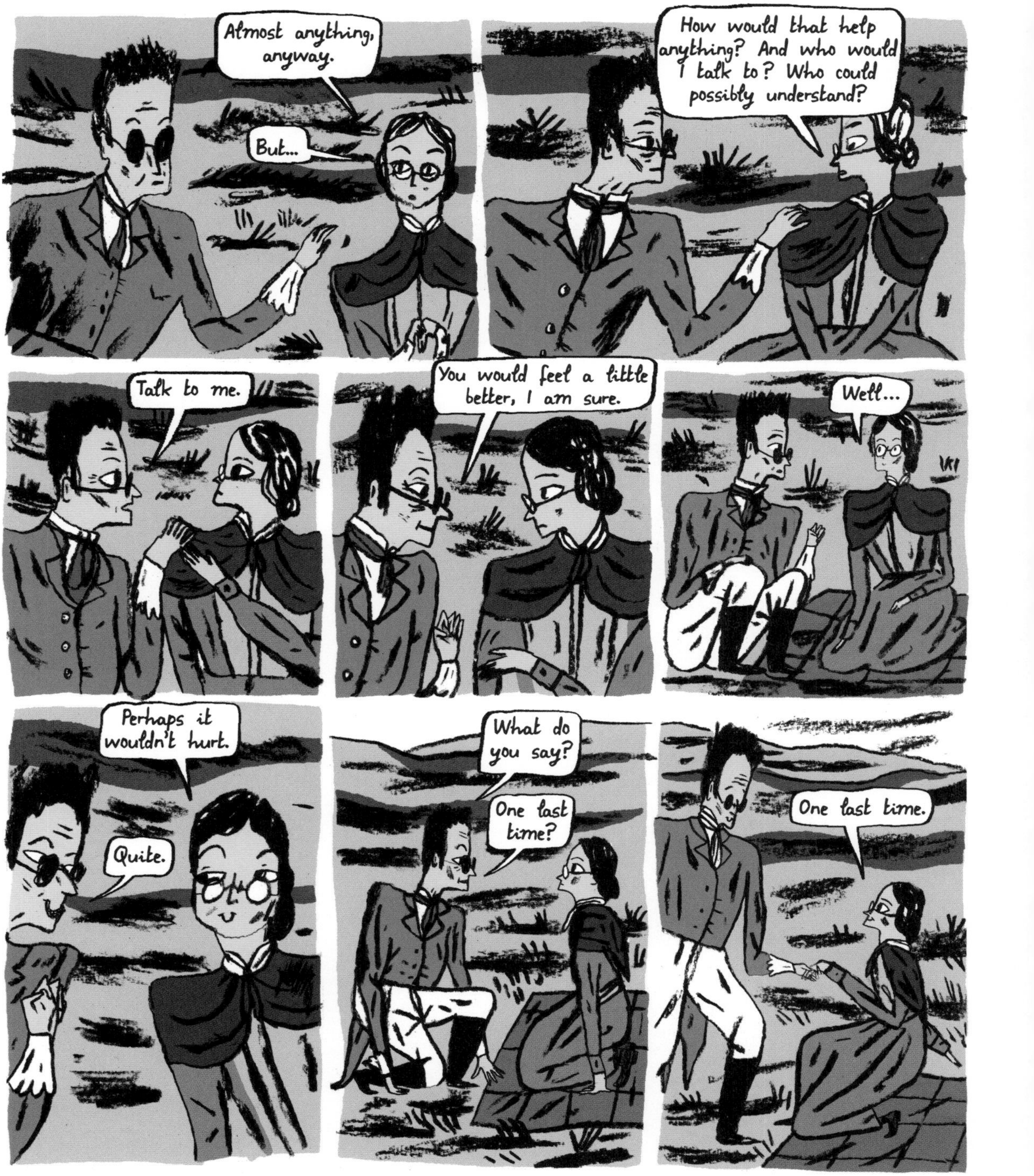
Almost anything, anyway.
But...
How would that help anything? And who would I talk to? Who could possibly understand?
Talk to me.
You would feel a little better, I am sure.
Well...
Perhaps it wouldn't hurt.
Quite.
What do you say?
One last time?
One last time.

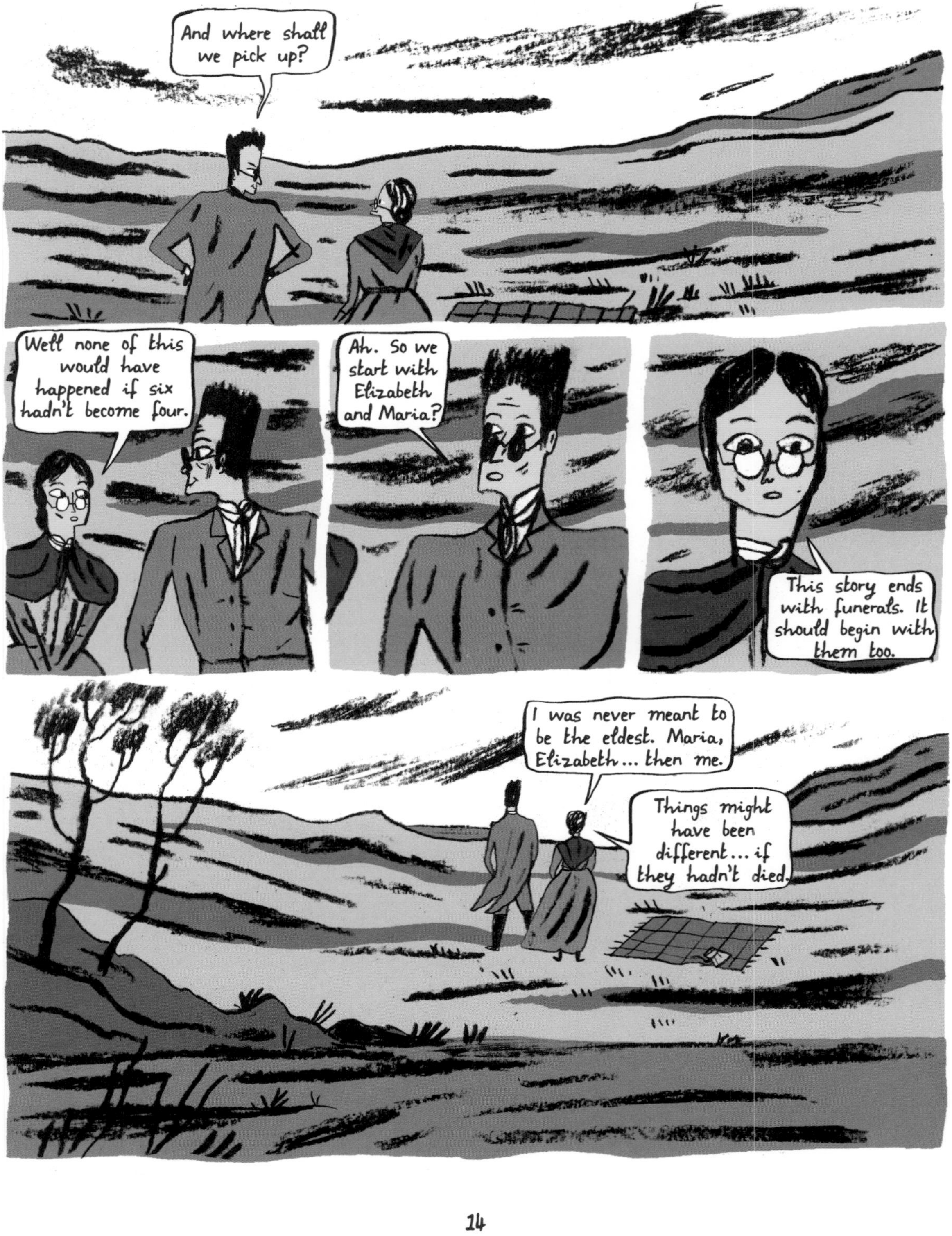
And where shall we pick up?
Well none of this would have happened if six hadn't become four.
Ah. So we start with Elizabeth and Maria?
This story ends with funerals. It should begin with them too.
I was never meant to be the eldest. Maria, Elizabeth... then me.
Things might have been different... if they hadn't died.

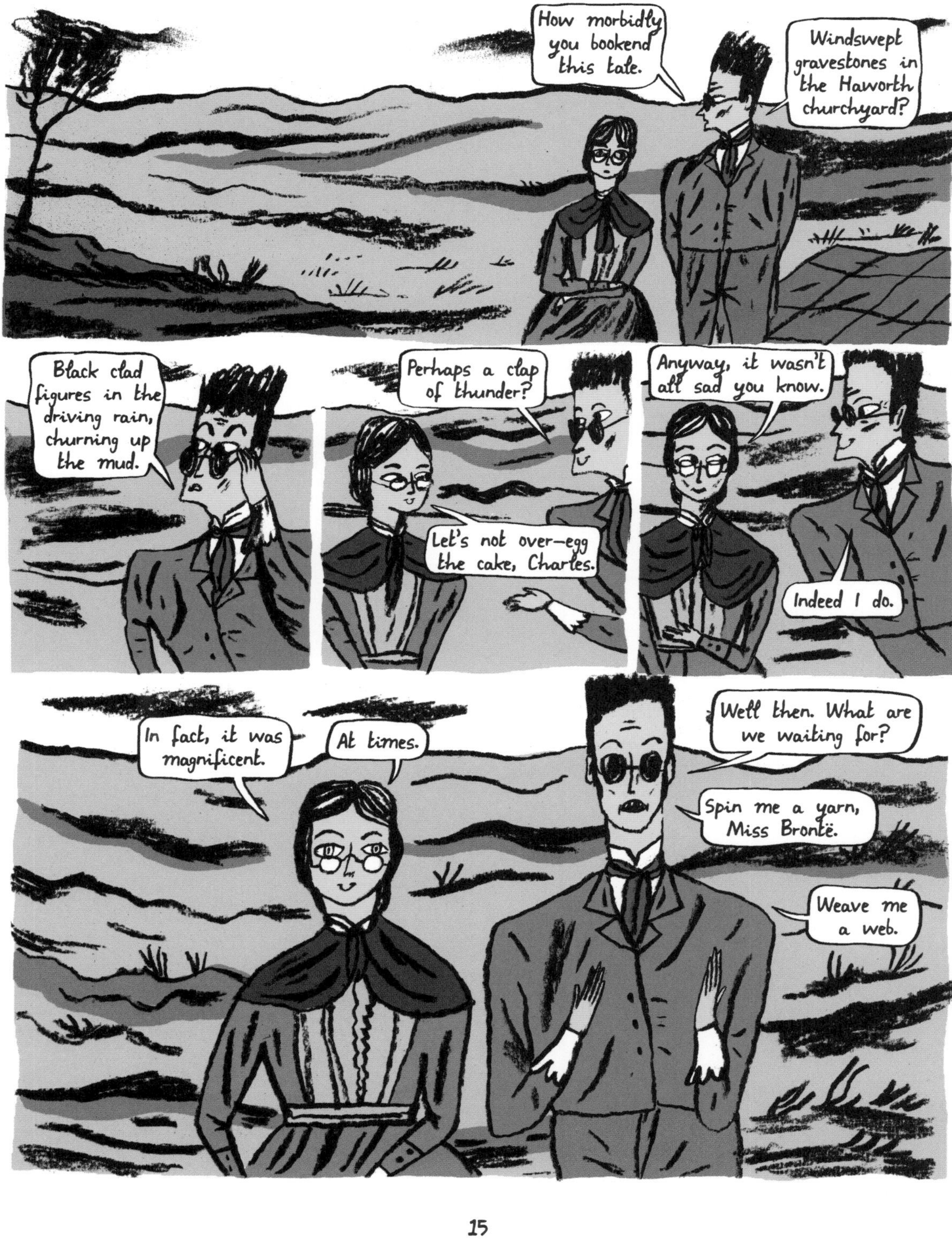
How morbidly you bookend this tale.
Windswept gravestones in the Haworth churchyard?
Black clad figures in the driving rain, churning up the mud.
Perhaps a clap of thunder?
Let's not over-egg the cake, Charles.
Anyway, it wasn't all sad you know.
Indeed I do.
In fact, it was magnificent.
At times.
Well then. What are we waiting for?
Spin me a yarn, Miss Brontë.
Weave me a web.

CHAPTER ONE

1825–1831

Weird Writings

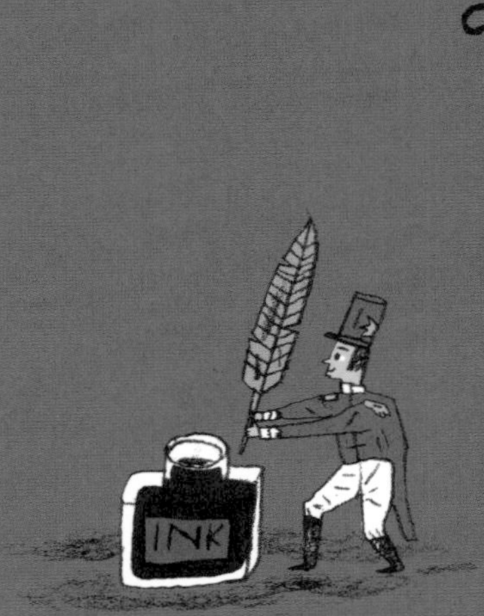
INK

The last house in Haworth was the parsonage. Its front faced out to the graveyard, to the grey roofs and sloping lanes of the town. But behind the house, there was nothing but the moors. Mile upon mile of wildness. There it teetered, and at night its windows were the only light before a great and infinite blackness.

Four children lived in that house.

And their names were Charlotte, Branwell, Emily and Anne.

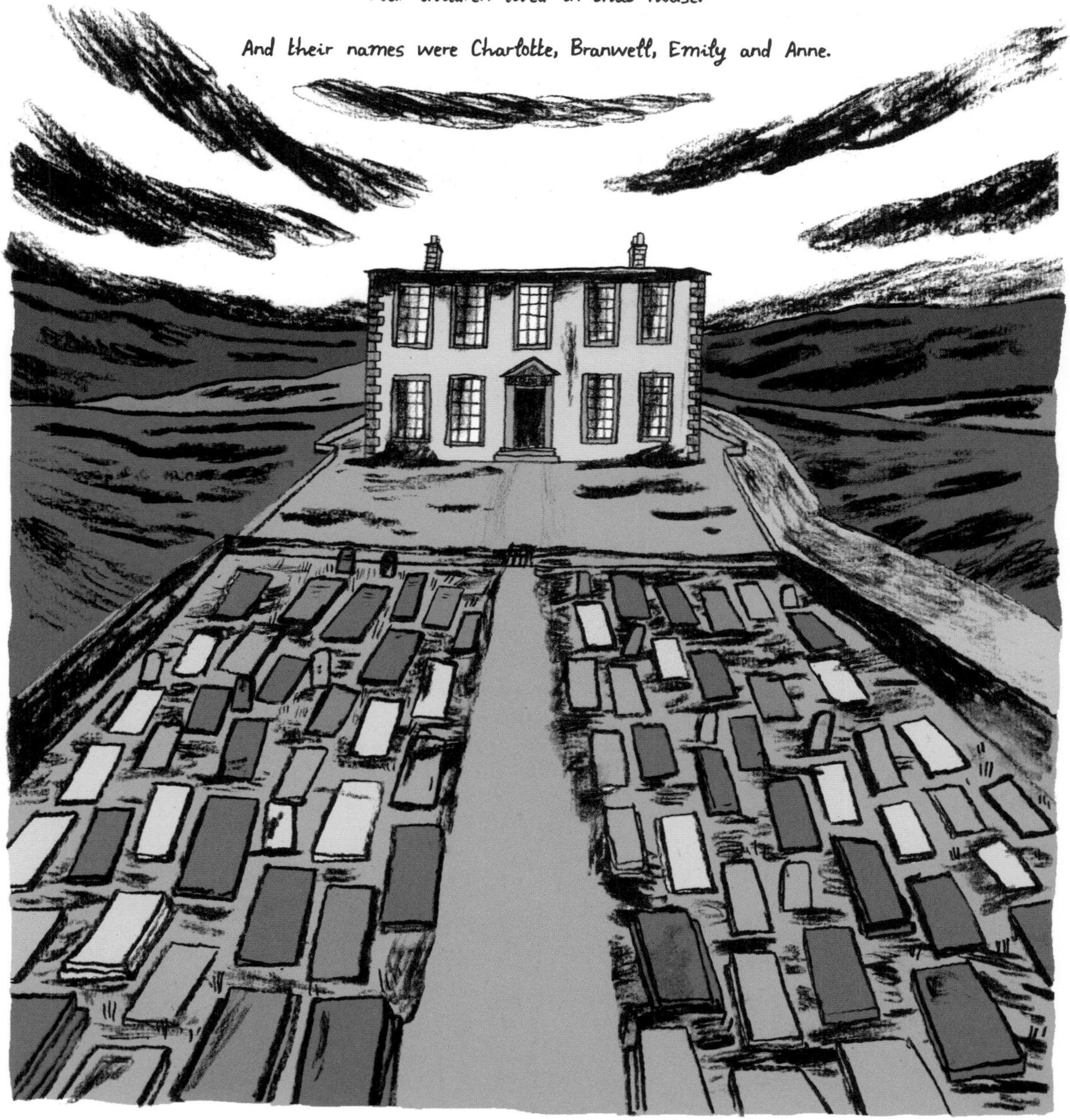

That's them there. Four forlorn little figures dressed in black.

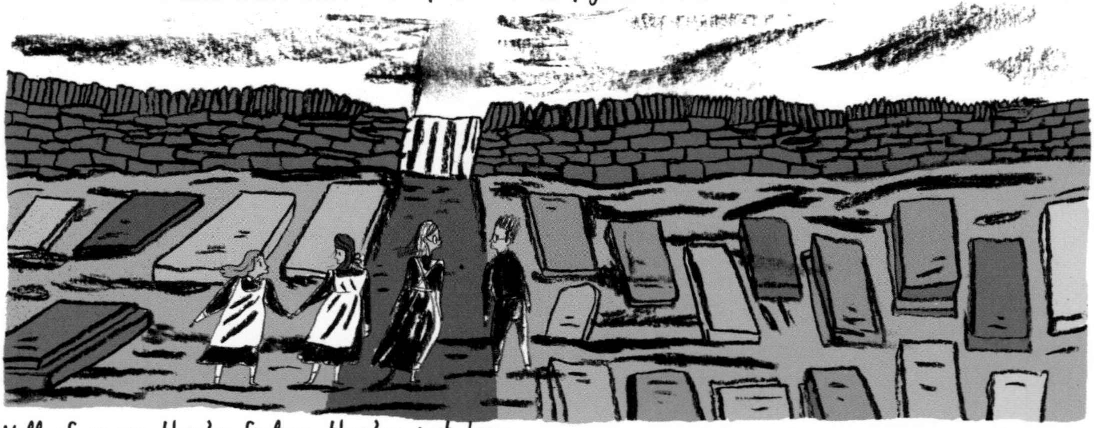

Well of course they're forlorn, they've just been to a funeral.

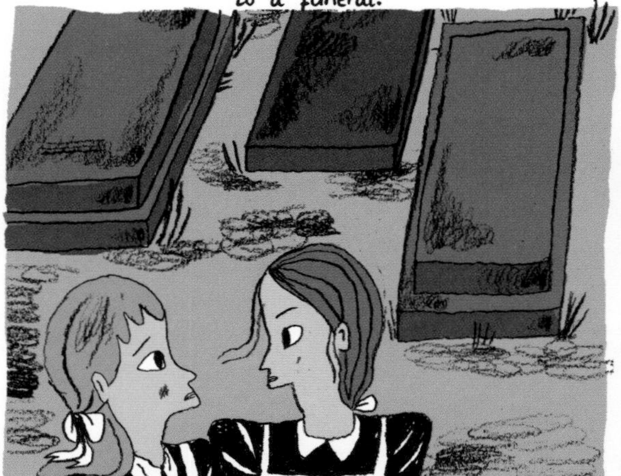

The second funeral in as many months.

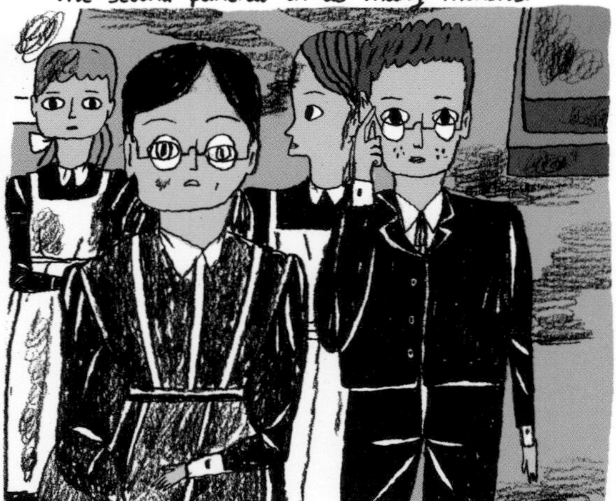

First Maria, then Elizabeth had returned home sick from Cowan Bridge School. And died.
The six Brontë siblings, who had already lost their mother, had become four.

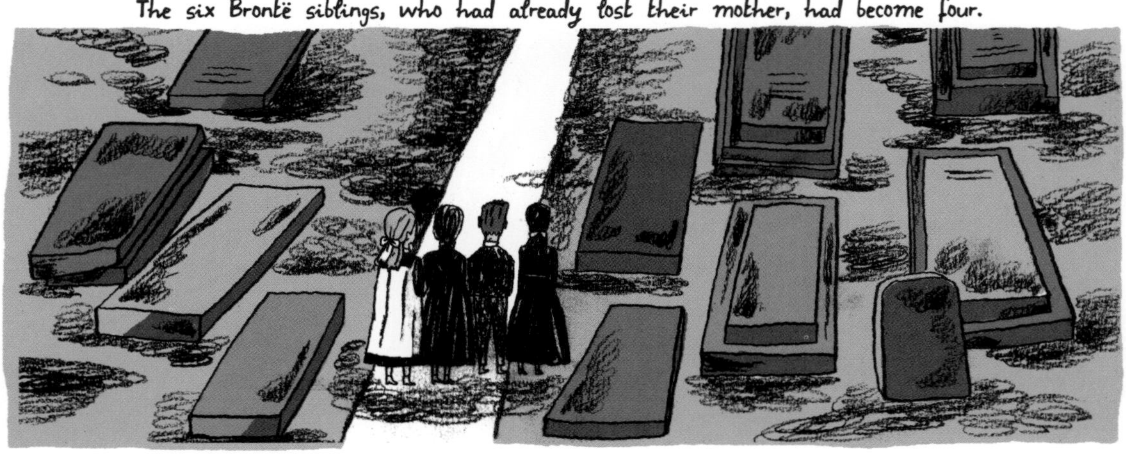

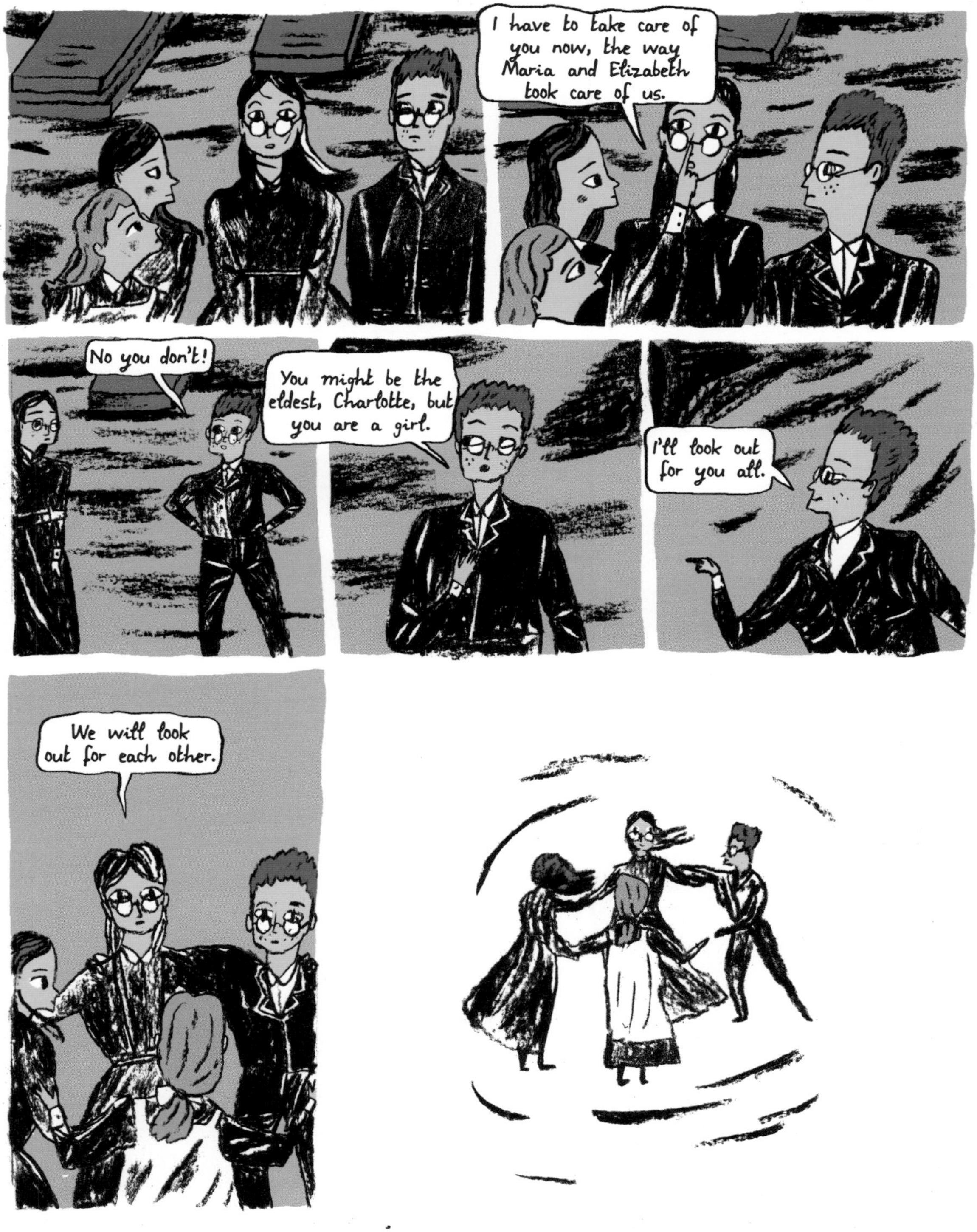
I have to take care of you now, the way Maria and Elizabeth took care of us.
No you don't!
You might be the eldest, Charlotte, but you are a girl.
I'll look out for you all.
We will look out for each other.

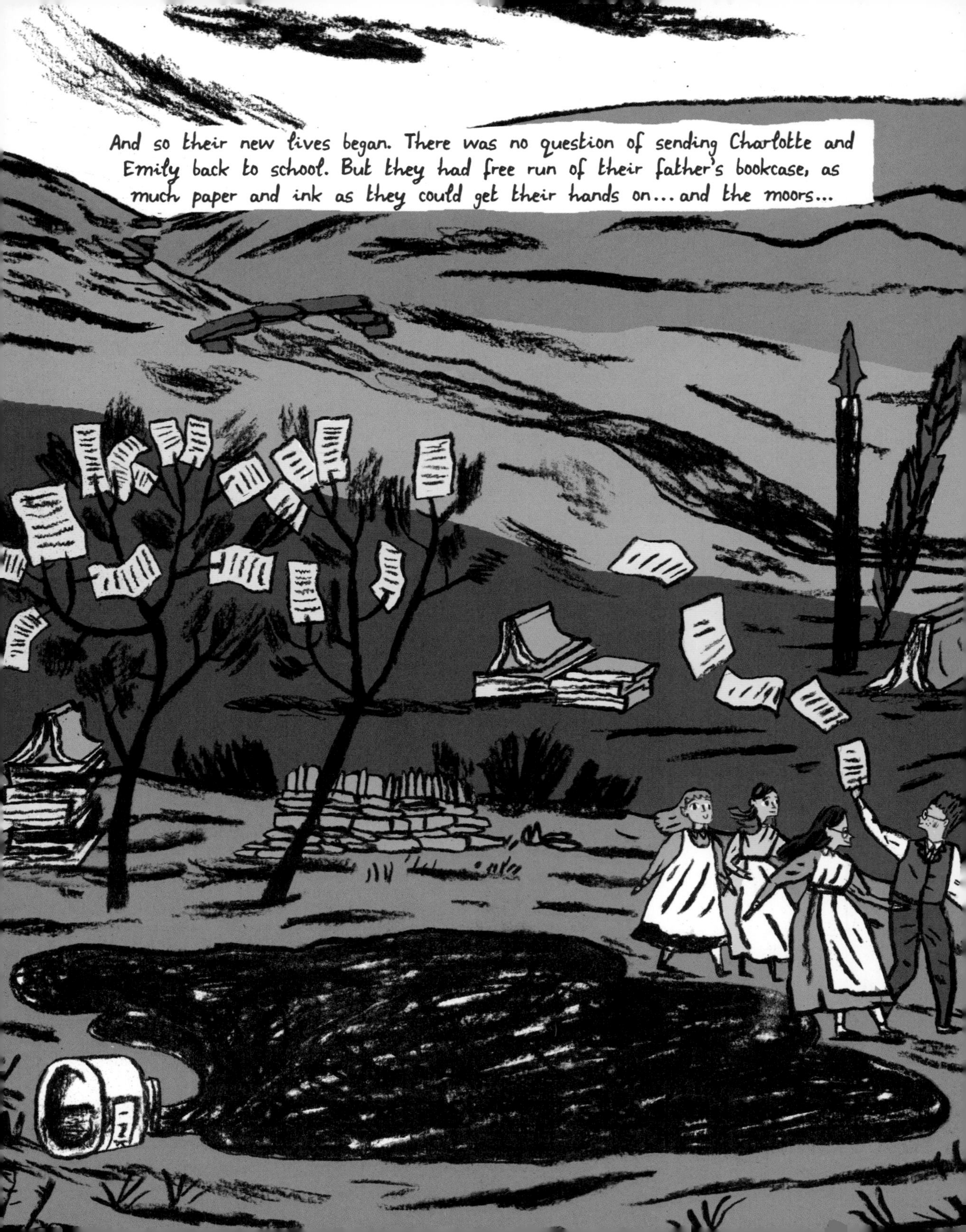
And so their new lives began. There was no question of sending Charlotte and Emily back to school. But they had free run of their father's bookcase, as much paper and ink as they could get their hands on... and the moors...

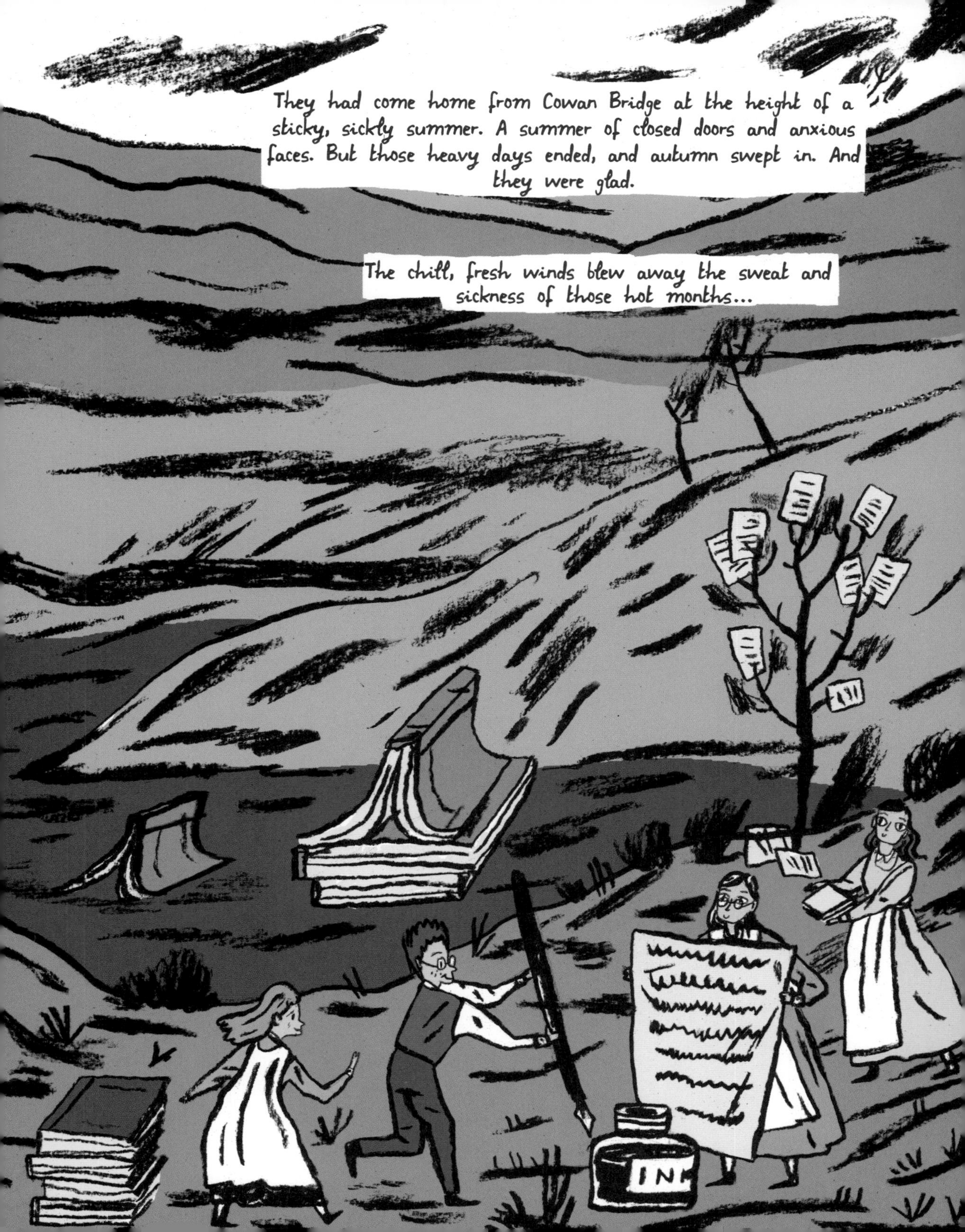
They had come home from Cowan Bridge at the height of a sticky, sickly summer. A summer of closed doors and anxious faces. But those heavy days ended, and autumn swept in. And they were glad.
The chill, fresh winds blew away the sweat and sickness of those hot months...
INK

And left them raw and chafed, but new.

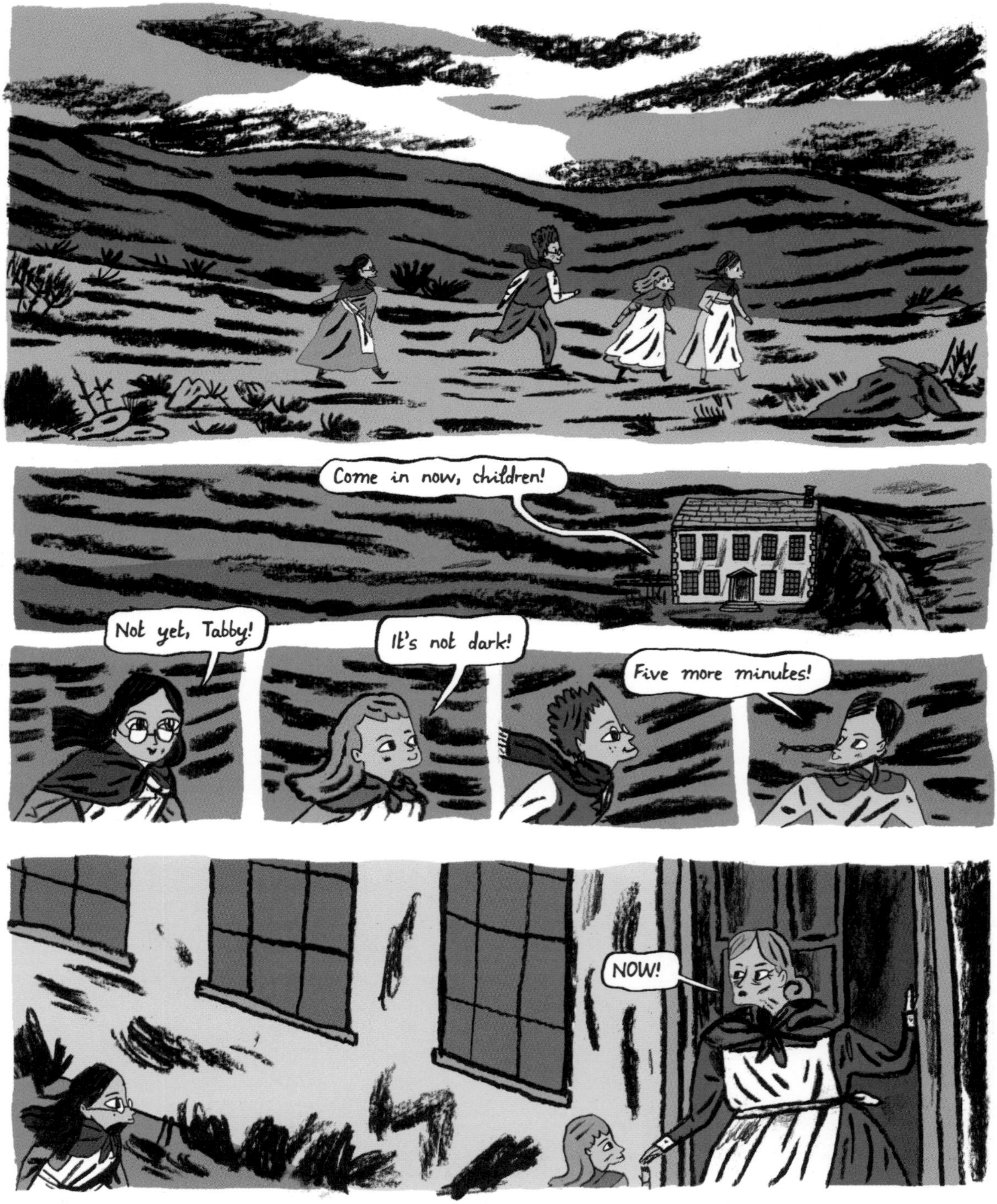
Come in now, children!
Not yet, Tabby!
It's not dark!
Five more minutes!
NOW!

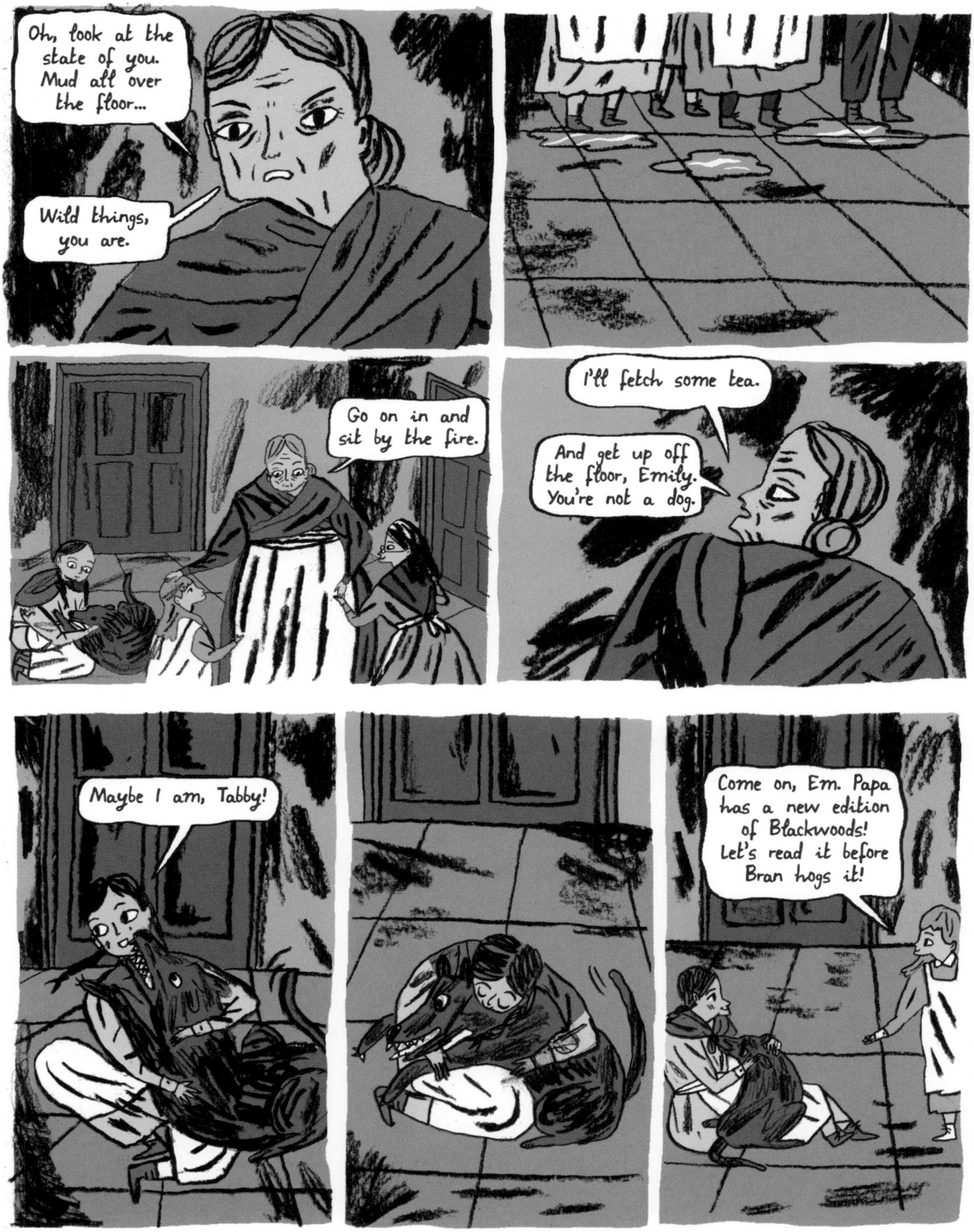
Oh, look at the state of you. Mud all over the floor...
Wild things, you are.
Go on in and sit by the fire.
I'll fetch some tea.
And get up off the floor, Emily. You're not a dog.
Maybe I am, Tabby!
Come on, Em. Papa has a new edition of Blackwoods! Let's read it before Bran hogs it!

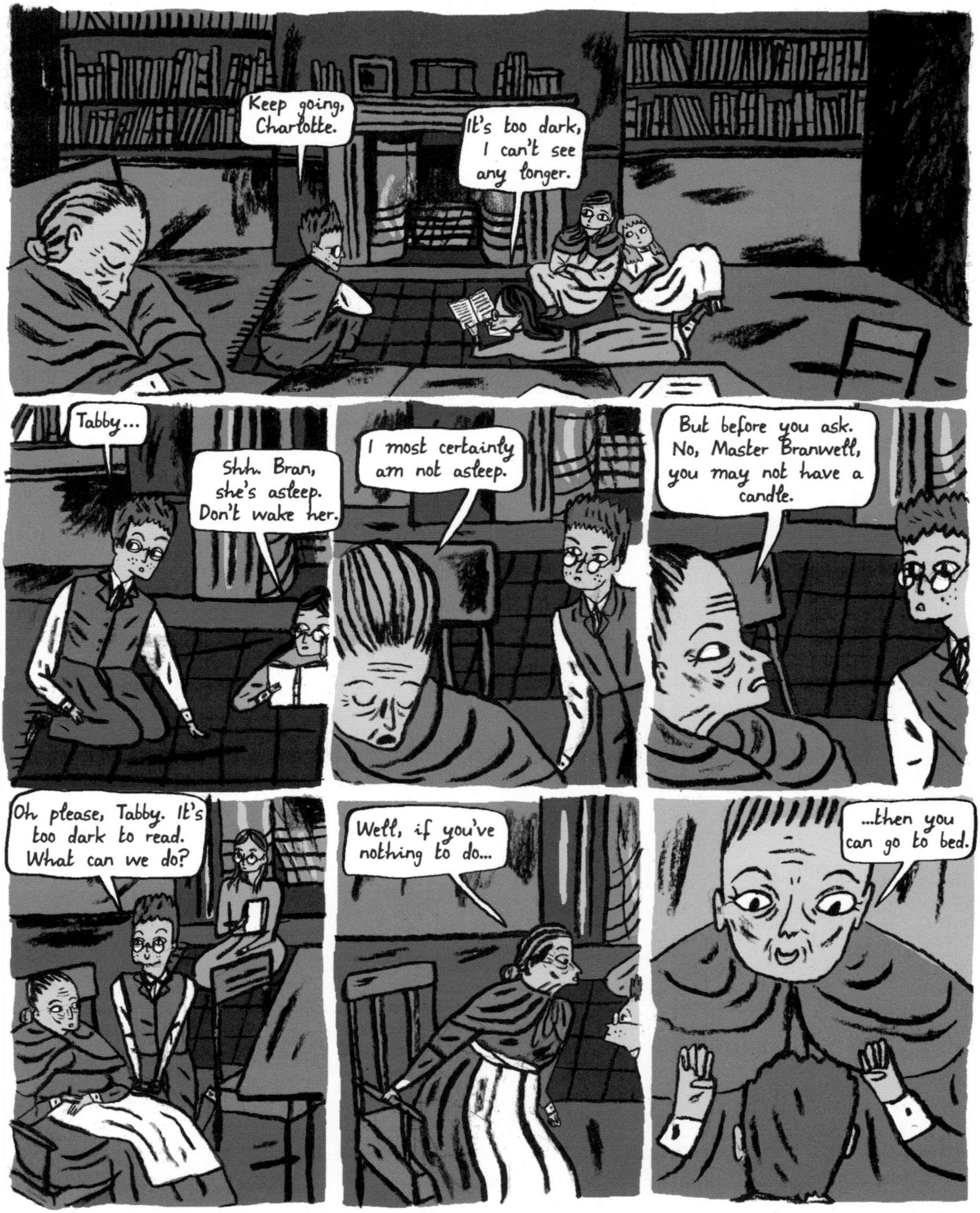
Keep going, Charlotte.
It's too dark, I can't see any longer.
Tabby...
Shh. Bran, she's asleep. Don't wake her.
I most certainly am not asleep.
But before you ask. No, Master Branwell, you may not have a candle.
Oh please, Tabby. It's too dark to read. What can we do?
Well, if you've nothing to do...
...then you can go to bed.

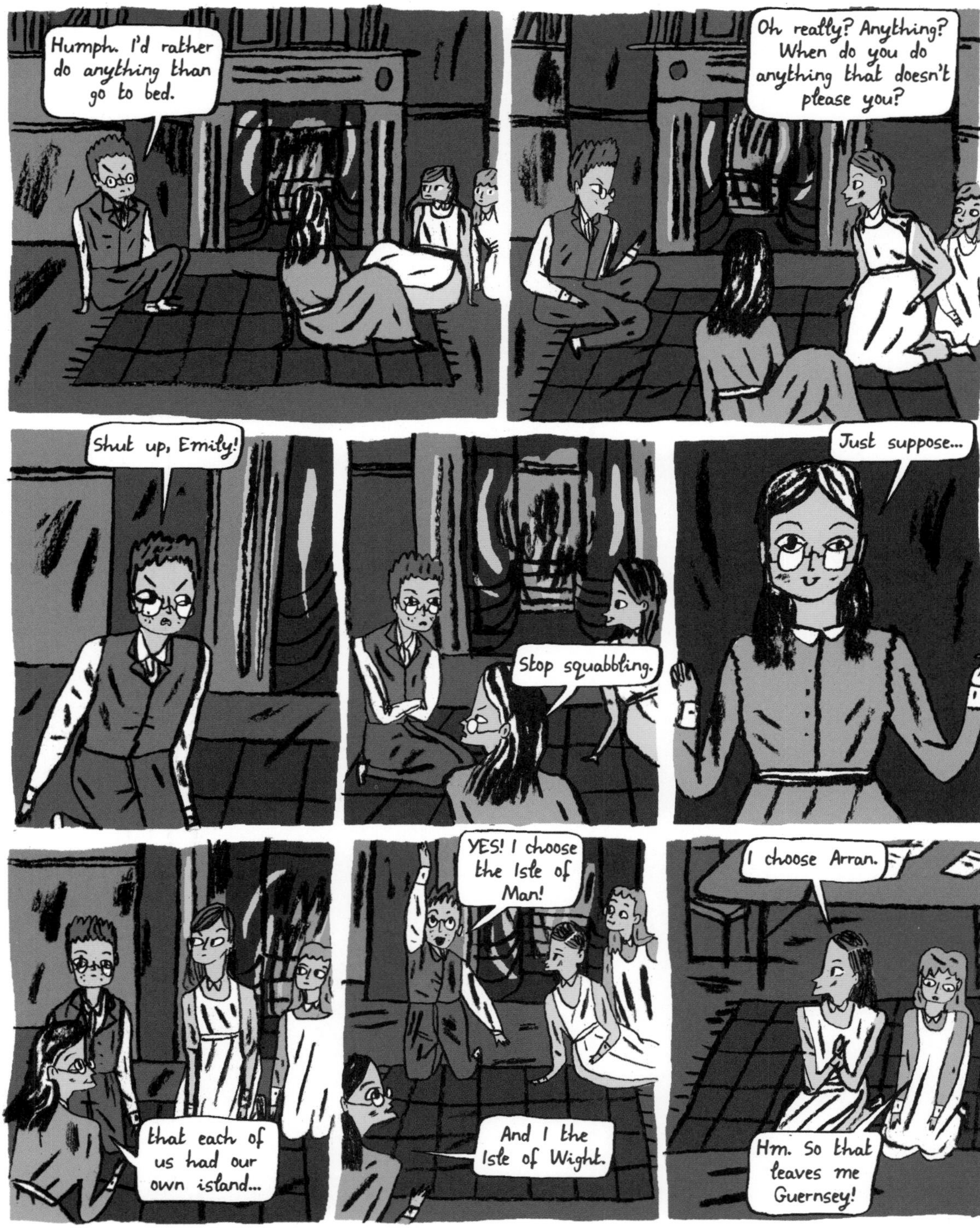
Humph. I'd rather do anything than go to bed.
Oh really? Anything? When do you do anything that doesn't please you?
Shut up, Emily!
Stop squabbling.
Just suppose...
that each of us had our own island...
YES! I choose the Isle of Man!
And I the Isle of Wight.
I choose Arran.
Hm. So that leaves me Guernsey!

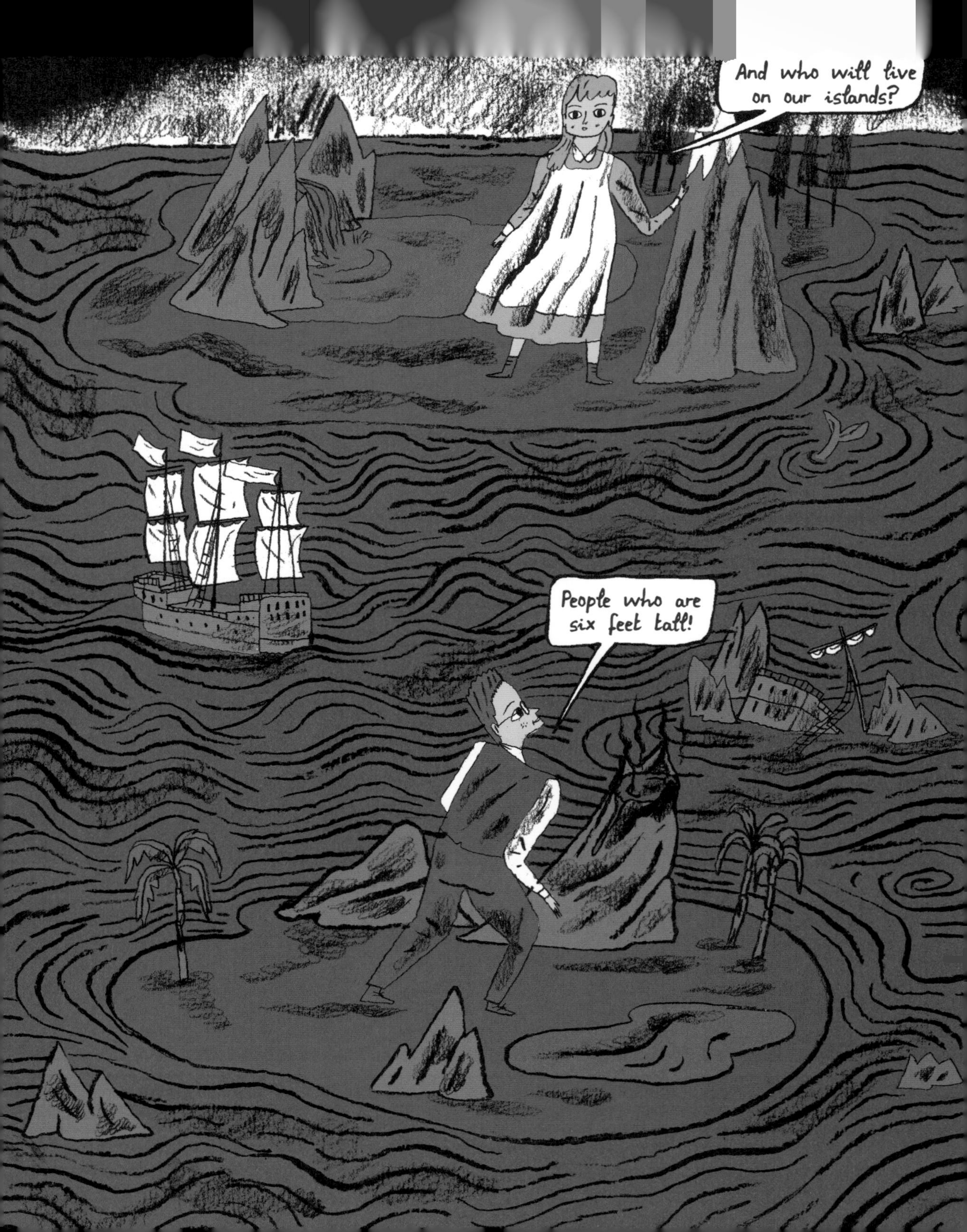
And who will live on our islands?
People who are six feet tall!

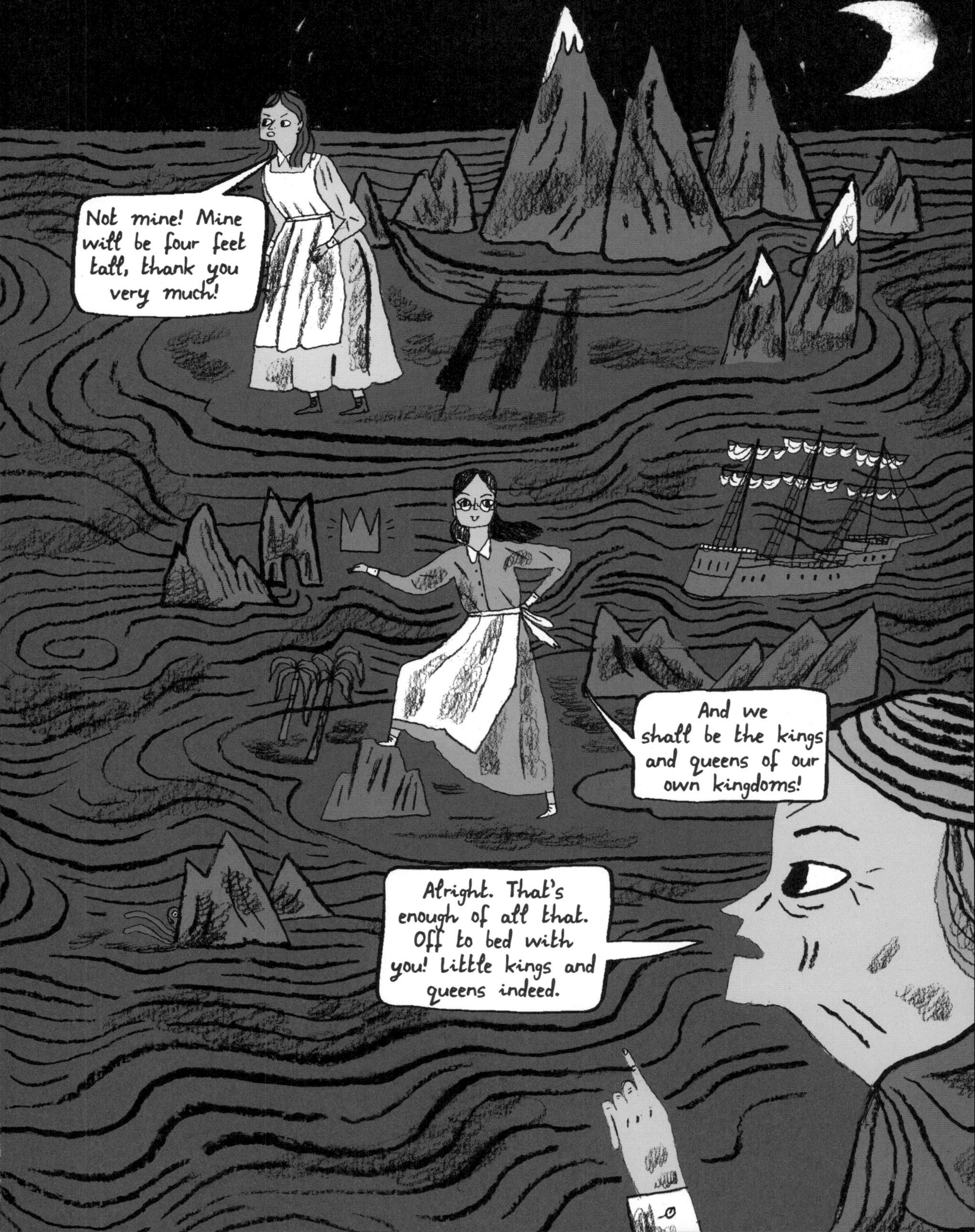
Not mine! Mine will be four feet tall, thank you very much!
And we shall be the kings and queens of our own kingdoms!
Alright. That's enough of all that. Off to bed with you! Little kings and queens indeed.

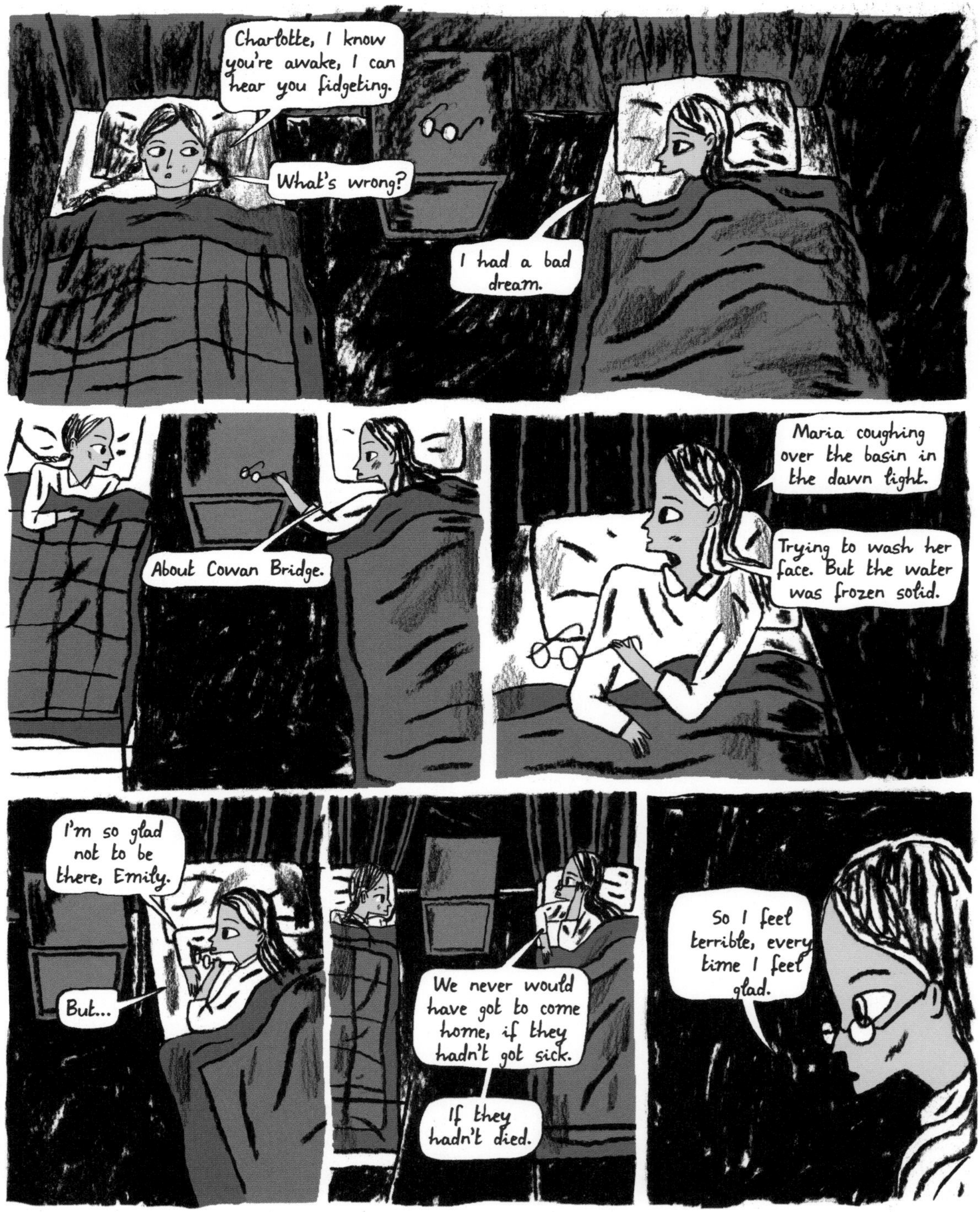
Charlotte, I know you're awake, I can hear you fidgeting.
What's wrong?
I had a bad dream.
About Cowan Bridge.
Maria coughing over the basin in the dawn light.
Trying to wash her face. But the water was frozen solid.
I'm so glad not to be there, Emily.
But...
We never would have got to come home, if they hadn't got sick.
If they hadn't died.
So I feel terrible, every time I feel glad.

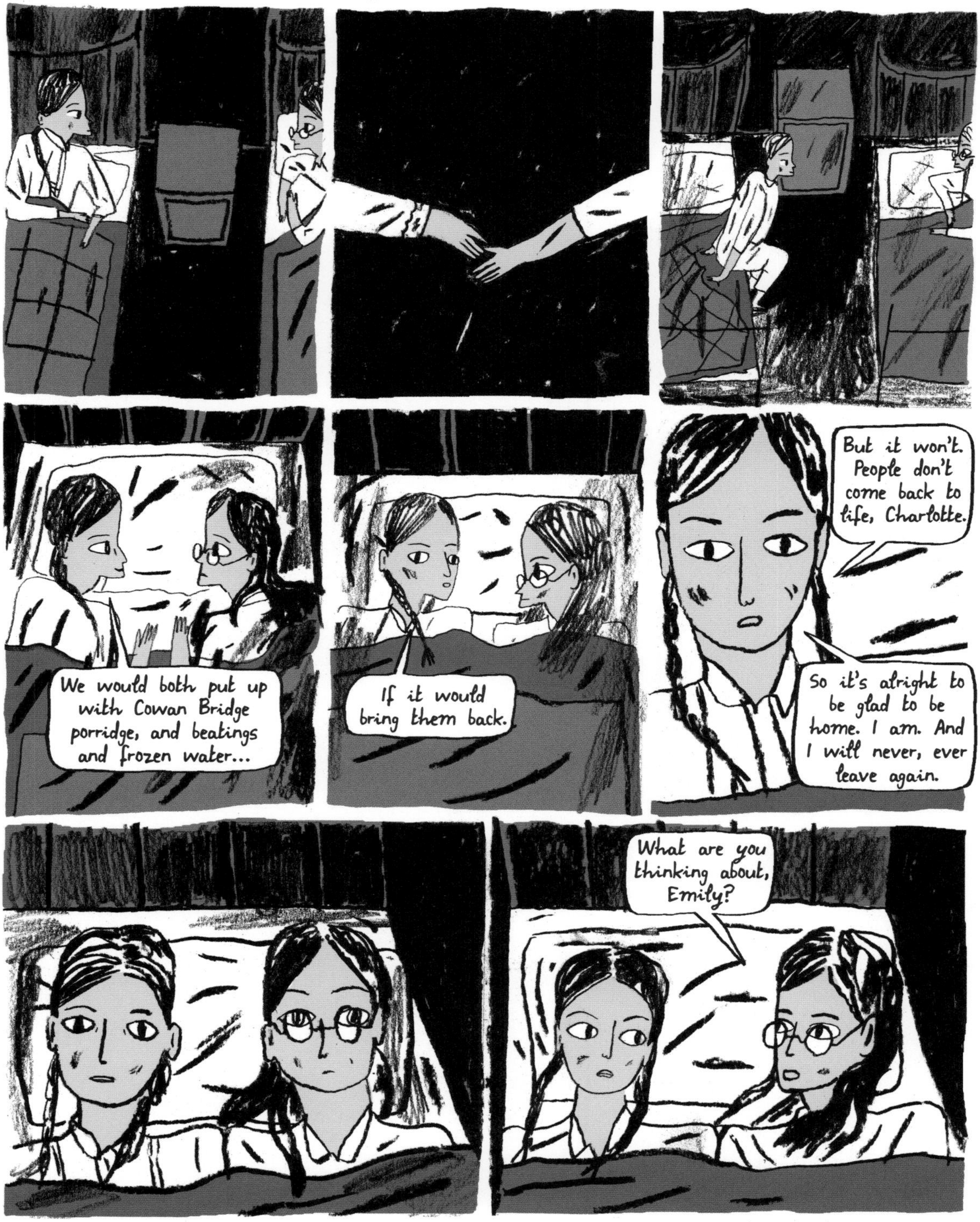
We would both put up with Cowan Bridge porridge, and beatings and frozen water...
If it would bring them back.
But it won't. People don't come back to life, Charlotte.
So it's alright to be glad to be home. I am. And I will never, ever leave again.
What are you thinking about, Emily?

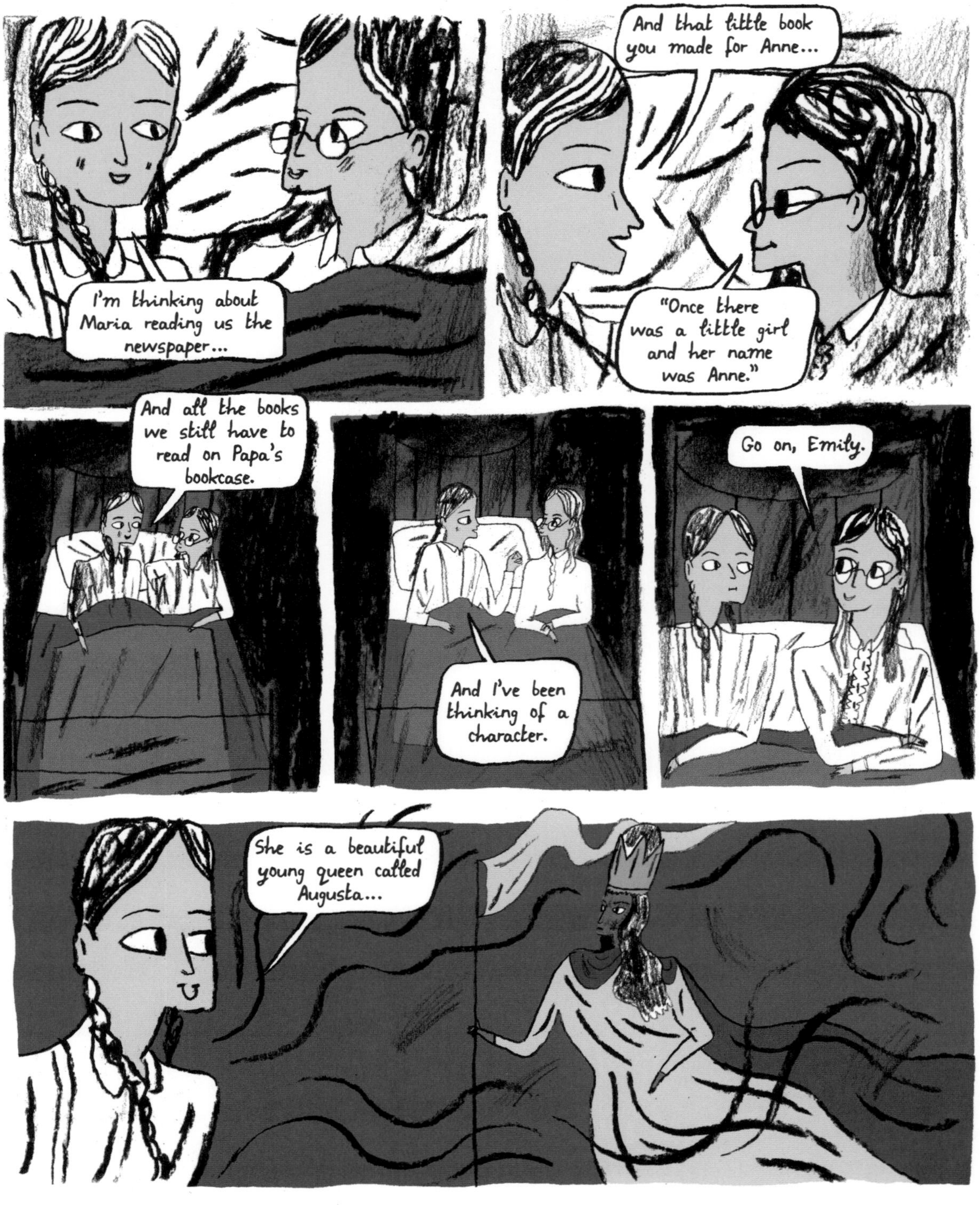
I'm thinking about Maria reading us the newspaper...
And that little book you made for Anne...
"Once there was a little girl and her name was Anne."
And all the books we still have to read on Papa's bookcase.
And I've been thinking of a character.
Go on, Emily.
She is a beautiful young queen called Augusta...

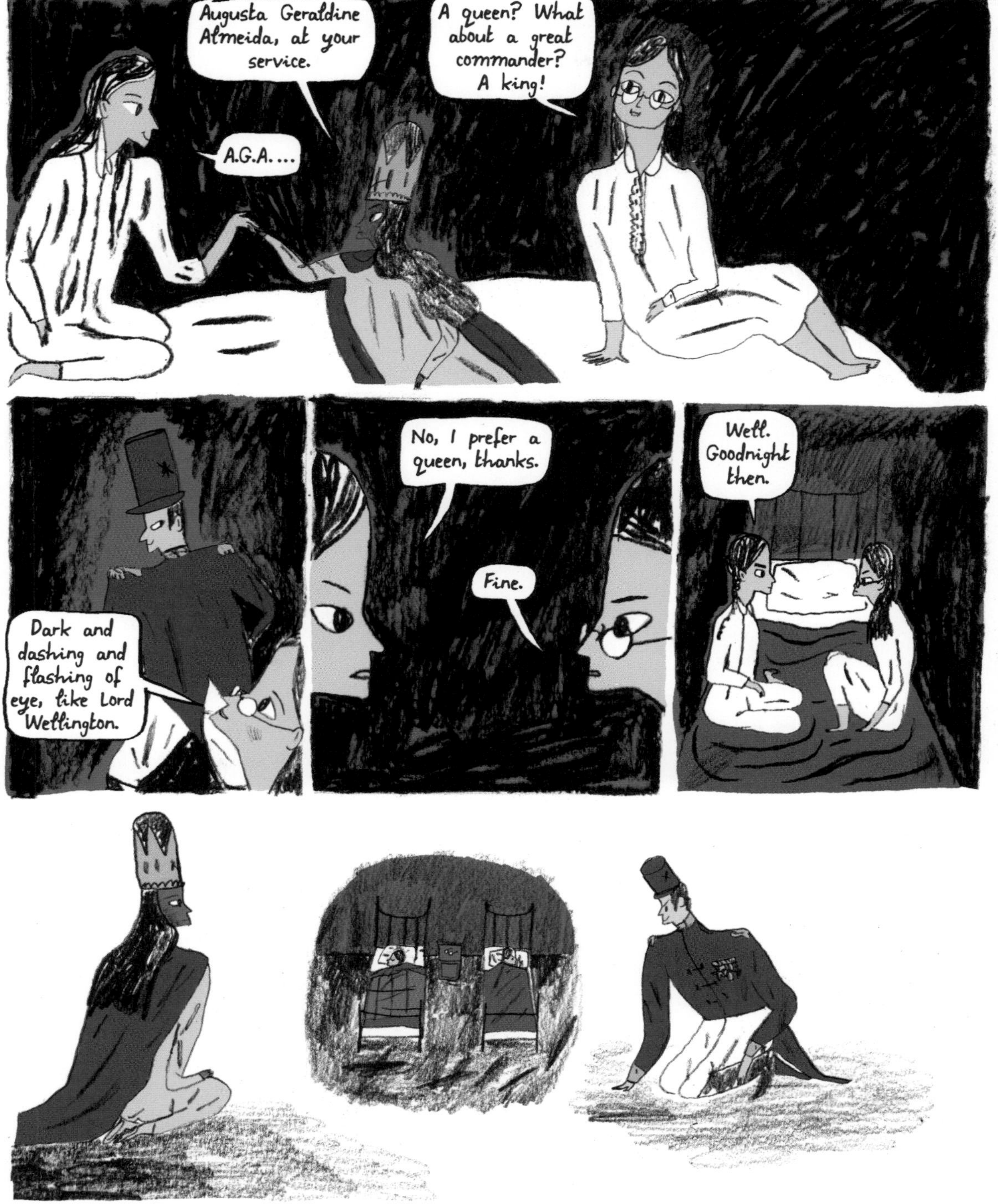
Augusta Geraldine Almeida, at your service.
A.G.A....
A queen? What about a great commander? A king!
Dark and dashing and flashing of eye, like Lord Wellington.
No, I prefer a queen, thanks.
Fine.
Well. Goodnight then.

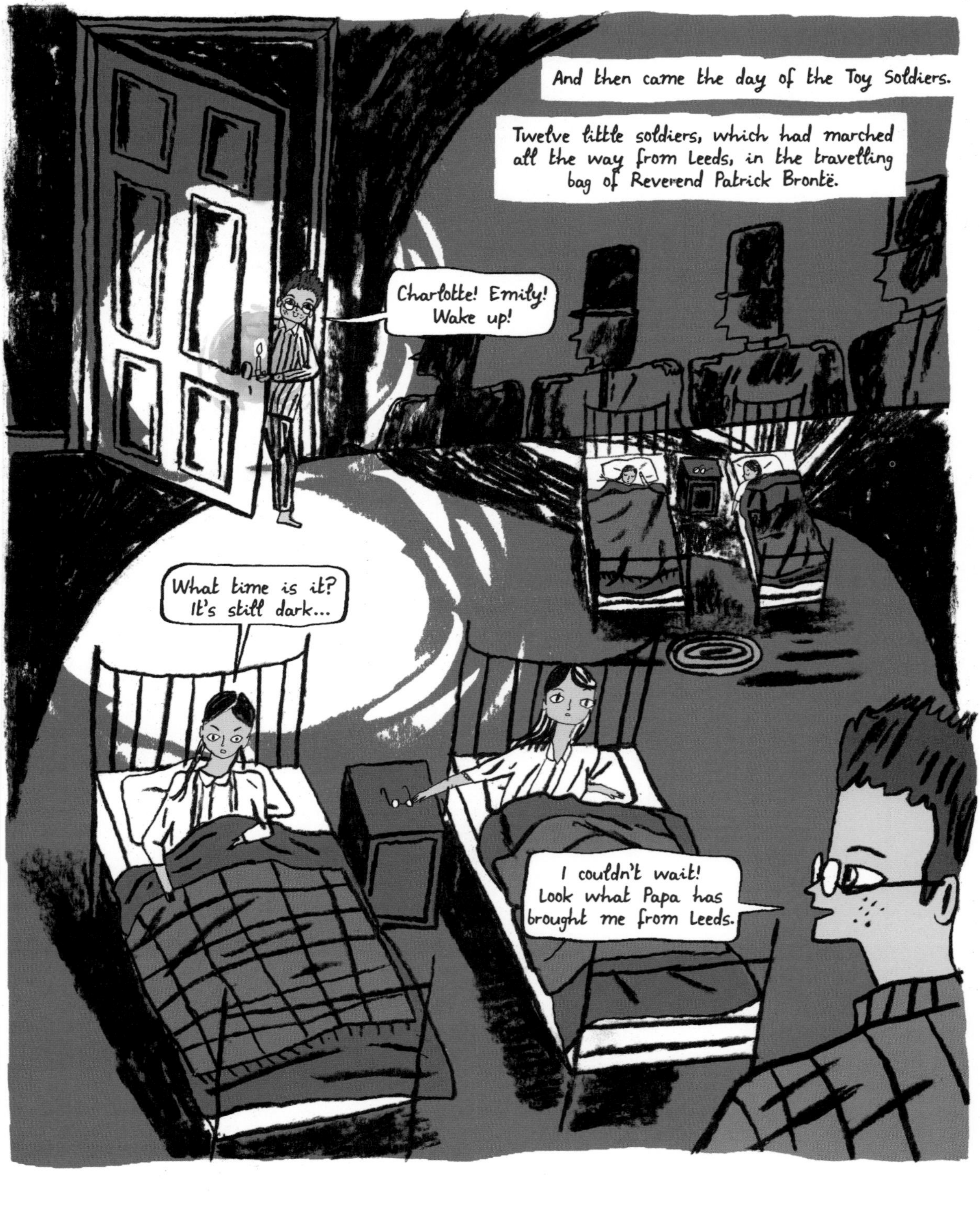
And then came the day of the Toy Soldiers.
Twelve little soldiers, which had marched all the way from Leeds, in the travelling bag of Reverend Patrick Brontë.
Charlotte! Emily! Wake up!
What time is it? It's still dark...
I couldn't wait! Look what Papa has brought me from Leeds.

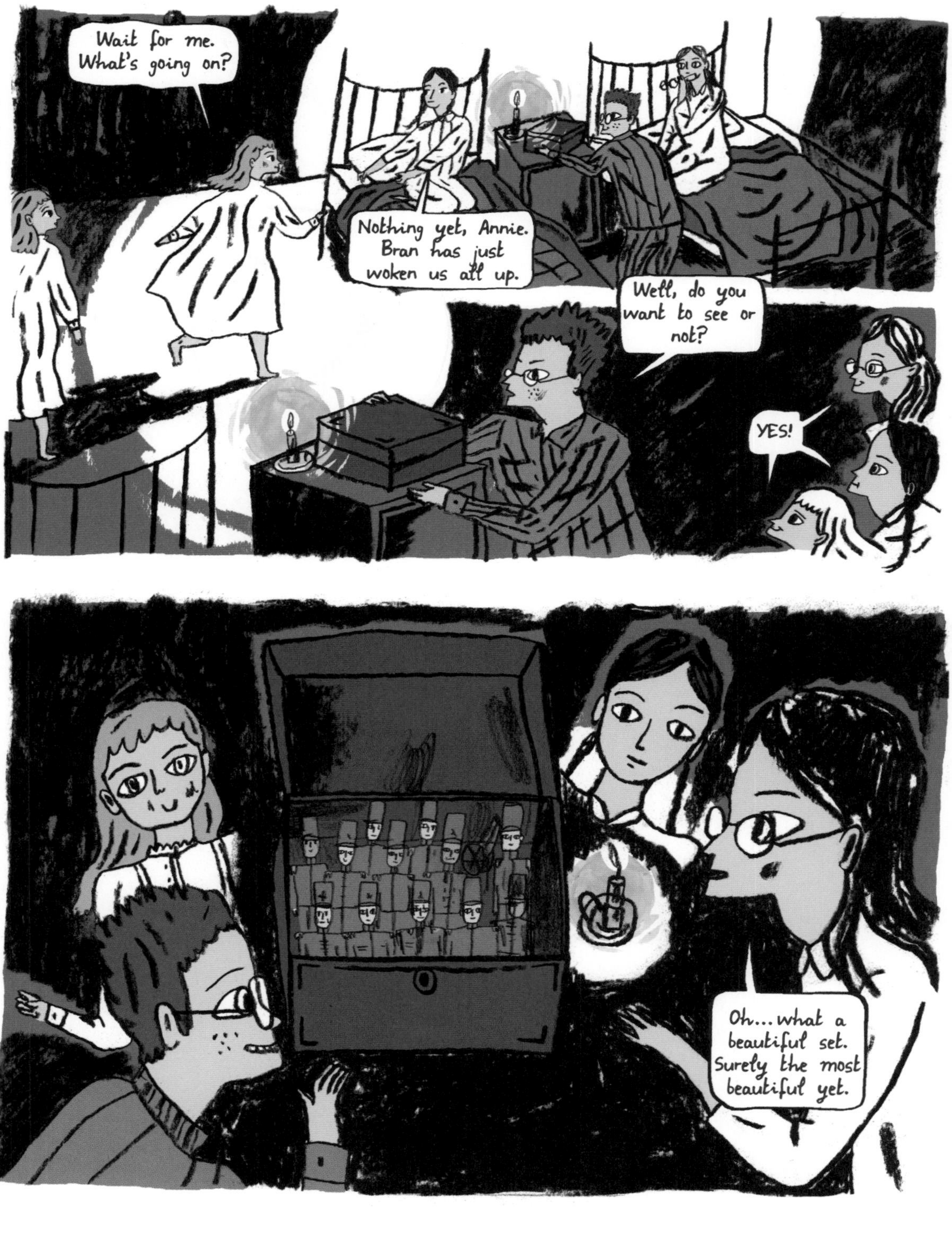
Wait for me. What's going on?
Nothing yet, Annie. Bran has just woken us all up.
Well, do you want to see or not?
YES!
Oh... what a beautiful set. Surely the most beautiful yet.

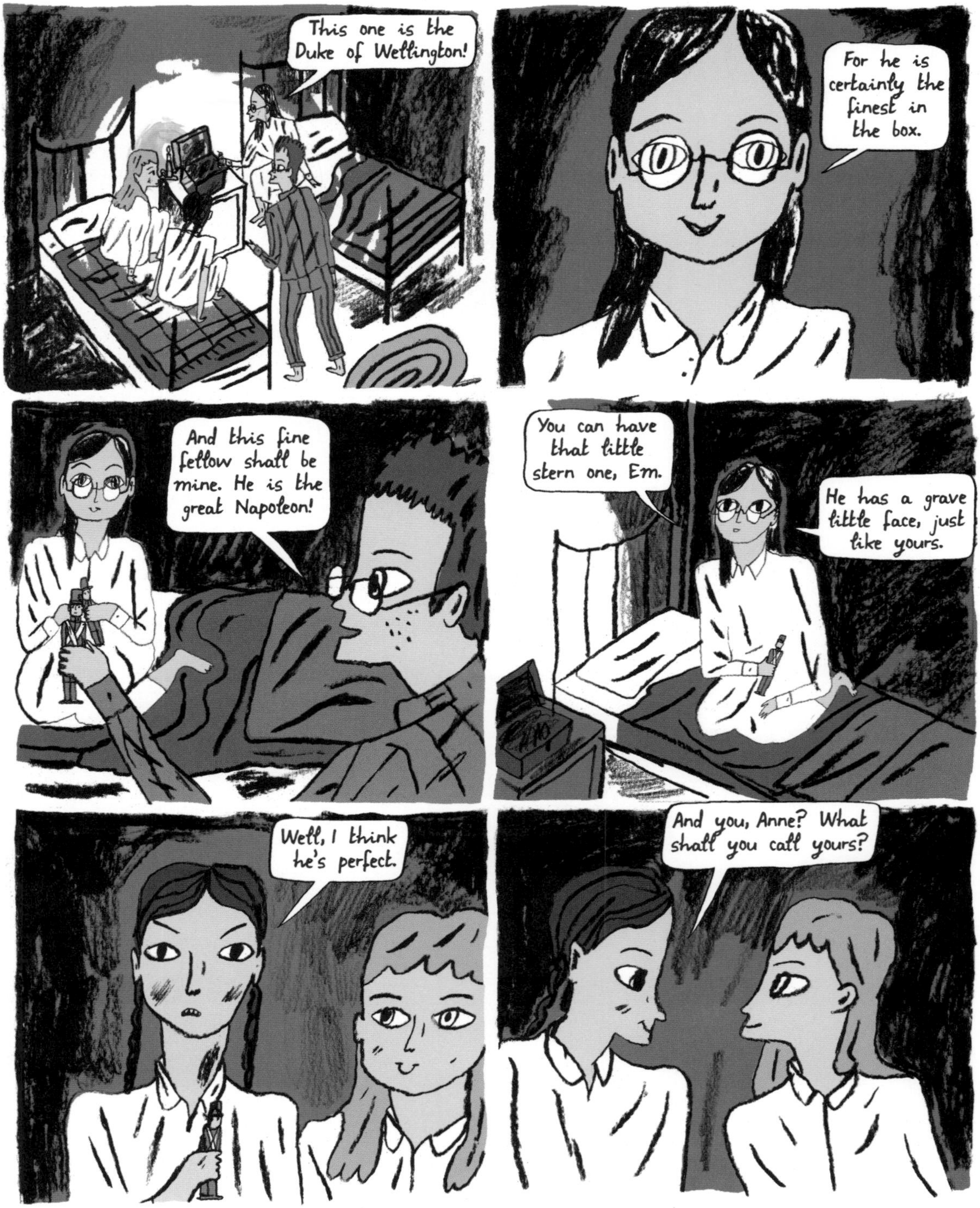
This one is the Duke of Wellington!
For he is certainly the finest in the box.
And this fine fellow shall be mine. He is the great Napoleon!
You can have that little stern one, Em.
He has a grave little face, just like yours.
Well, I think he's perfect.
And you, Anne? What shall you call yours?

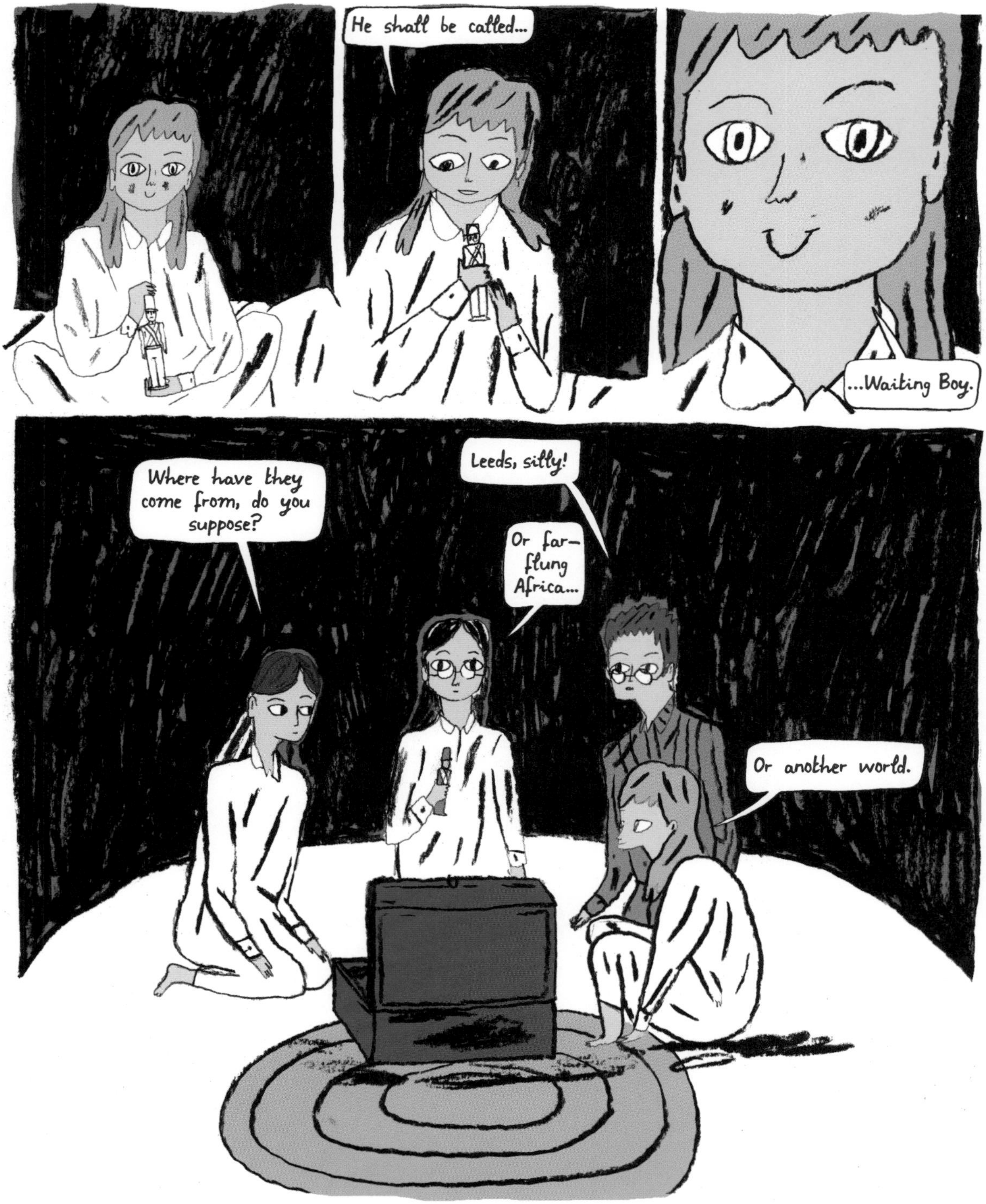
He shall be called...
...Waiting Boy.
Where have they come from, do you suppose?
Leeds, silly!
Or far-flung Africa...
Or another world.

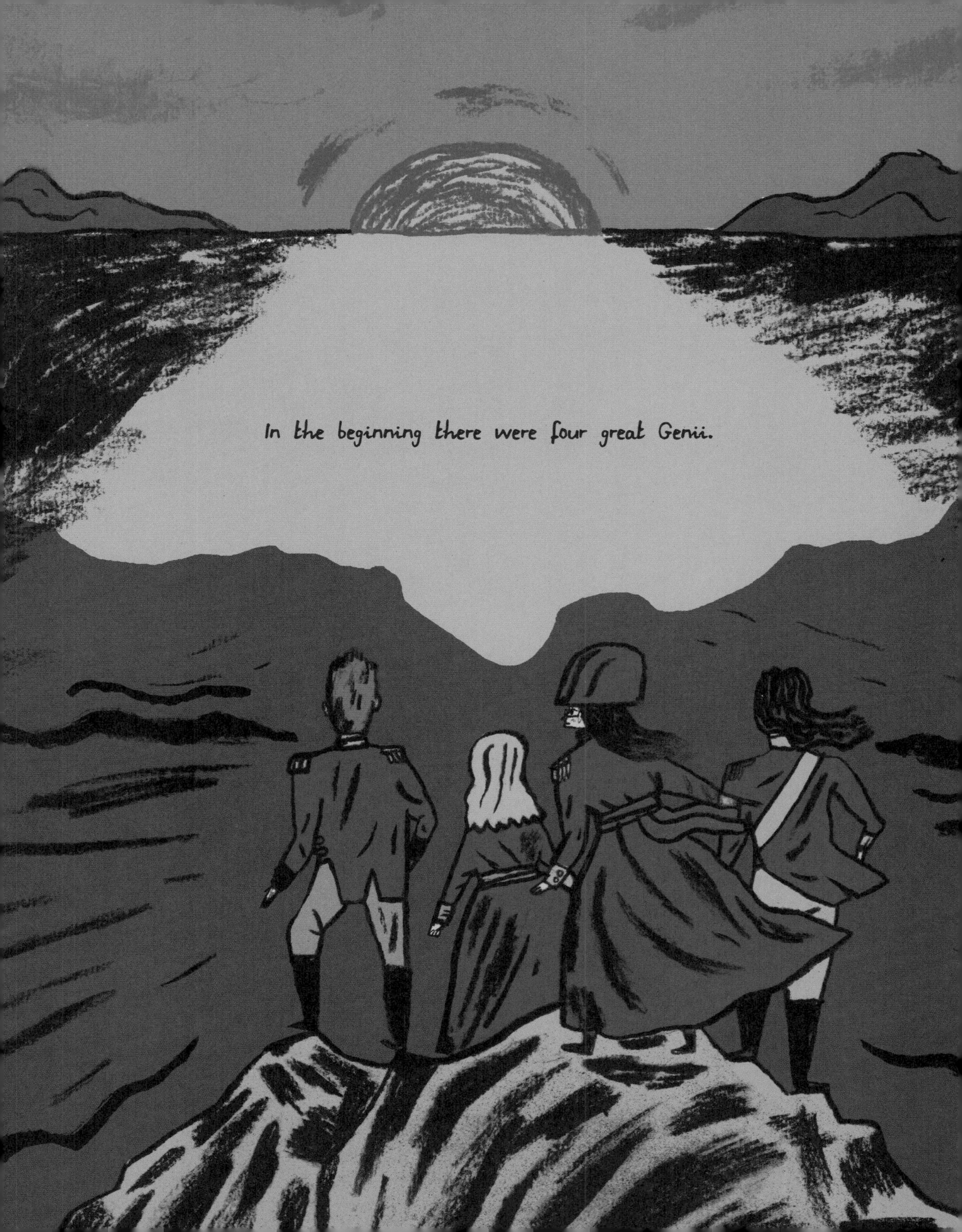
In the beginning there were four great Genii.

And their names were Tallii, Brannii, Emmii and Annii.

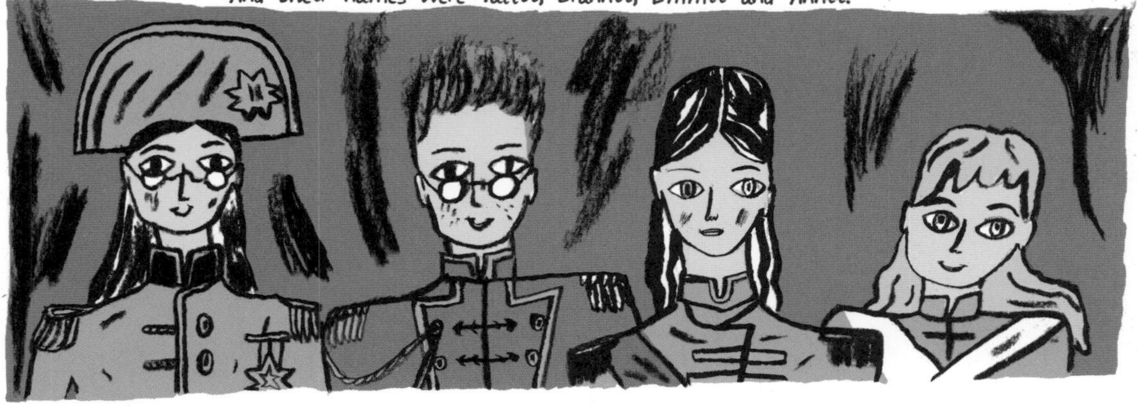

They dwelt at the top of Mount Atos, the highest of all the mountains of the Jibbel Kumri (or Mountains of the Moon, to those not fluent in the dialects of Angria).

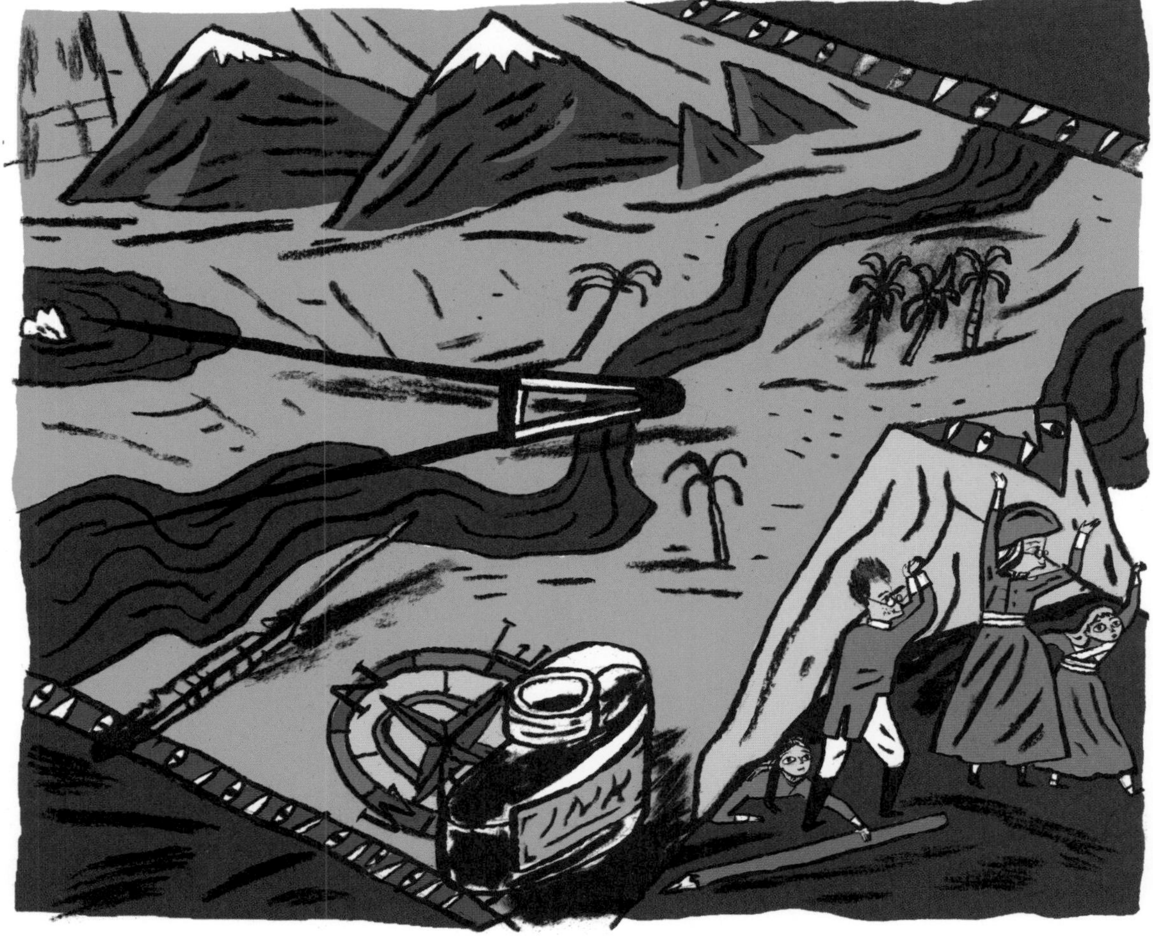
INK

One fine day the Genii received a votive offering from a mysterious source.

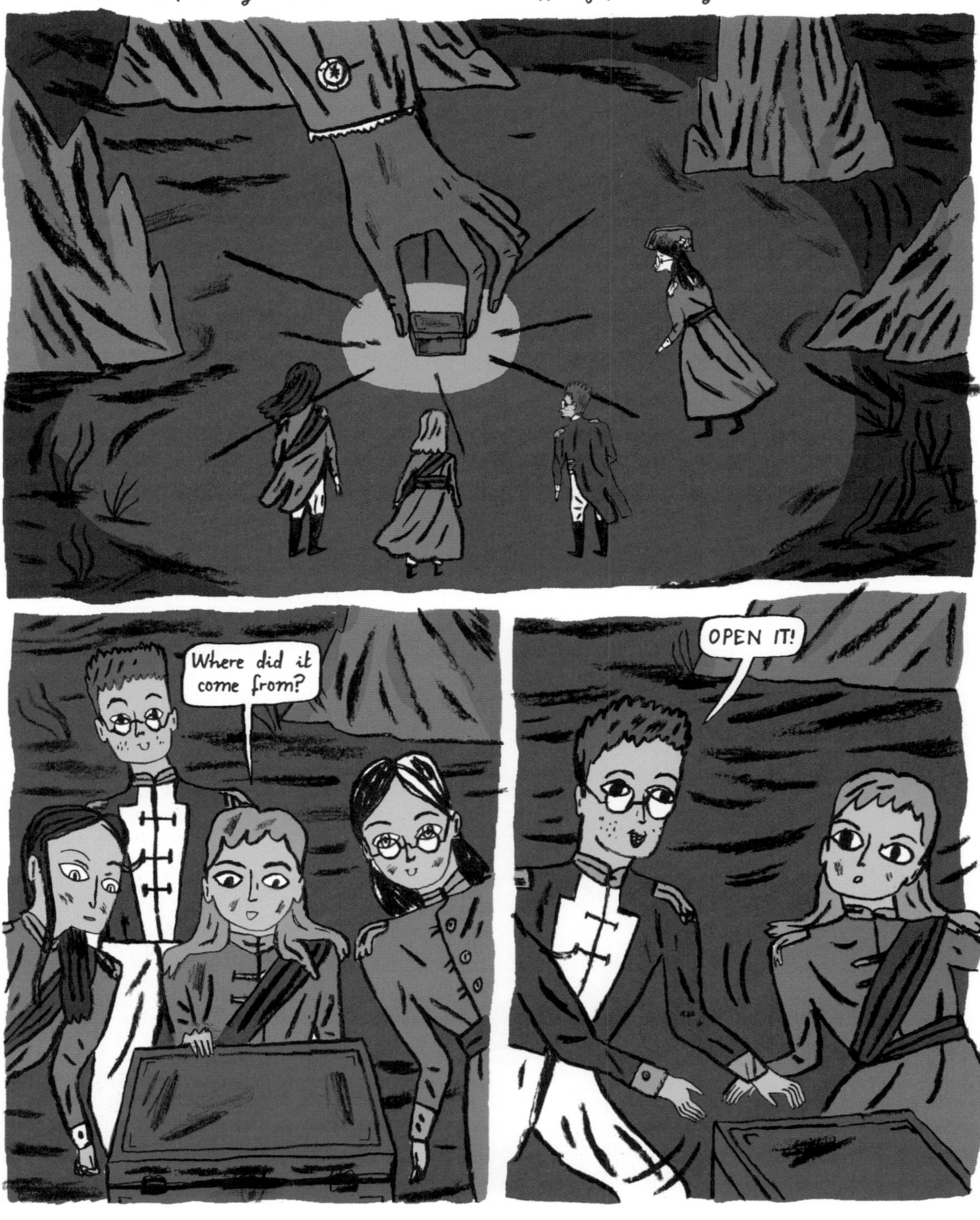
Where did it come from?
OPEN IT!

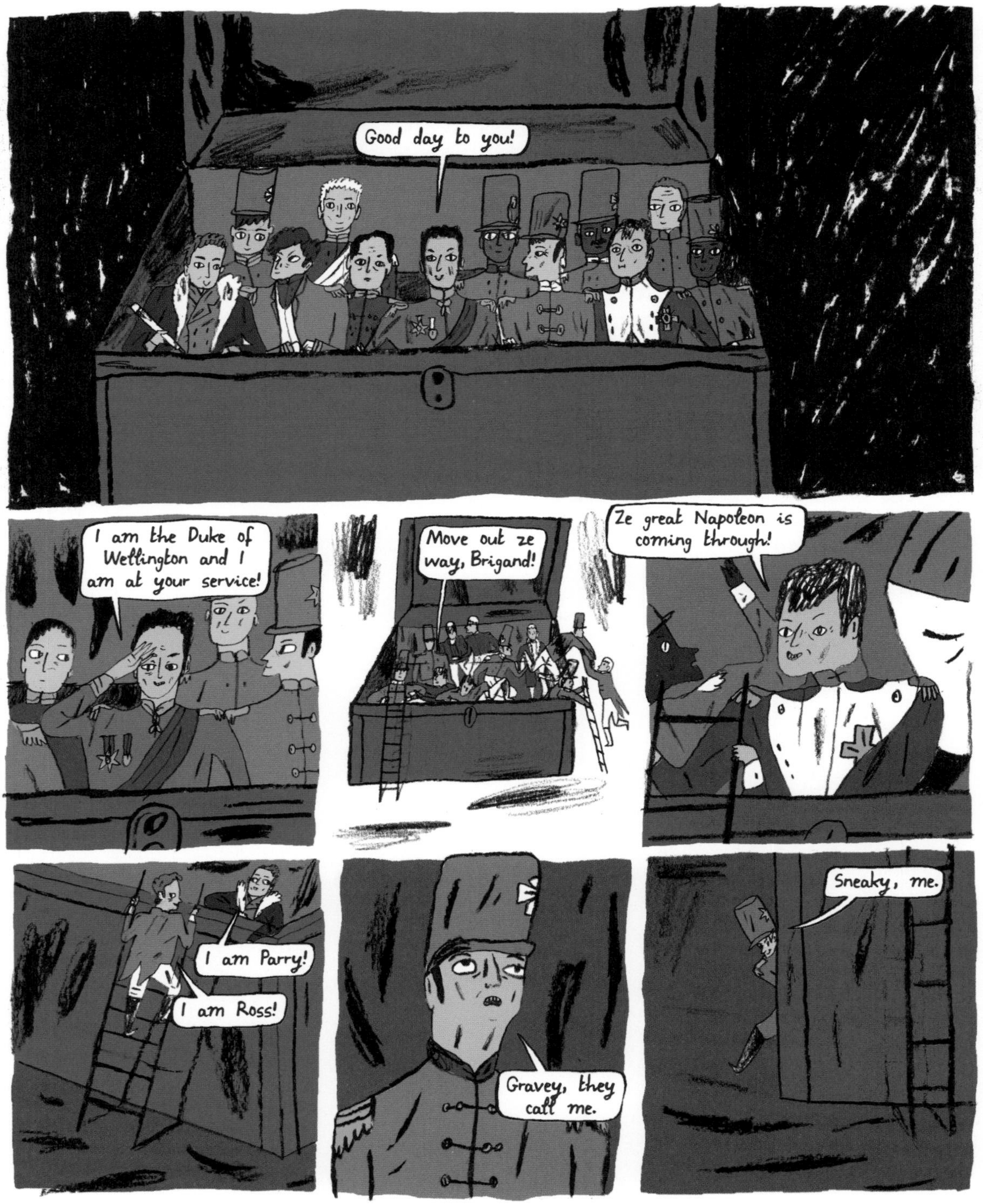
Good day to you!
I am the Duke of Wellington and I am at your service!
Move out ze way, Brigand!
Ze great Napoleon is coming through!
I am Parry!
I am Ross!
Gravey, they call me.
Sneaky, me.

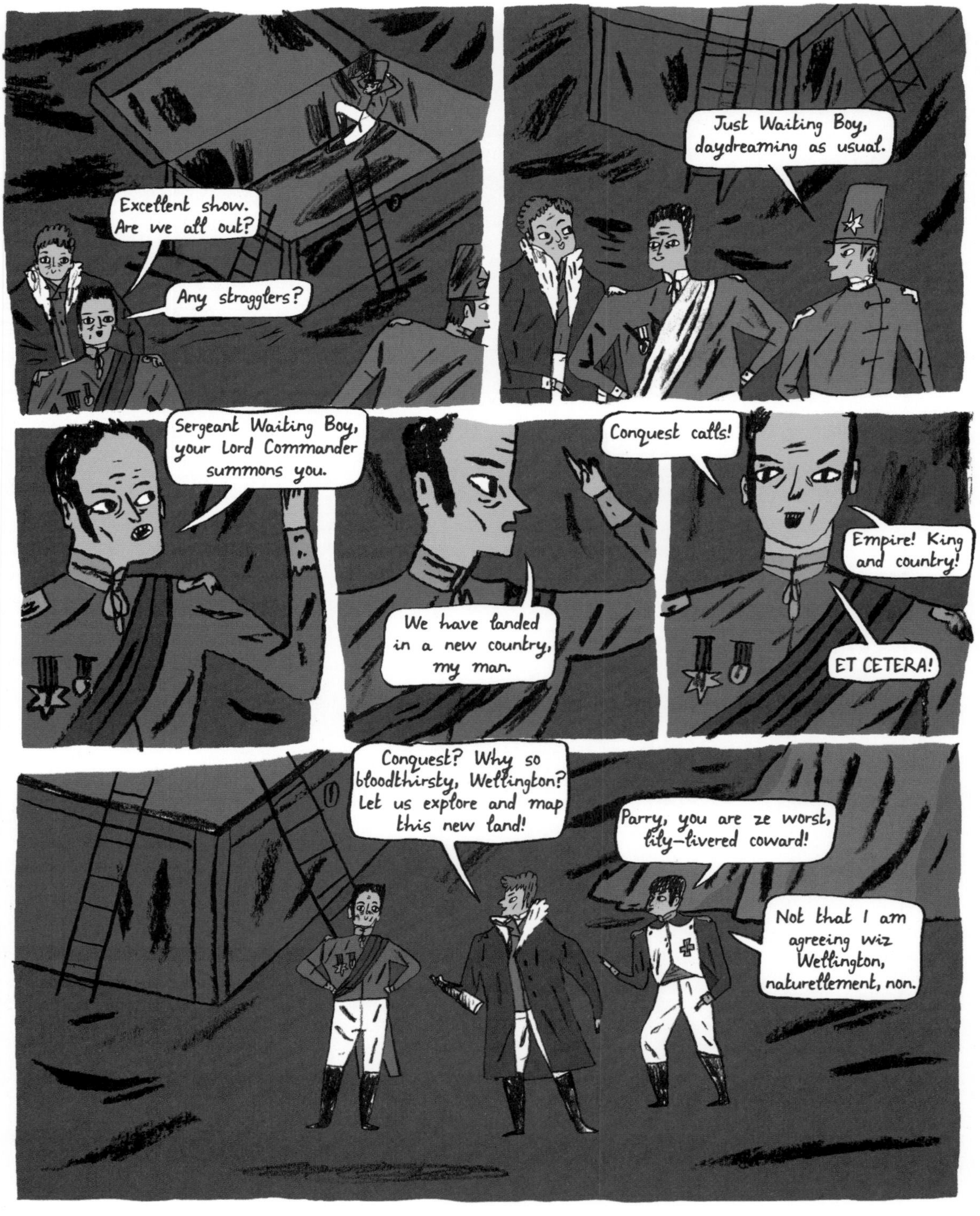
Excellent show. Are we all out?
Any stragglers?
Just Waiting Boy, daydreaming as usual.
Sergeant Waiting Boy, your Lord Commander summons you.
We have landed in a new country, my man.
Conquest calls!
Empire! King and country!
ET CETERA!
Conquest? Why so bloodthirsty, Wellington? Let us explore and map this new land!
Parry, you are ze worst, lily-livered coward!
Not that I am agreeing wiz Wellington, naturellement, non.

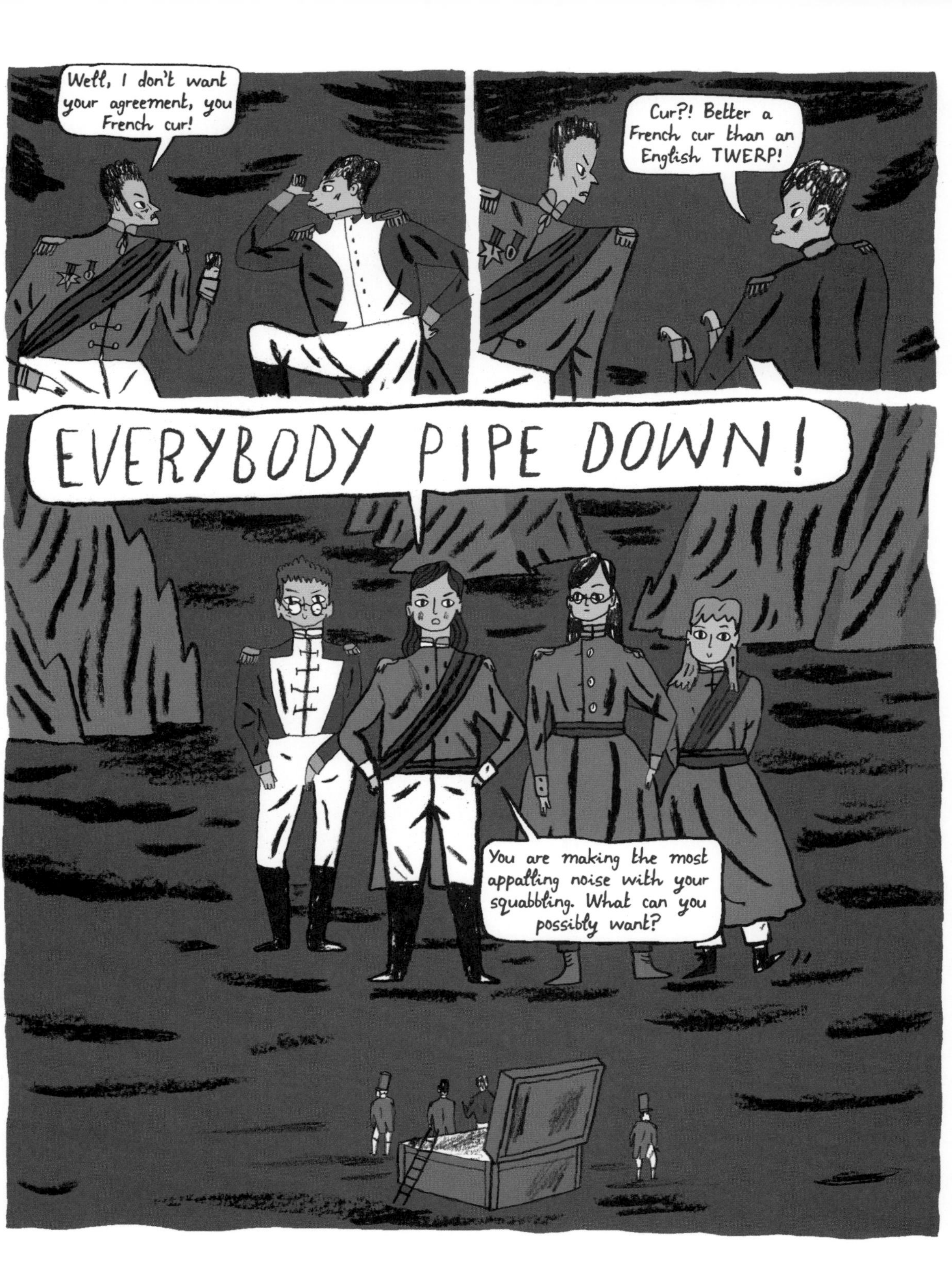
Well, I don't want your agreement, you French cur!
Cur?! Better a French cur than an English TWERP!
EVERYBODY PIPE DOWN!
You are making the most appalling noise with your squabbling. What can you possibly want?

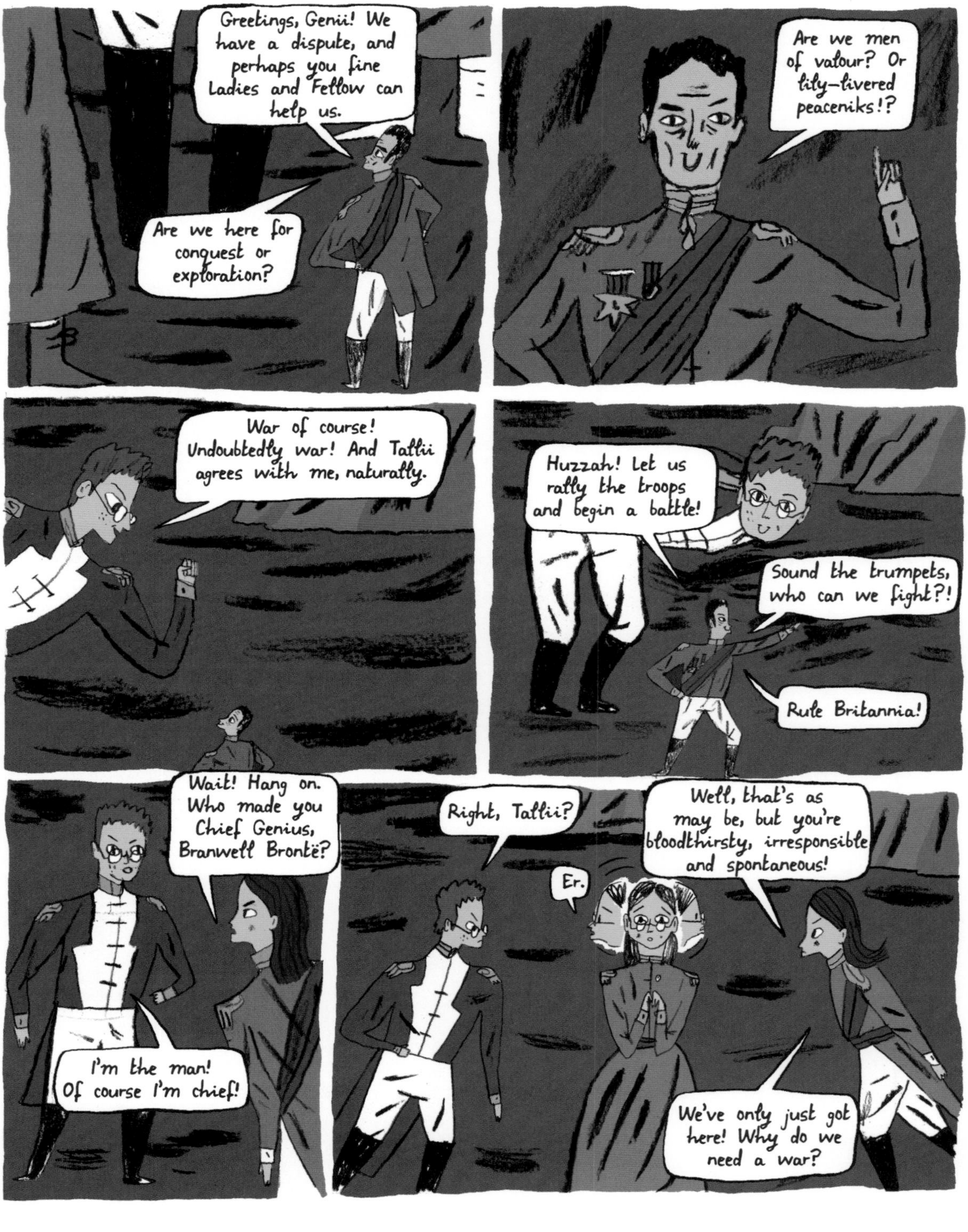
Greetings, Genii! We have a dispute, and perhaps you fine Ladies and Fellow can help us.
Are we here for conquest or exploration?
Are we men of valour? Or lily-livered peaceniks!?
War of course! Undoubtedly war! And Tallii agrees with me, naturally.
Huzzah! Let us rally the troops and begin a battle!
Sound the trumpets, who can we fight?!
Rule Britannia!
Wait! Hang on. Who made you Chief Genius, Branwell Brontë?
I'm the man! Of course I'm chief!
Right, Tallii?
Er.
Well, that's as may be, but you're bloodthirsty, irresponsible and spontaneous!
We've only just got here! Why do we need a war?

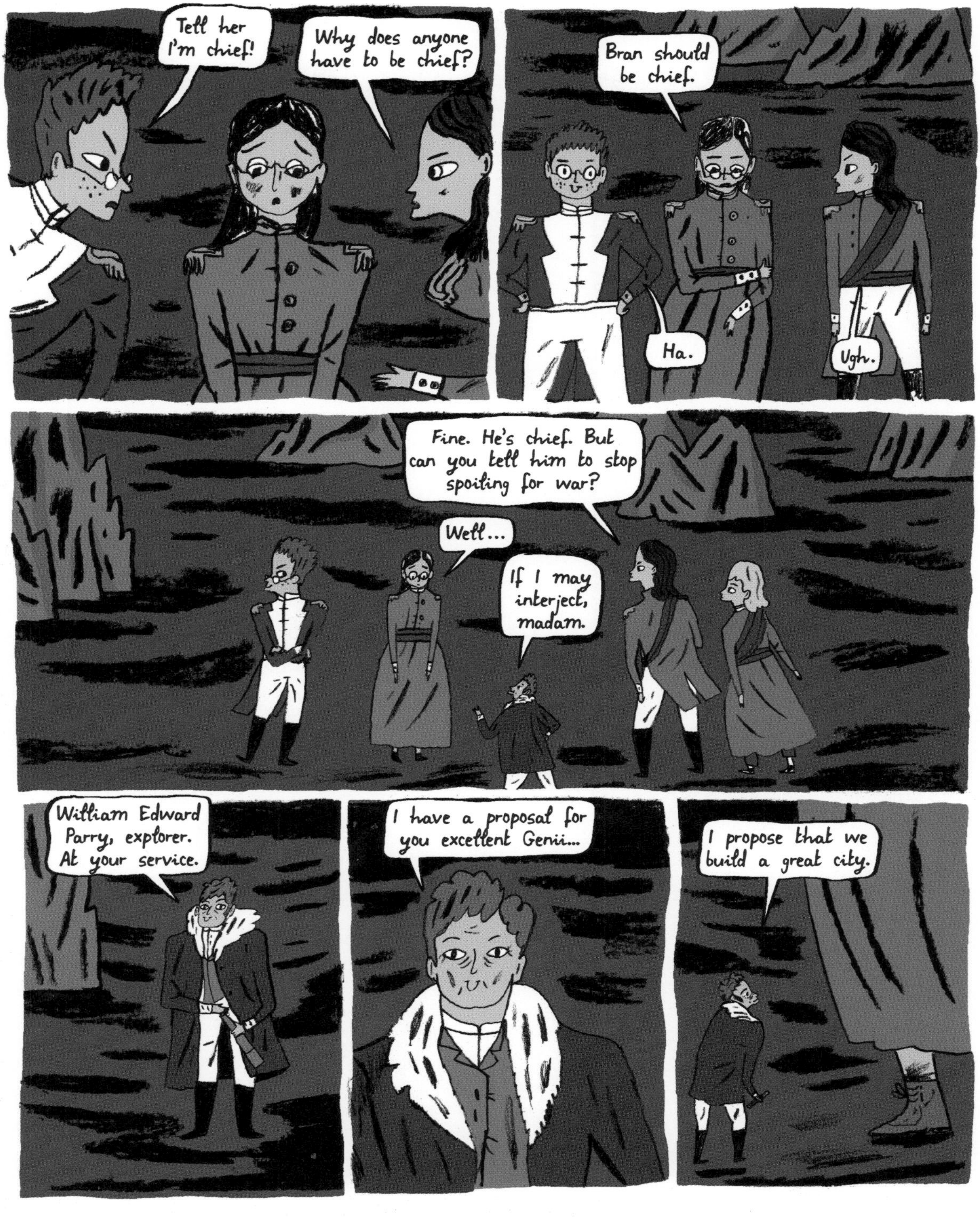
Tell her I'm chief!
Why does anyone have to be chief?
Bran should be chief.
Ha.
Ugh.
Fine. He's chief. But can you tell him to stop spoiling for war?
Well...
If I may interject, madam.
William Edward Parry, explorer. At your service.
I have a proposal for you excellent Genii...
I propose that we build a great city.

The four Genii held a quick Genii Conclave to discuss the suggestion.

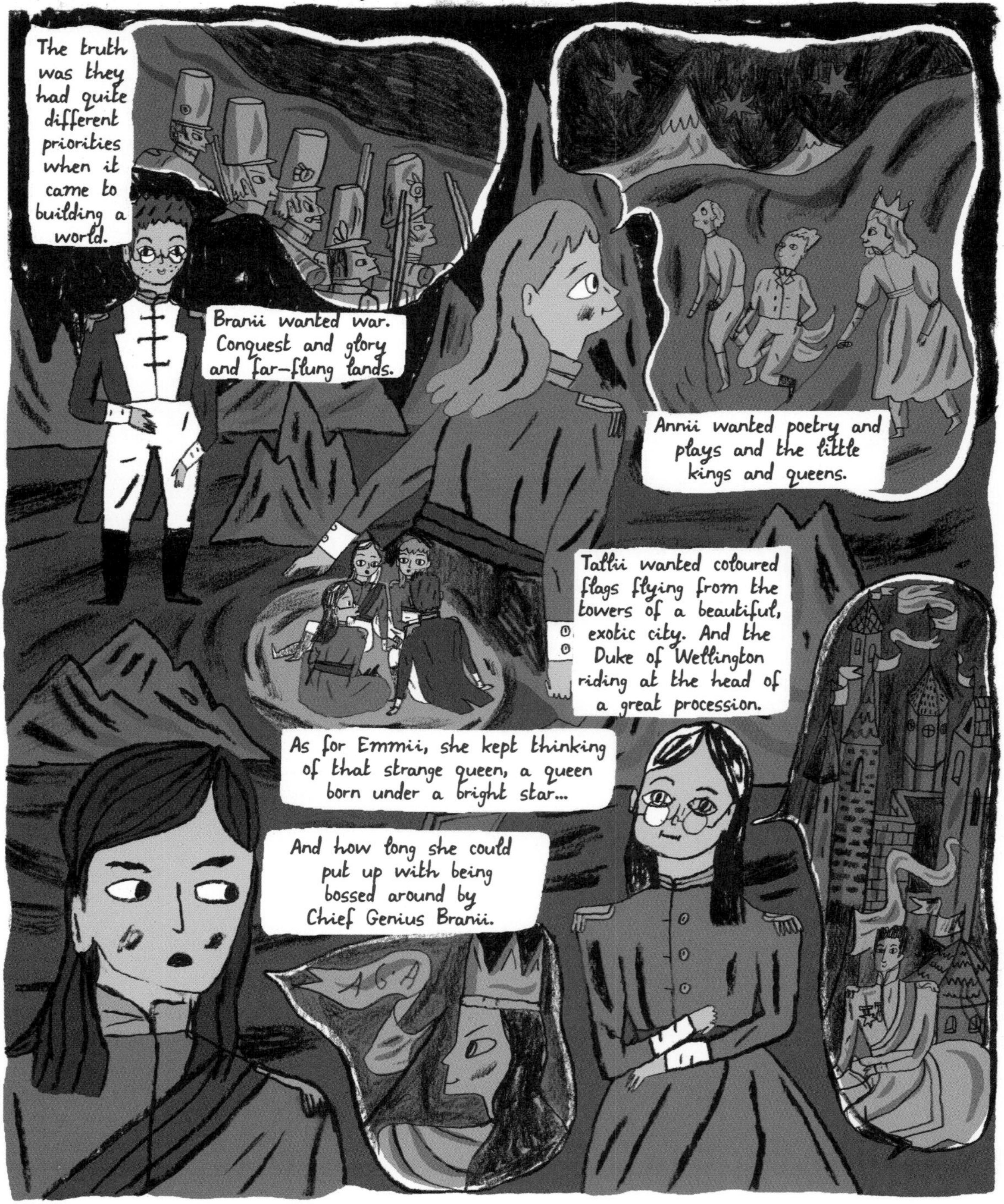
The truth was they had quite different priorities when it came to building a world.
Branii wanted war. Conquest and glory and far-flung lands.
Annii wanted poetry and plays and the little kings and queens.
Tallii wanted coloured flags flying from the towers of a beautiful, exotic city. And the Duke of Wellington riding at the head of a great procession.
As for Emmii, she kept thinking of that strange queen, a queen born under a bright star...
And how long she could put up with being bossed around by Chief Genius Branii.
AGA

But for now it seemed like building a city might have something in it for everyone.

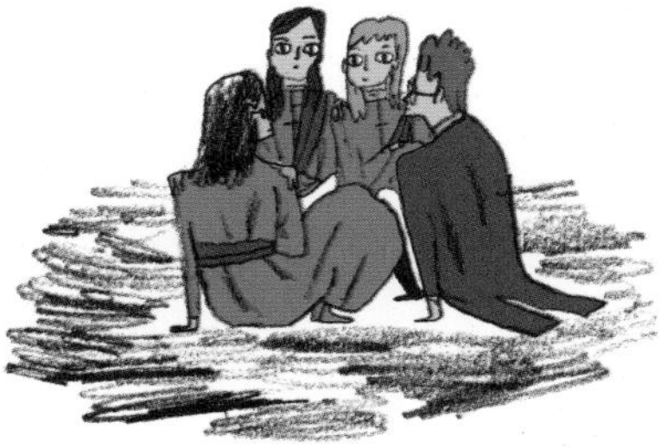

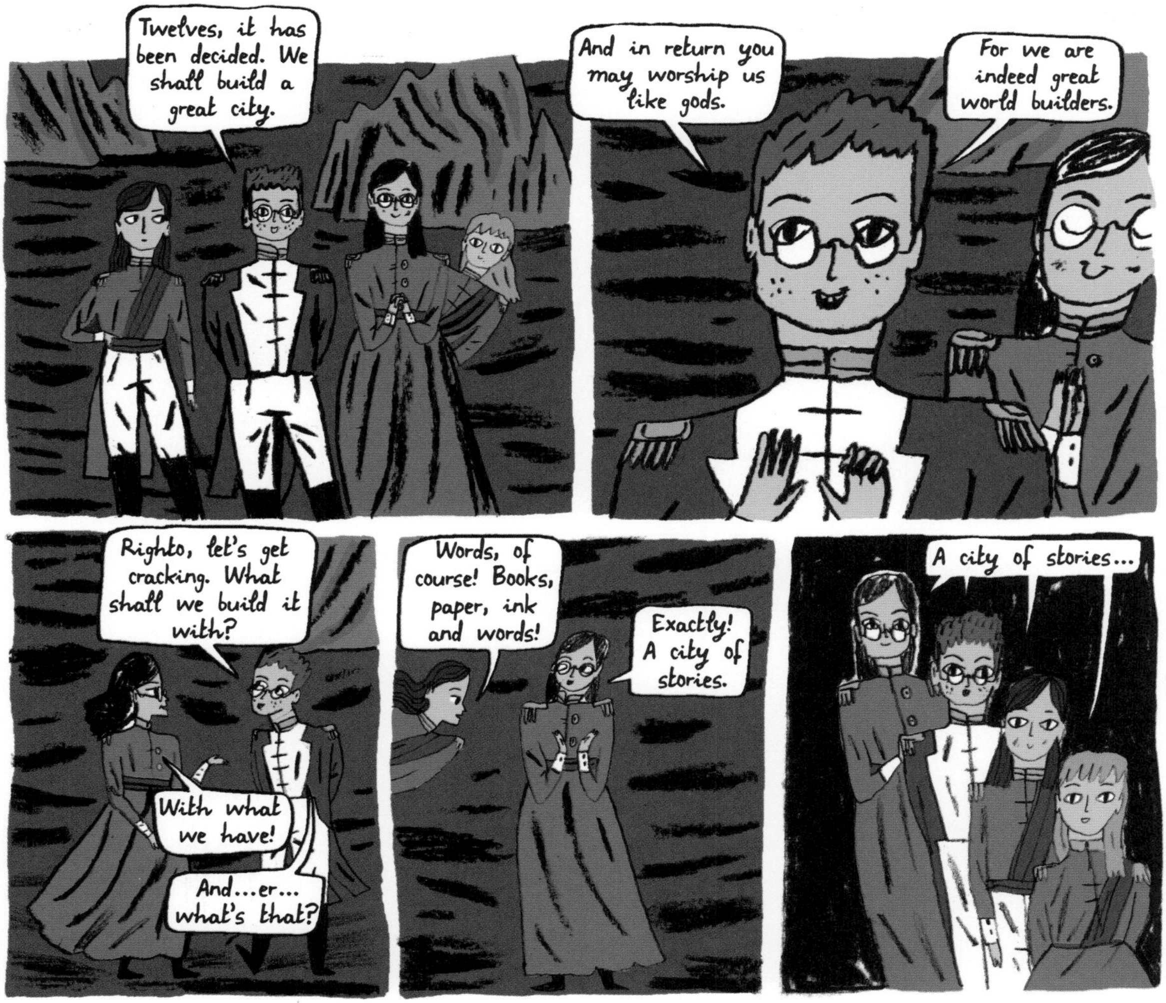
Twelves, it has been decided. We shall build a great city.
And in return you may worship us like gods.
For we are indeed great world builders.
Righto, let's get cracking. What shall we build it with?
With what we have!
And...er... what's that?
Words, of course! Books, paper, ink and words!
Exactly! A city of stories.
A city of stories...

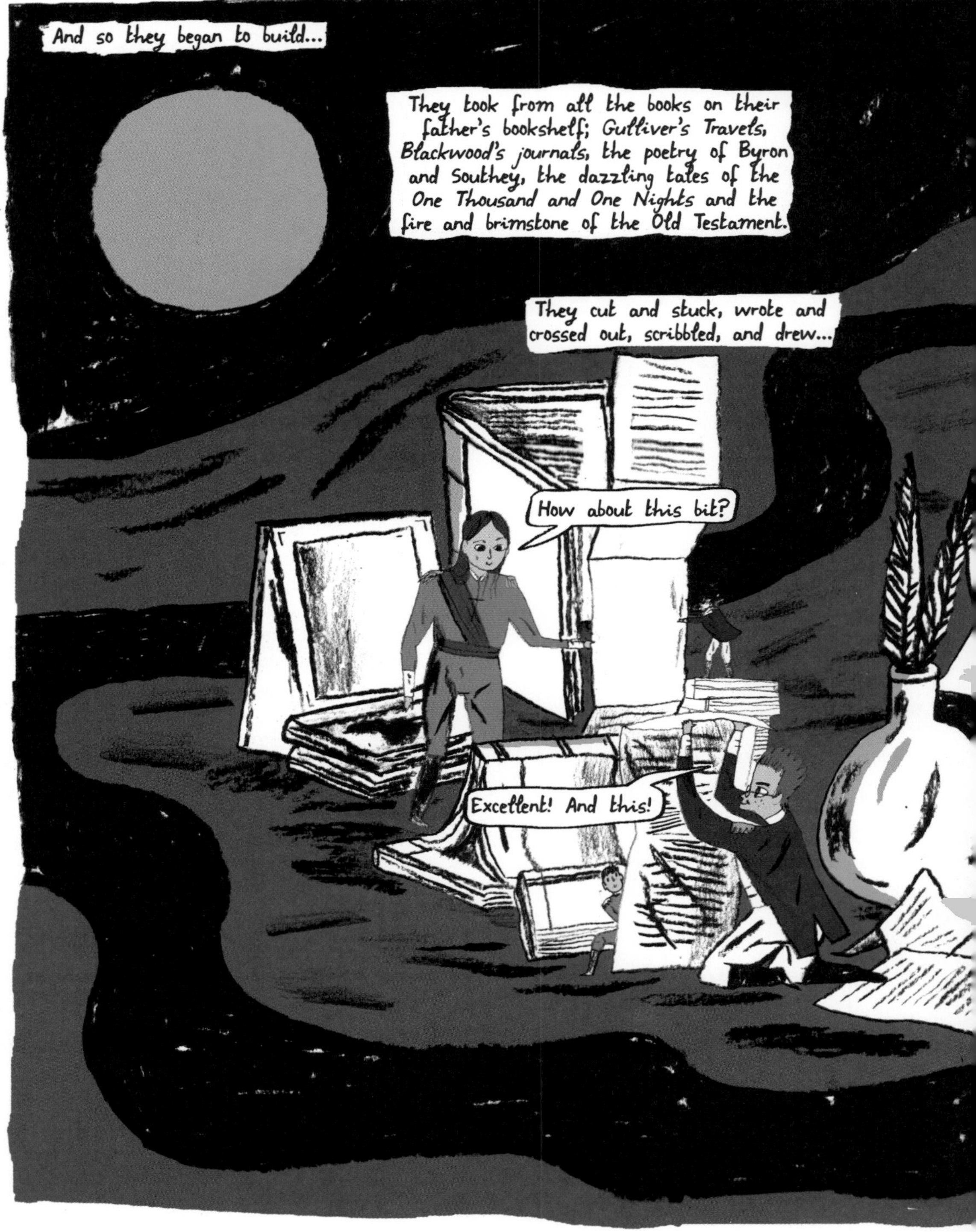
And so they began to build...
They took from all the books on their father's bookshelf; Gulliver's Travels, Blackwood's journals, the poetry of Byron and Southey, the dazzling tales of the One Thousand and One Nights and the fire and brimstone of the Old Testament.
They cut and stuck, wrote and crossed out, scribbled, and drew...
How about this bit?
Excellent! And this!

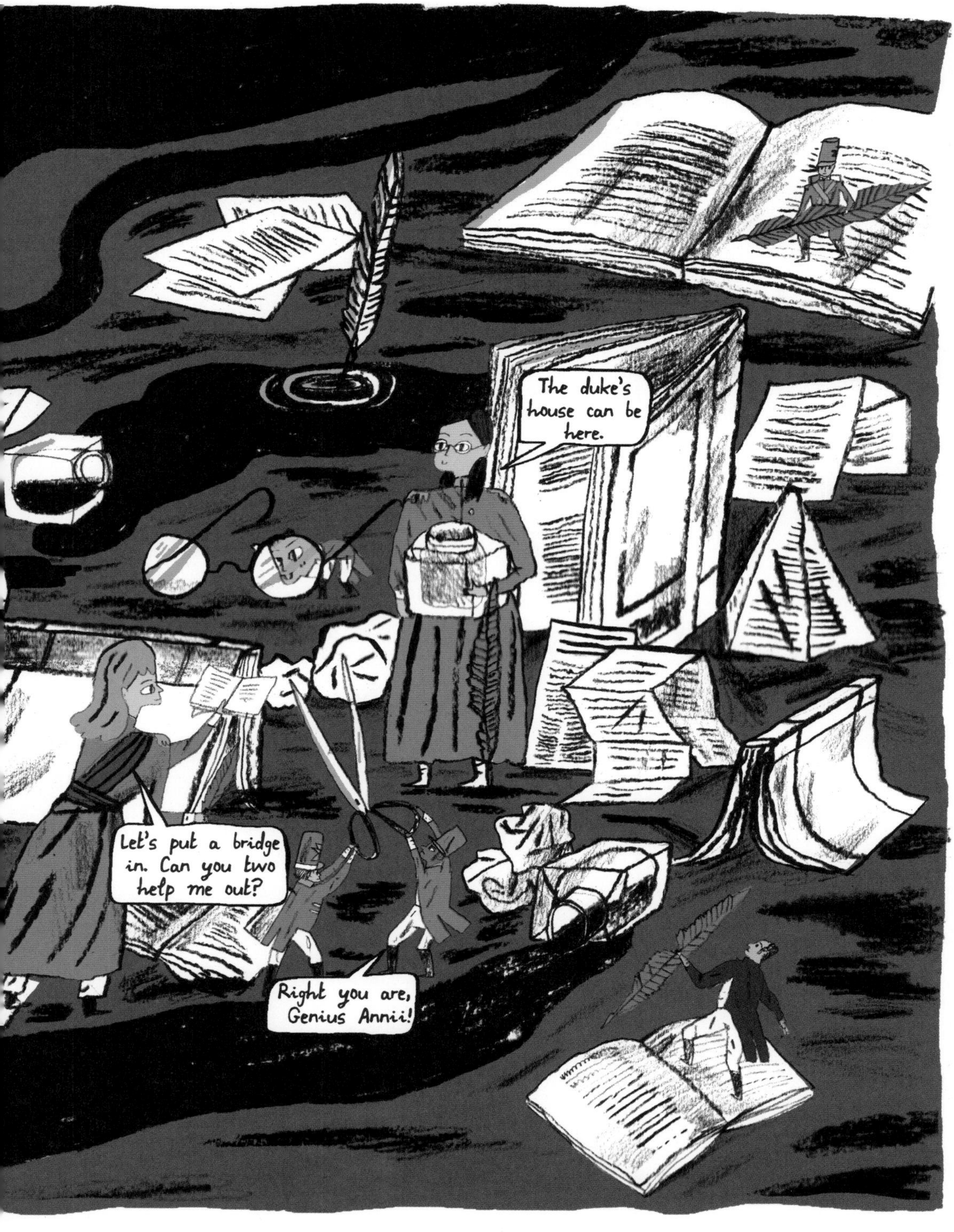
The duke's house can be here.
Let's put a bridge in. Can you two help me out?
Right you are, Genius Annii!

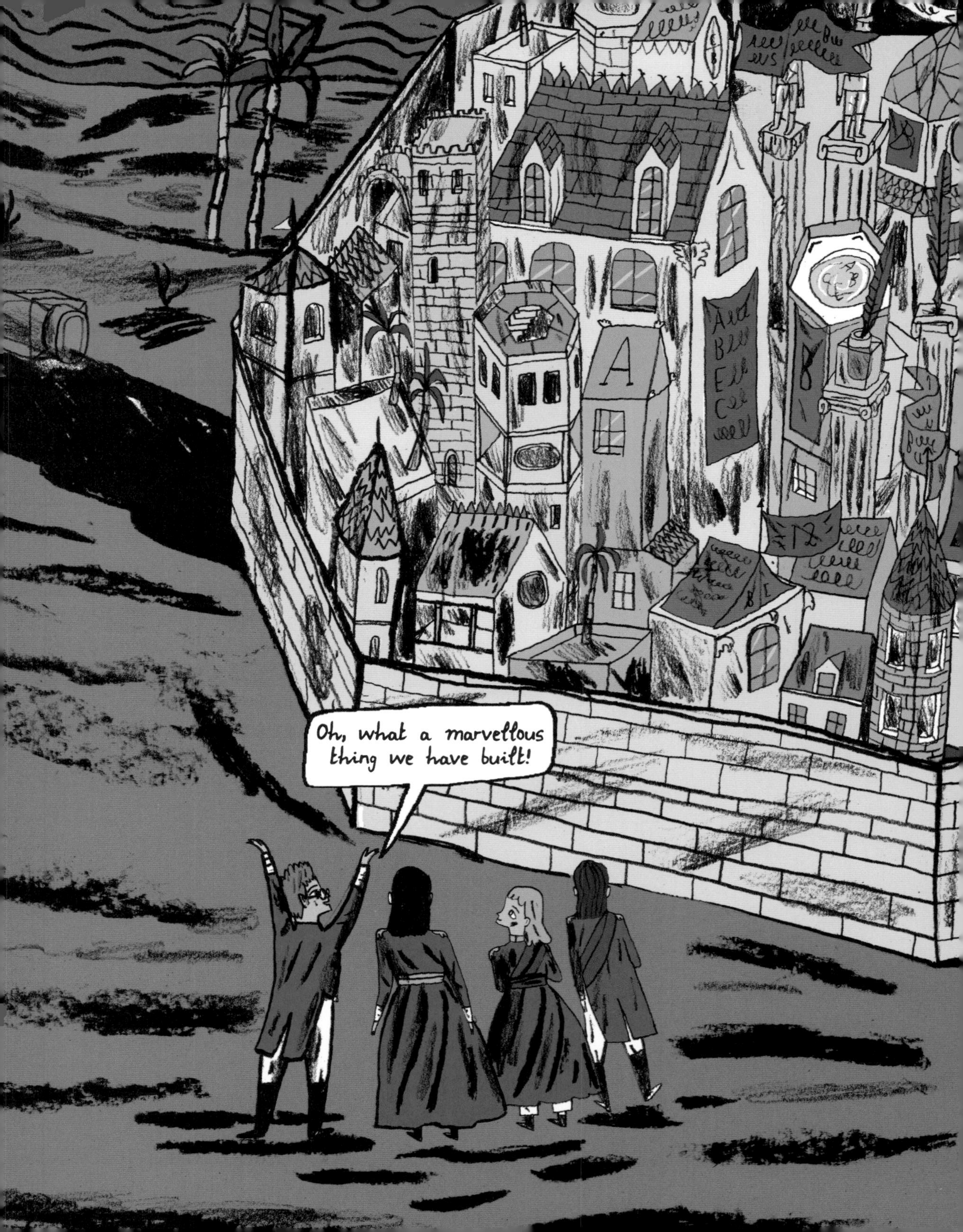
Oh, what a marvellous thing we have built!

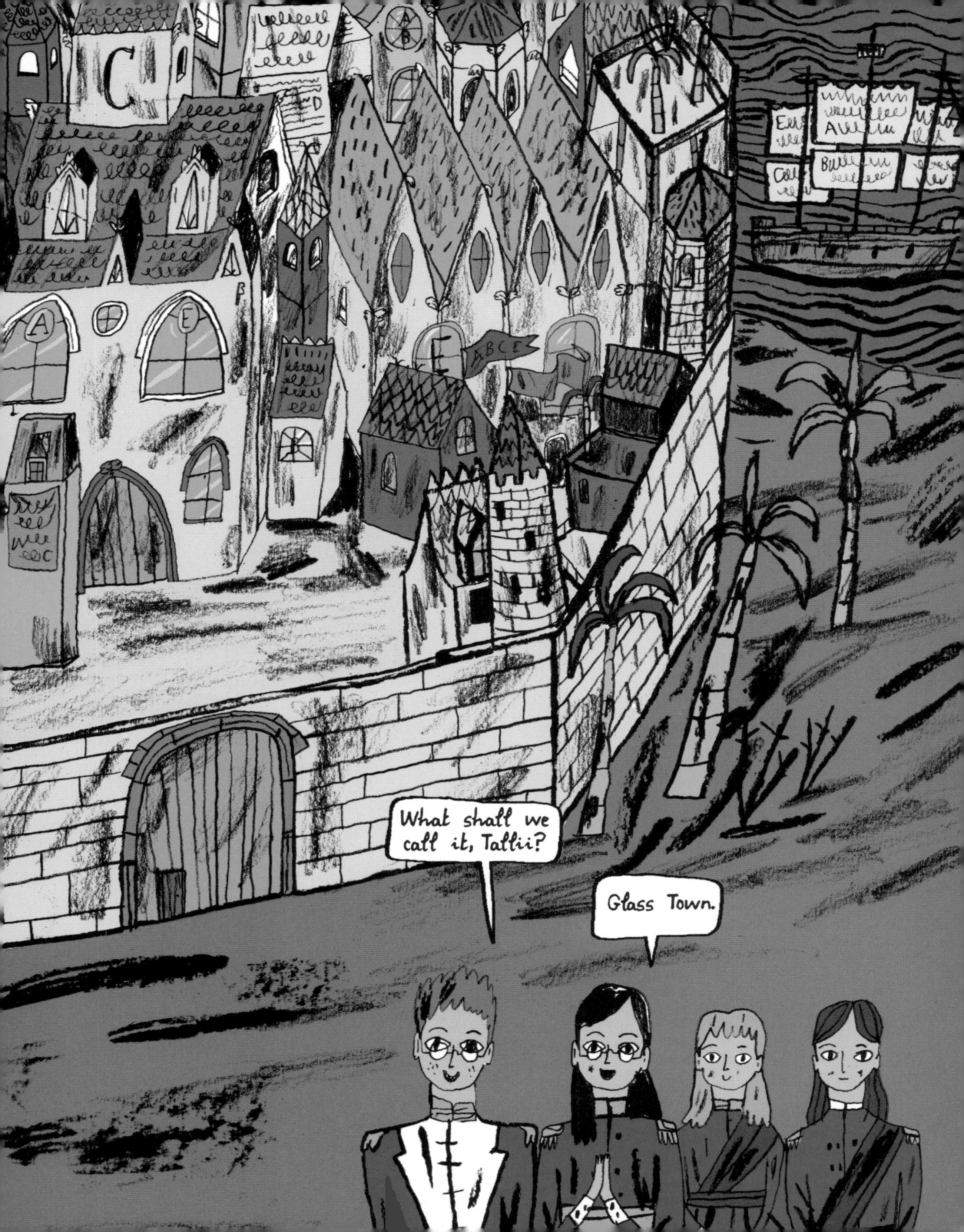
What shall we call it, Tallii?
Glass Town.

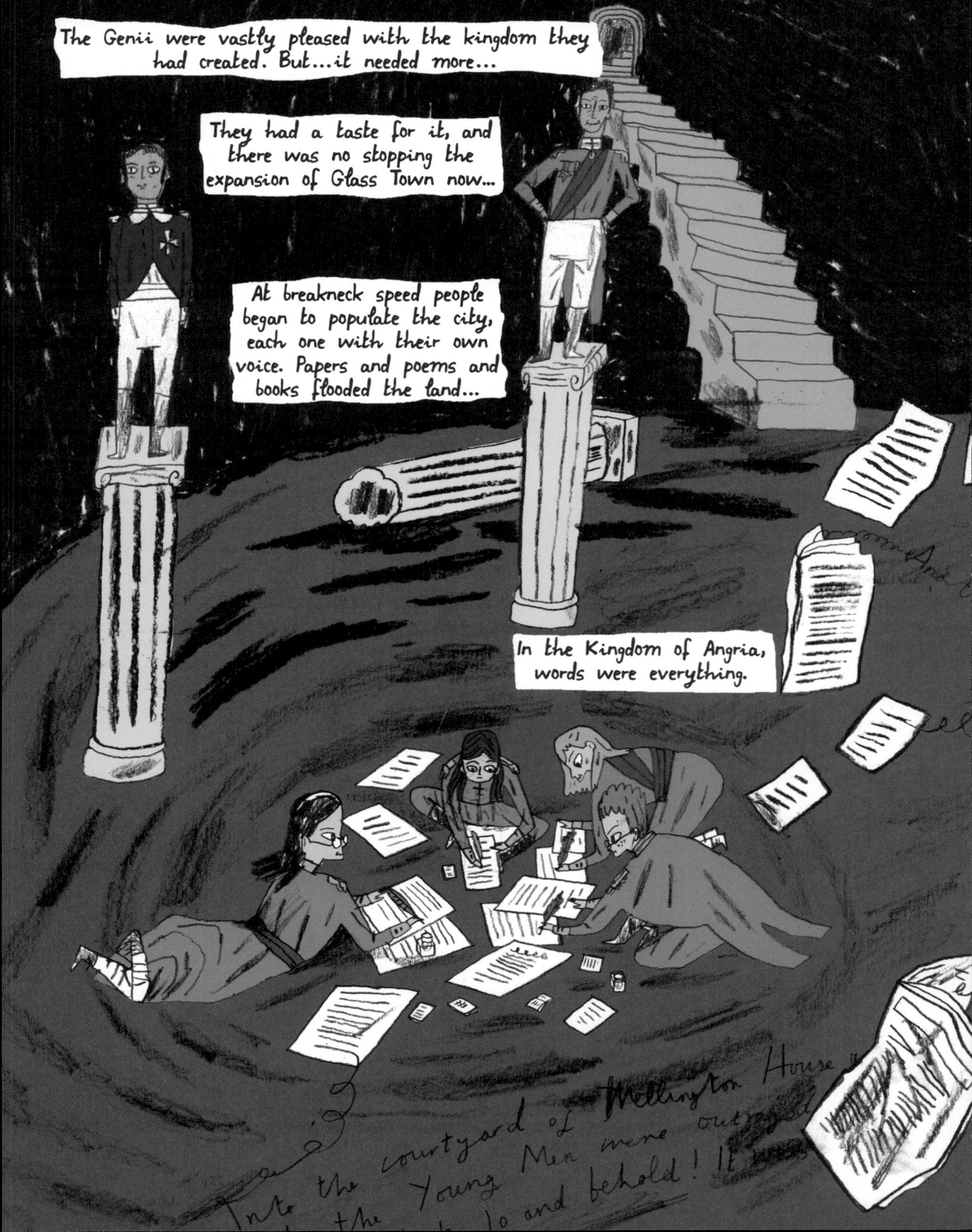
The Genii were vastly pleased with the kingdom they had created. But...it needed more...
They had a taste for it, and there was no stopping the expansion of Glass Town now...
At breakneck speed people began to populate the city, each one with their own voice. Papers and poems and books flooded the land...
In the Kingdom of Angria, words were everything.

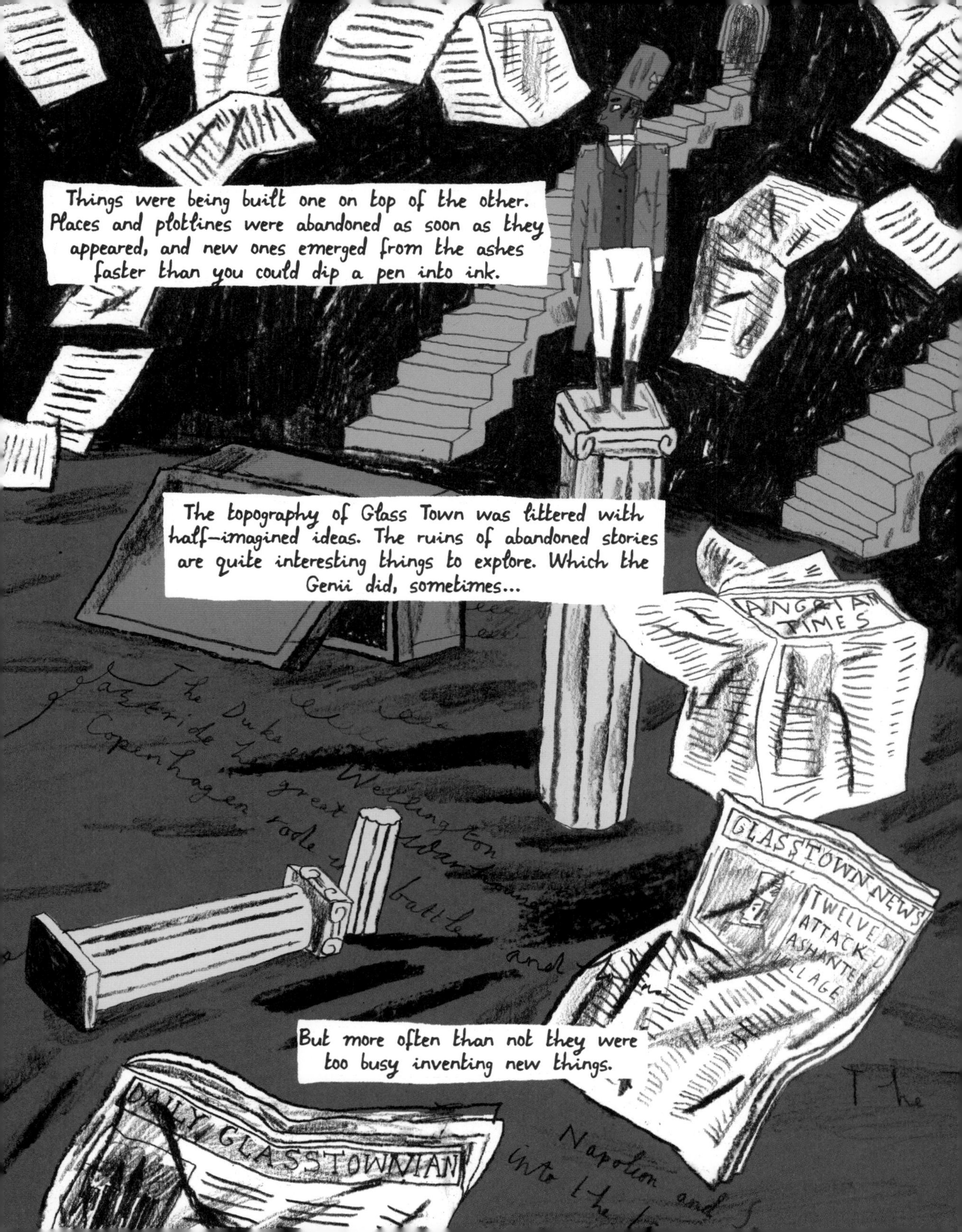
Things were being built one on top of the other. Places and plotlines were abandoned as soon as they appeared, and new ones emerged from the ashes faster than you could dip a pen into ink.
The topography of Glass Town was littered with half-imagined ideas. The ruins of abandoned stories are quite interesting things to explore. Which the Genii did, sometimes...
ANGRIAN TIMES
GLASSTOWN NEWS
TWELVES ATTACKED
But more often than not they were too busy inventing new things.
DAILY GLASSTOWNIAN

A new cast of Glass Towners had arrived. The Twelves, though venerated as founding fathers, had been consigned to become great marble statues in the Hall of Ideas Past. The four Genii had new people to take care of...

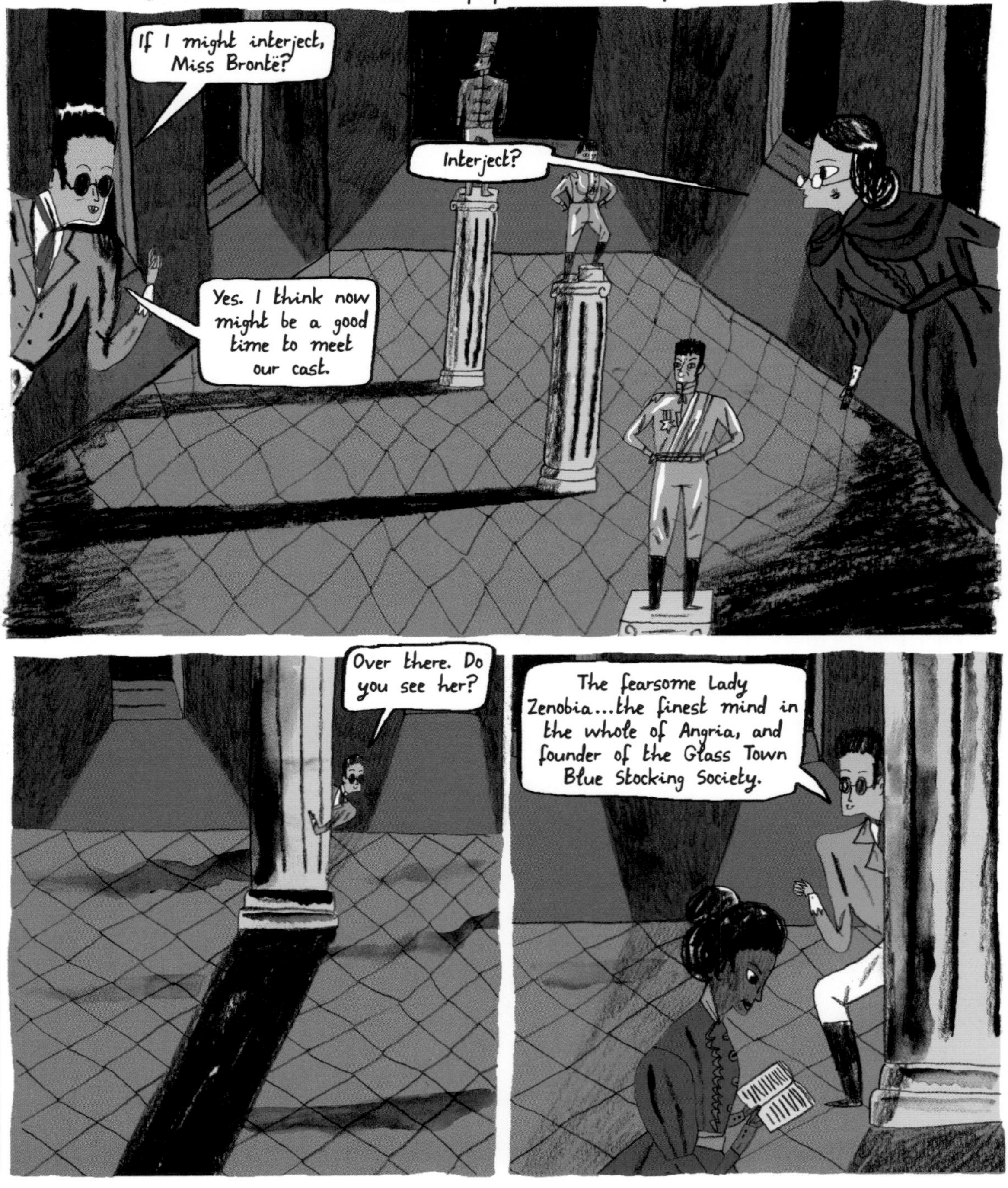
If I might interject, Miss Brontë?
Interject?
Yes. I think now might be a good time to meet our cast.
Over there. Do you see her?
The fearsome Lady Zenobia...the finest mind in the whole of Angria, and founder of the Glass Town Blue Stocking Society.

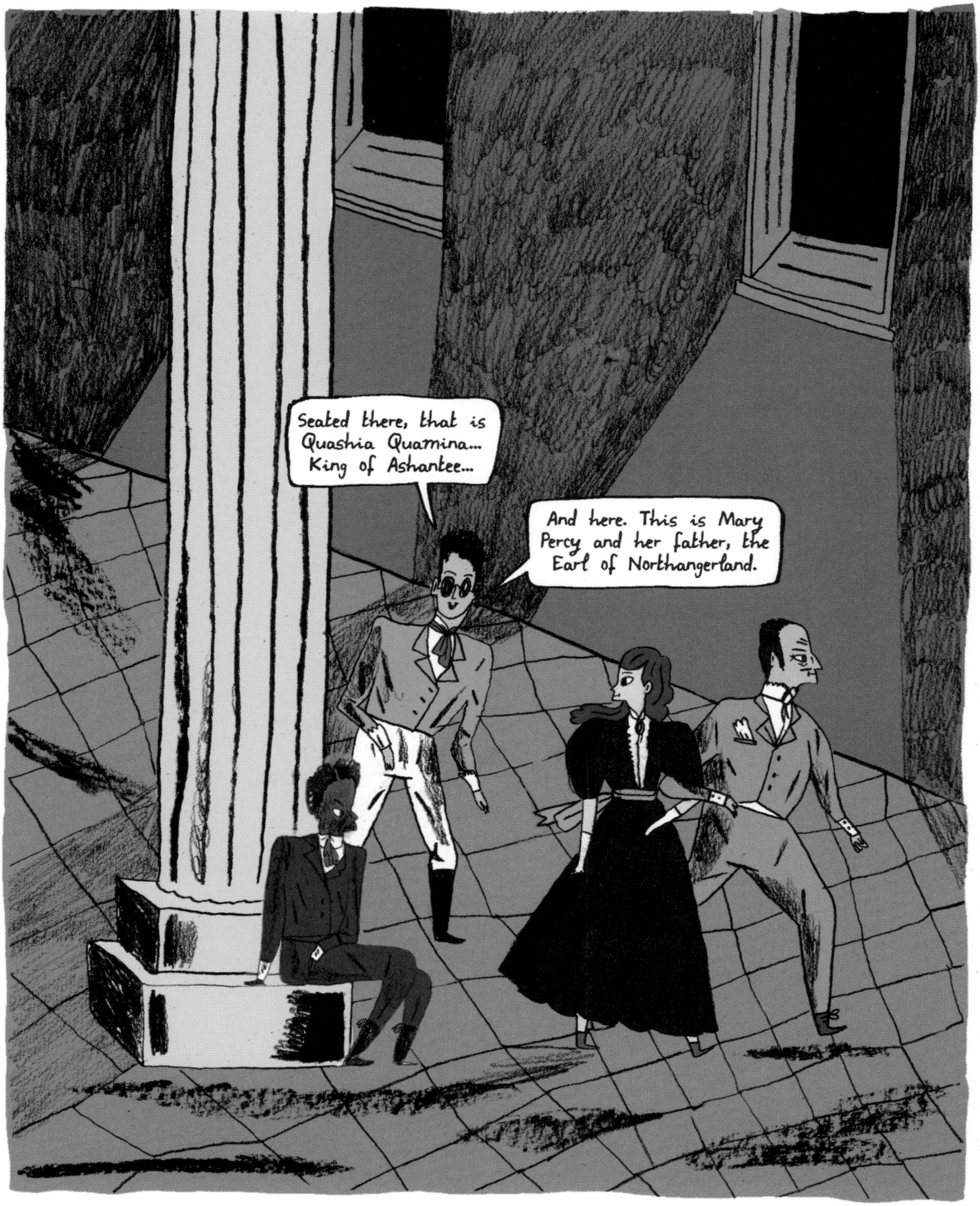
Seated there, that is Quashia Quamina... King of Ashantee...
And here. This is Mary Percy and her father, the Earl of Northangerland.

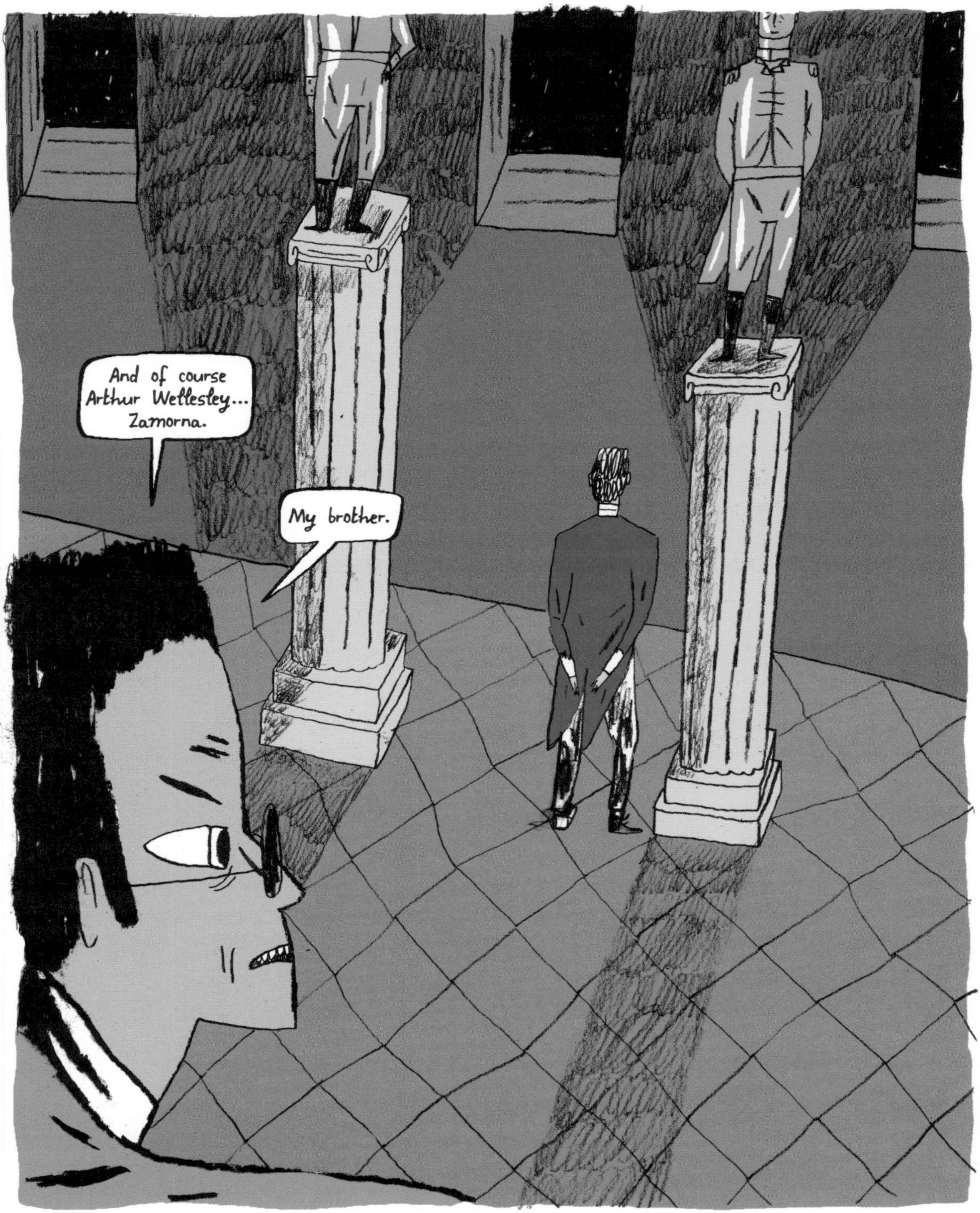
And of course Arthur Wellesley... Zamorna.
My brother.

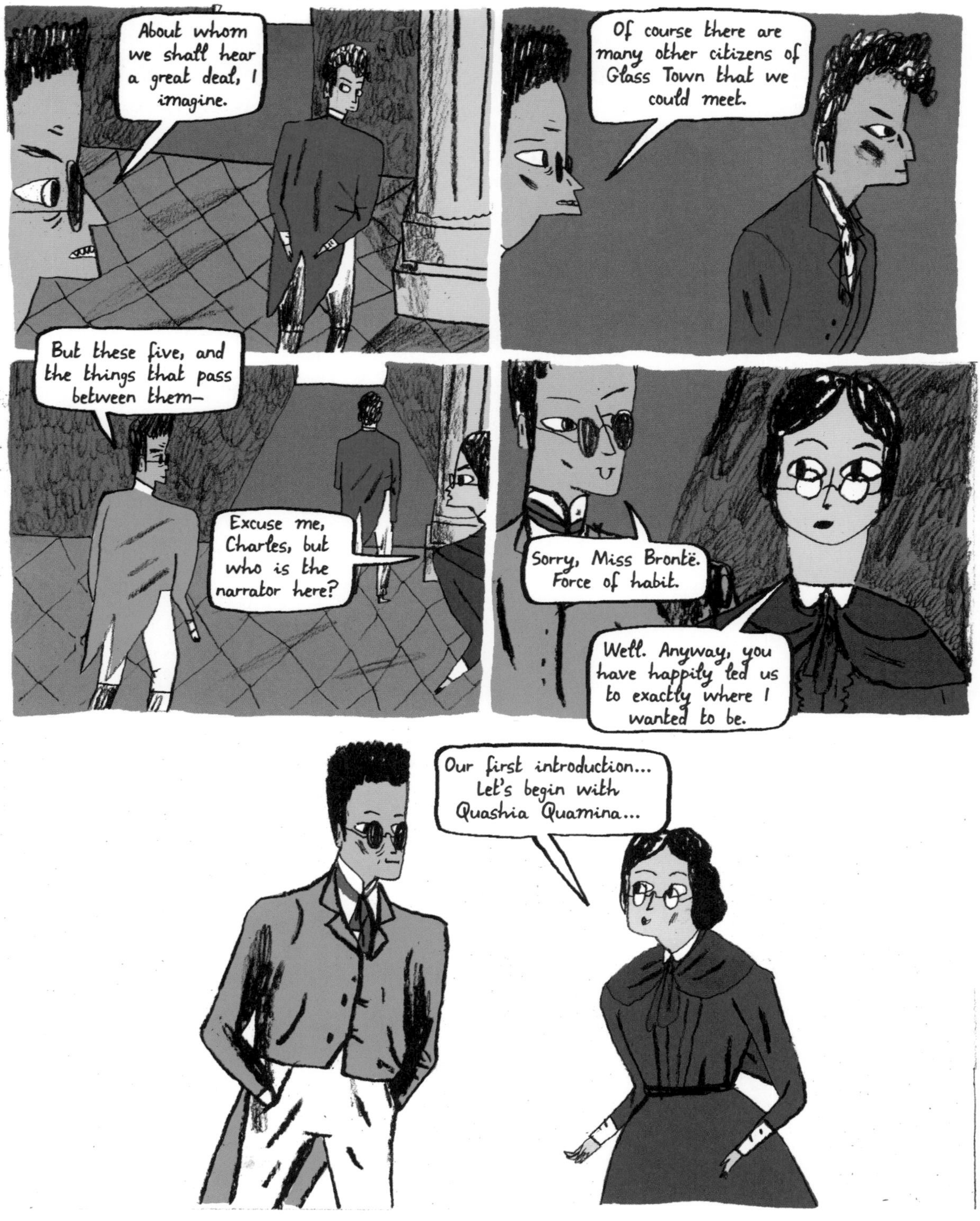
About whom we shall hear a great deal, I imagine.
Of course there are many other citizens of Glass Town that we could meet.
But these five, and the things that pass between them—
Excuse me, Charles, but who is the narrator here?
Sorry, Miss Brontë. Force of habit.
Well. Anyway, you have happily led us to exactly where I wanted to be.
Our first introduction... Let's begin with Quashia Quamina...

Quashia Quamina

Quashia Quamina was the son of the king of the Ashantee people, who had lived in the Kingdom of Angria for as long as time. When the Duke of Wellington arrived with the Twelves, and the terrible Ashantee Wars began, they were driven from their homes. With the Duke at their head, the English troops ravaged and slaughtered and pillaged and enslaved.

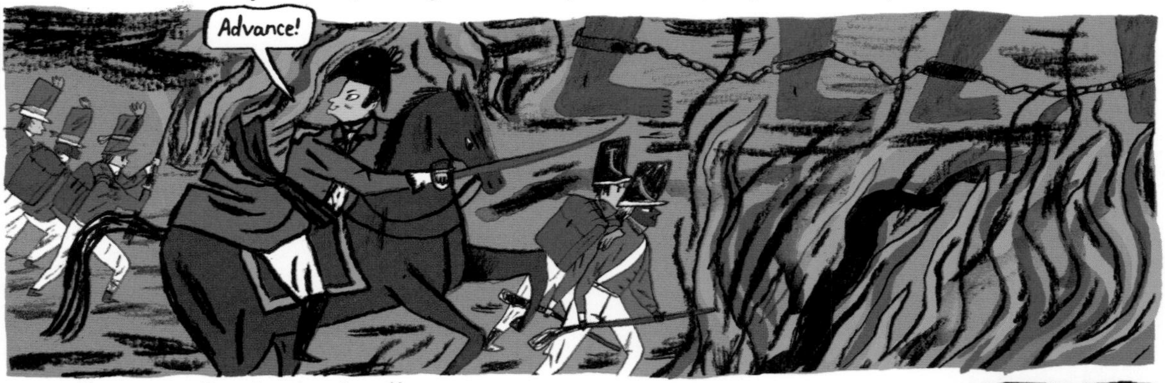
Advance!

In the ruins of a burnt-out village Wellington himself came upon the little boy, Quashia Quamina.

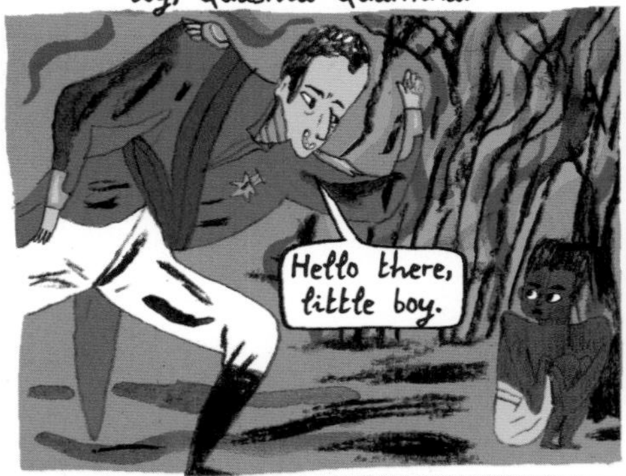
Hello there, little boy.

His father had been killed, his mother, his brothers, his sisters...

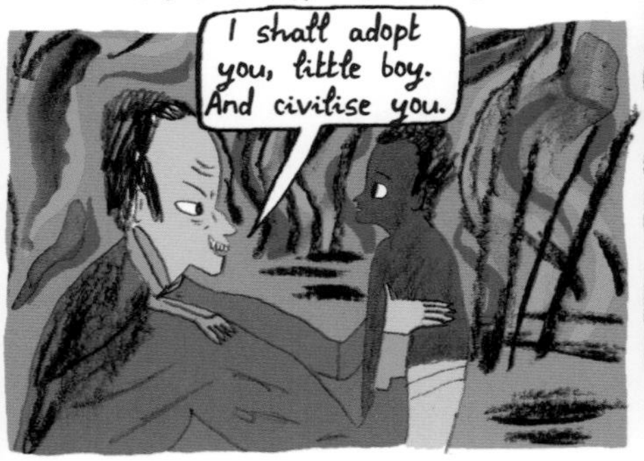
I shall adopt you, little boy. And civilise you.

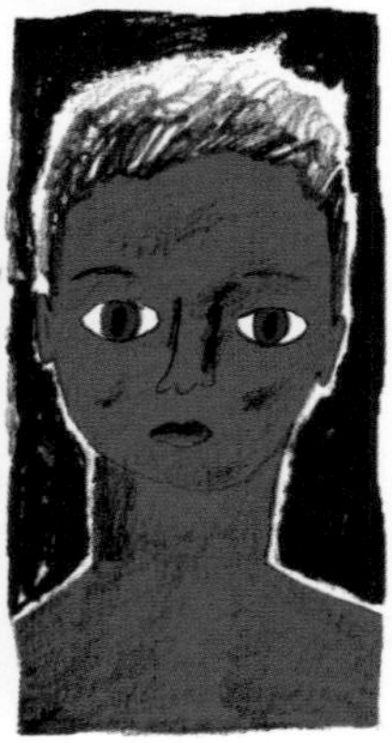

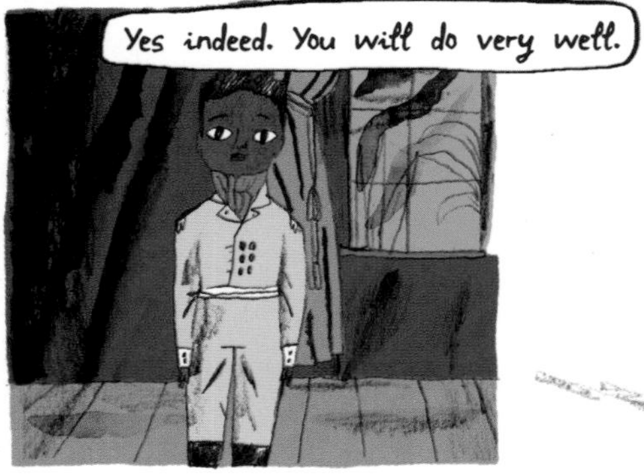
Yes indeed. You will do very well.

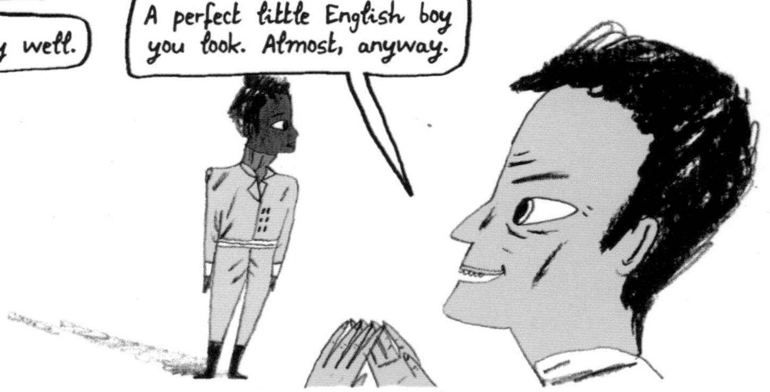
A perfect little English boy you look. Almost, anyway.

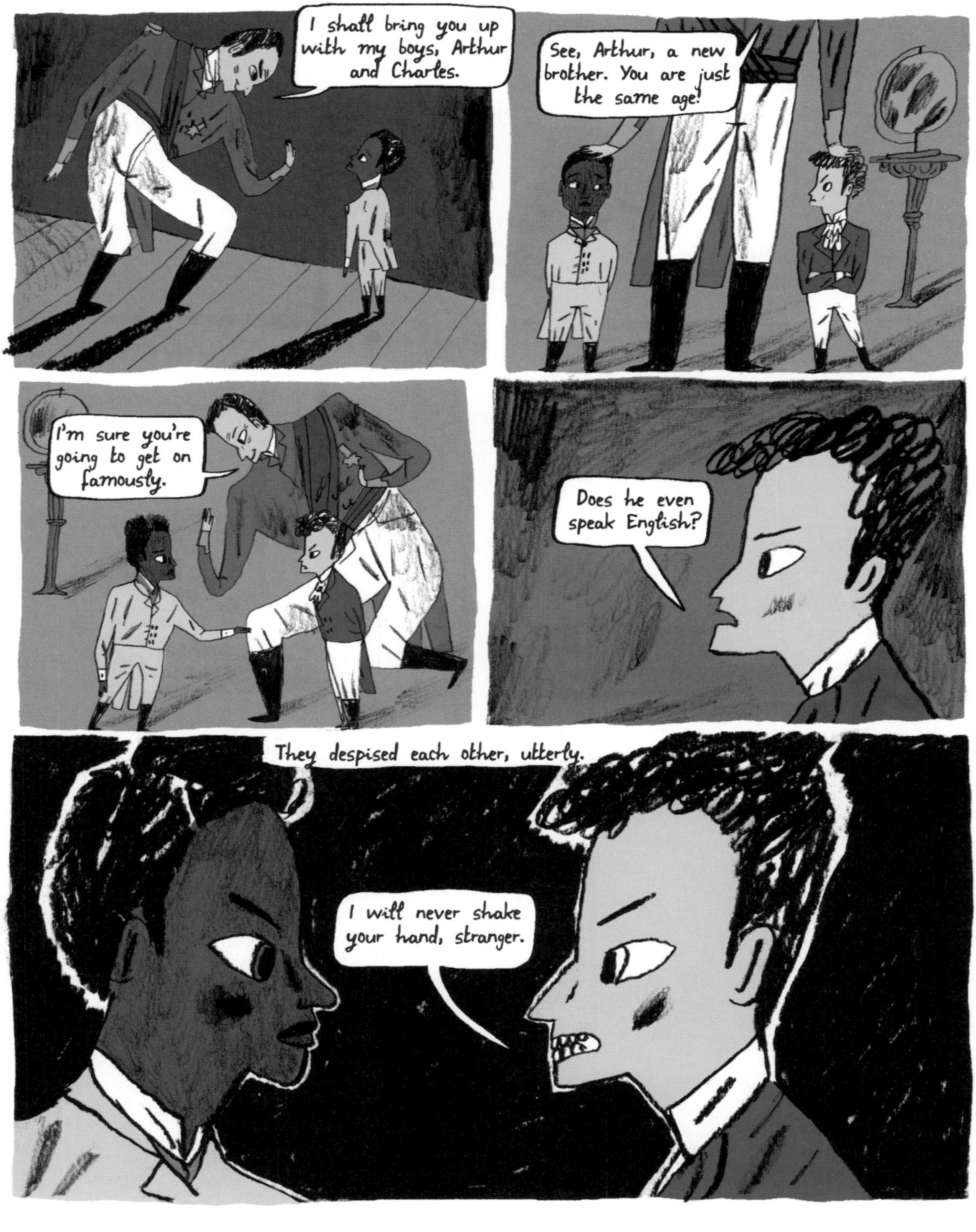
I shall bring you up with my boys, Arthur and Charles.
See, Arthur, a new brother. You are just the same age!
I'm sure you're going to get on famously.
Does he even speak English?
They despised each other, utterly.
I will never shake your hand, stranger.

As they grew, their hatred of each other only increased.

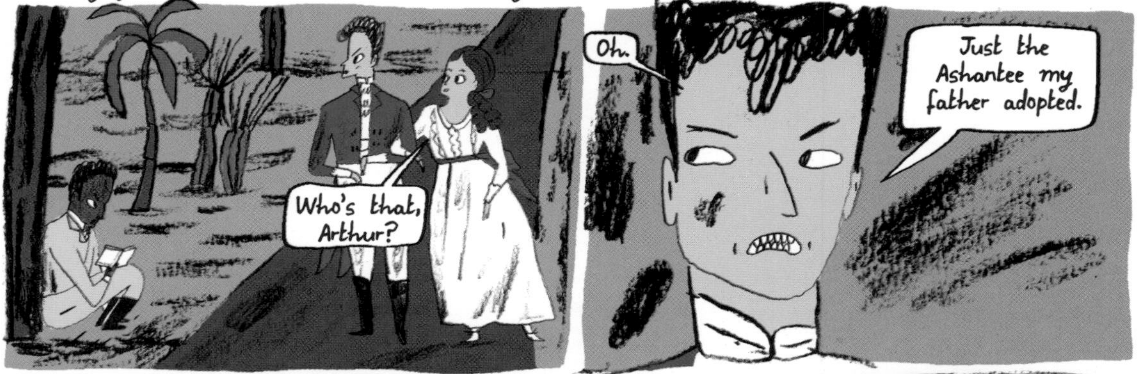
Who's that, Arthur?
Oh.
Just the Ashantee my father adopted.

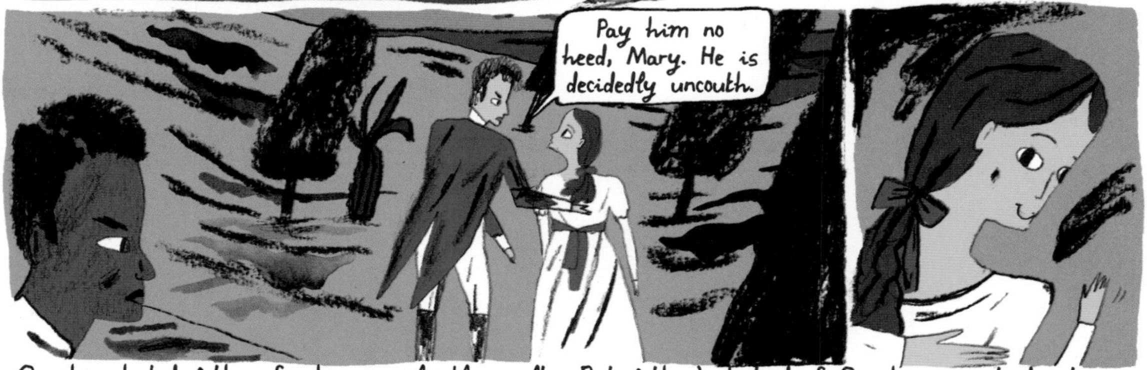
Pay him no heed, Mary. He is decidedly uncouth.

Quashia hated Arthur for his inexplicable cruelty. But Arthur's hatred of Quashia was tied into a jealousy that ran deep and fast. For his father loved Quashia and his brother loved Quashia. And that Arthur could not bear.

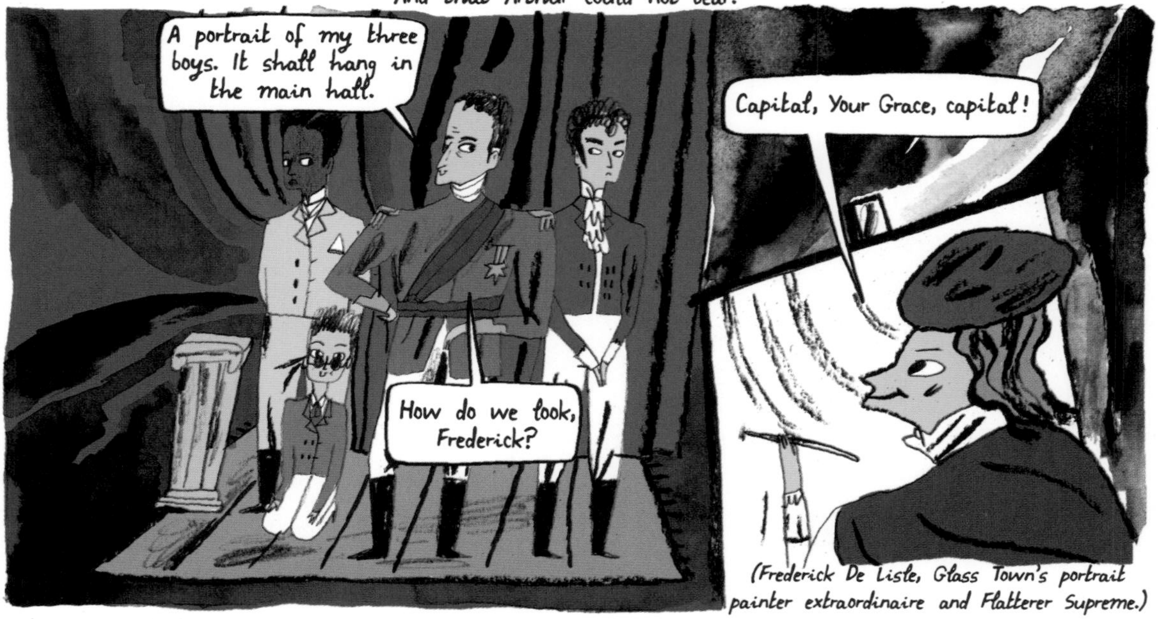
A portrait of my three boys. It shall hang in the main hall.
How do we look, Frederick?
Capital, Your Grace, capital!

(Frederick De Lisle, Glass Town's portrait painter extraordinaire and Flatterer Supreme.)

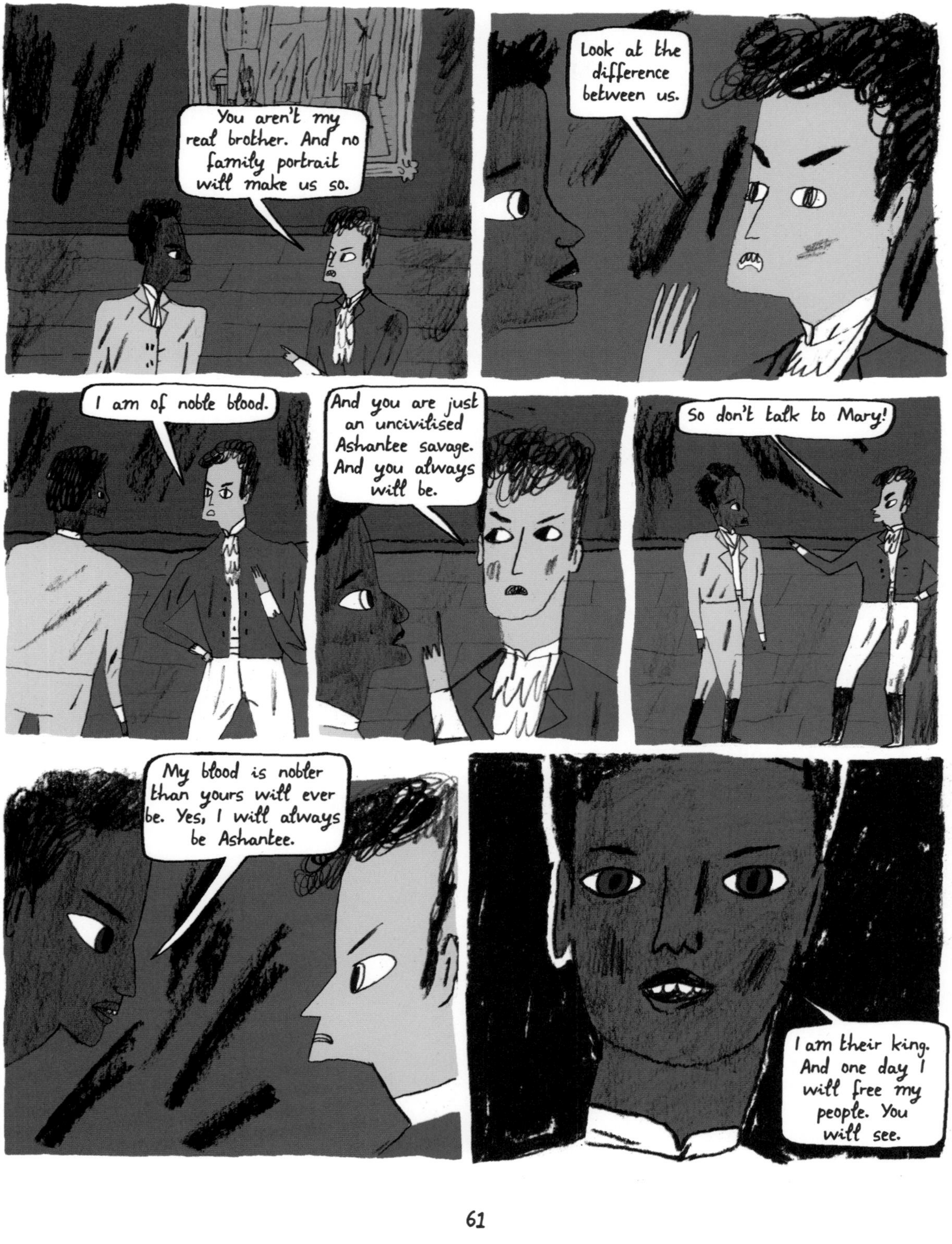
You aren't my real brother. And no family portrait will make us so.
Look at the difference between us.
I am of noble blood.
And you are just an uncivilised Ashantee savage. And you always will be.
So don't talk to Mary!
My blood is nobler than yours will ever be. Yes, I will always be Ashantee.
I am their king. And one day I will free my people. You will see.

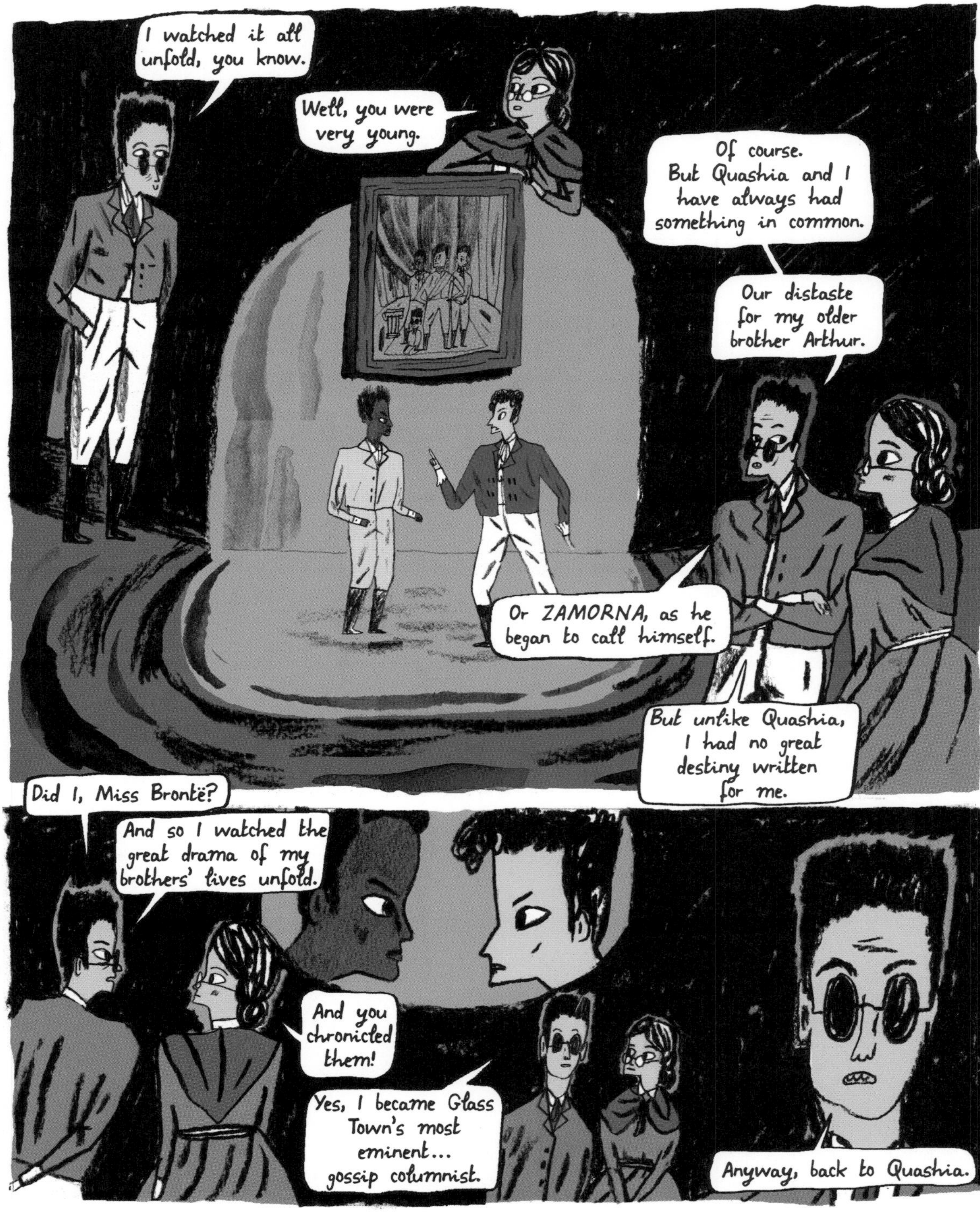
I watched it all unfold, you know.
Well, you were very young.
Of course. But Quashia and I have always had something in common.
Our distaste for my older brother Arthur.
Or ZAMORNA, as he began to call himself.
But unlike Quashia, I had no great destiny written for me.
Did I, Miss Brontë?
And so I watched the great drama of my brothers' lives unfold.
And you chronicled them!
Yes, I became Glass Town's most eminent... gossip columnist.
Anyway, back to Quashia.

As soon as Quashia came of age he ran away. He left the splendours of Glass Town behind. The city that had been built on the lands of his ancestors.

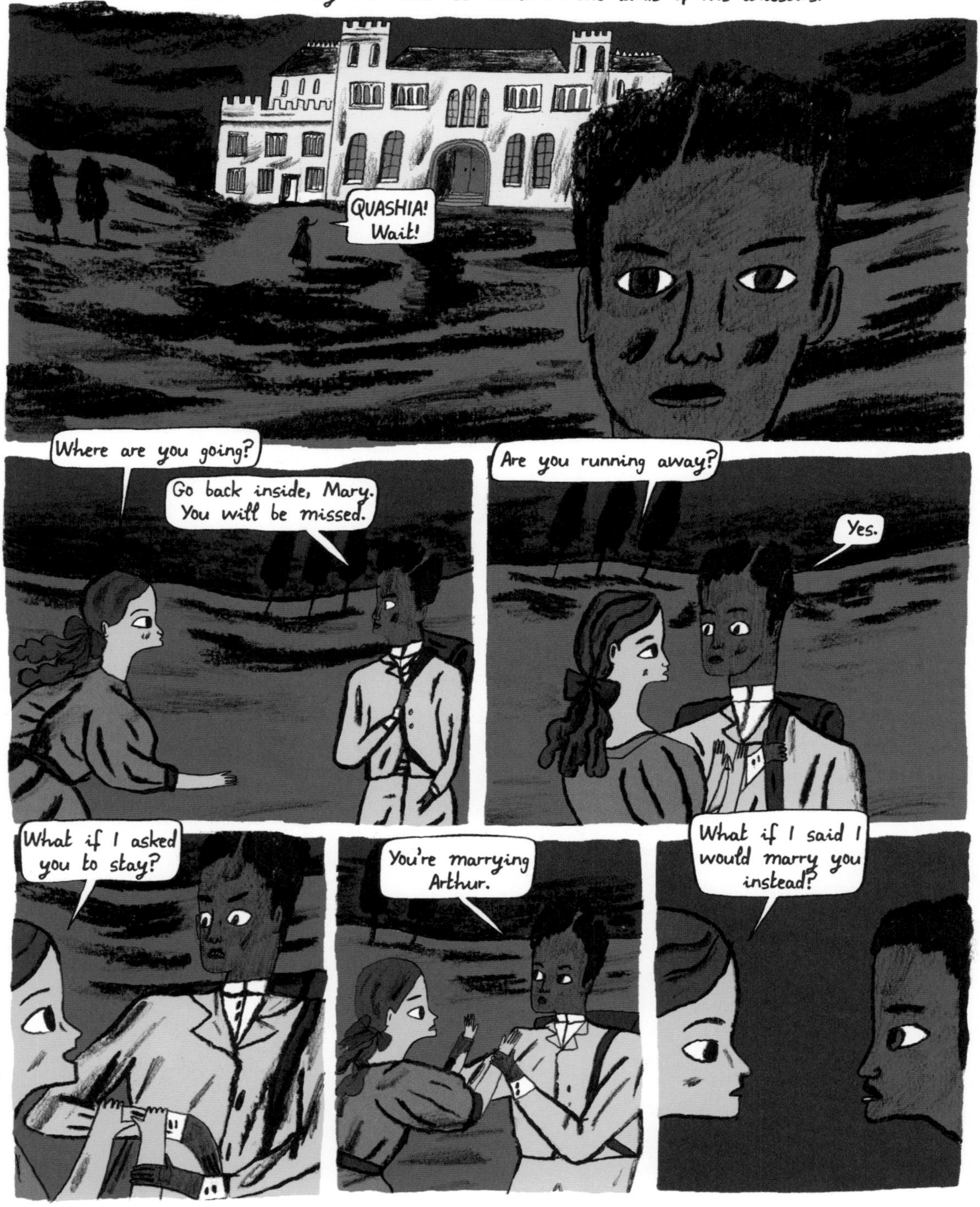
QUASHIA! Wait!
Where are you going?
Go back inside, Mary. You will be missed.
Are you running away?
Yes.
What if I asked you to stay?
You're marrying Arthur.
What if I said I would marry you instead?

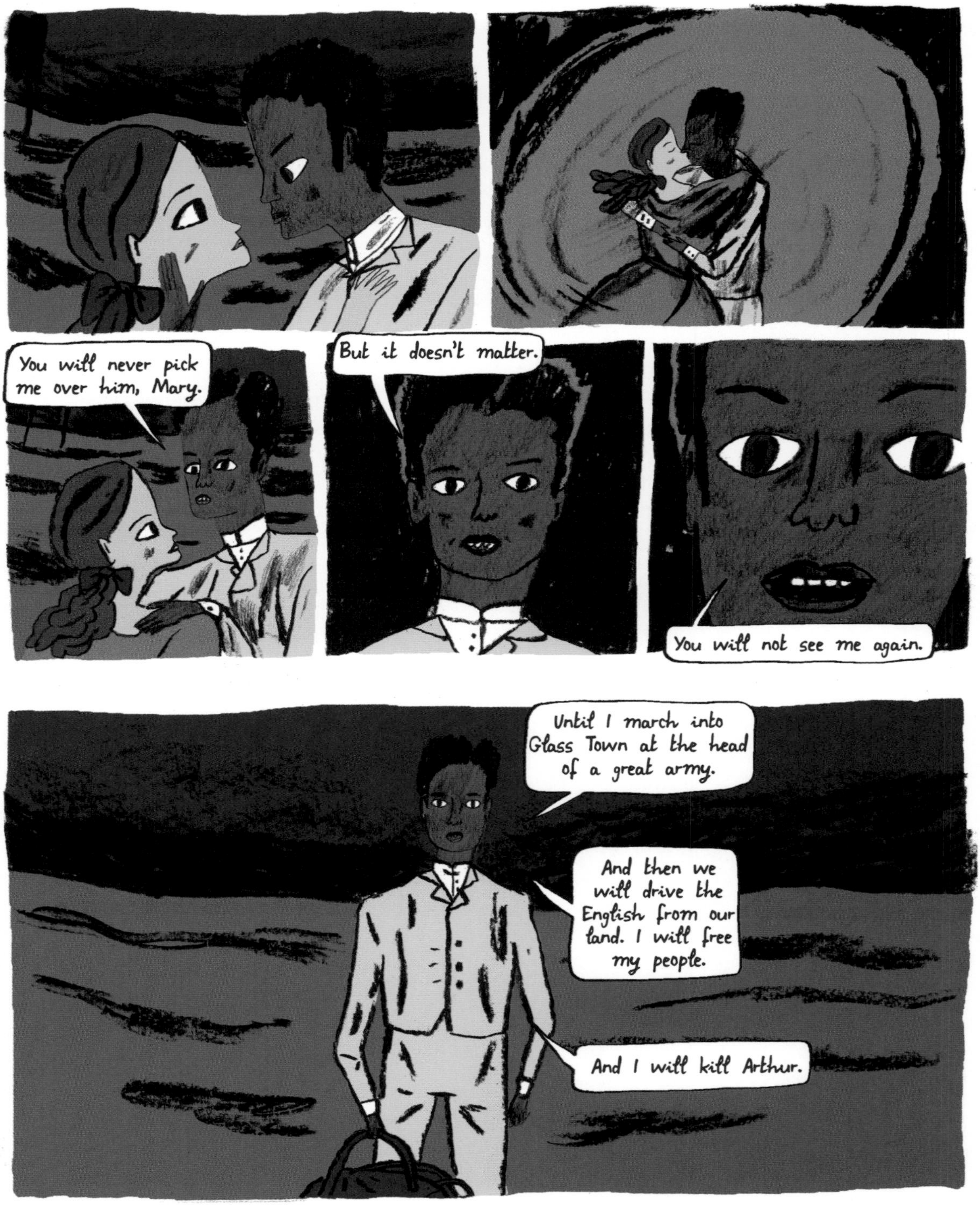
You will never pick me over him, Mary.
But it doesn't matter.
You will not see me again.
Until I march into Glass Town at the head of a great army.
And then we will drive the English from our land. I will free my people.
And I will kill Arthur.

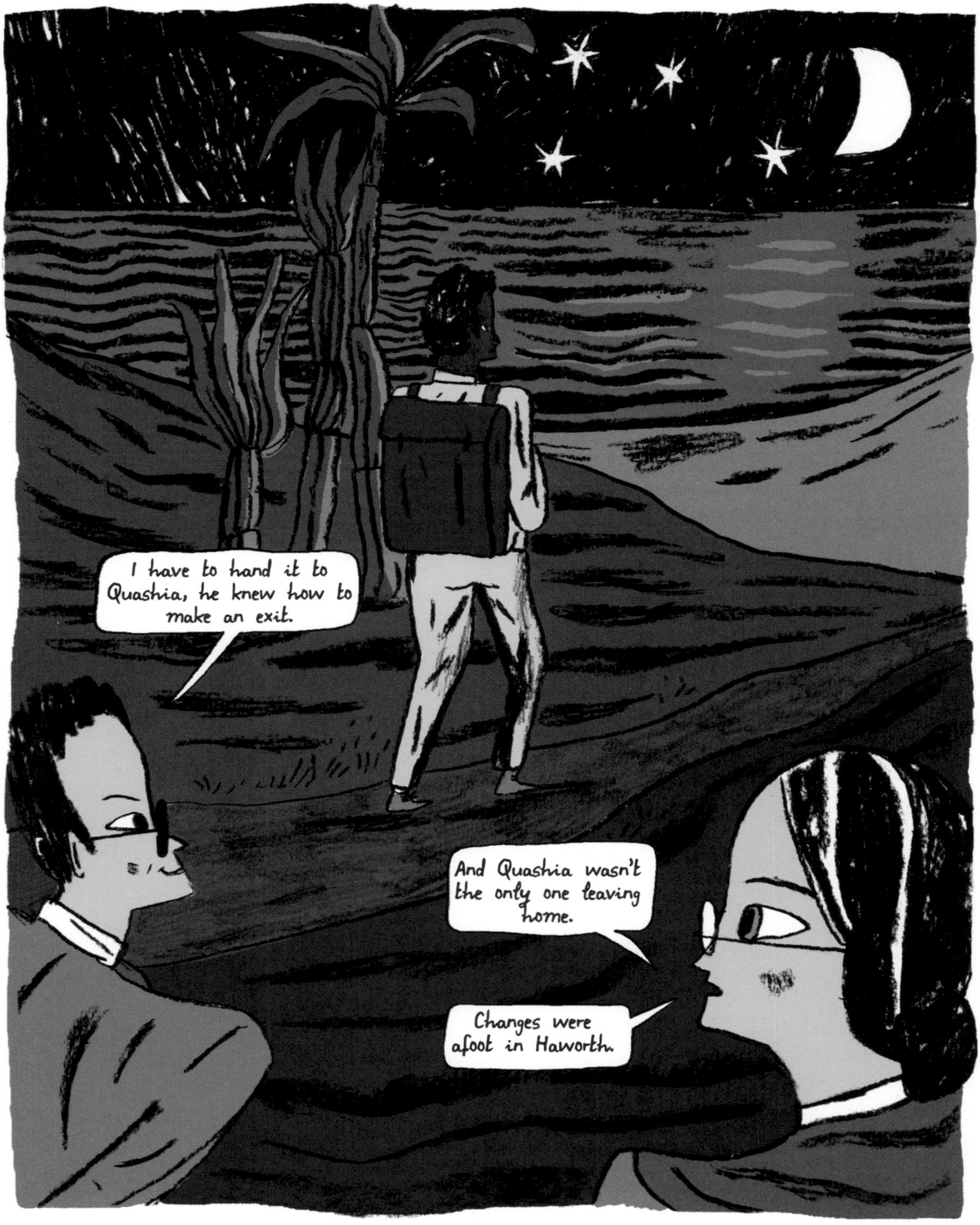
I have to hand it to Quashia, he knew how to make an exit.
And Quashia wasn't the only one leaving home.
Changes were afoot in Haworth.

CHAPTER TWO

1831 - 1835

Angrians Arise!

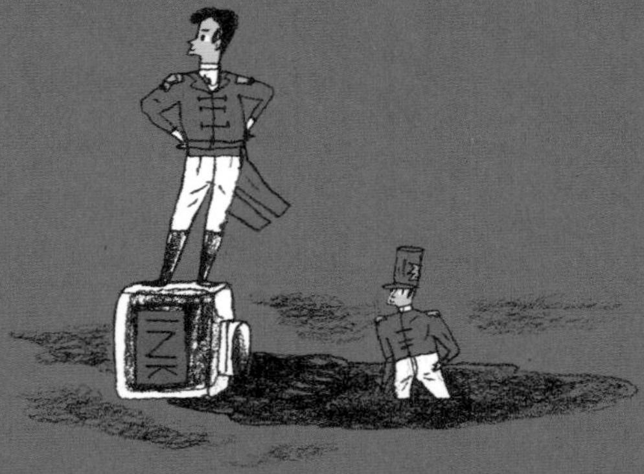
INK

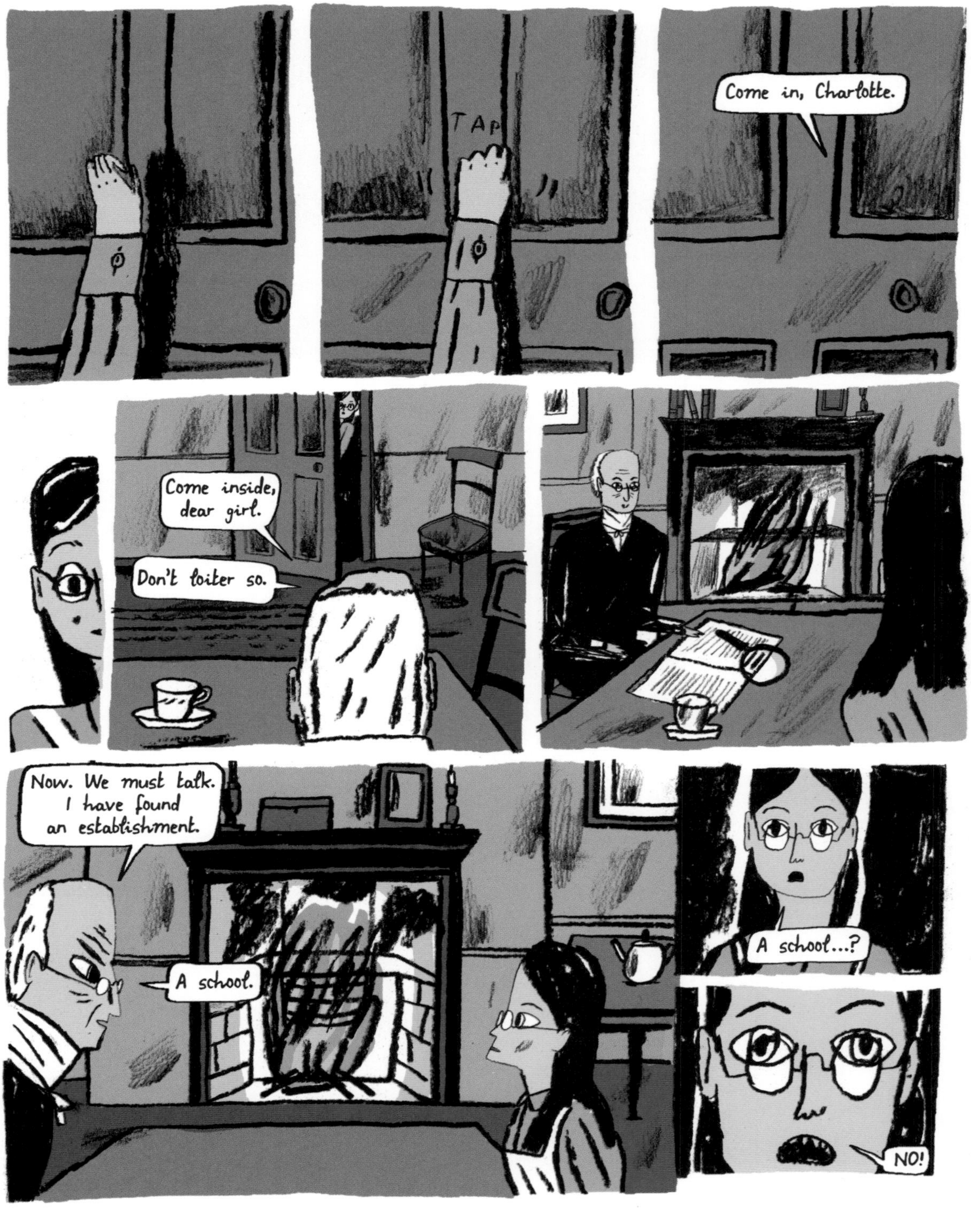
TAp
Come in, Charlotte.
Come inside, dear girl.
Don't loiter so.
Now. We must talk. I have found an establishment.
A school.
A school...?
NO!

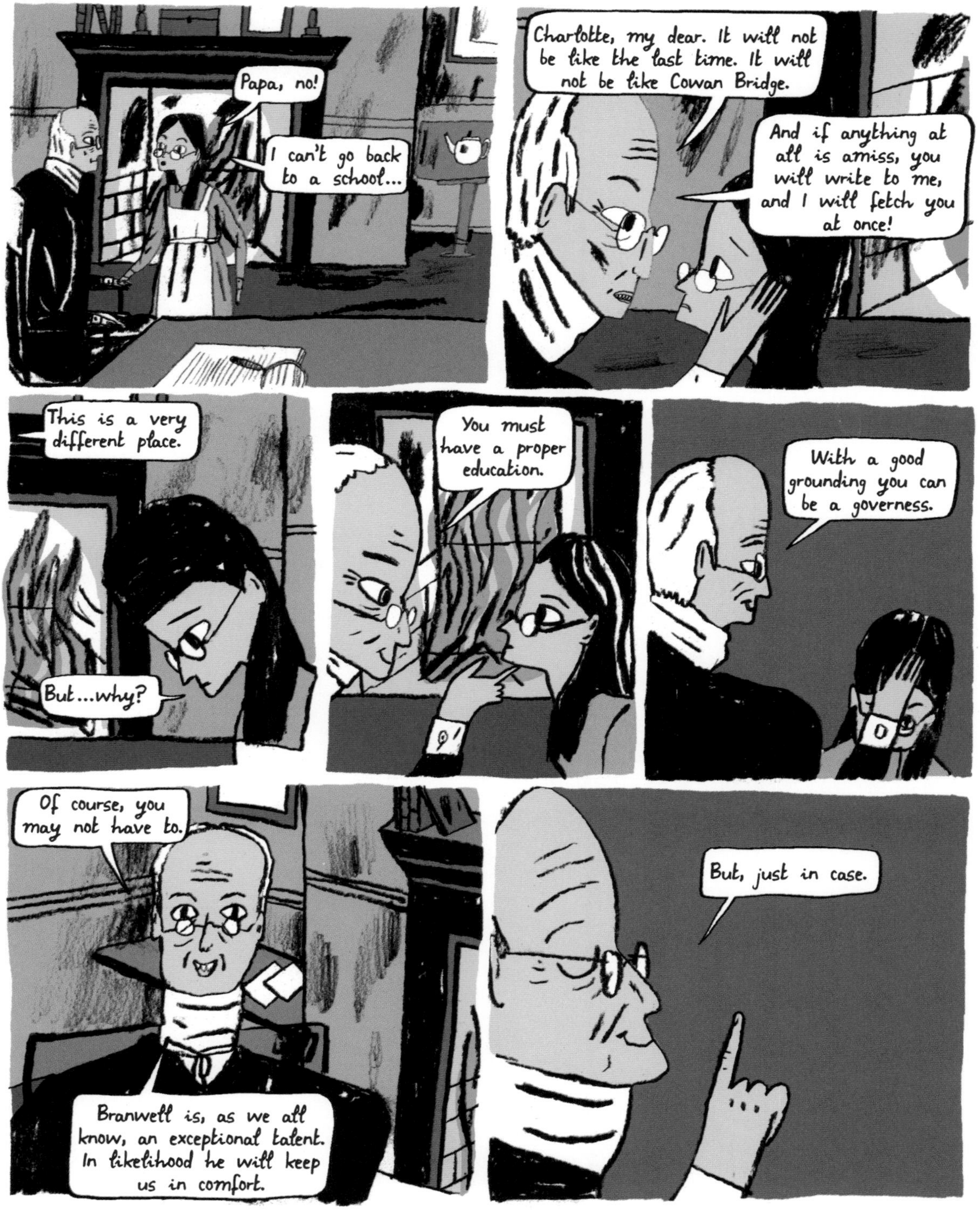

Papa, no!
I can't go back to a school...
Charlotte, my dear. It will not be like the last time. It will not be like Cowan Bridge.
And if anything at all is amiss, you will write to me, and I will fetch you at once!
This is a very different place.
But...why?
You must have a proper education.
With a good grounding you can be a governess.
Of course, you may not have to.
Branwell is, as we all know, an exceptional talent. In likelihood he will keep us in comfort.
But, just in case.

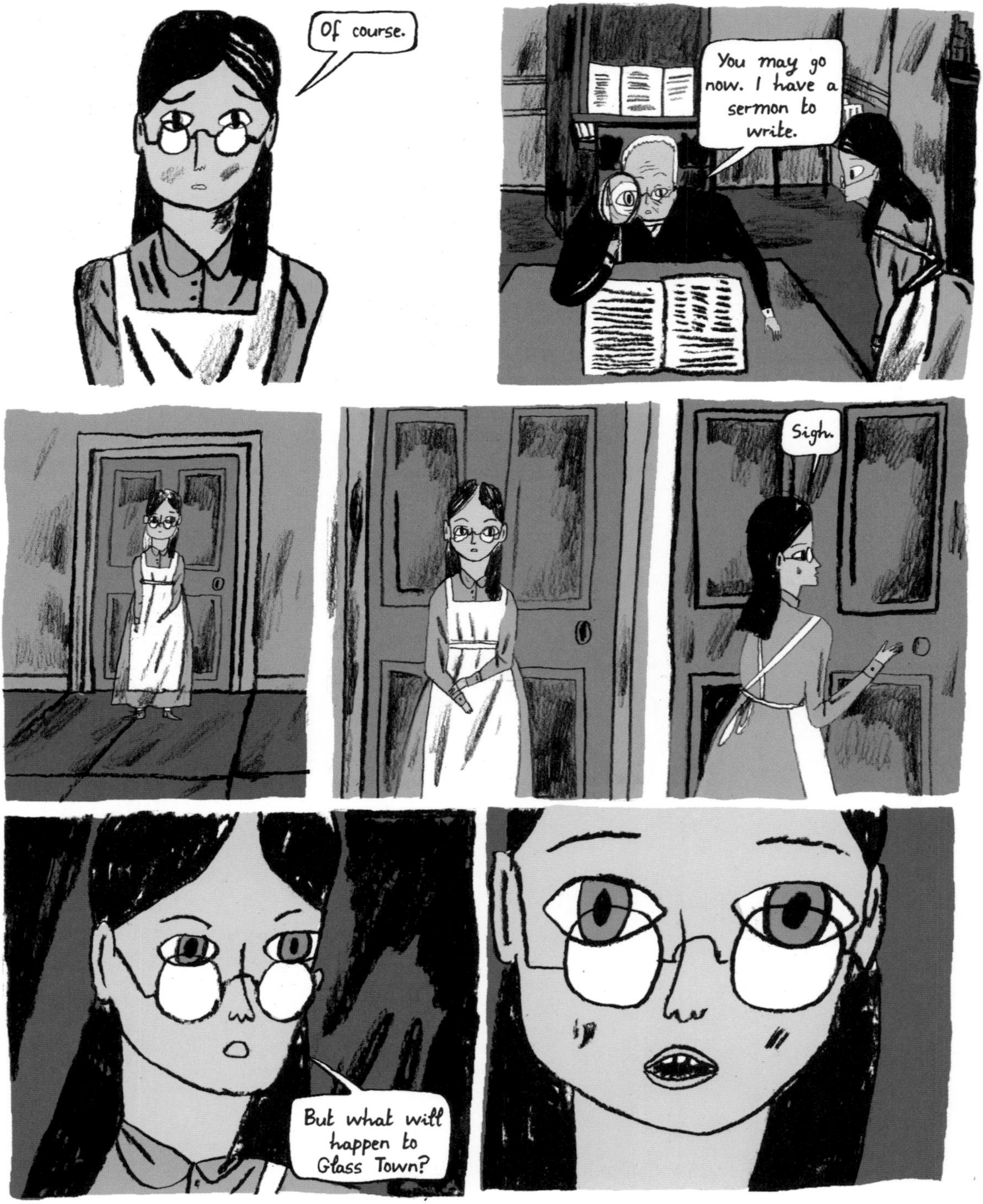
Of course.
You may go now. I have a sermon to write.
Sigh.
But what will happen to Glass Town?

So the Genii called a conclave around the dining-room table.

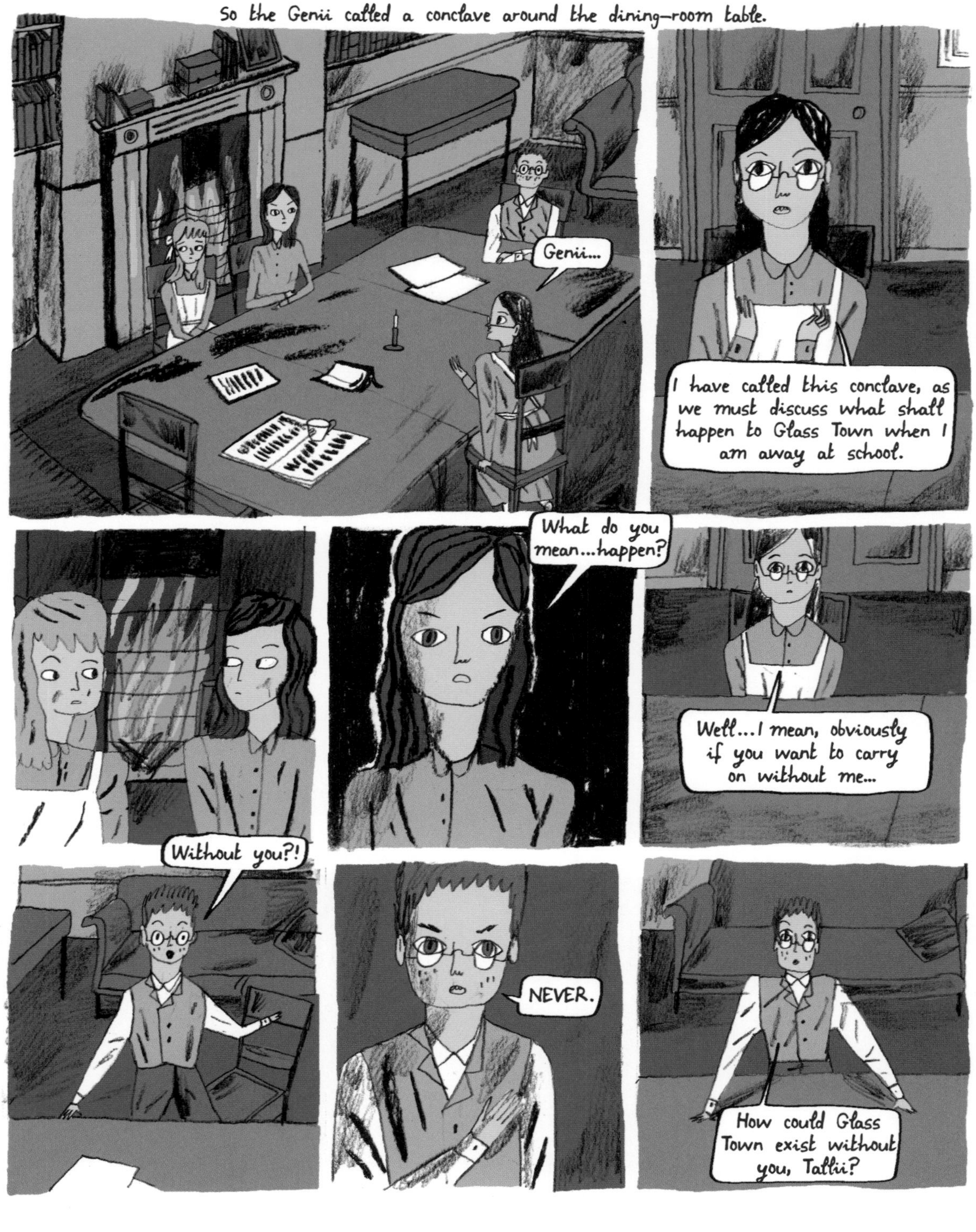
Genii...
I have called this conclave, as we must discuss what shall happen to Glass Town when I am away at school.
What do you mean...happen?
Well...I mean, obviously if you want to carry on without me...
Without you?!
NEVER.
How could Glass Town exist without you, Tallii?

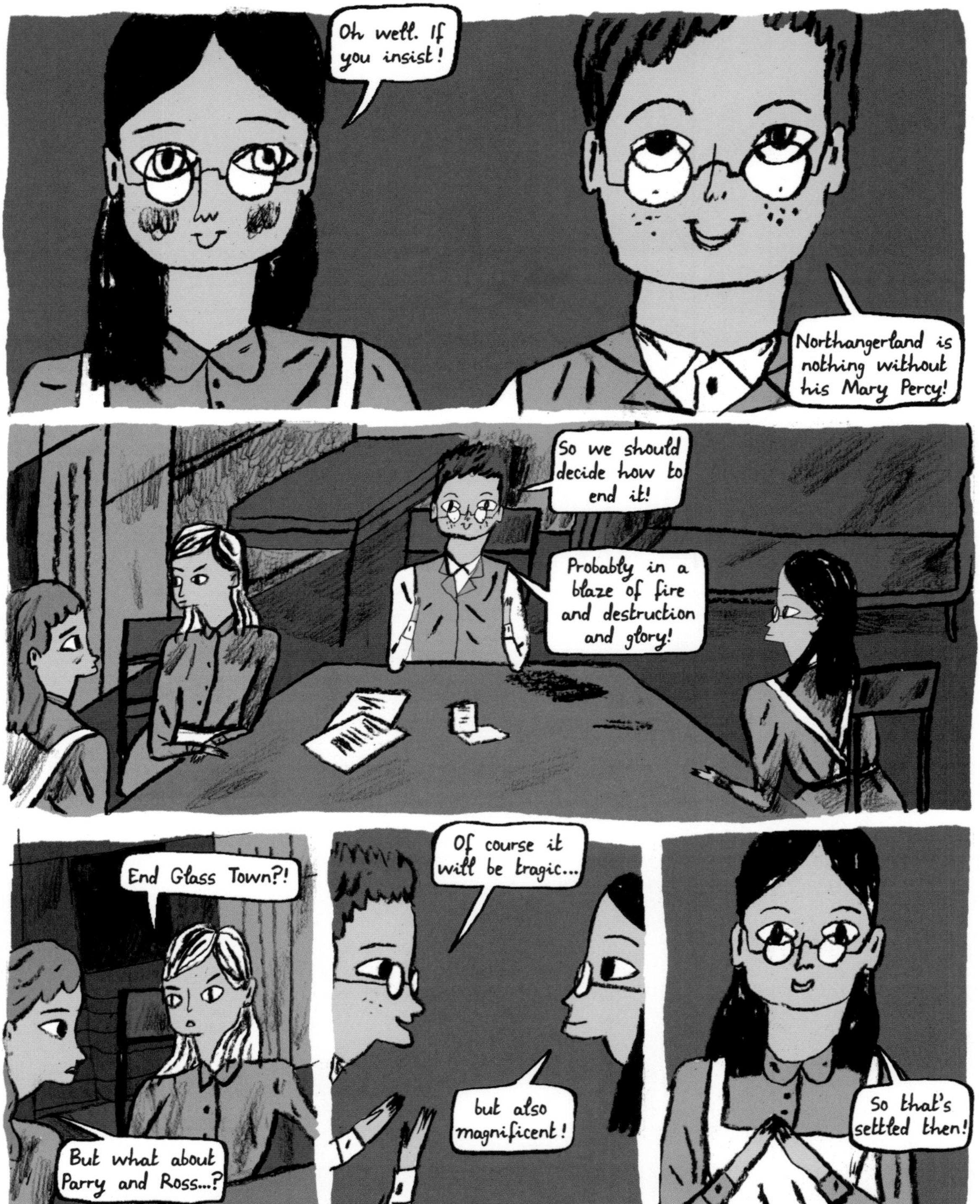
Oh well. If you insist!
Northangerland is nothing without his Mary Percy!
So we should decide how to end it!
Probably in a blaze of fire and destruction and glory!
End Glass Town?!
But what about Parry and Ross...?
Of course it will be tragic...
but also magnificent!
So that's settled then!

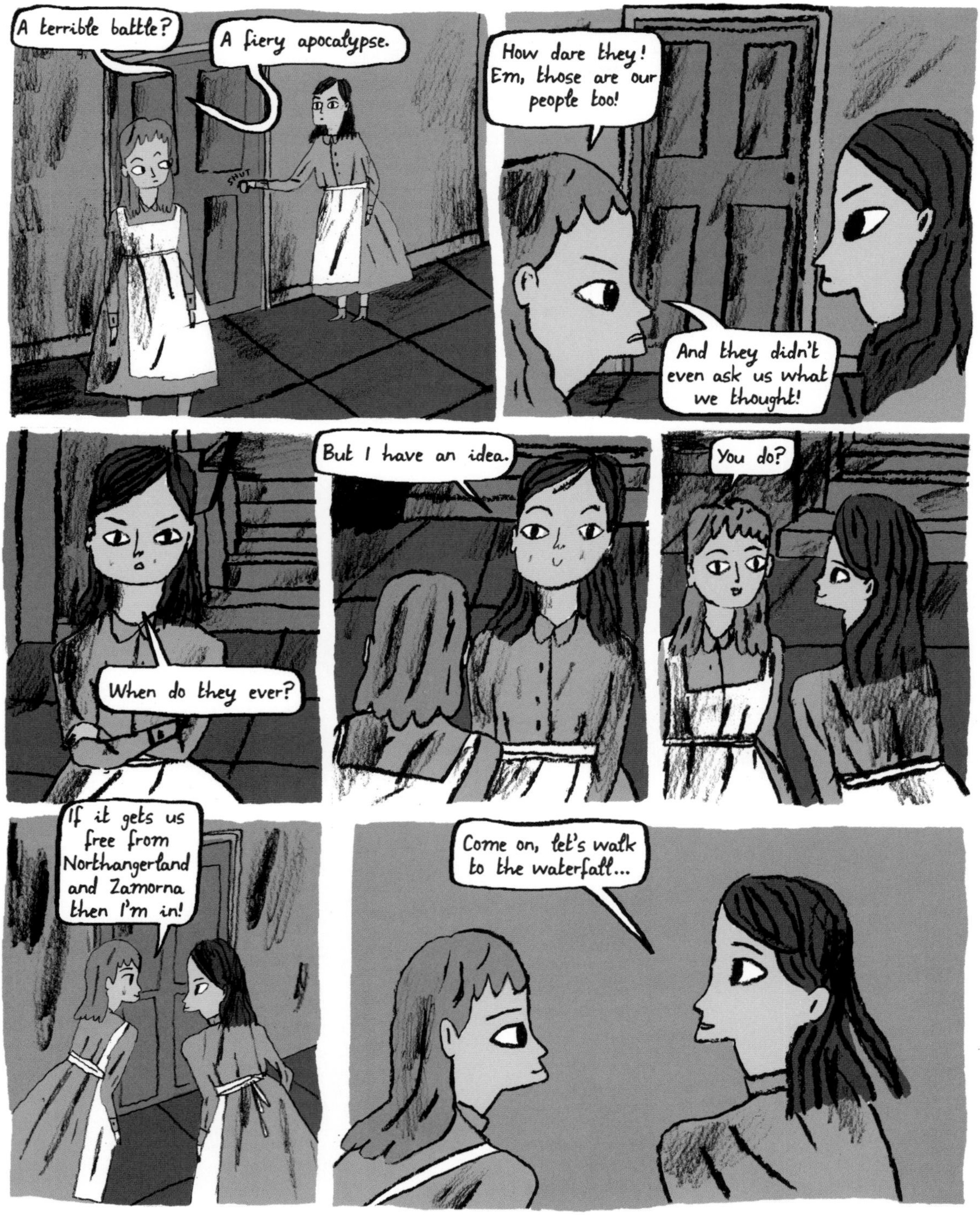
A terrible battle?
A fiery apocalypse.
SHUT
How dare they! Em, those are our people too!
And they didn't even ask us what we thought!
When do they ever?
But I have an idea.
You do?
If it gets us free from Northangerland and Zamorna then I'm in!
Come on, let's walk to the waterfall...

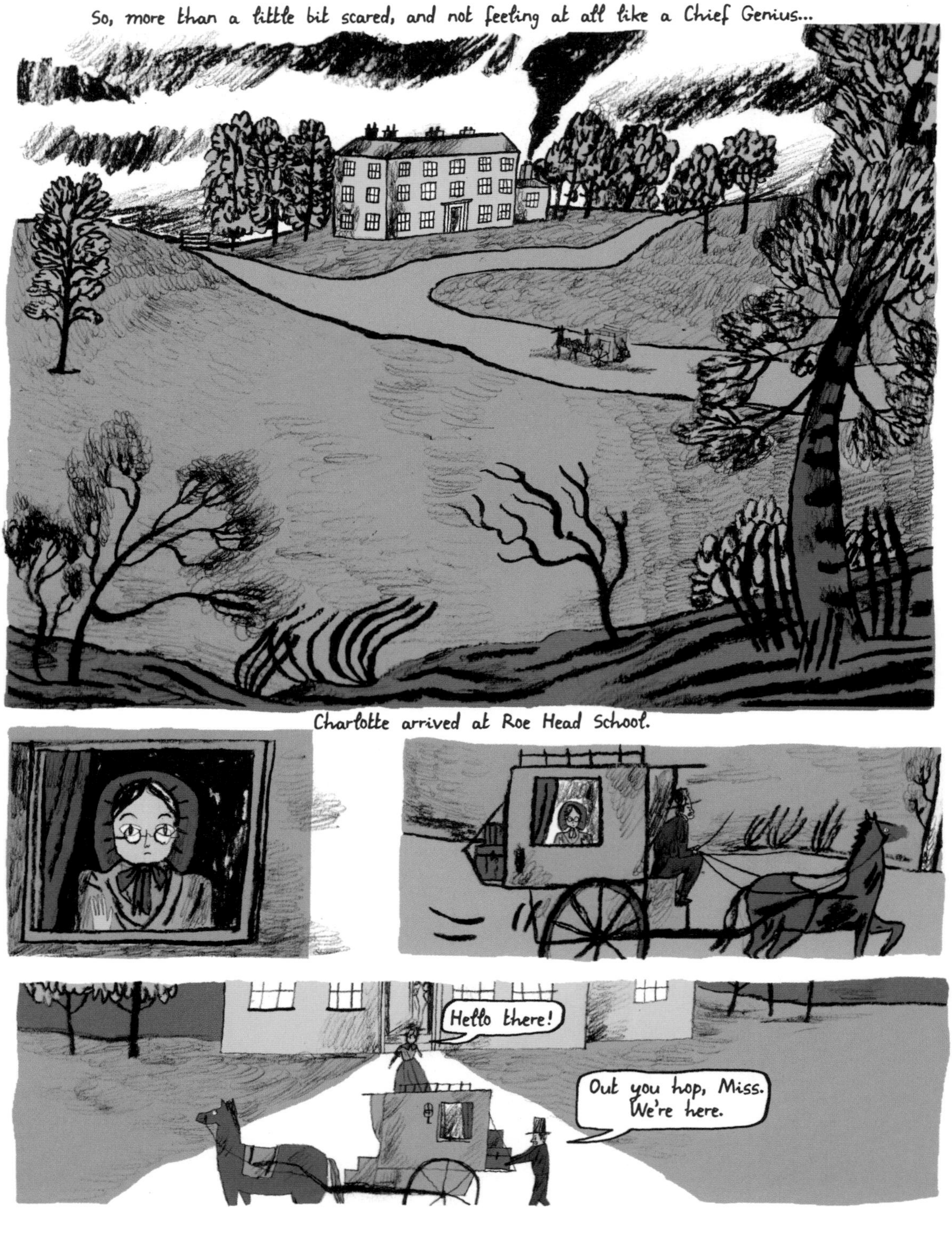
So, more than a little bit scared, and not feeling at all like a Chief Genius...
Charlotte arrived at Roe Head School.
Hello there!
Out you hop, Miss. We're here.

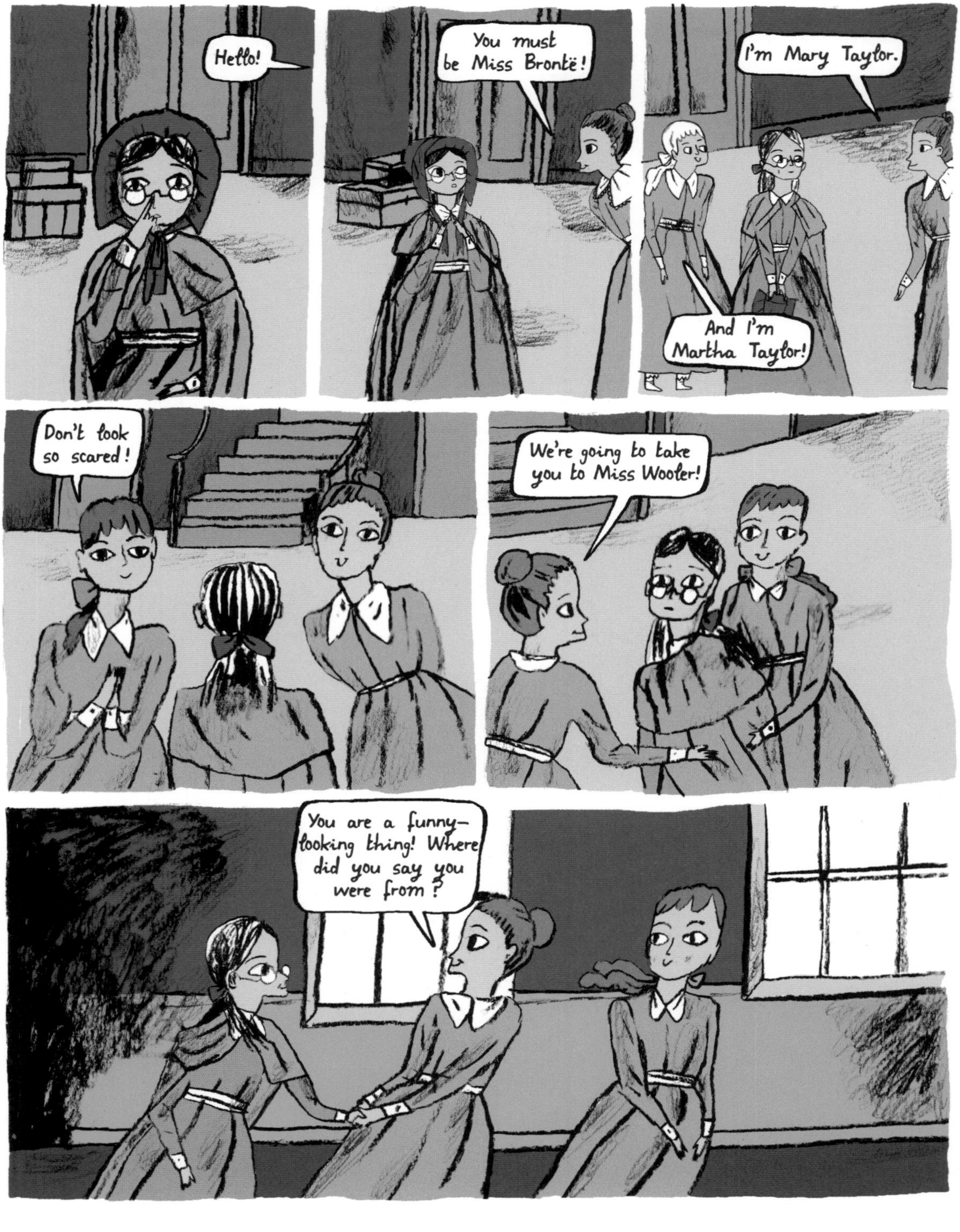
Hello!
You must be Miss Brontë!
I'm Mary Taylor.
And I'm Martha Taylor!
Don't look so scared!
We're going to take you to Miss Wooler!
You are a funny-looking thing! Where did you say you were from?

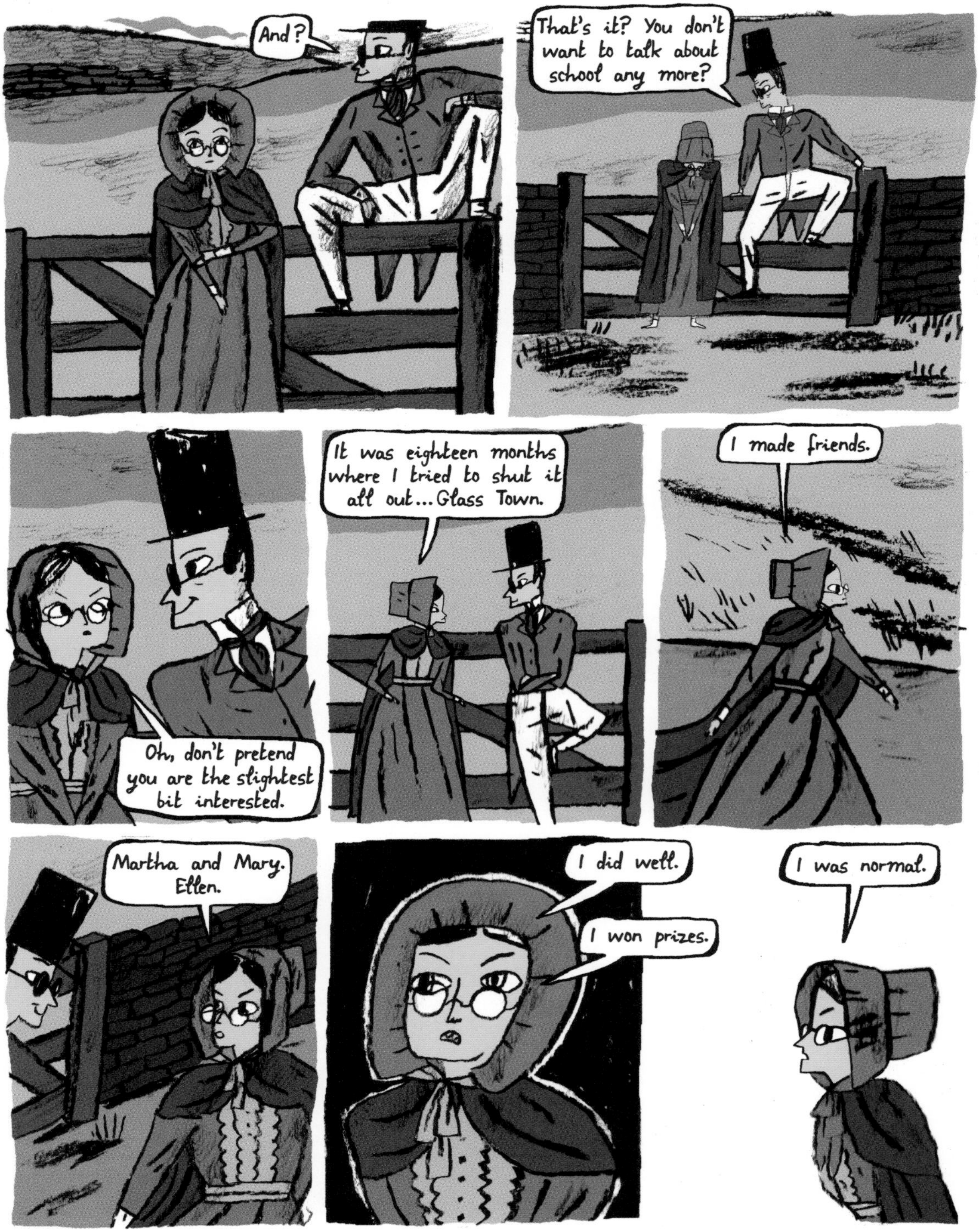
And?
That's it? You don't want to talk about school any more?
Oh, don't pretend you are the slightest bit interested.
It was eighteen months where I tried to shut it all out... Glass Town.
I made friends.
Martha and Mary. Ellen.
I did well.
I won prizes.
I was normal.

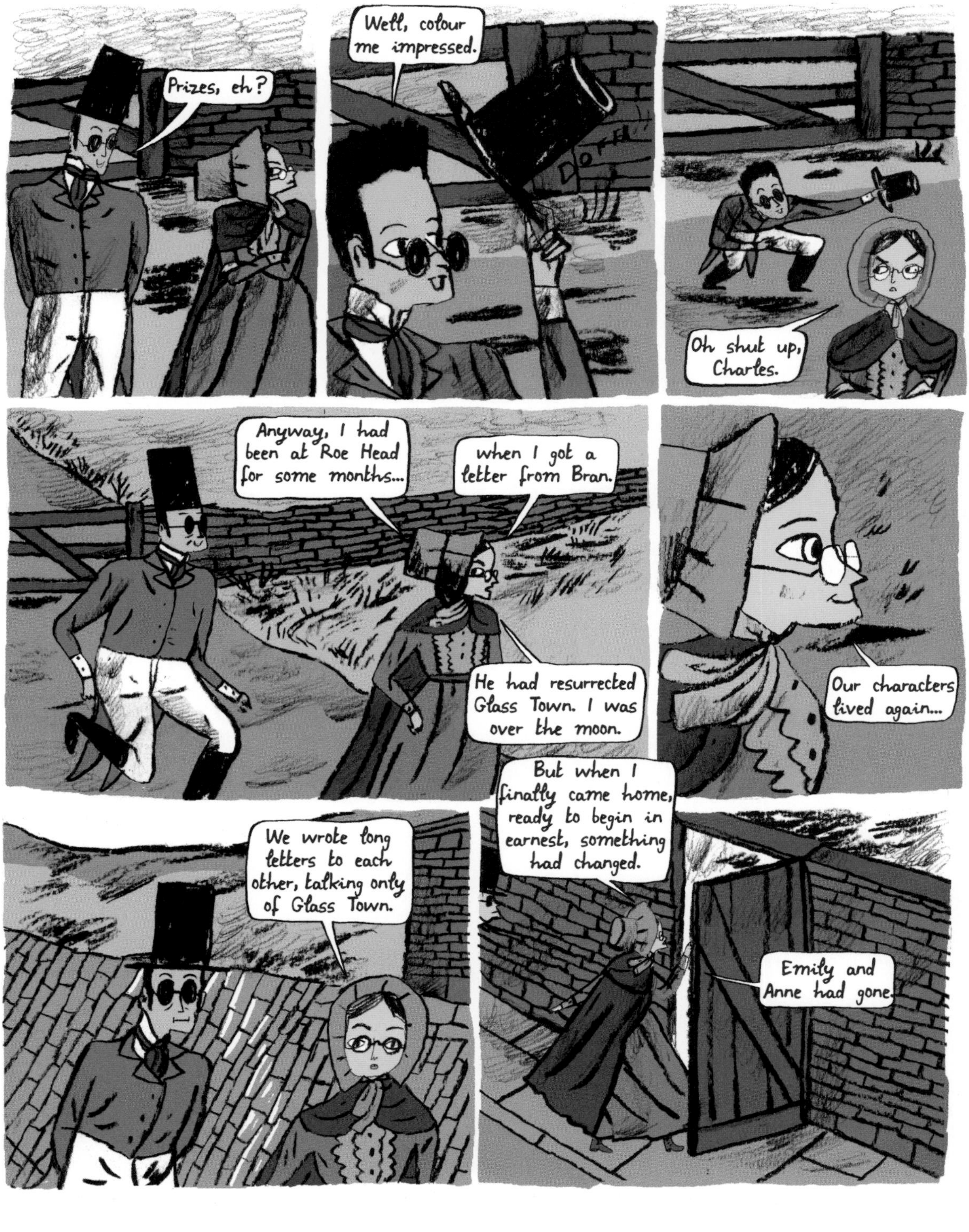
Prizes, eh?
Well, colour me impressed.
DOFF
Oh shut up, Charles.
Anyway, I had been at Roe Head for some months...
when I got a letter from Bran.
He had resurrected Glass Town. I was over the moon.
Our characters lived again...
We wrote long letters to each other, talking only of Glass Town.
But when I finally came home, ready to begin in earnest, something had changed.
Emily and Anne had gone.

As the saying goes, too many Gods can spoil a stew... or... How many Genii does it take to overpopulate a small universe, is another. And the answer might be four. On Charlotte's return from school, Emily and Anne called a Genii Conclave.

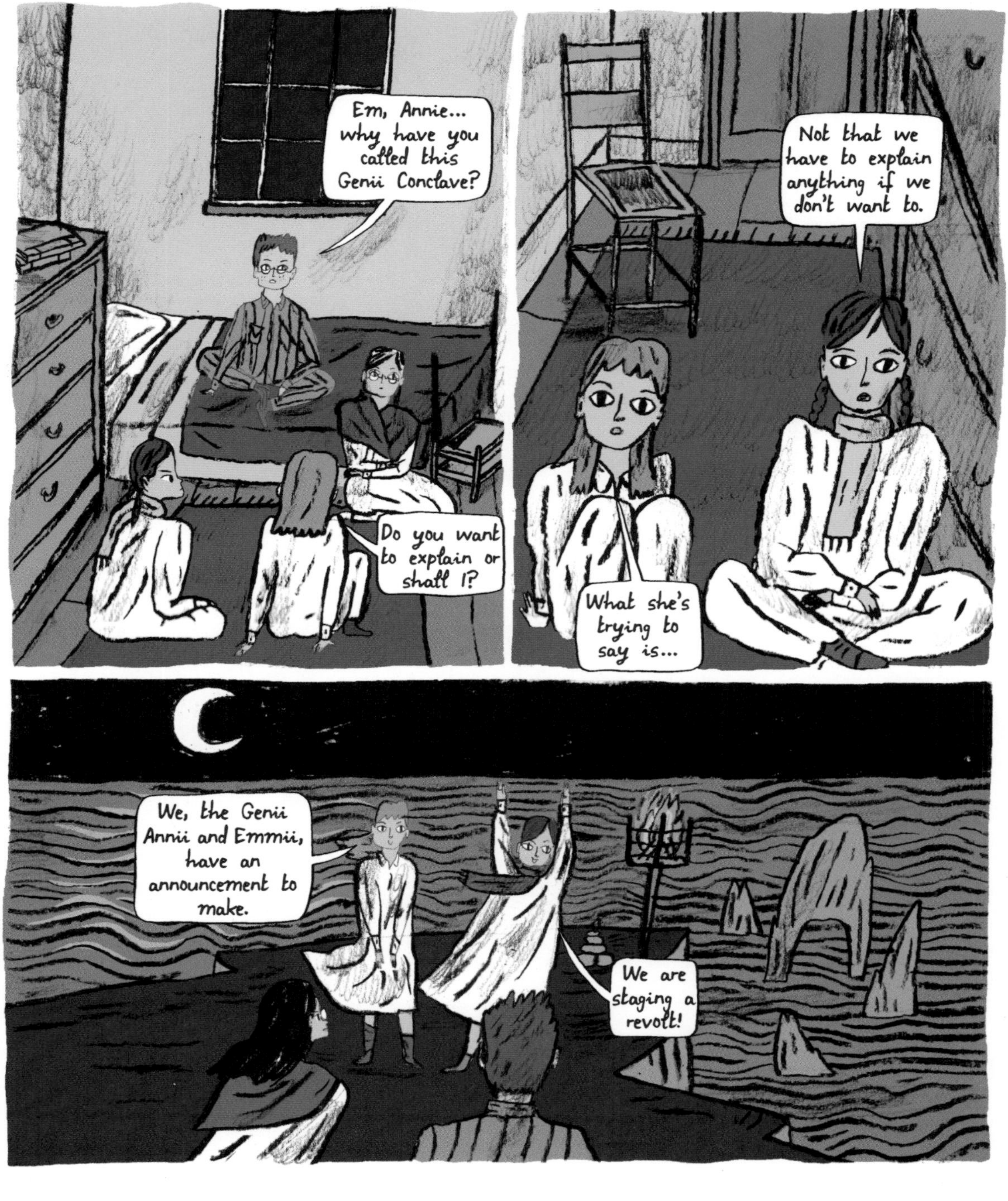

Em, Annie... why have you called this Genii Conclave?
Do you want to explain or shall I?
Not that we have to explain anything if we don't want to.
What she's trying to say is...
We, the Genii Annii and Emmii, have an announcement to make.
We are staging a revolt!

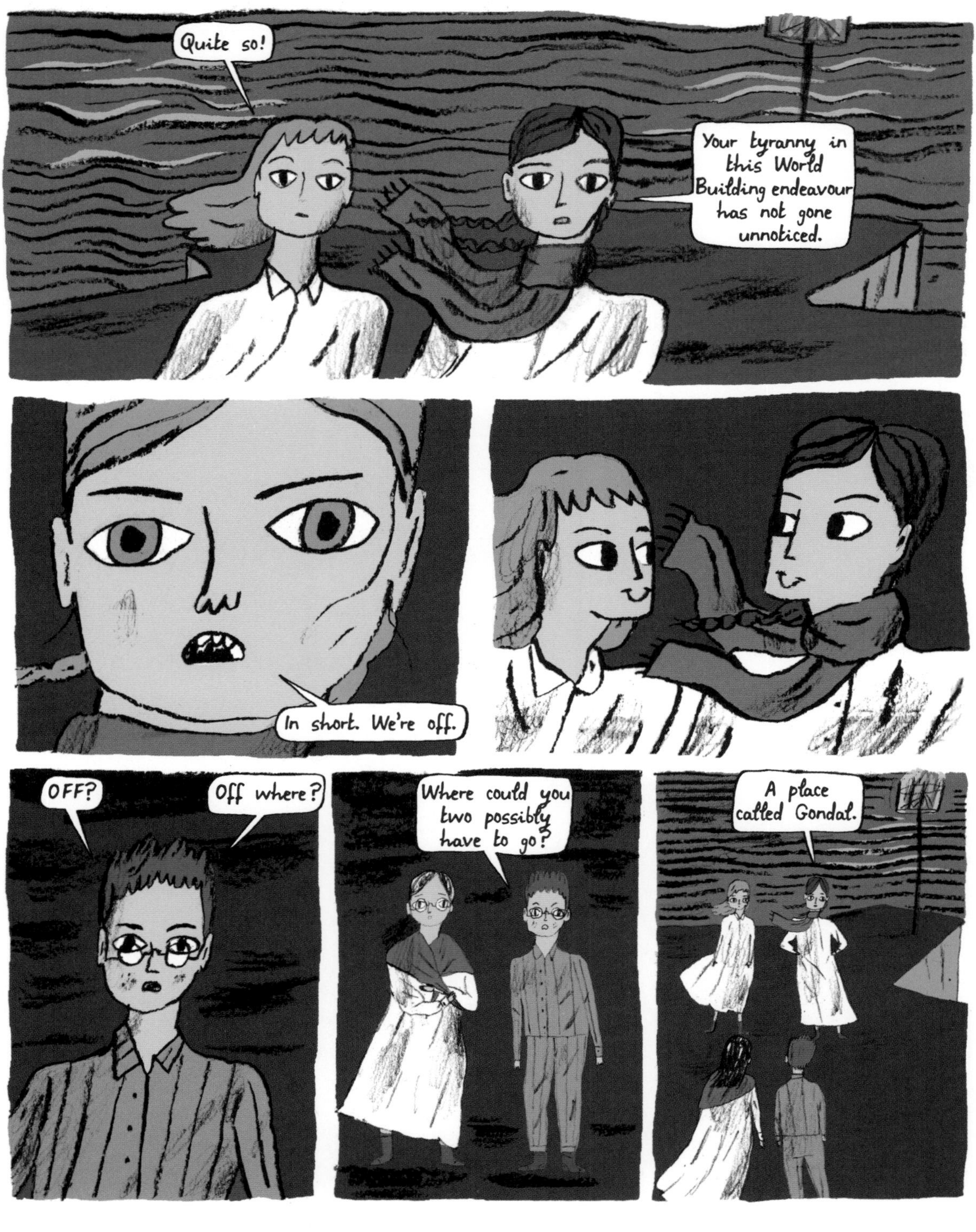
Quite so!
Your tyranny in this World Building endeavour has not gone unnoticed.
In short. We're off.
OFF?
Off where?
Where could you two possibly have to go?
A place called Gondal.

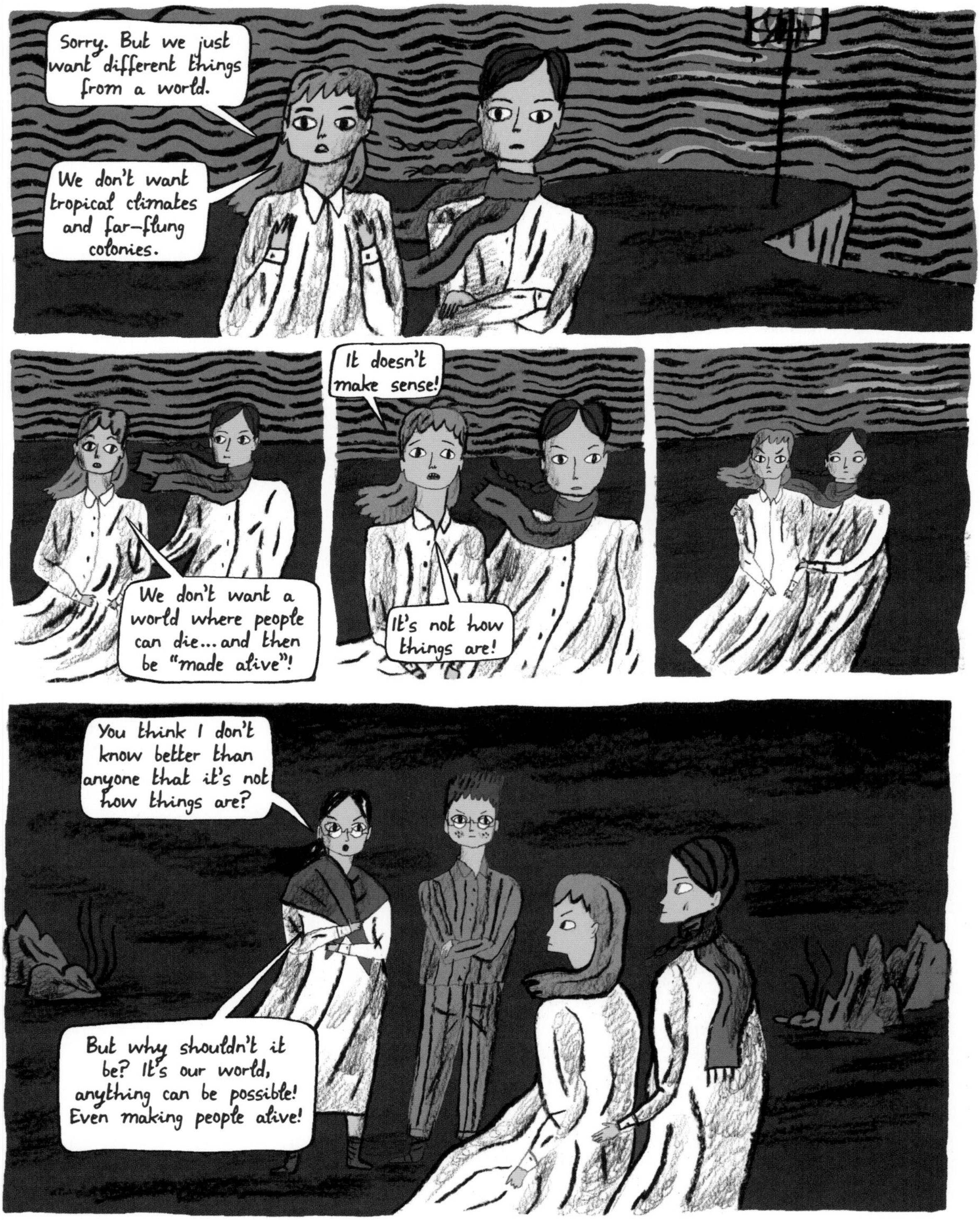
Sorry. But we just want different things from a world.
We don't want tropical climates and far-flung colonies.
We don't want a world where people can die... and then be "made alive"!
It doesn't make sense!
It's not how things are!
You think I don't know better than anyone that it's not how things are?
But why shouldn't it be? It's our world, anything can be possible! Even making people alive!

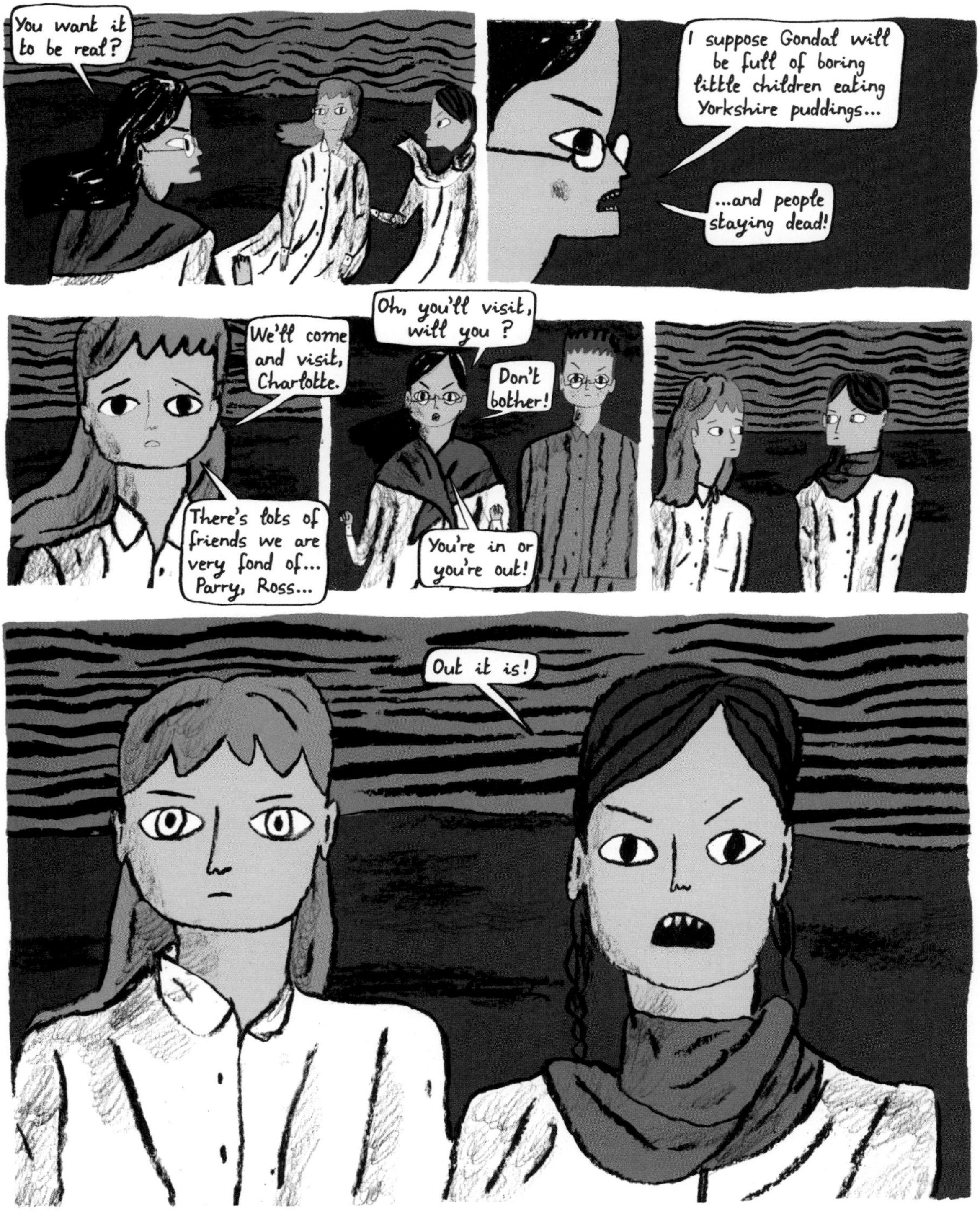
You want it to be real?
I suppose Gondal will be full of boring little children eating Yorkshire puddings...
...and people staying dead!
We'll come and visit, Charlotte.
There's lots of friends we are very fond of... Parry, Ross...
Oh, you'll visit, will you ?
Don't bother!
You're in or you're out!
Out it is!

Thus the Genii Emmii and Annii boarded a ship. Out of the harbour of Great Glass Town it slid, and into the inky sea. Tallii and Brannii watched it until it was a pinprick on the horizon.

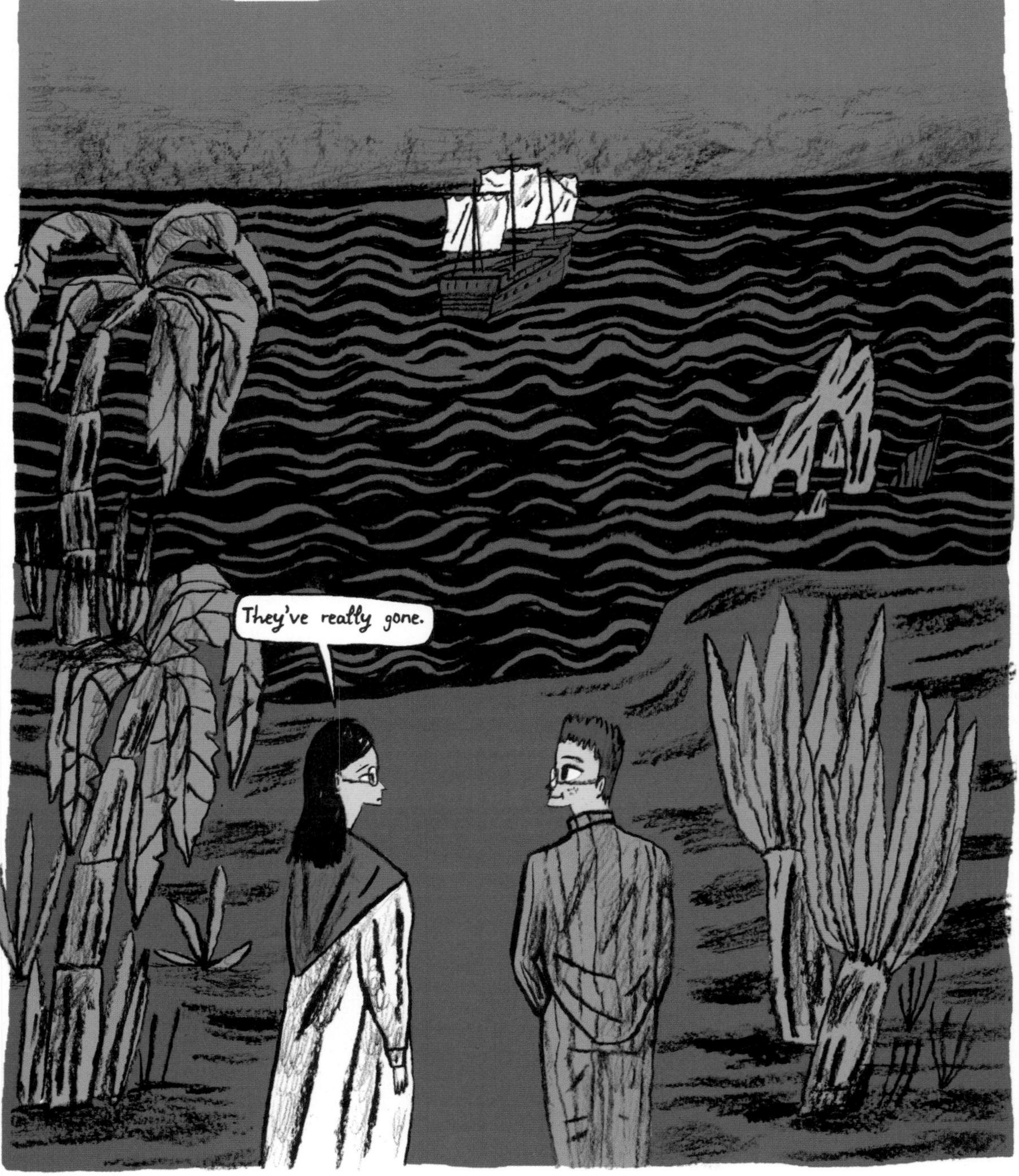
They've really gone.

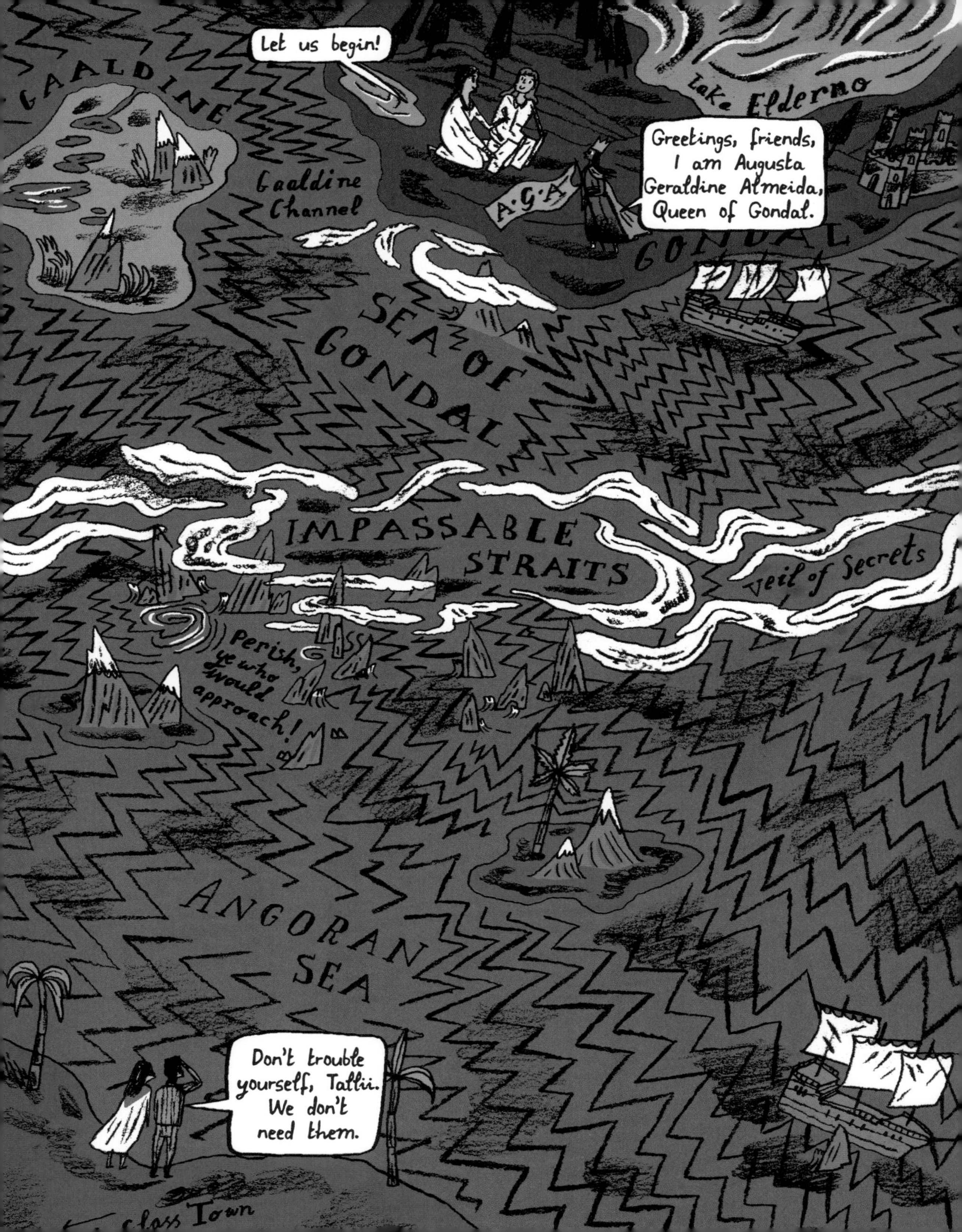

GAALDINE
Let us begin!
Lake Elderno
Gaaldine Channel
A·G·A
Greetings, friends, I am Augusta Geraldine Almeida, Queen of Gondal.
GONDAL
SEA OF GONDAL
IMPASSABLE STRAITS
Veil of Secrets
Perish, ye who would approach!
ANGORAN SEA
Don't trouble yourself, Tallii. We don't need them.
Glass Town

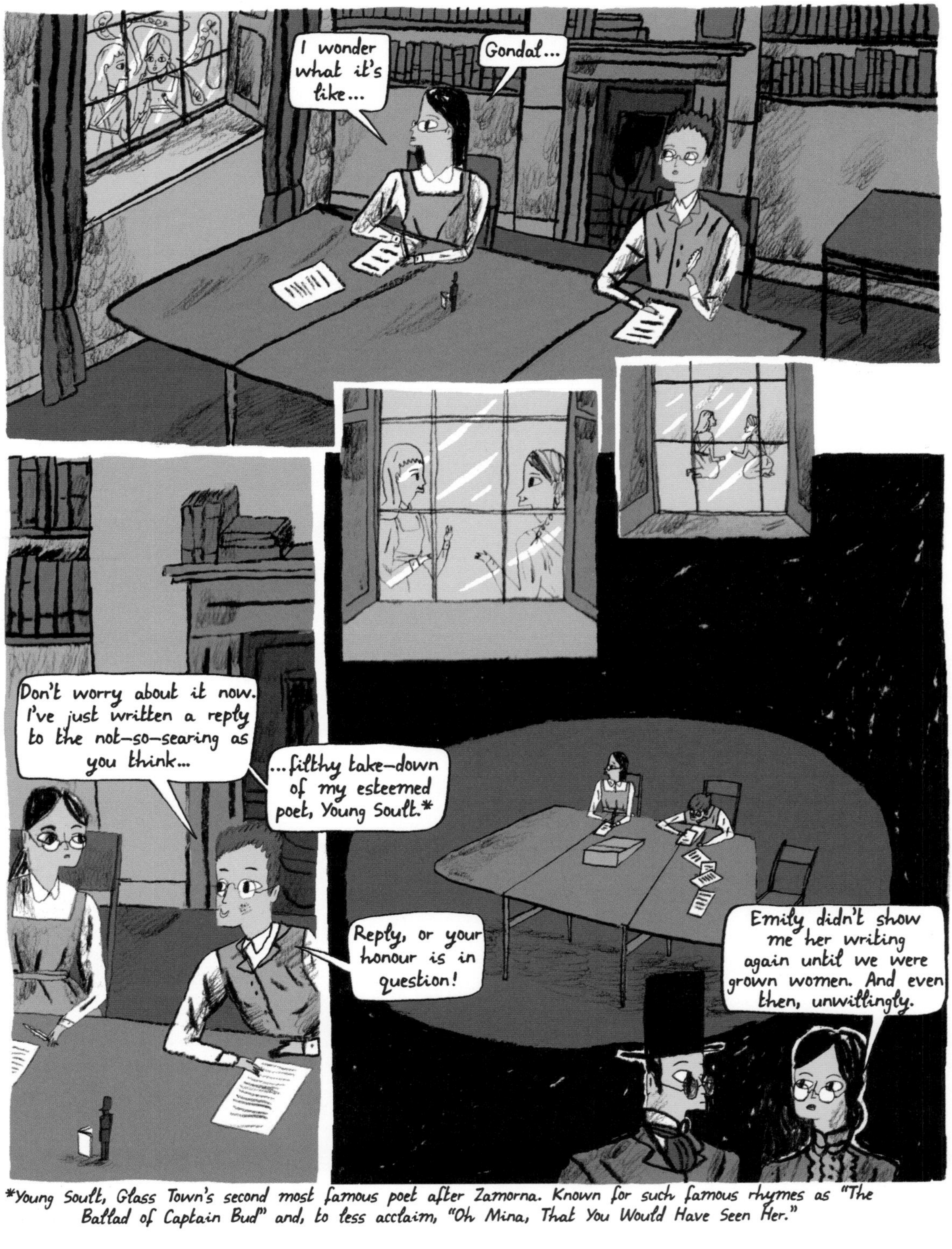
I wonder what it's like...
Gondal...
Don't worry about it now. I've just written a reply to the not-so-searing as you think...
...filthy take-down of my esteemed poet, Young Soult.*
Reply, or your honour is in question!
Emily didn't show me her writing again until we were grown women. And even then, unwillingly.

*Young Soult, Glass Town's second most famous poet after Zamorna. Known for such famous rhymes as "The Ballad of Captain Bud" and, to less acclaim, "Oh Mina, That You Would Have Seen Her."

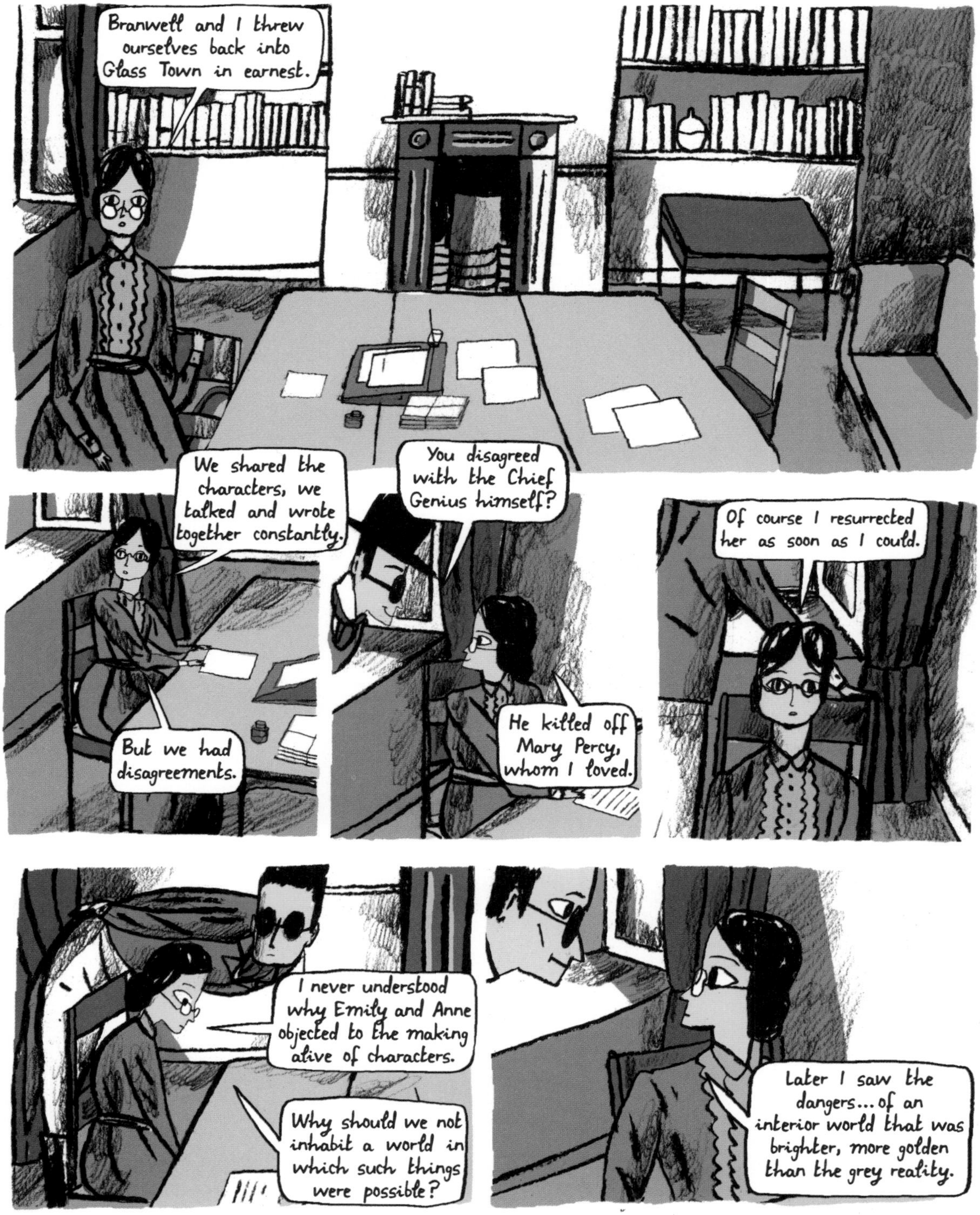
Branwell and I threw ourselves back into Glass Town in earnest.
We shared the characters, we talked and wrote together constantly.
But we had disagreements.
You disagreed with the Chief Genius himself?
He killed off Mary Percy, whom I loved.
Of course I resurrected her as soon as I could.
I never understood why Emily and Anne objected to the making alive of characters.
Why should we not inhabit a world in which such things were possible?
Later I saw the dangers... of an interior world that was brighter, more golden than the grey reality.

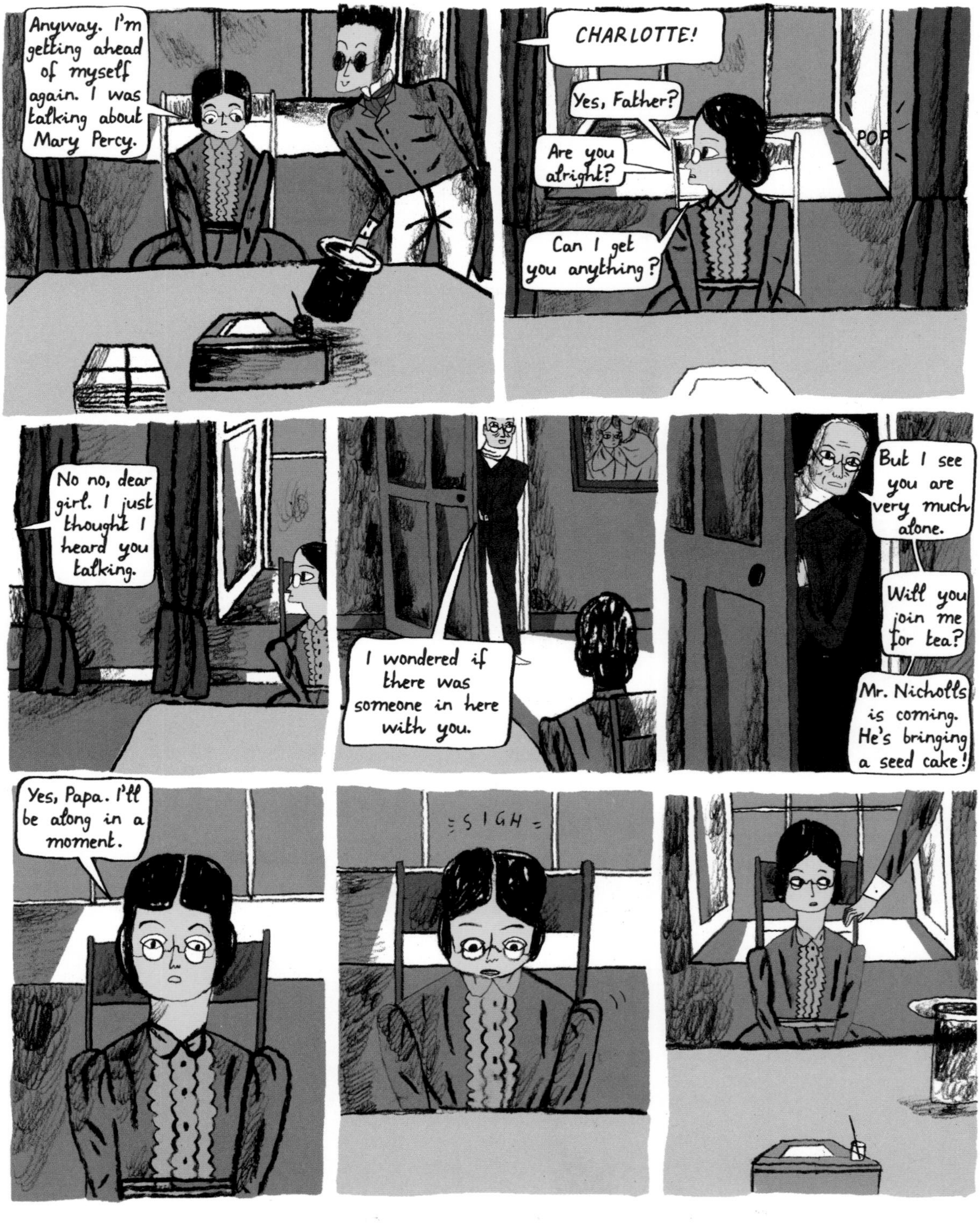
Anyway. I'm getting ahead of myself again. I was talking about Mary Percy.
CHARLOTTE!
Yes, Father?
Are you alright?
Can I get you anything?
POP
No no, dear girl. I just thought I heard you talking.
I wondered if there was someone in here with you.
But I see you are very much alone.
Will you join me for tea?
Mr. Nicholls is coming. He's bringing a seed cake!
Yes, Papa. I'll be along in a moment.
SIGH

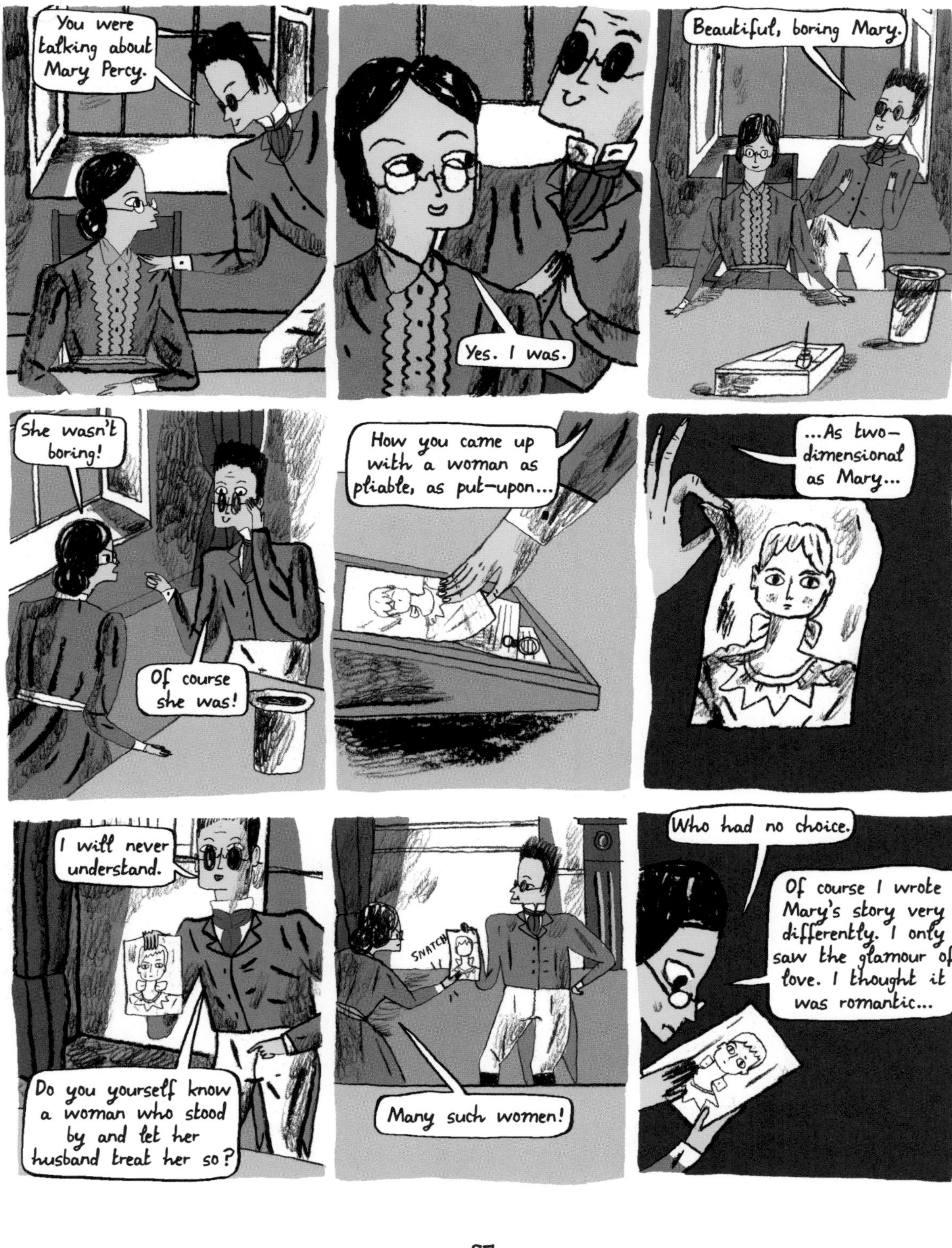
You were talking about Mary Percy.
Yes. I was.
Beautiful, boring Mary.
She wasn't boring!
Of course she was!
How you came up with a woman as pliable, as put-upon...
...As two-dimensional as Mary...
I will never understand.
Do you yourself know a woman who stood by and let her husband treat her so?
SNATCH
Many such women!
Who had no choice.
Of course I wrote Mary's story very differently. I only saw the glamour of love. I thought it was romantic...

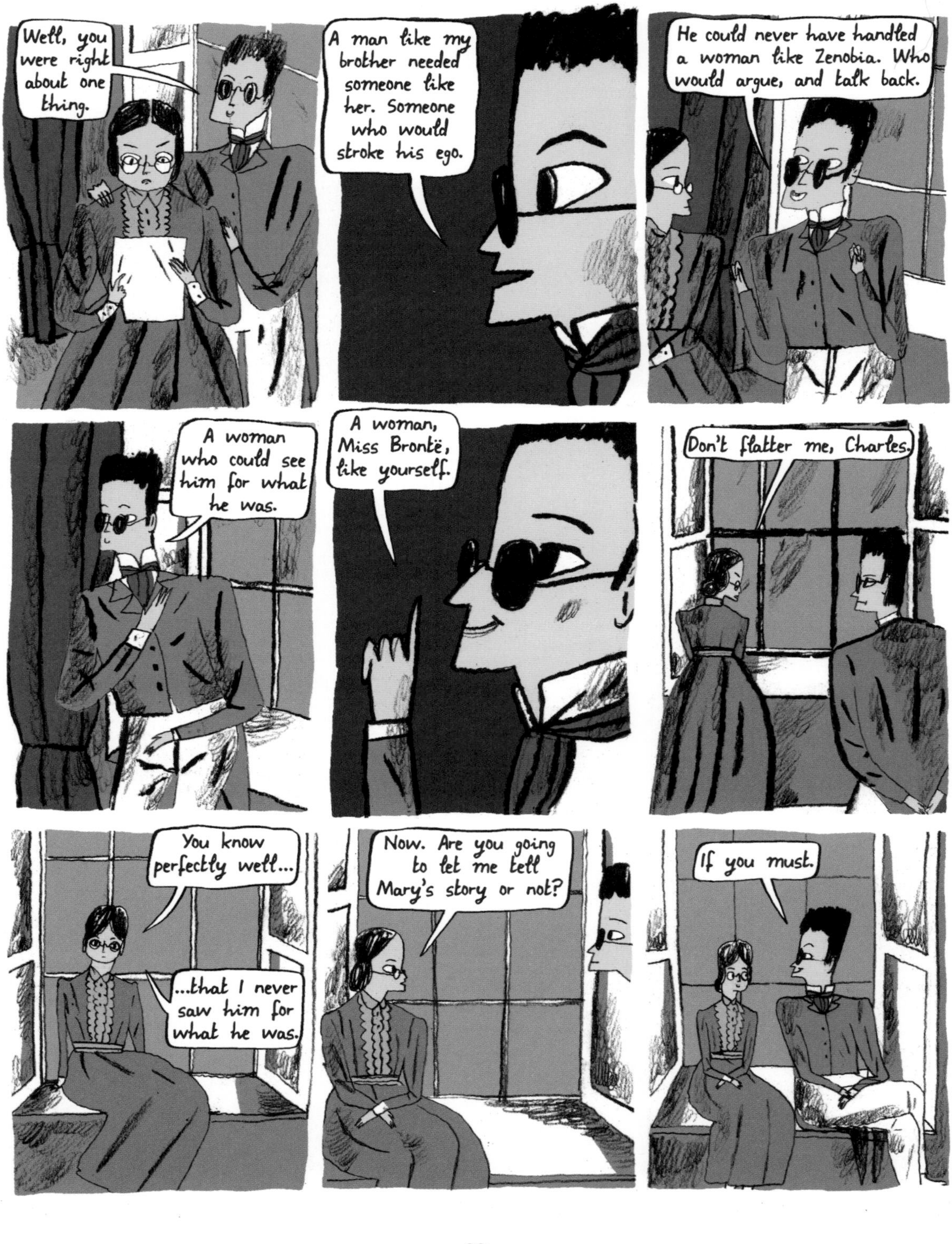
Well, you were right about one thing.
A man like my brother needed someone like her. Someone who would stroke his ego.
He could never have handled a woman like Zenobia. Who would argue, and talk back.
A woman who could see him for what he was.
A woman, Miss Brontë, like yourself.
Don't flatter me, Charles.
You know perfectly well...
...that I never saw him for what he was.
Now. Are you going to let me tell Mary's story or not?
If you must.

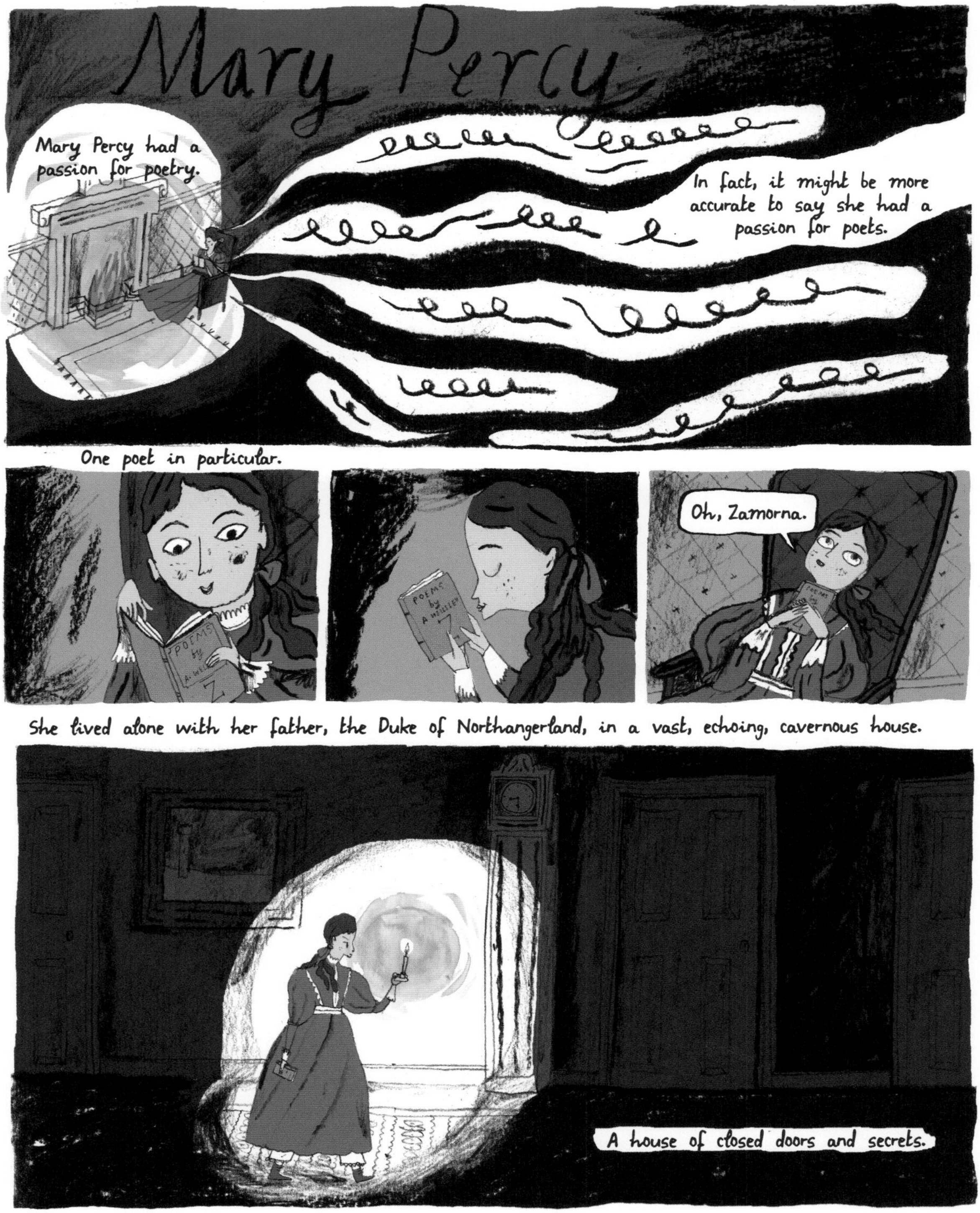
Mary Percy
Mary Percy had a passion for poetry.
In fact, it might be more accurate to say she had a passion for poets.
One poet in particular.
Oh, Zamorna.
She lived alone with her father, the Duke of Northangerland, in a vast, echoing, cavernous house.
A house of closed doors and secrets.

She had once had three brothers, but they had died as children in mysterious circumstances.

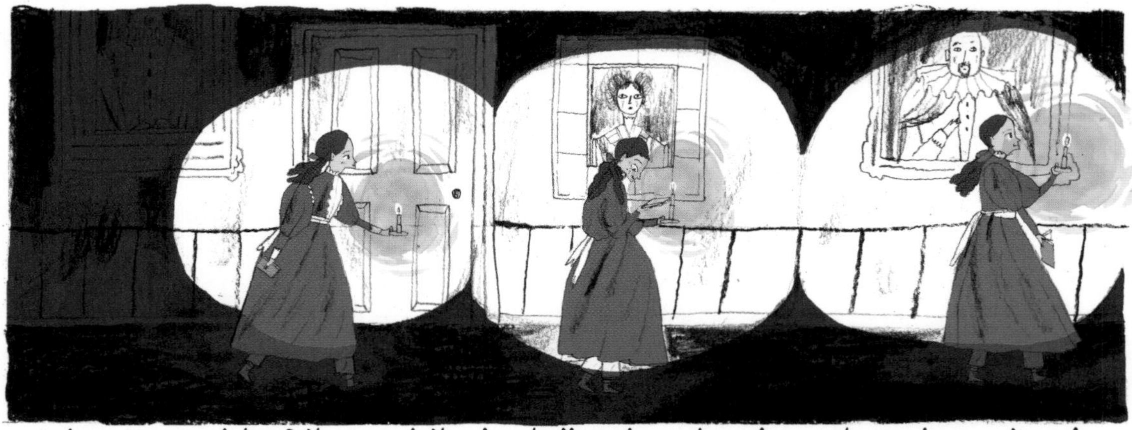

And so Mary and her father paced the long halls and corridors alone, each guarding a strangely similar secret.

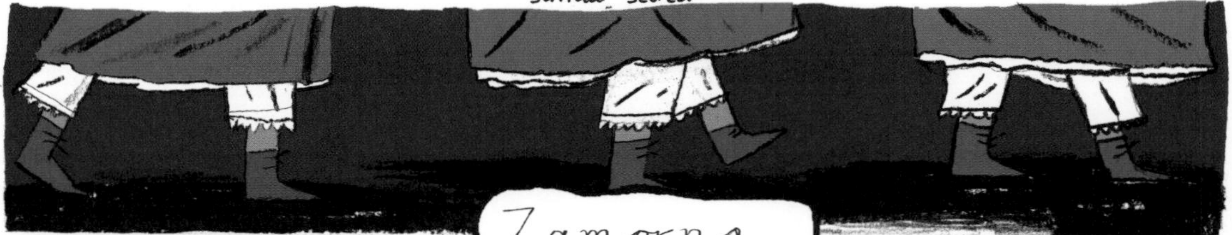

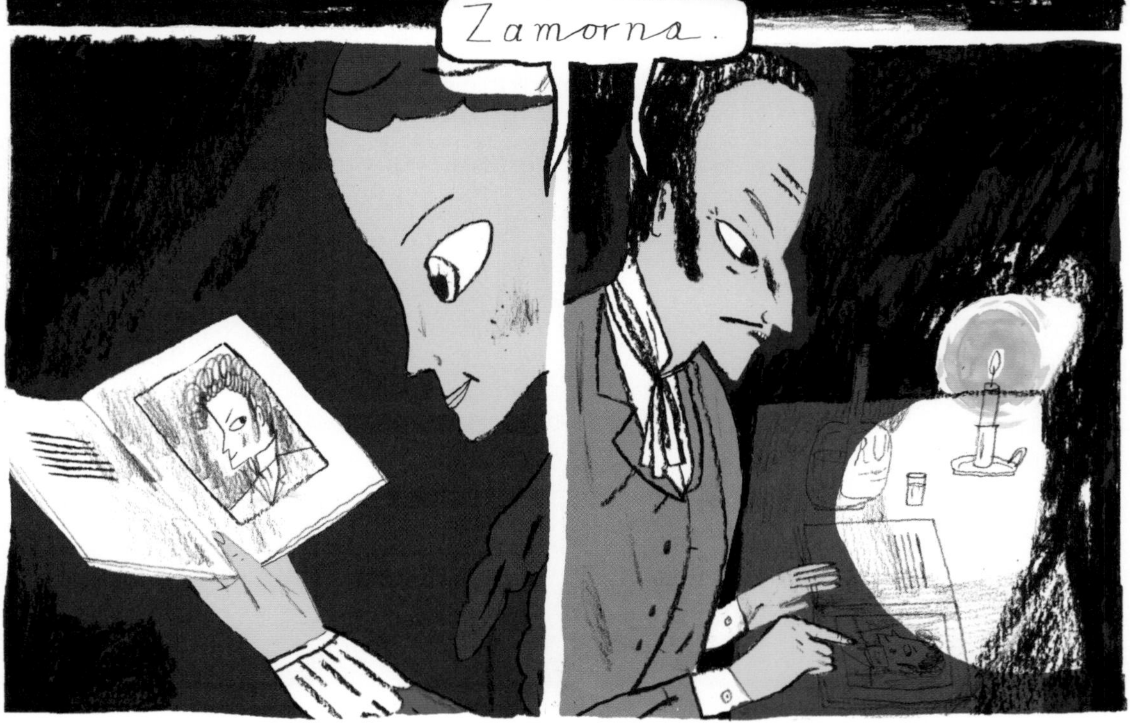
Zamorna.

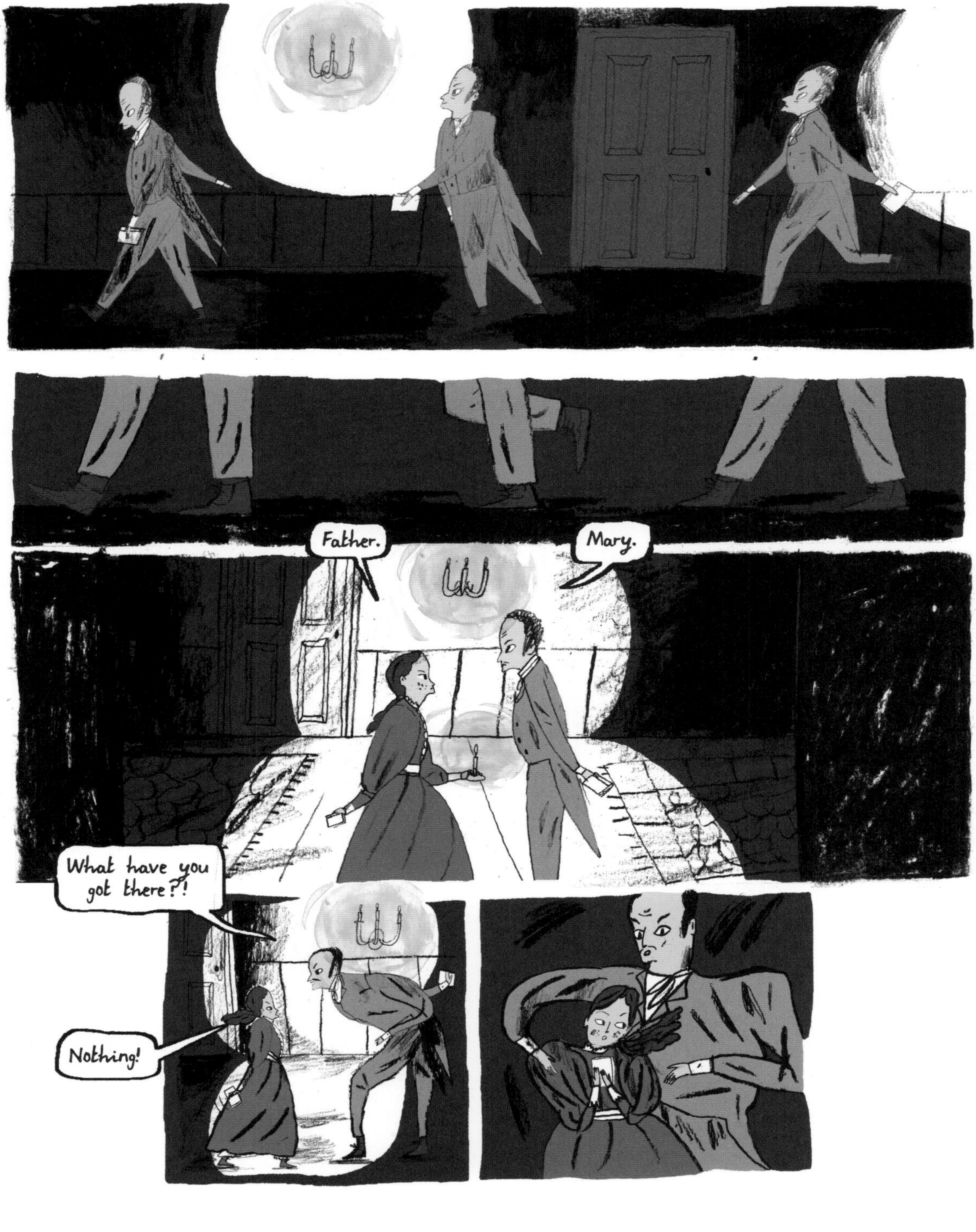
Father.
Mary.
What have you got there?!
Nothing!

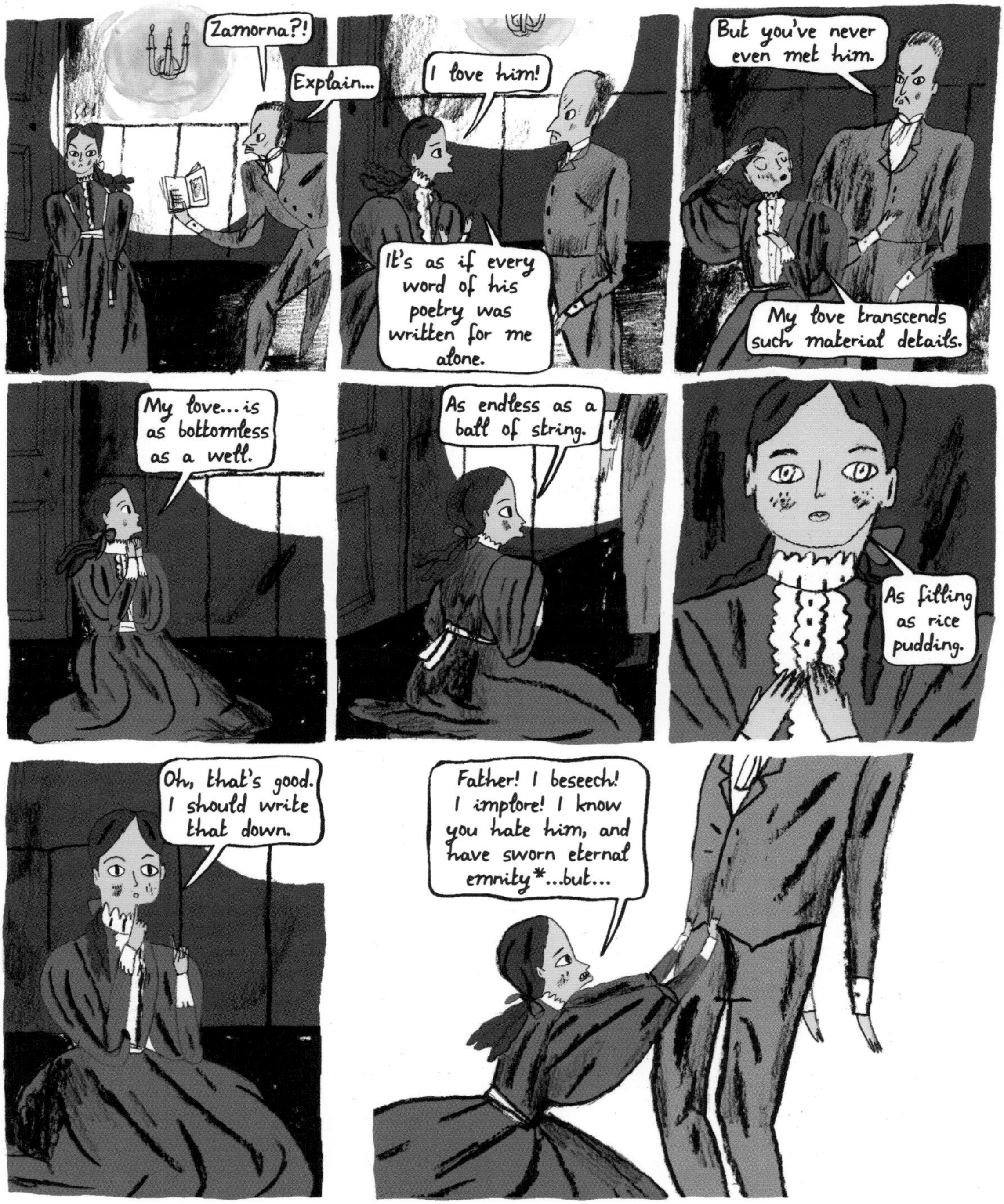
Zamorna?!
Explain...
I love him!
It's as if every word of his poetry was written for me alone.
But you've never even met him.
My love transcends such material details.
My love... is as bottomless as a well.
As endless as a ball of string.
As fitting as rice pudding.
Oh, that's good. I should write that down.
Father! I beseech! I implore! I know you hate him, and have sworn eternal emnity*...but...

*The feud between Zamorna and Northangerland is said to have begun during a rivalry for the attentions of the beautiful Mina Laury. Z won, despite being a boy of fifteen, and N twice his age. N has never recovered from this humiliation.

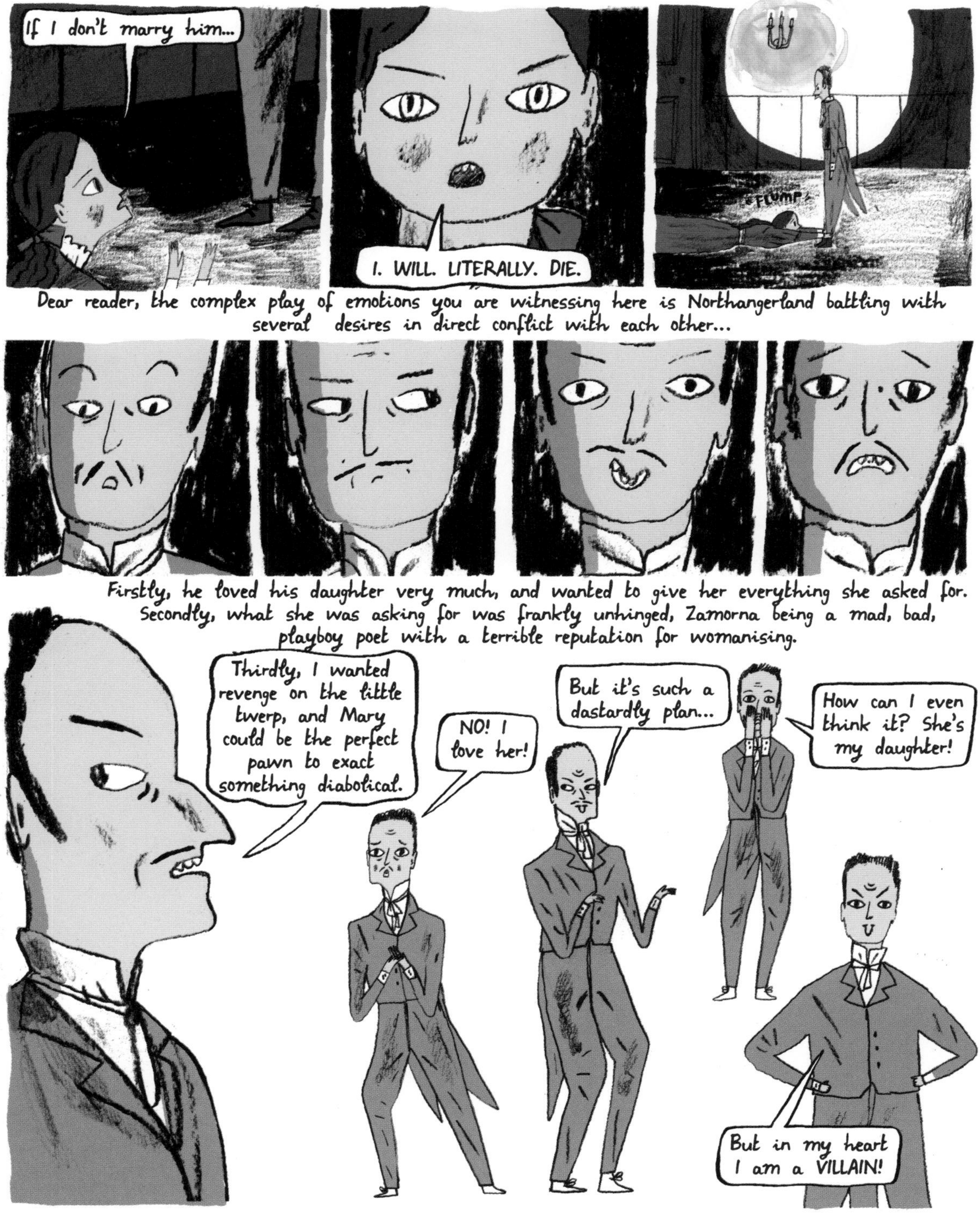
If I don't marry him...
I. WILL. LITERALLY. DIE.
FLUMP
Dear reader, the complex play of emotions you are witnessing here is Northangerland battling with several desires in direct conflict with each other...
Firstly, he loved his daughter very much, and wanted to give her everything she asked for. Secondly, what she was asking for was frankly unhinged, Zamorna being a mad, bad, playboy poet with a terrible reputation for womanising.
Thirdly, I wanted revenge on the little twerp, and Mary could be the perfect pawn to exact something diabolical.
NO! I love her!
But it's such a dastardly plan...
How can I even think it? She's my daughter!
But in my heart I am a VILLAIN!

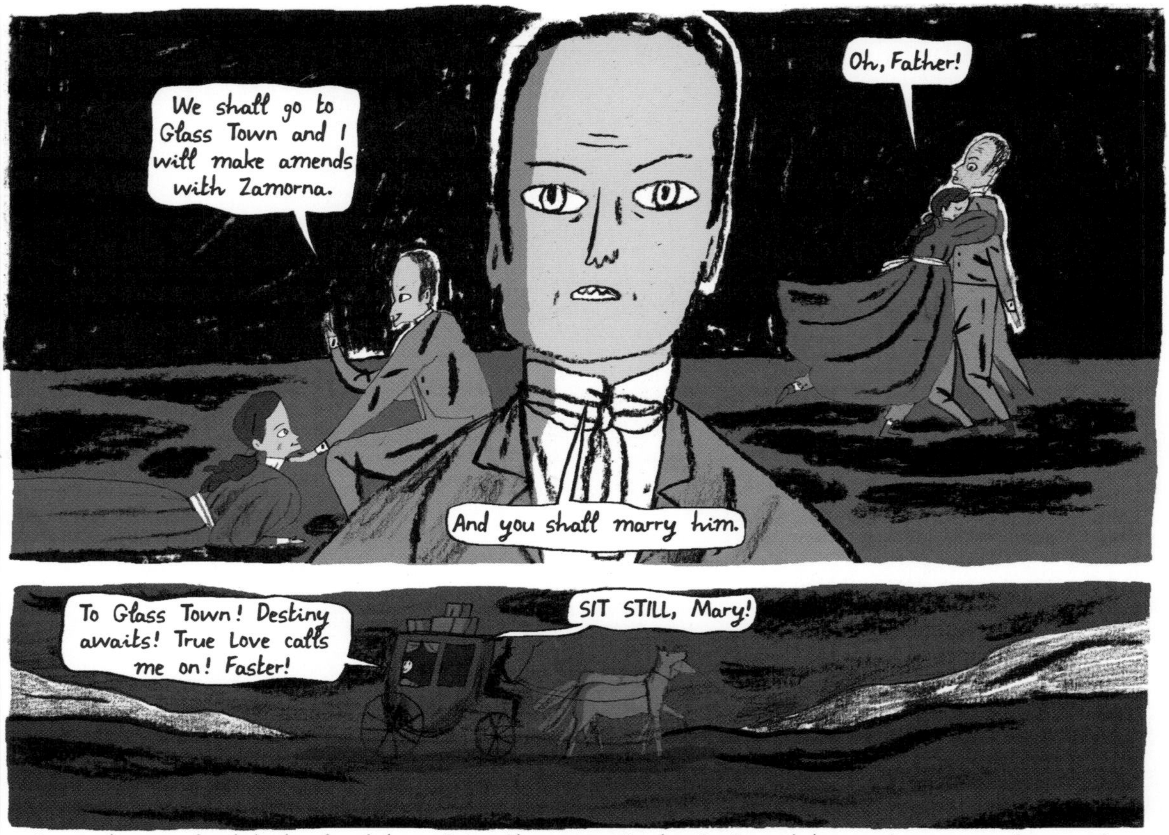
We shall go to Glass Town and I will make amends with Zamorna.
Oh, Father!
And you shall marry him.
To Glass Town! Destiny awaits! True Love calls me on! Faster!
SIT STILL, Mary!

Mary, having decided she loved him from the moment she first read his poetry, was not going to let anything stand in her way. Not his reputation, not his previous two dead wives, and certainly not the trifling matter of his personality.

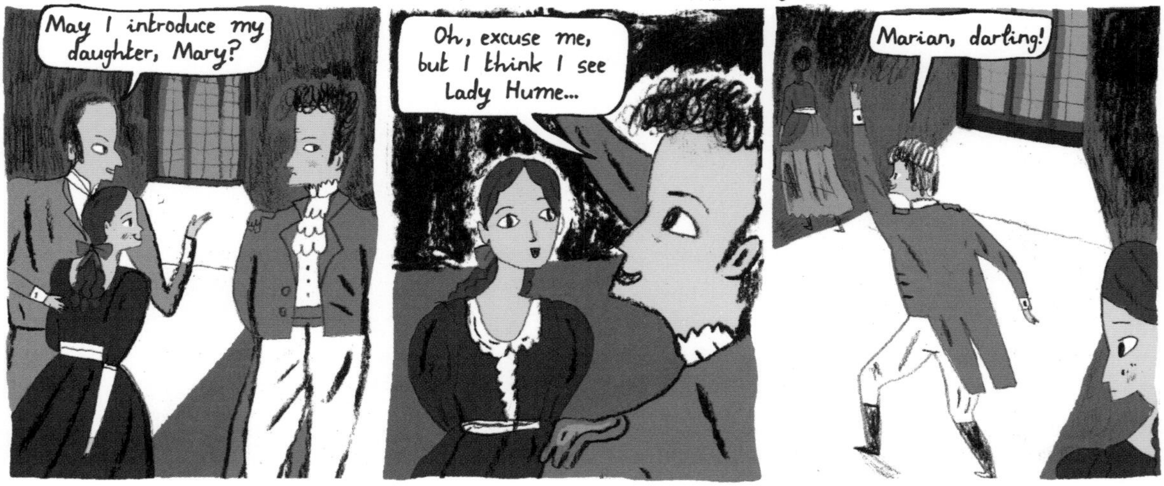
May I introduce my daughter, Mary?
Oh, excuse me, but I think I see Lady Hume...
Marian, darling!

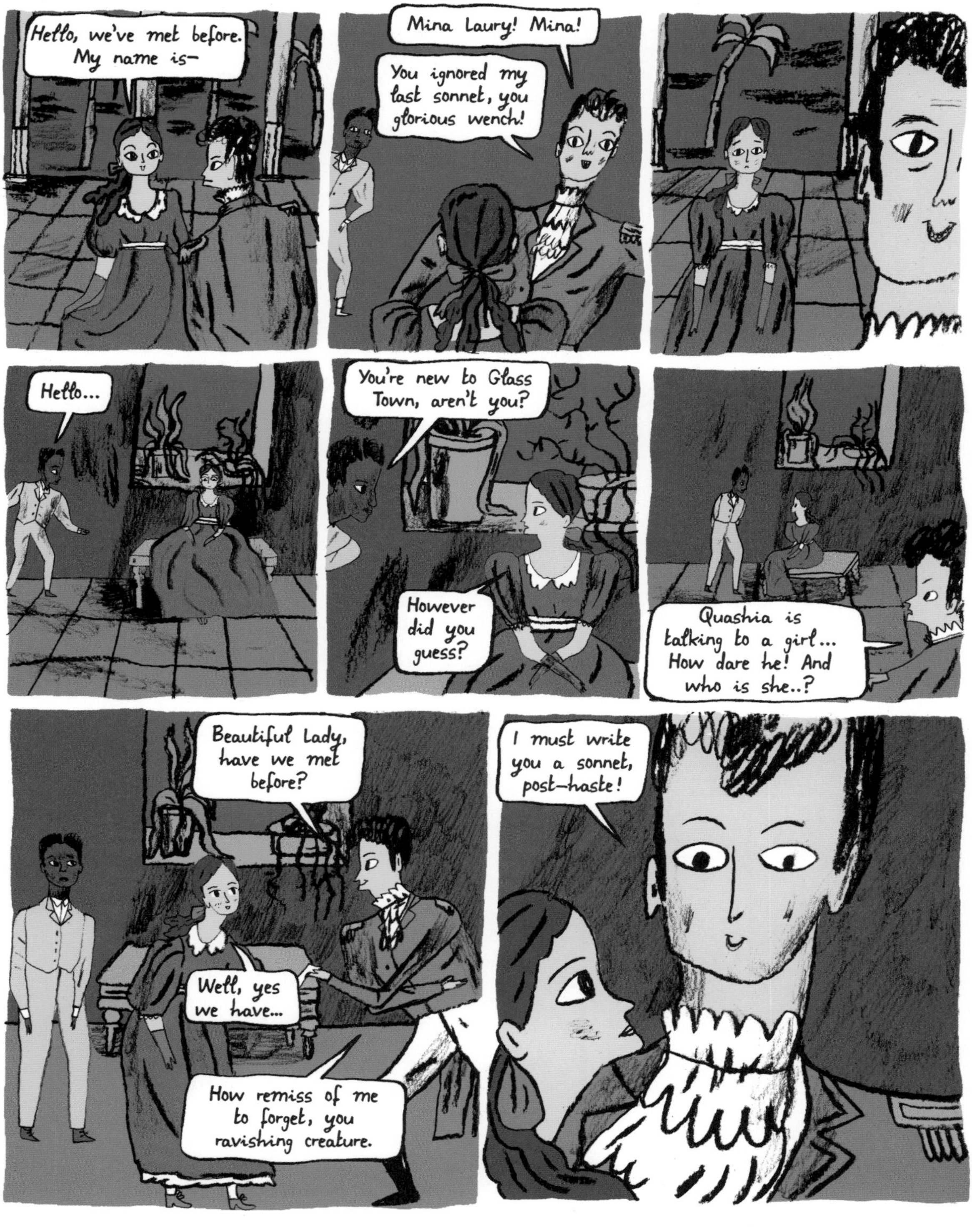
Hello, we've met before. My name is—
Mina Laury! Mina!
You ignored my last sonnet, you glorious wench!
Hello...
You're new to Glass Town, aren't you?
However did you guess?
Quashia is talking to a girl... How dare he! And who is she..?
Beautiful Lady, have we met before?
Well, yes we have...
How remiss of me to forget, you ravishing creature.
I must write you a sonnet, post-haste!

And so that brings us back to the day in the garden, when Mary and Zamorna came upon Quashia.

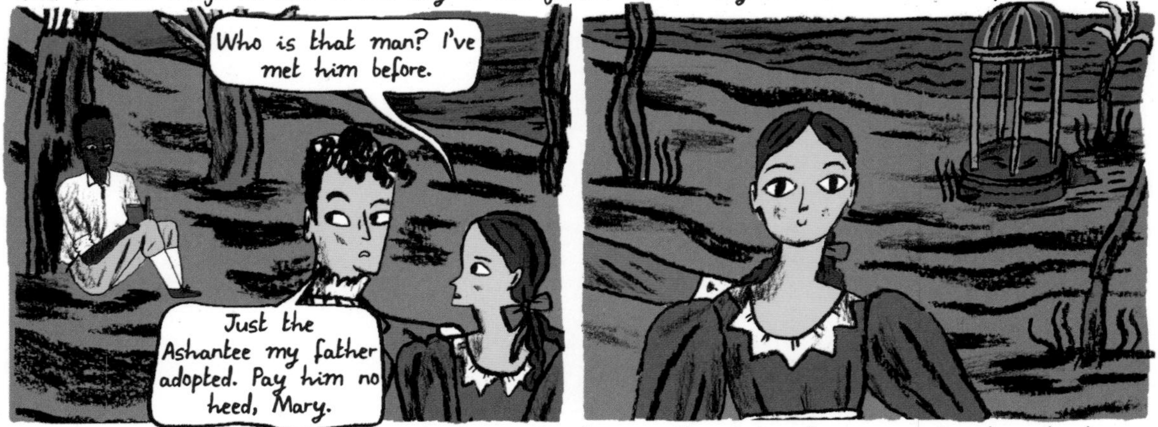
Who is that man? I've met him before.
Just the Ashantee my father adopted. Pay him no heed, Mary.

But Mary and Quashia became friends, during the long months of Mary's engagement, when she hung around Wellington House, hoping Zamorna would come back from his carousing in Glass Town.

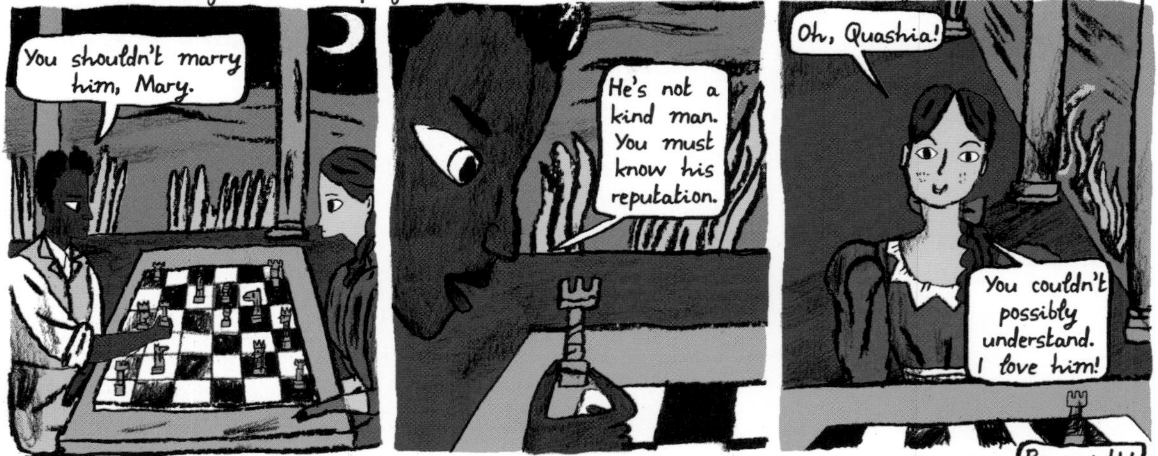
You shouldn't marry him, Mary.
He's not a kind man. You must know his reputation.
Oh, Quashia!
You couldn't possibly understand. I love him!

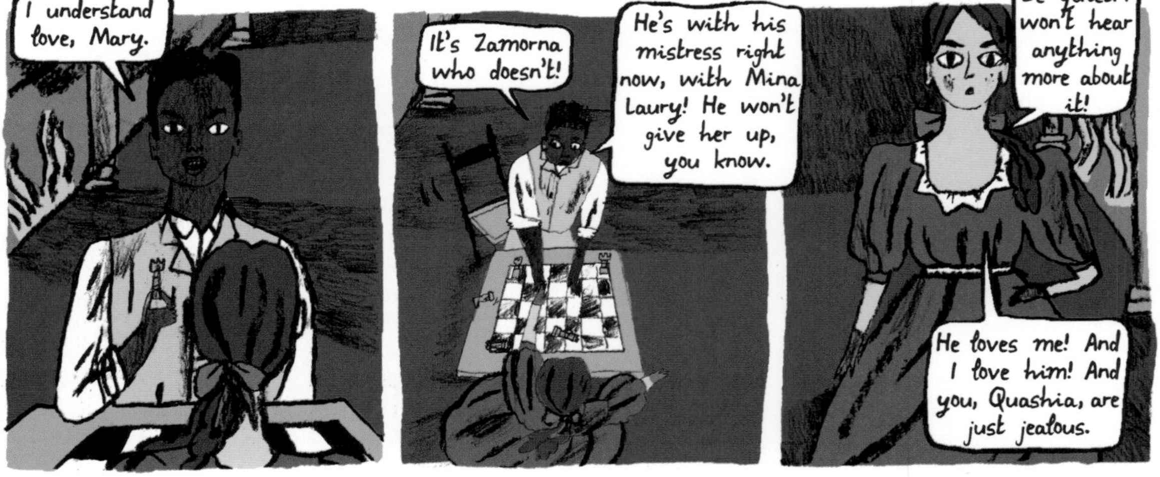
I understand love, Mary.
It's Zamorna who doesn't!
He's with his mistress right now, with Mina Laury! He won't give her up, you know.
Be quiet! I won't hear anything more about it!
He loves me! And I love him! And you, Quashia, are just jealous.

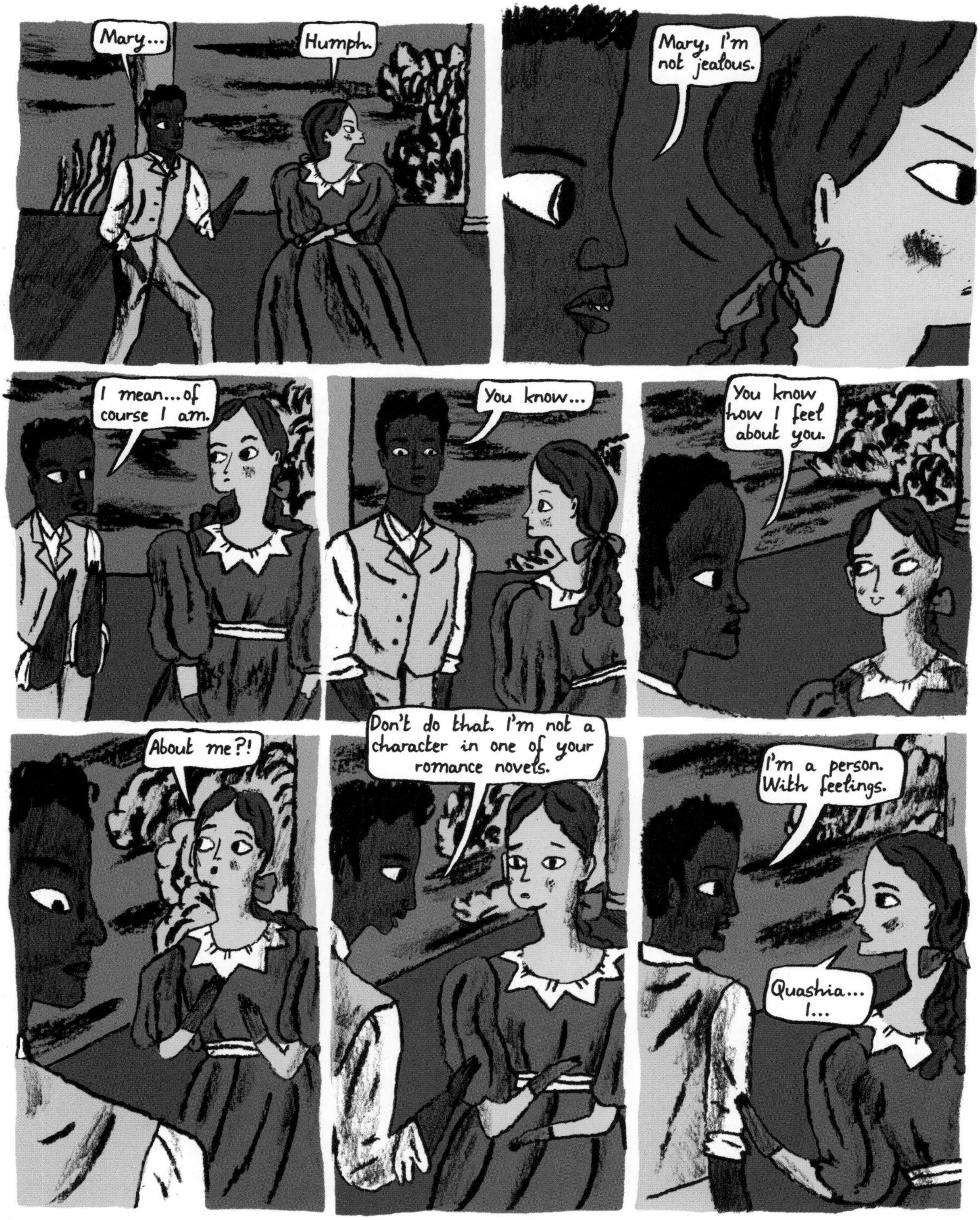
Mary...
Humph.
Mary, I'm not jealous.
I mean... of course I am.
You know...
You know how I feel about you.
About me?!
Don't do that. I'm not a character in one of your romance novels.
I'm a person. With feelings.
Quashia... I...

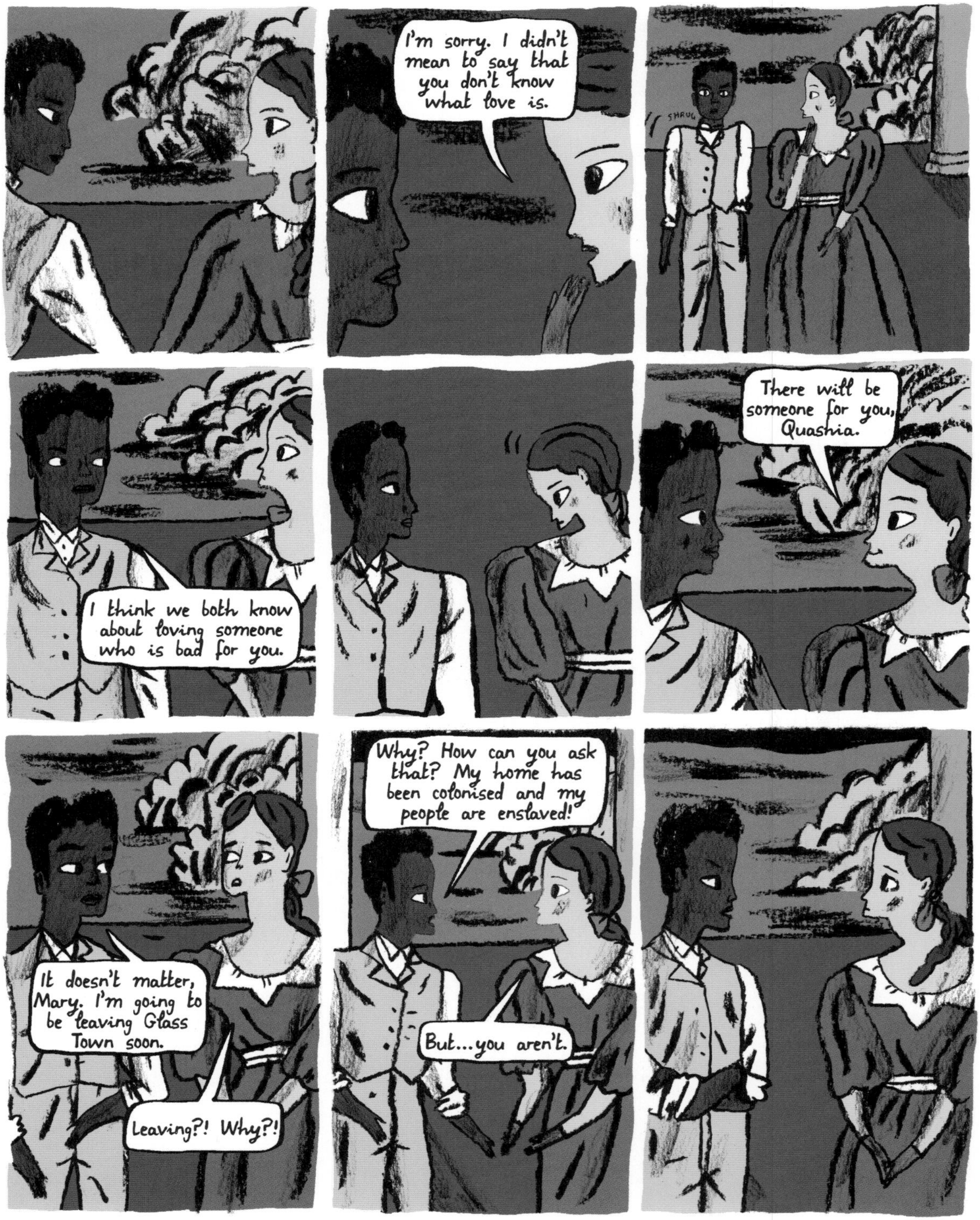
I'm sorry. I didn't mean to say that you don't know what love is.
SHRUG
I think we both know about loving someone who is bad for you.
There will be someone for you, Quashia.
It doesn't matter, Mary. I'm going to be leaving Glass Town soon.
Leaving?! Why?!
Why? How can you ask that? My home has been colonised and my people are enslaved!
But...you aren't.

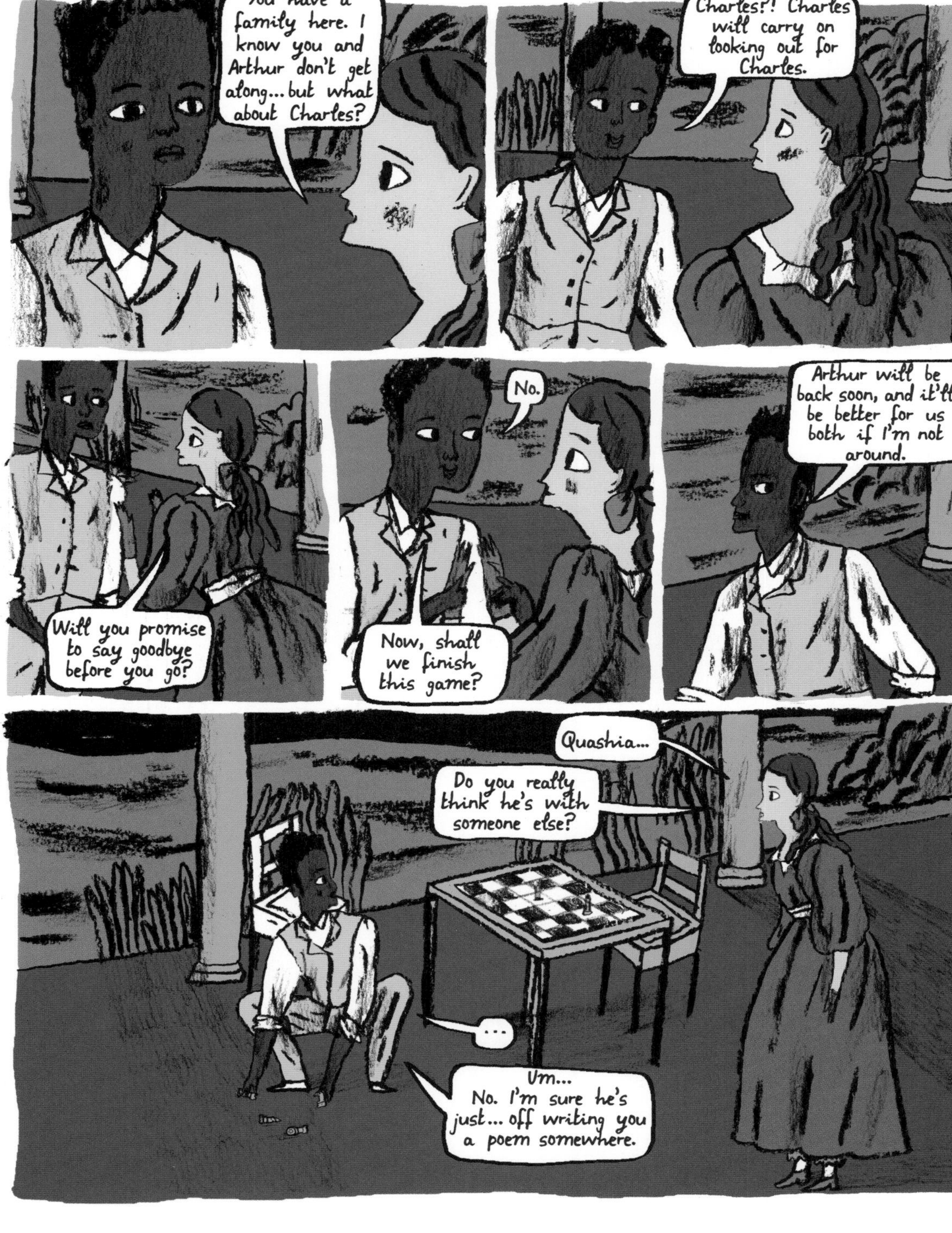
You have a family here. I know you and Arthur don't get along... but what about Charles?
Charles?! Charles will carry on looking out for Charles.
Will you promise to say goodbye before you go?
No.
Now, shall we finish this game?
Arthur will be back soon, and it'll be better for us both if I'm not around.
Quashia...
Do you really think he's with someone else?
...
Um...
No. I'm sure he's just... off writing you a poem somewhere.

Lady Zenobia
~A most tragical tale~

Zenobia was brilliant. Zenobia was bright. She strode through the streets of Glass Town with a book in each hand and a glint in her eye.

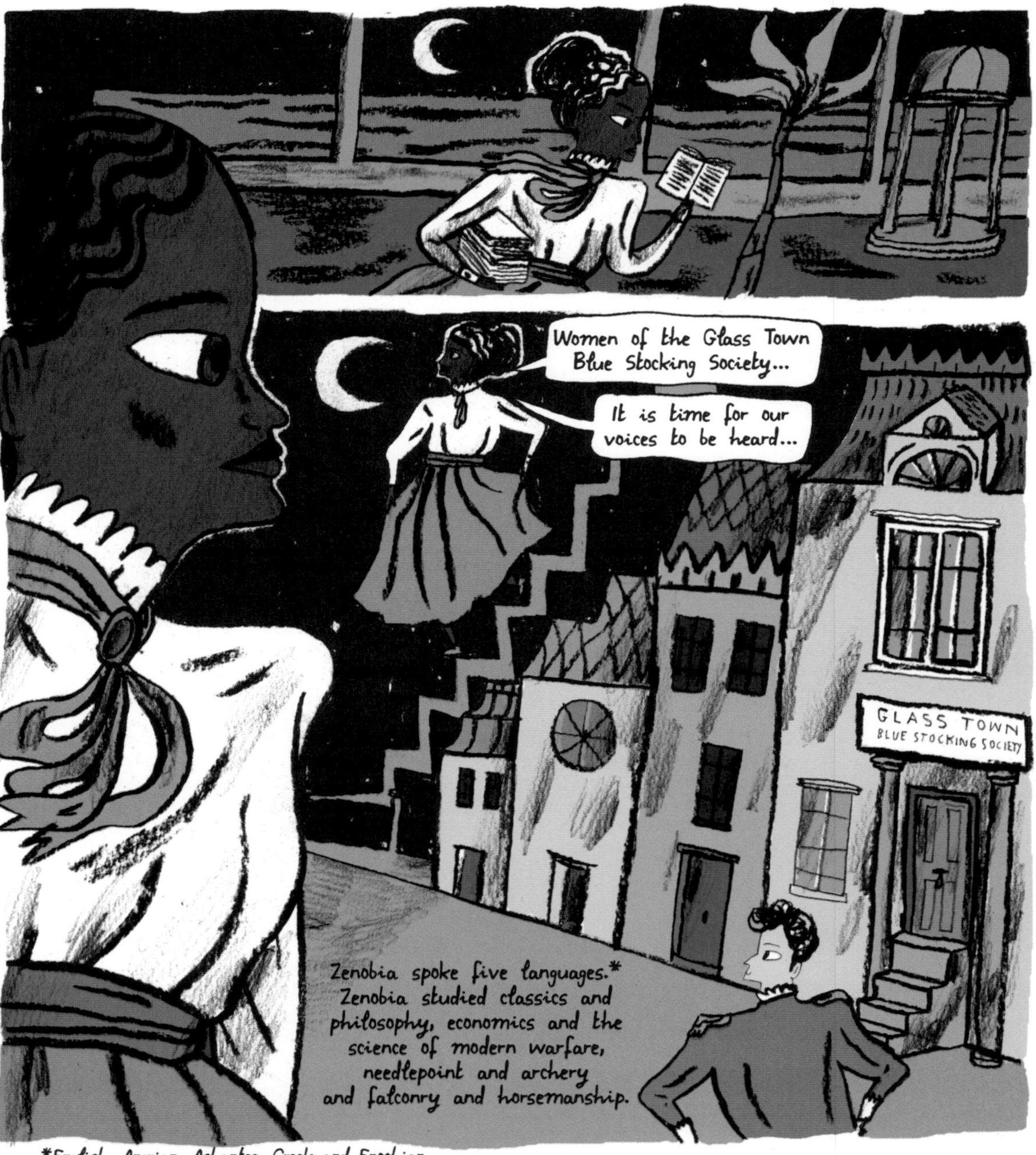
Women of the Glass Town Blue Stocking Society...
It is time for our voices to be heard...
GLASS TOWN
BLUE STOCKING SOCIETY
Zenobia spoke five languages.* Zenobia studied classics and philosophy, economics and the science of modern warfare, needlepoint and archery and falconry and horsemanship.

*English, Angrian, Ashantee, Greek and Enochian.

But then she met Zamorna.

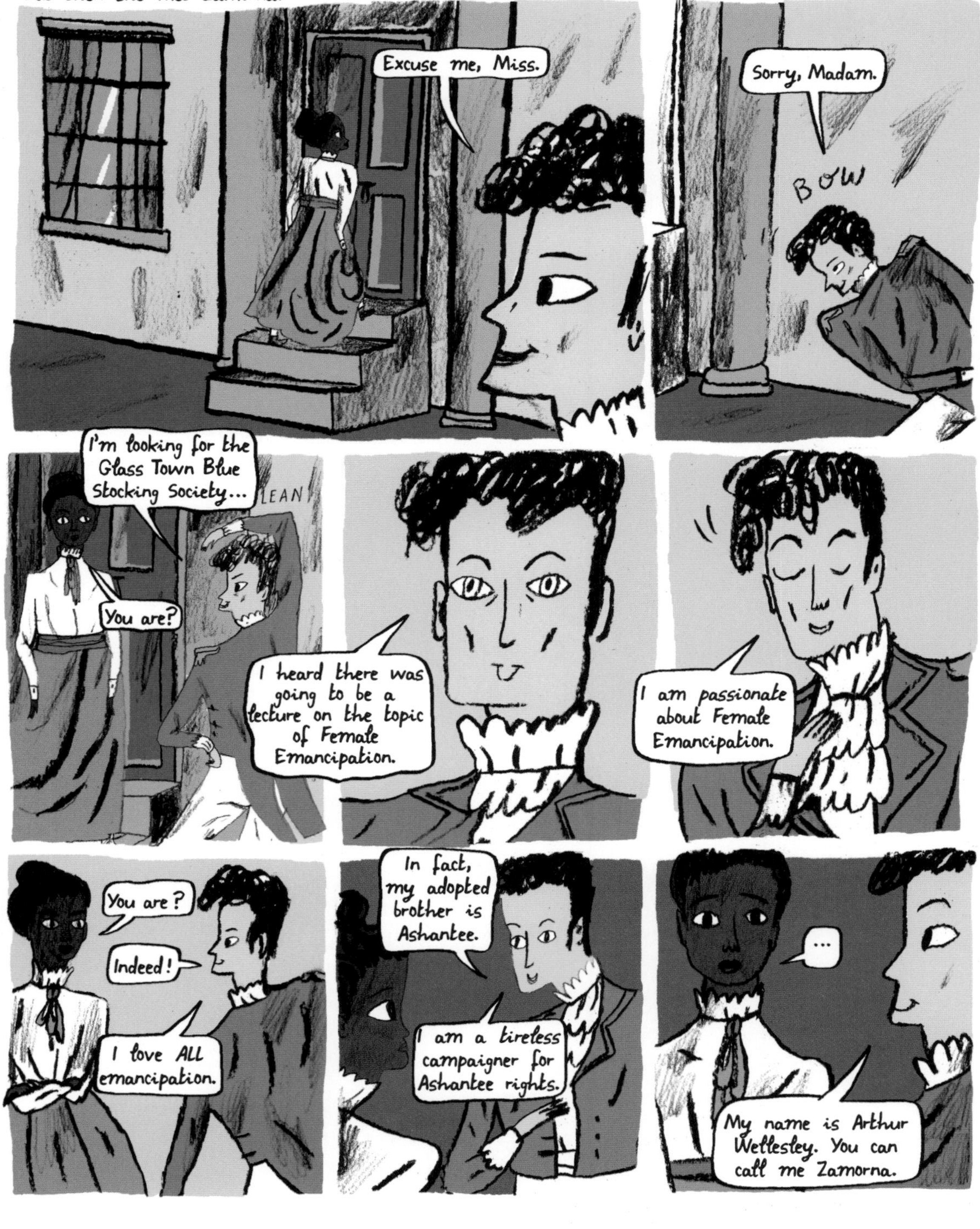
Excuse me, Miss.
Sorry, Madam.
BOW
I'm looking for the Glass Town Blue Stocking Society...
LEAN
You are?
I heard there was going to be a lecture on the topic of Female Emancipation.
I am passionate about Female Emancipation.
You are?
Indeed!
I love ALL emancipation.
In fact, my adopted brother is Ashantee.
I am a tireless campaigner for Ashantee rights.
...
My name is Arthur Wellesley. You can call me Zamorna.

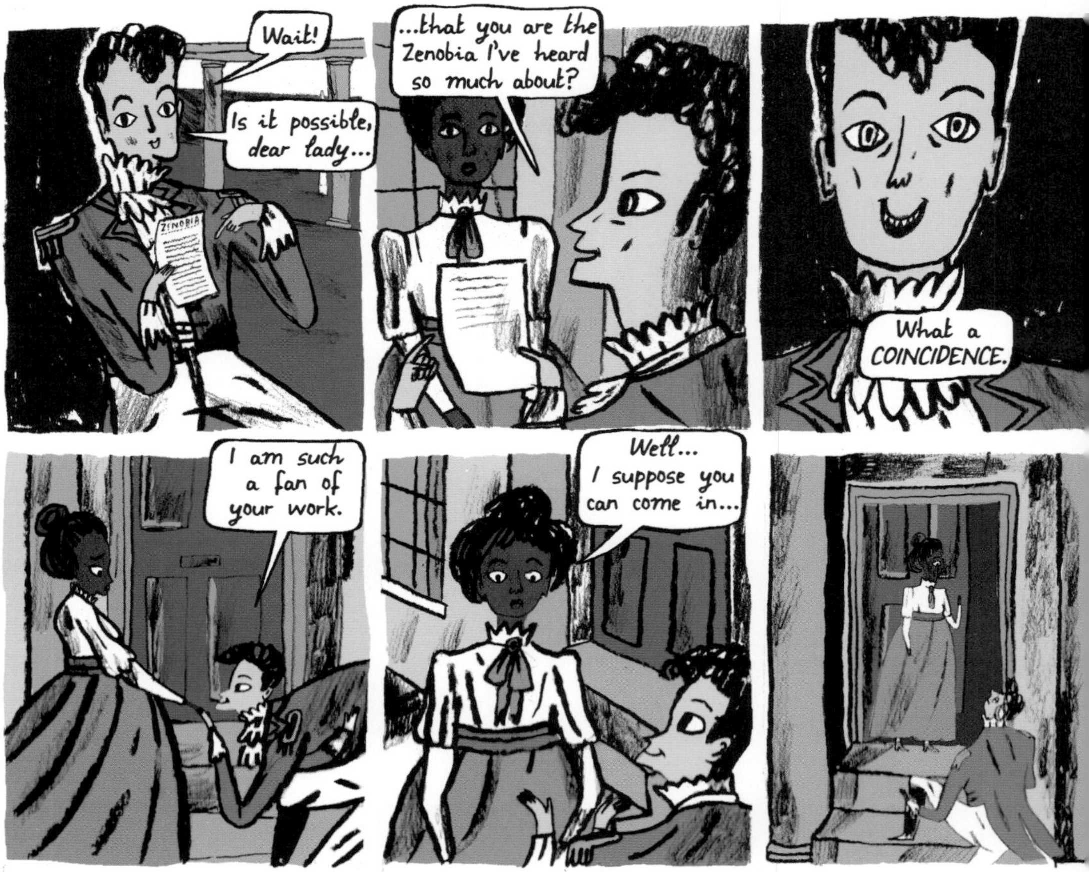
Wait!
Is it possible, dear lady...
...that you are the Zenobia I've heard so much about?
What a COINCIDENCE.
I am such a fan of your work.
Well... I suppose you can come in...

All that long summer he courted her. He called for her every day. They walked in the fragrant botanical gardens and along the golden lakeside parades.

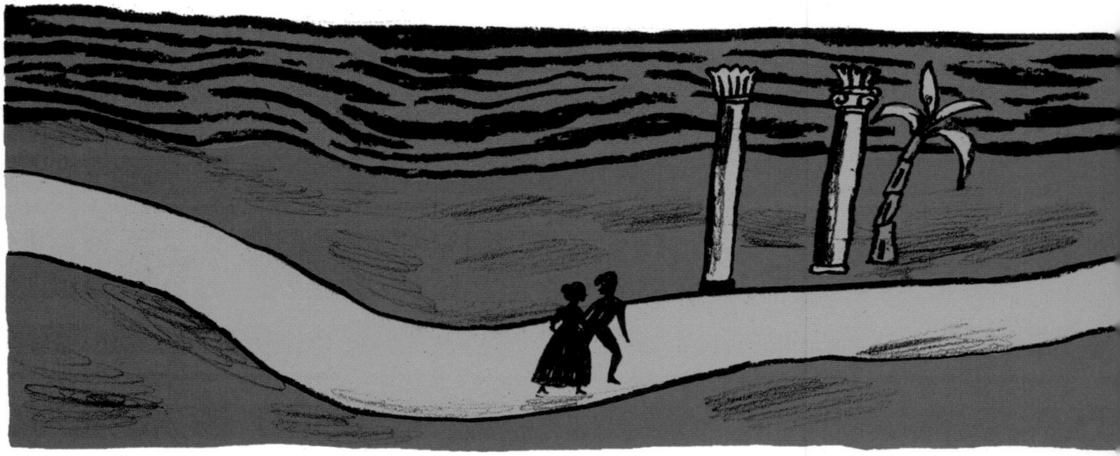

They talked of poetry and politics, the violent founding of Glass Town, the treatment of the Ashantee people. They talked about how they might change the world. And slowly, slowly, against all her better instincts, Zenobia began to trust him.

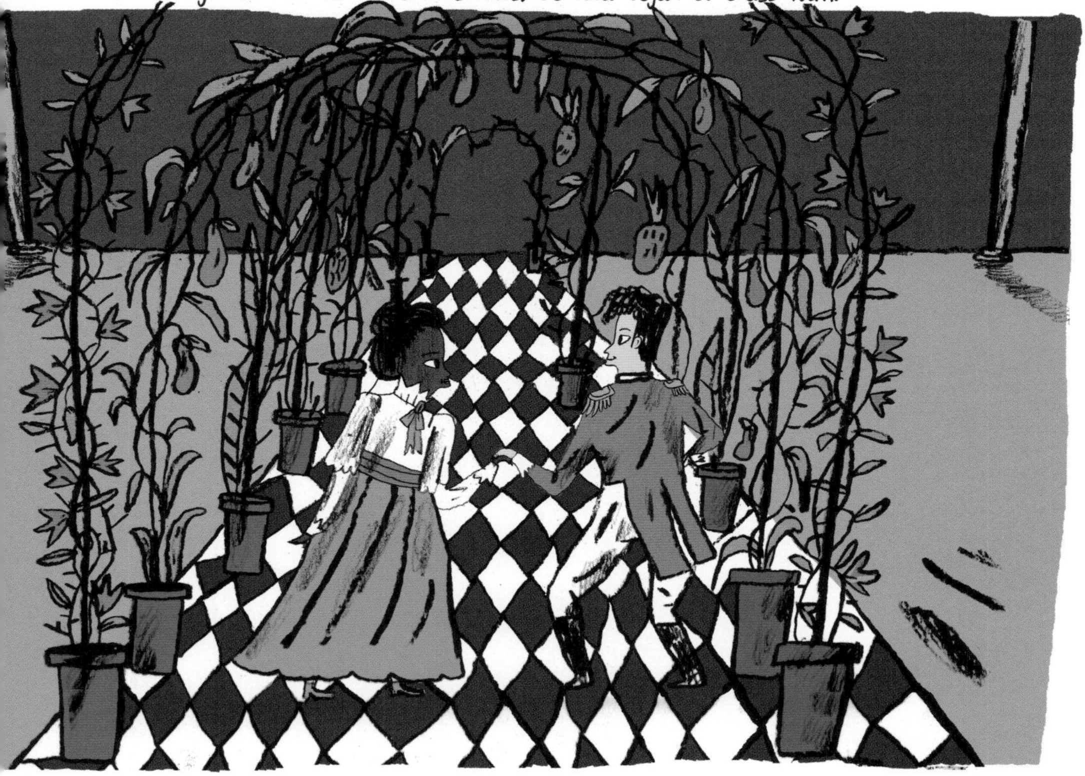

And then, when summer drew to a close, and a chill wind blew across the Angoran Sea from Gondal, whipping the palm trees into a frenzy and sending the parasols and hats and handkerchiefs of the promenading ladies flying...

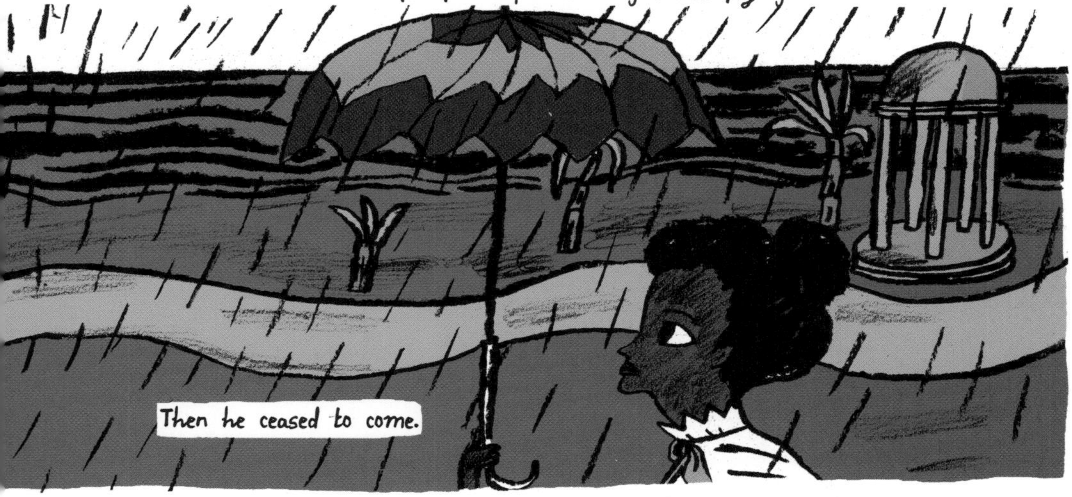
Then he ceased to come.

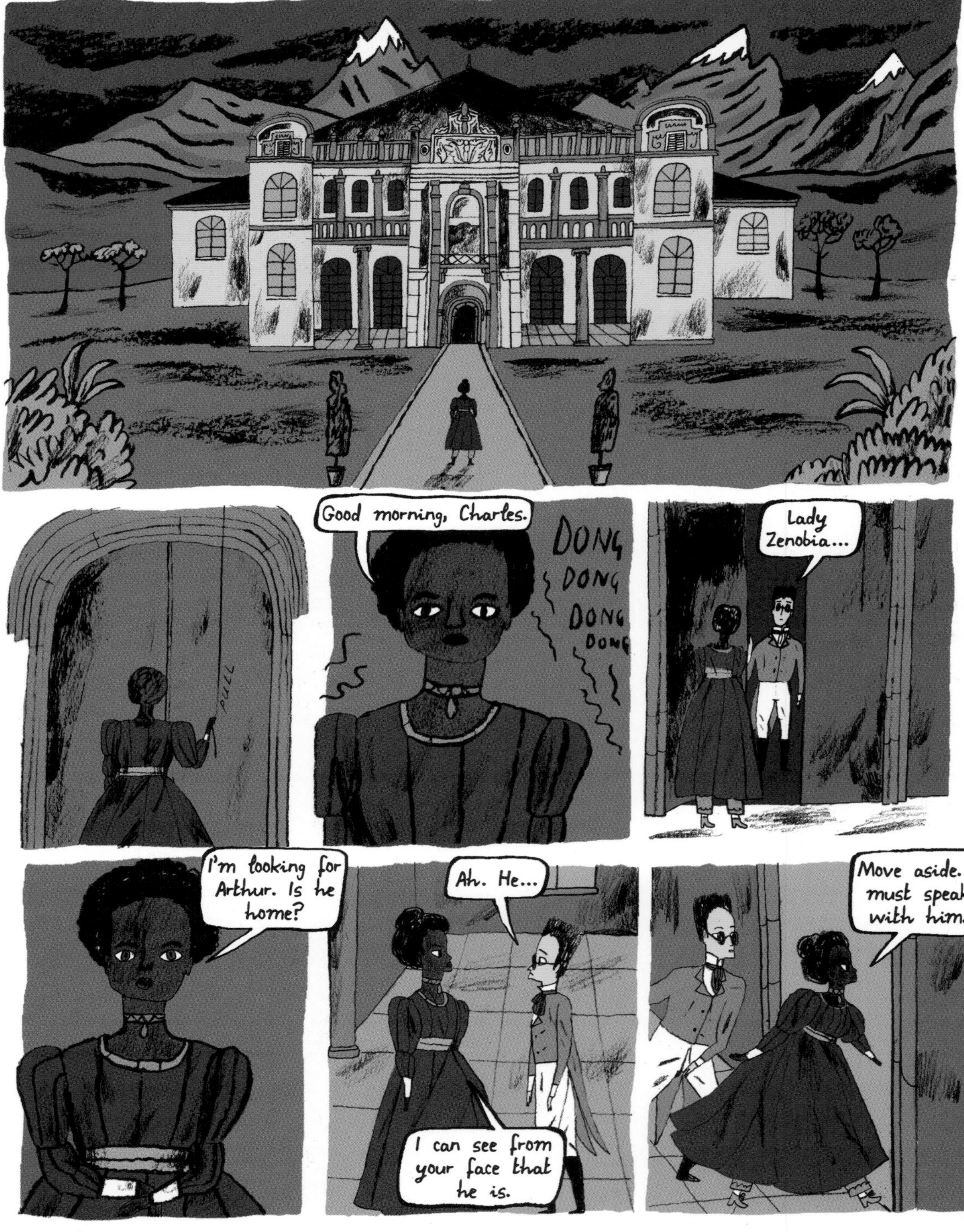
PULL
Good morning, Charles.
DONG
DONG
DONG
DONG
Lady Zenobia...
I'm looking for Arthur. Is he home?
Ah. He...
I can see from your face that he is.
Move aside. I must speak with him.

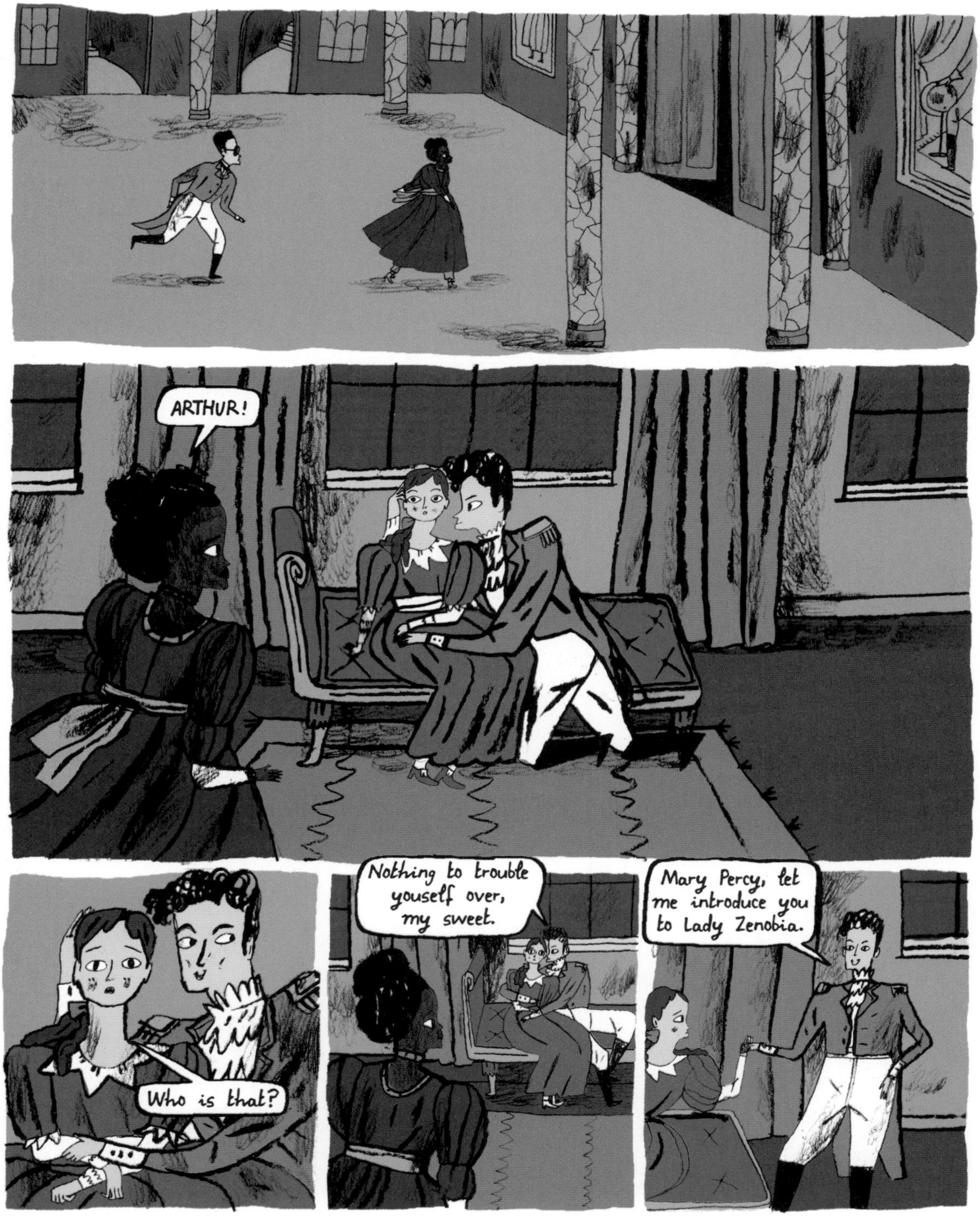
ARTHUR!
Who is that?
Nothing to trouble youself over, my sweet.
Mary Percy, let me introduce you to Lady Zenobia.

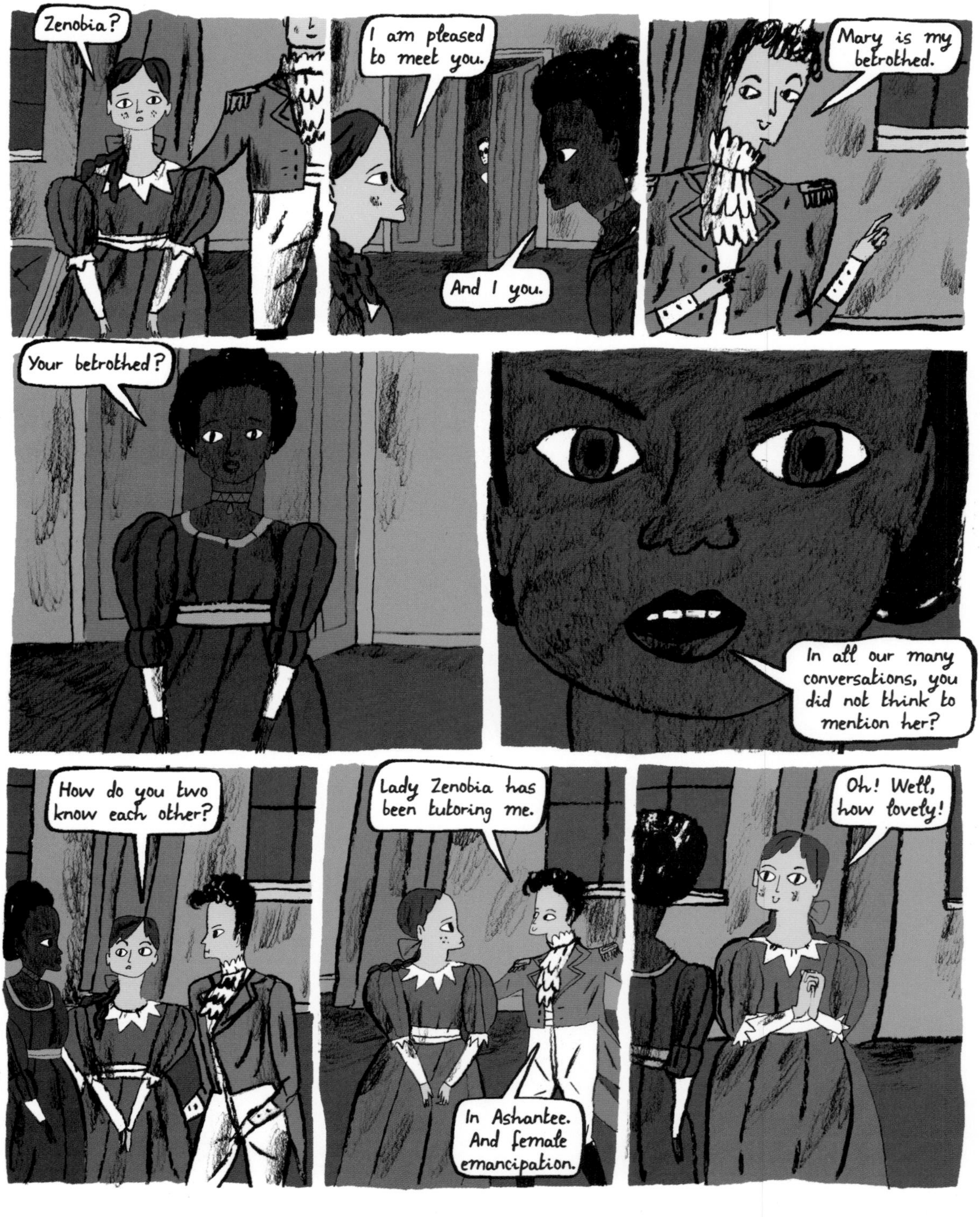
Zenobia?
I am pleased to meet you.
And I you.
Mary is my betrothed.
Your betrothed?
In all our many conversations, you did not think to mention her?
How do you two know each other?
Lady Zenobia has been tutoring me.
In Ashantee. And female emancipation.
Oh! Well, how lovely!

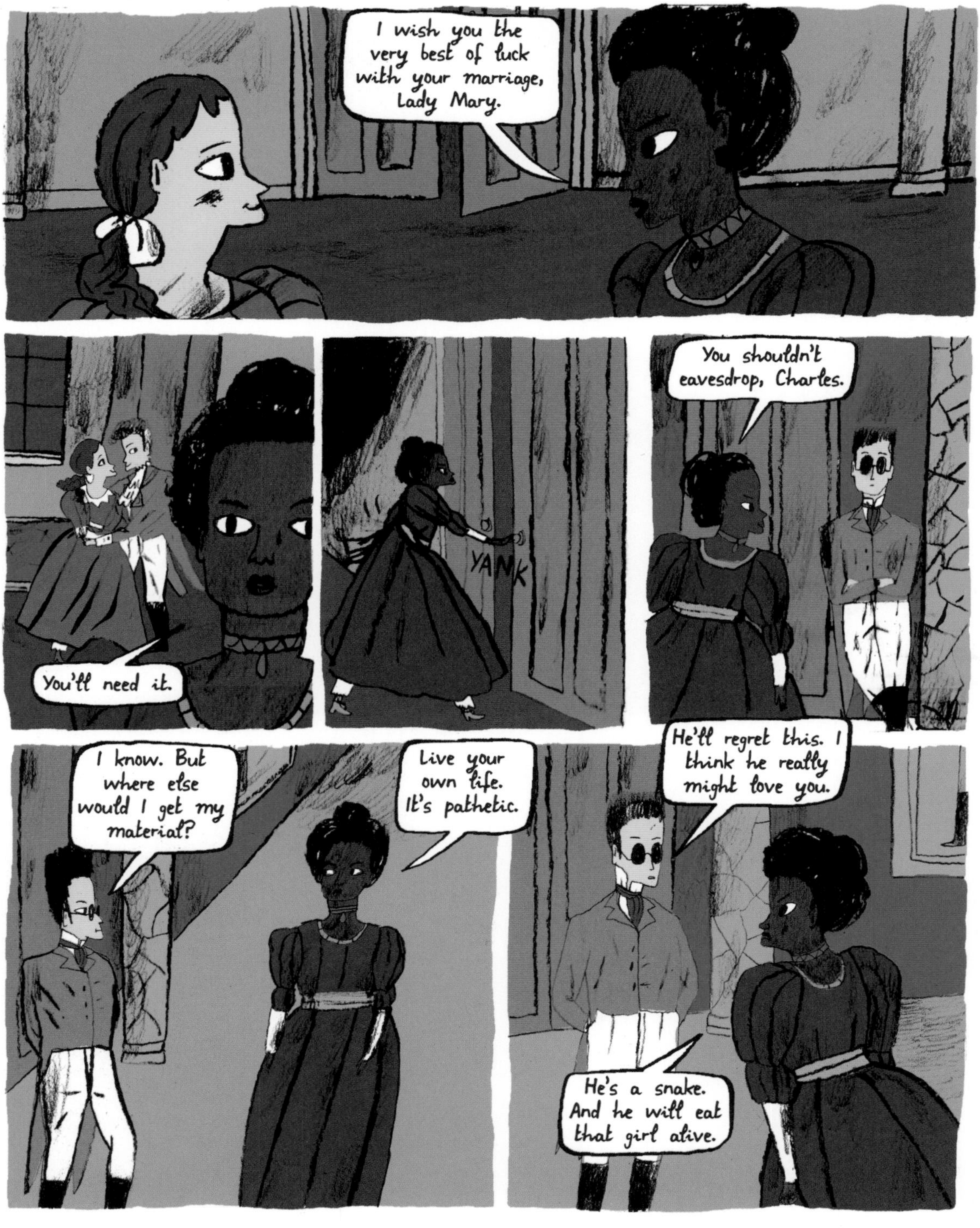
I wish you the very best of luck with your marriage, Lady Mary.
You'll need it.
YANK
You shouldn't eavesdrop, Charles.
I know. But where else would I get my material?
Live your own life. It's pathetic.
He'll regret this. I think he really might love you.
He's a snake. And he will eat that girl alive.

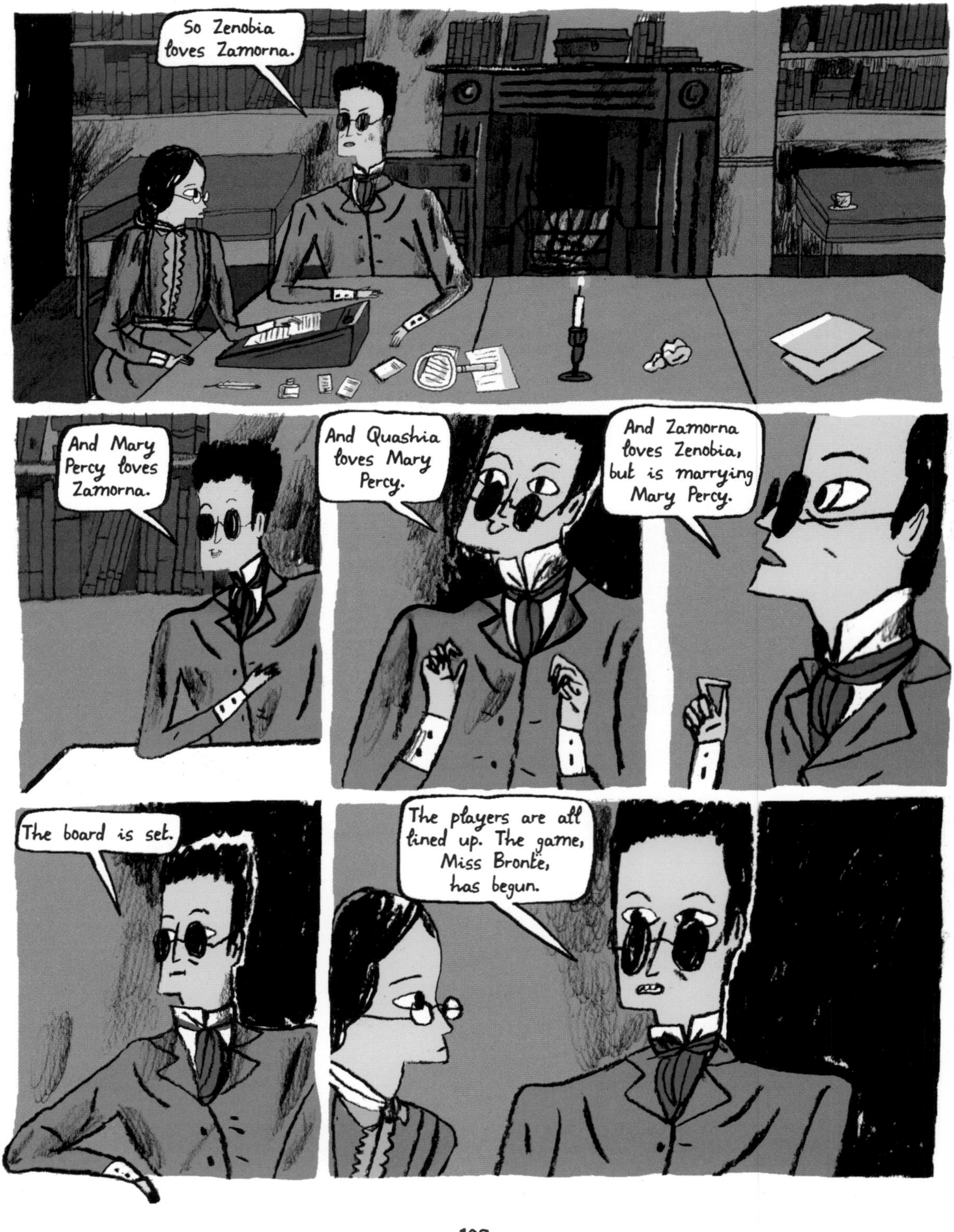
So Zenobia loves Zamorna.
And Mary Percy loves Zamorna.
And Quashia loves Mary Percy.
And Zamorna loves Zenobia, but is marrying Mary Percy.
The board is set.
The players are all lined up. The game, Miss Brontë, has begun.

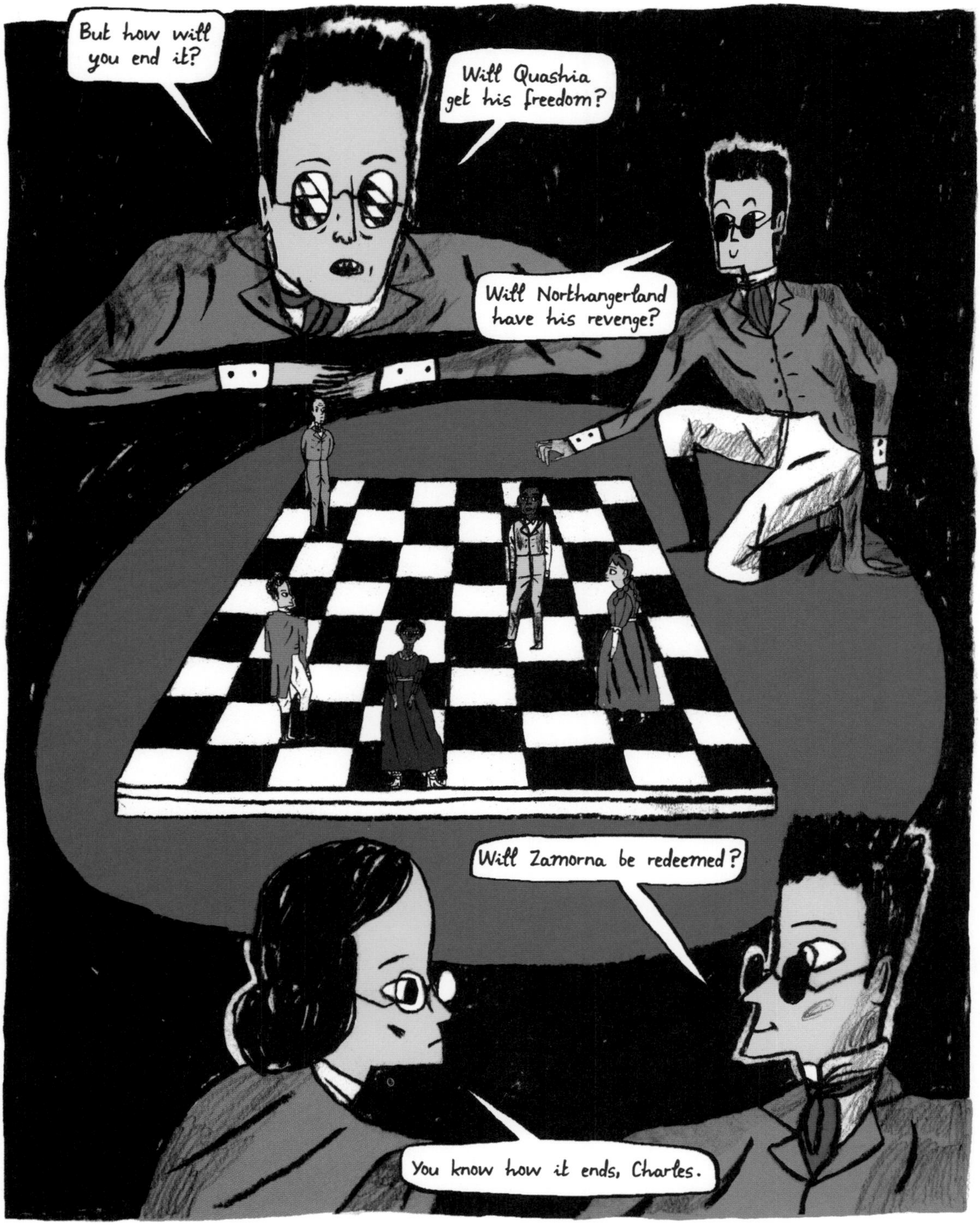
But how will you end it?
Will Quashia get his freedom?
Will Northangerland have his revenge?
Will Zamorna be redeemed?
You know how it ends, Charles.

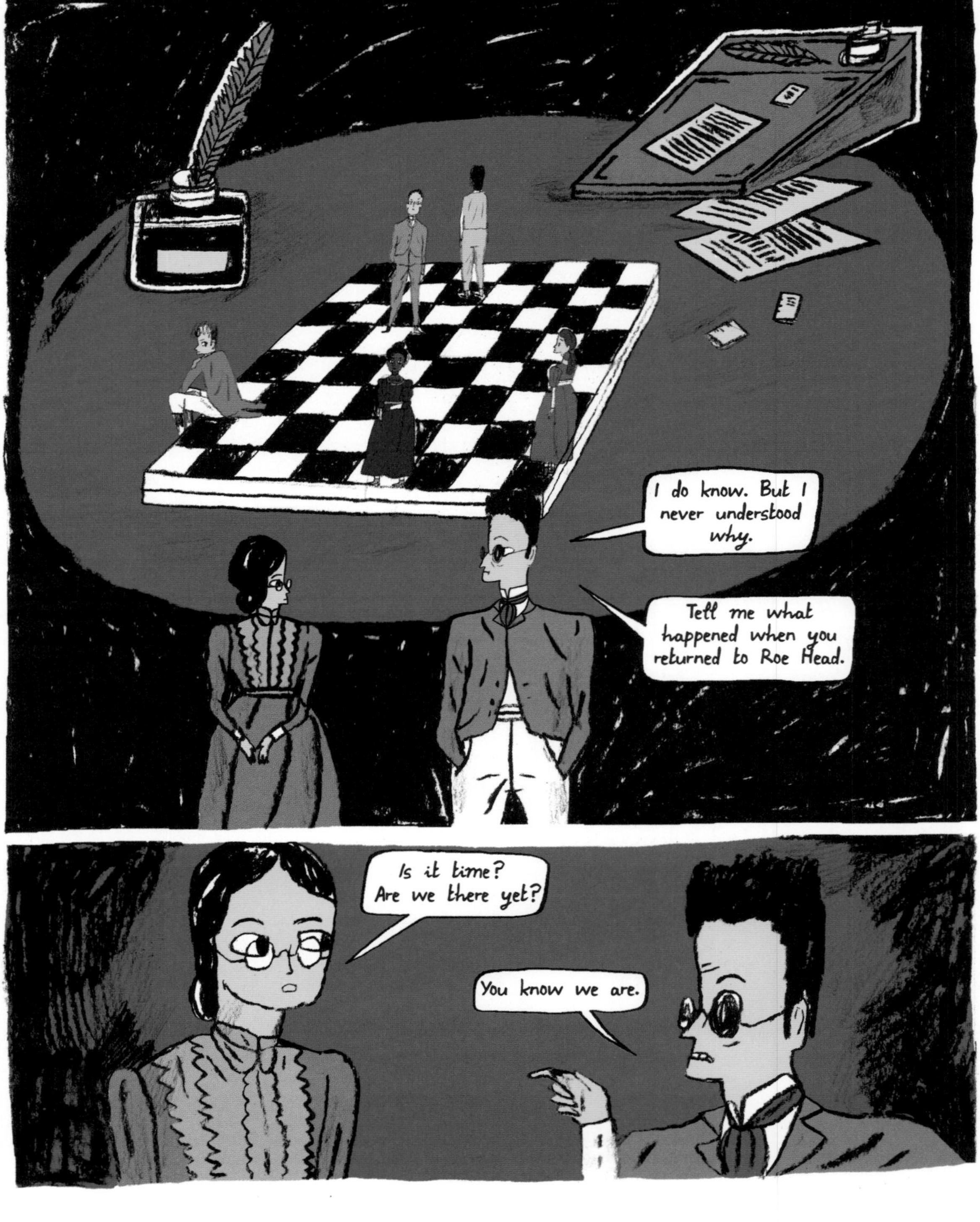
I do know. But I never understood why.
Tell me what happened when you returned to Roe Head.
Is it time? Are we there yet?
You know we are.

CHAPTER THREE

1835 - 1838

Scribblemania

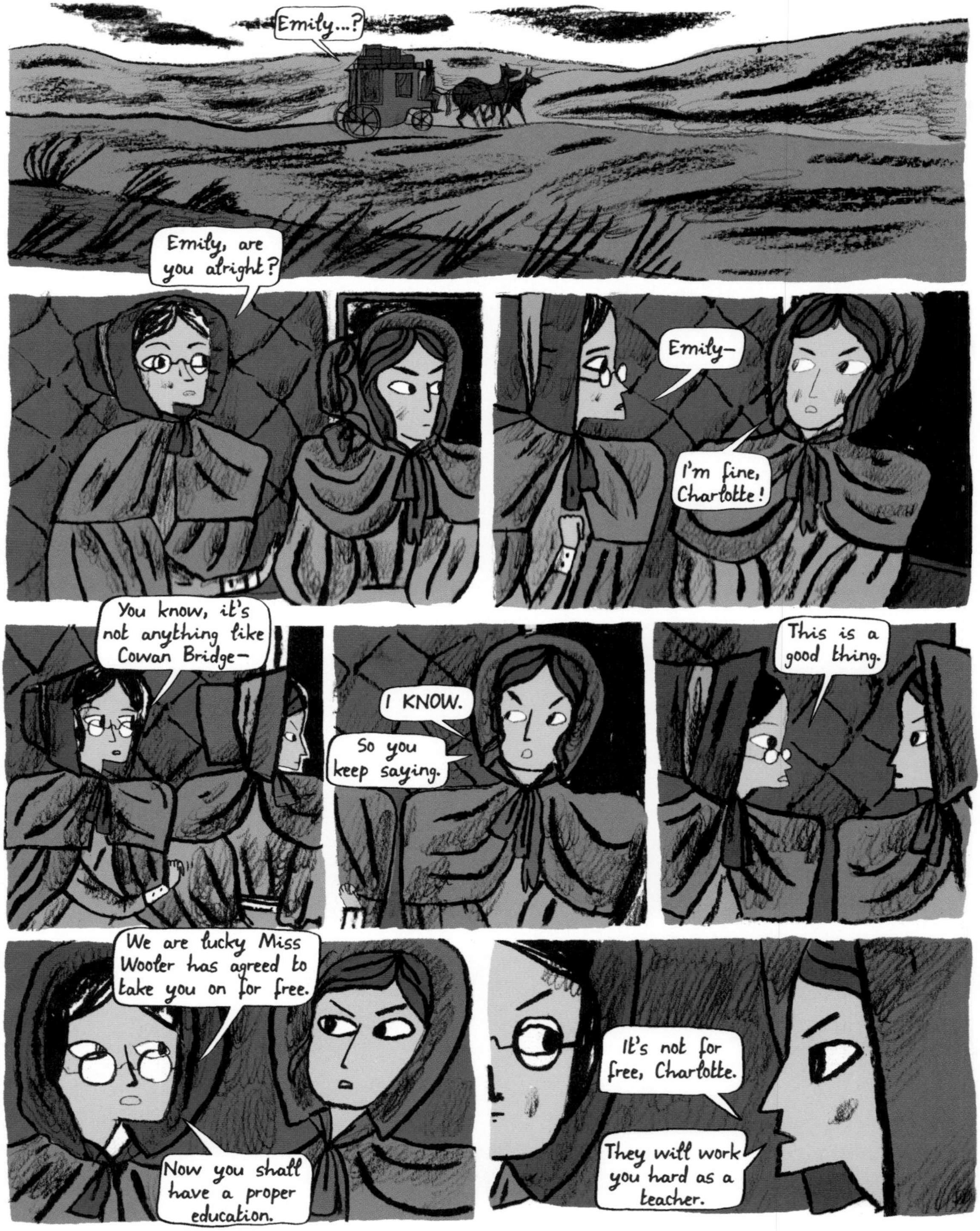
Emily...?
Emily, are you alright?
Emily-
I'm fine, Charlotte!
You know, it's not anything like Cowan Bridge-
I KNOW.
So you keep saying.
This is a good thing.
We are lucky Miss Wooler has agreed to take you on for free.
Now you shall have a proper education.
It's not for free, Charlotte.
They will work you hard as a teacher.

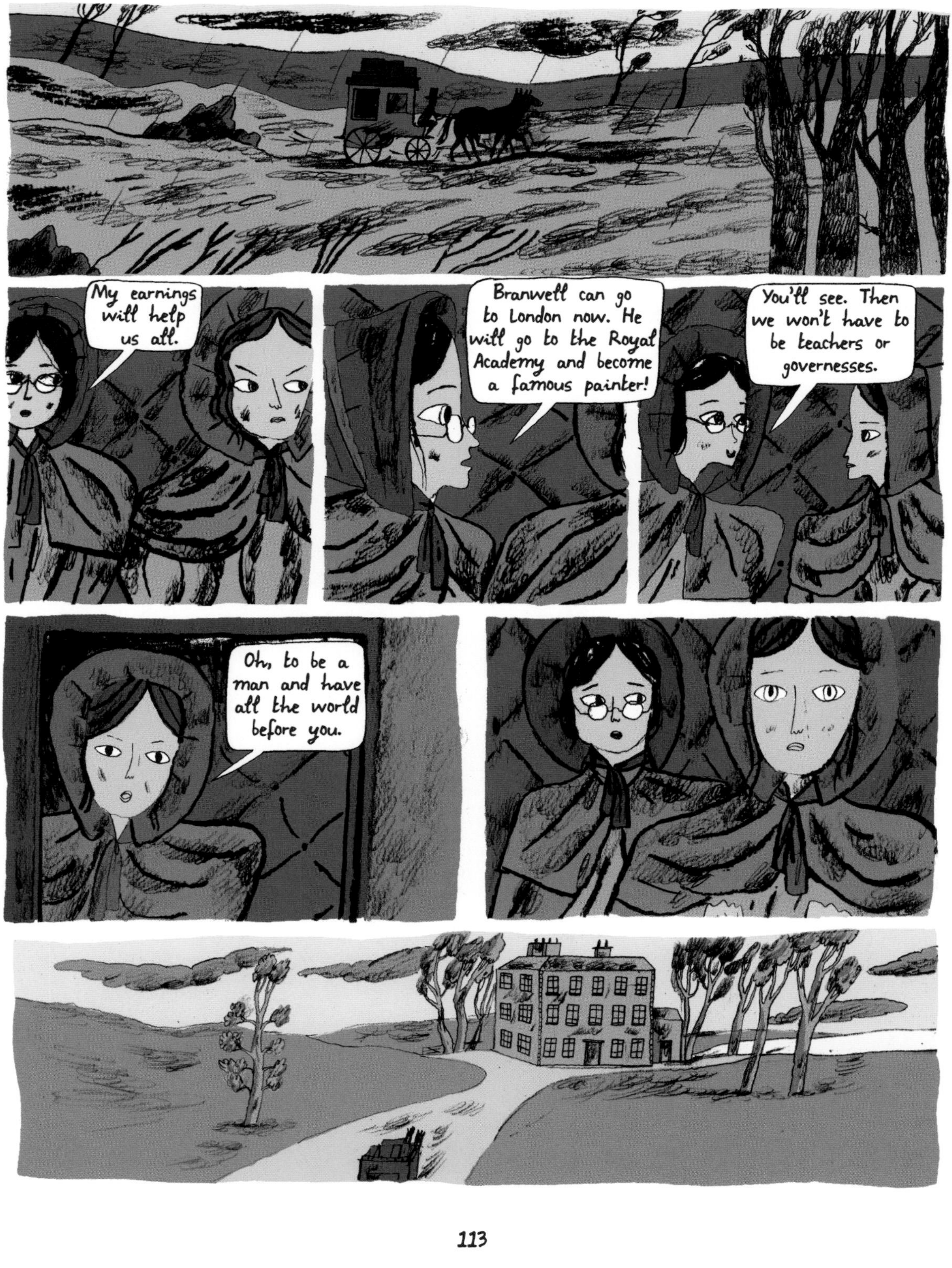
My earnings will help us all.
Branwell can go to London now. He will go to the Royal Academy and become a famous painter!
You'll see. Then we won't have to be teachers or governesses.
Oh, to be a man and have all the world before you.

But from the beginning it was not the same.

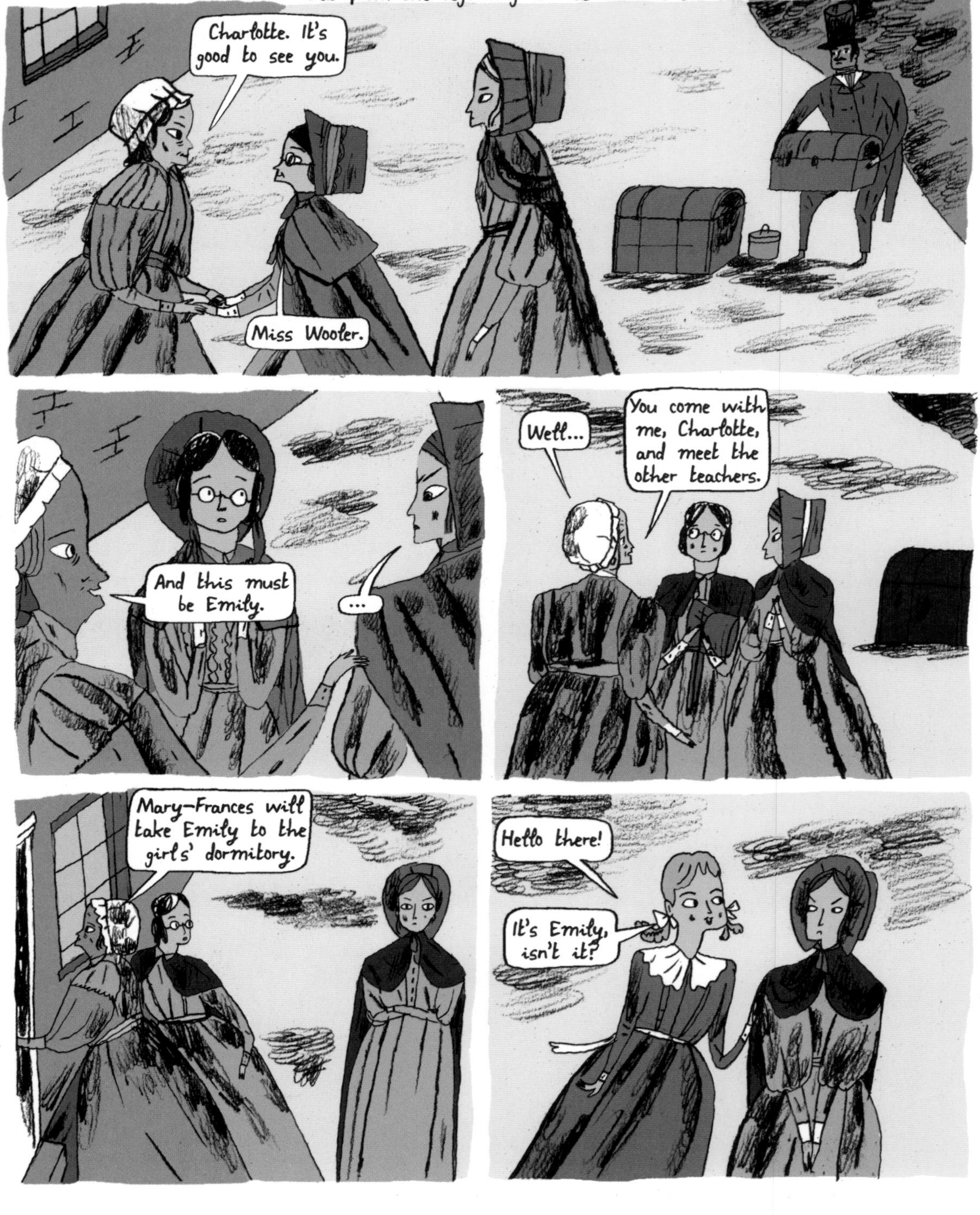

Charlotte. It's good to see you.
Miss Wooler.
And this must be Emily.
...
Well...
You come with me, Charlotte, and meet the other teachers.
Mary-Frances will take Emily to the girls' dormitory.
Hello there!
It's Emily, isn't it?

The Taylor sisters, and Ellen Nussey, Charlotte's great schoolfriends, had left. And she was a teacher now, with responsibilities.

Miss Brontë...

Miss Brontë?

MISS BRONTË!

What is it, Lucy? What do you want?

Can you help me untangle my yarn?

But, worst of all, the sisters were no solace to each other at all.

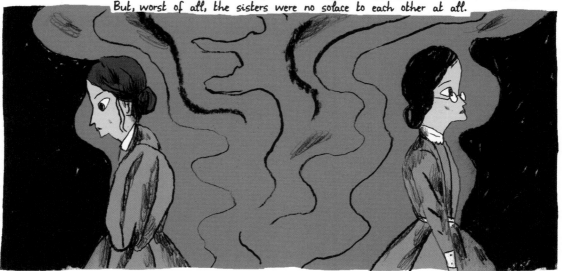

Within months, Emily's homesickness was so extreme that she had gone back to Haworth, and Anne had been sent to take her place.

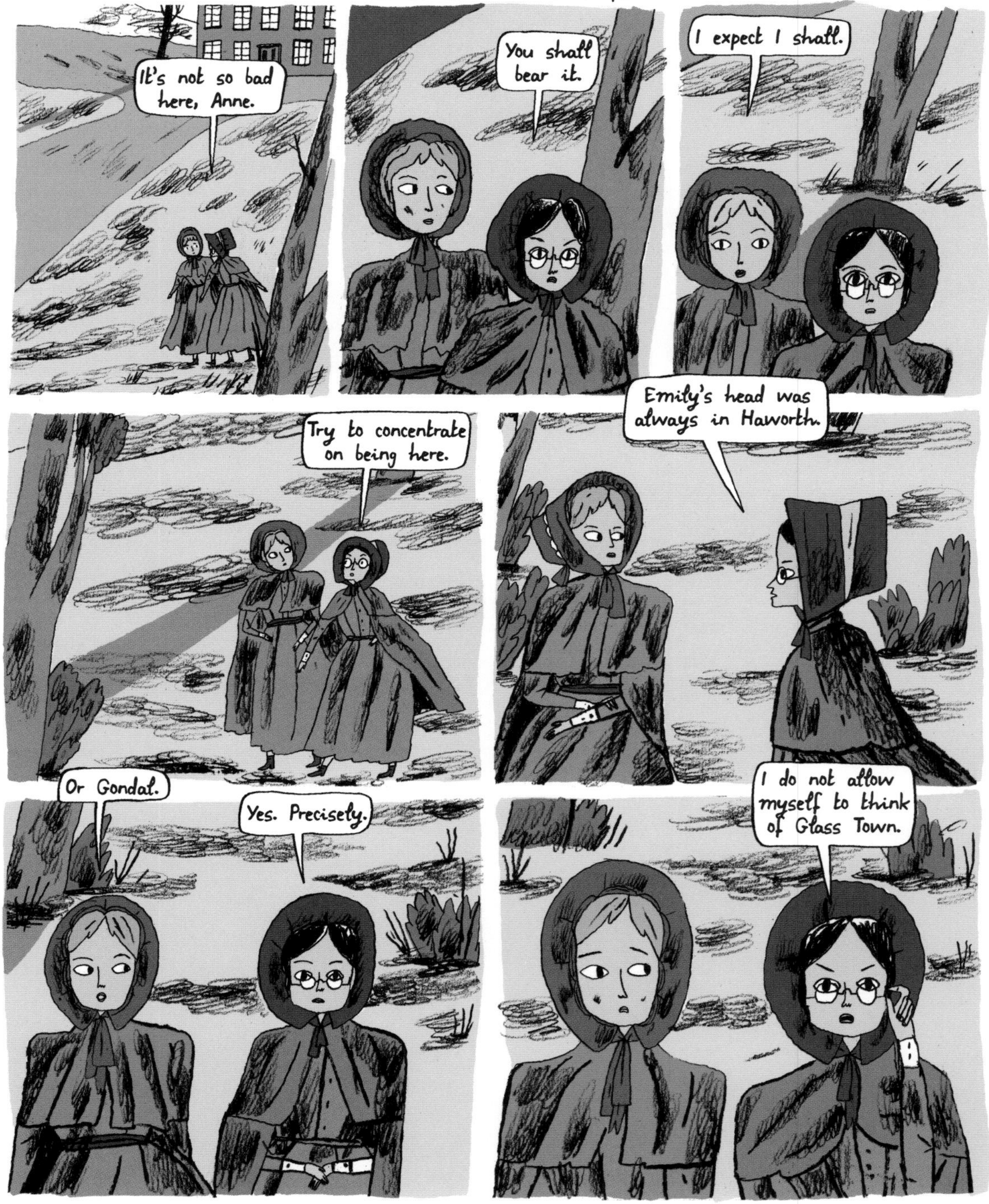
It's not so bad here, Anne.
You shall bear it.
I expect I shall.
Try to concentrate on being here.
Emily's head was always in Haworth.
Or Gondal.
Yes. Precisely.
I do not allow myself to think of Glass Town.

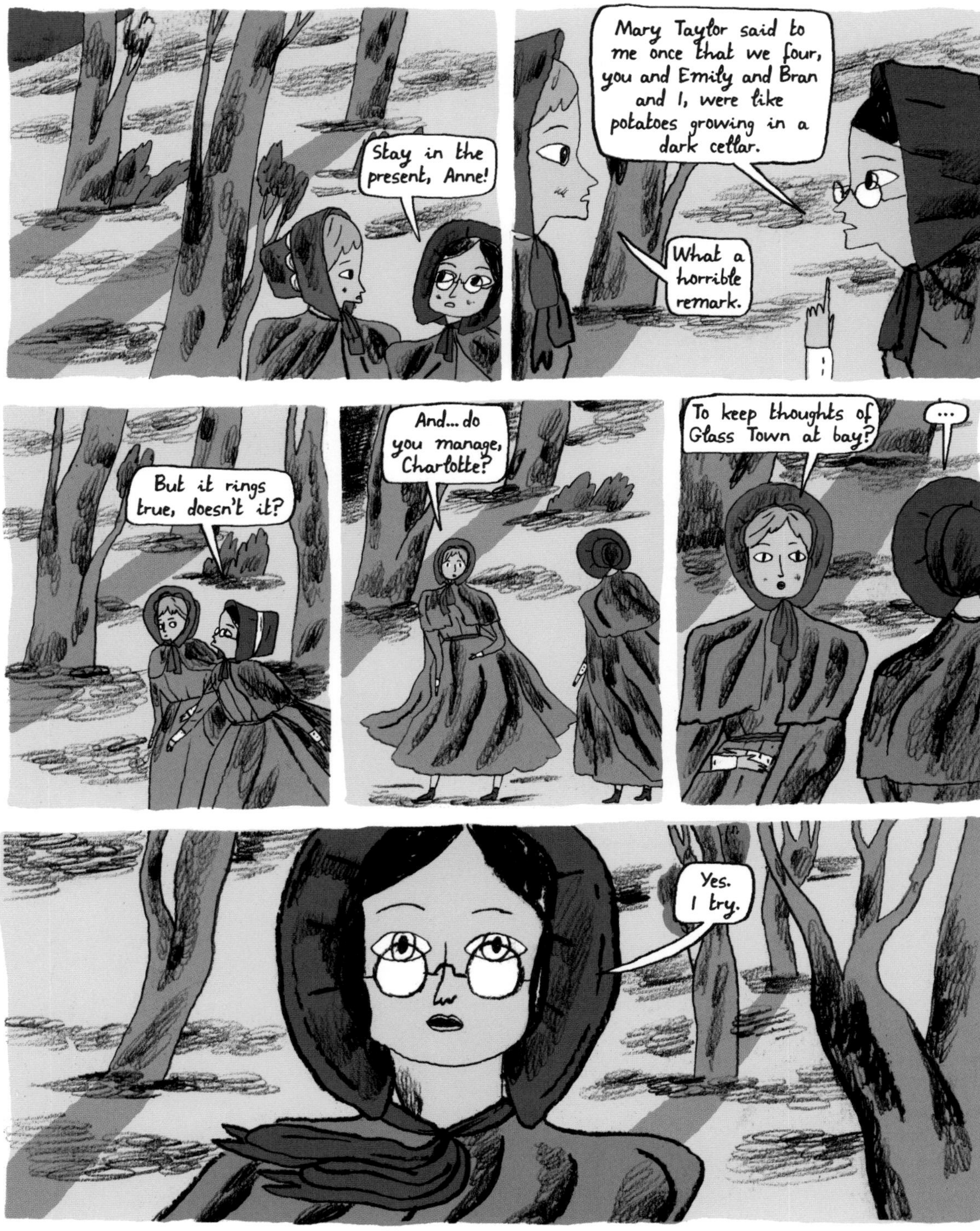
Stay in the present, Anne!
Mary Taylor said to me once that we four, you and Emily and Bran and I, were like potatoes growing in a dark cellar.
What a horrible remark.
But it rings true, doesn't it?
And... do you manage, Charlotte?
To keep thoughts of Glass Town at bay?
...
Yes. I try.

This could not have been further from the truth. In fact something had begun to creep over Charlotte in those last few months.

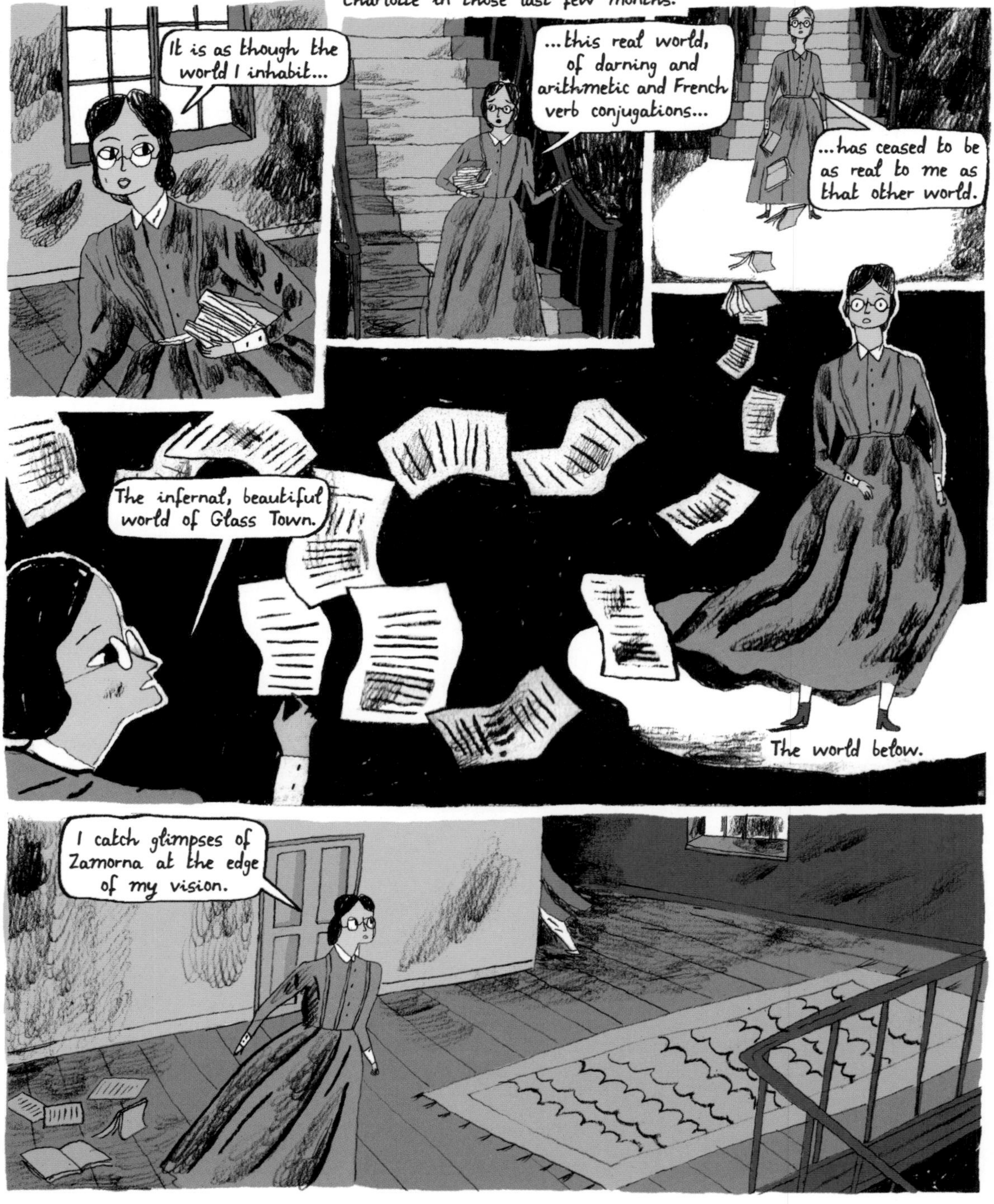
It is as though the world I inhabit...
...this real world, of darning and arithmetic and French verb conjugations...
...has ceased to be as real to me as that other world.
The infernal, beautiful world of Glass Town.
The world below.
I catch glimpses of Zamorna at the edge of my vision.

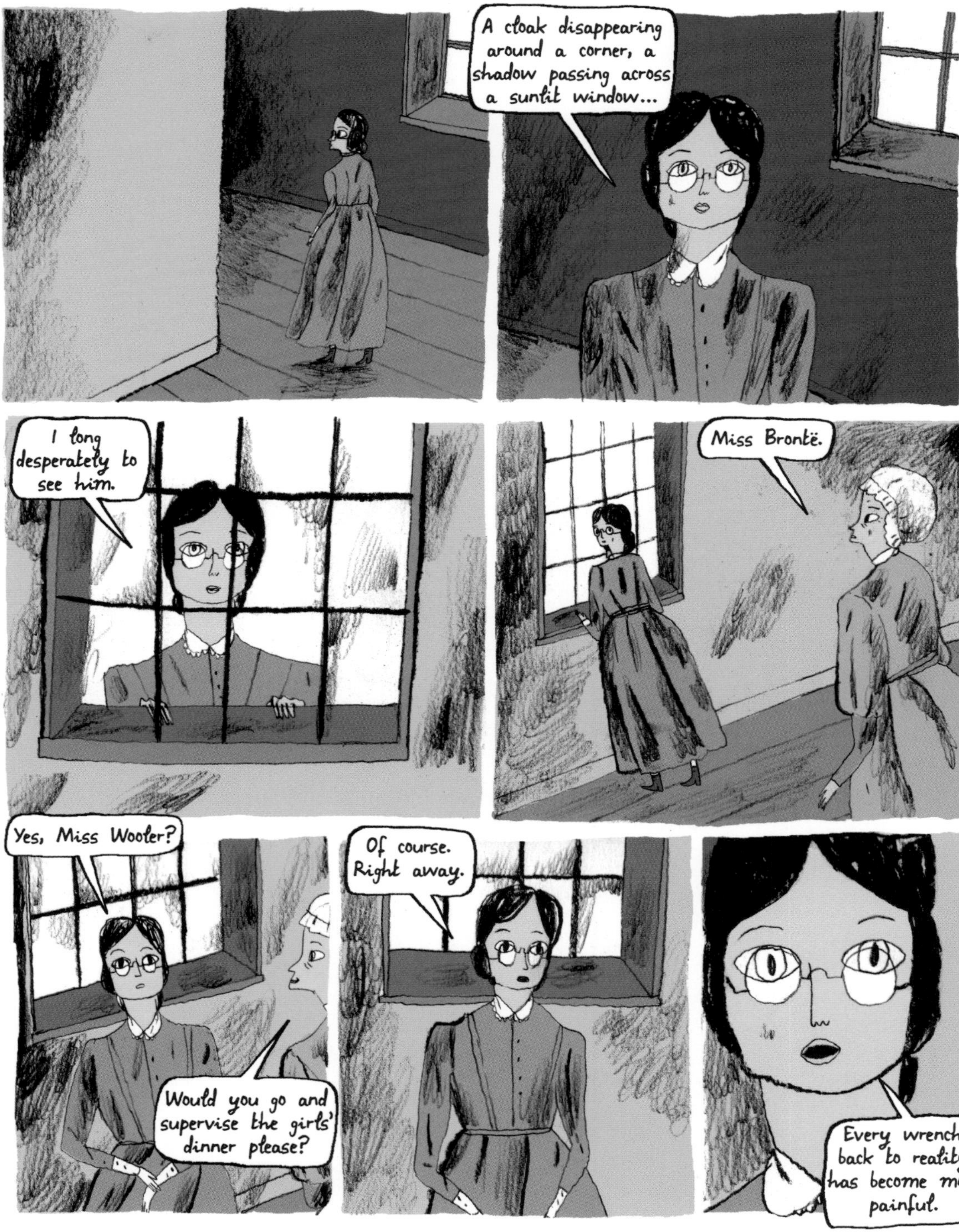
A cloak disappearing around a corner, a shadow passing across a sunlit window...
I long desperately to see him.
Miss Brontë.
Yes, Miss Wooler?
Would you go and supervise the girls' dinner please?
Of course. Right away.
Every wrench back to reality has become more painful.

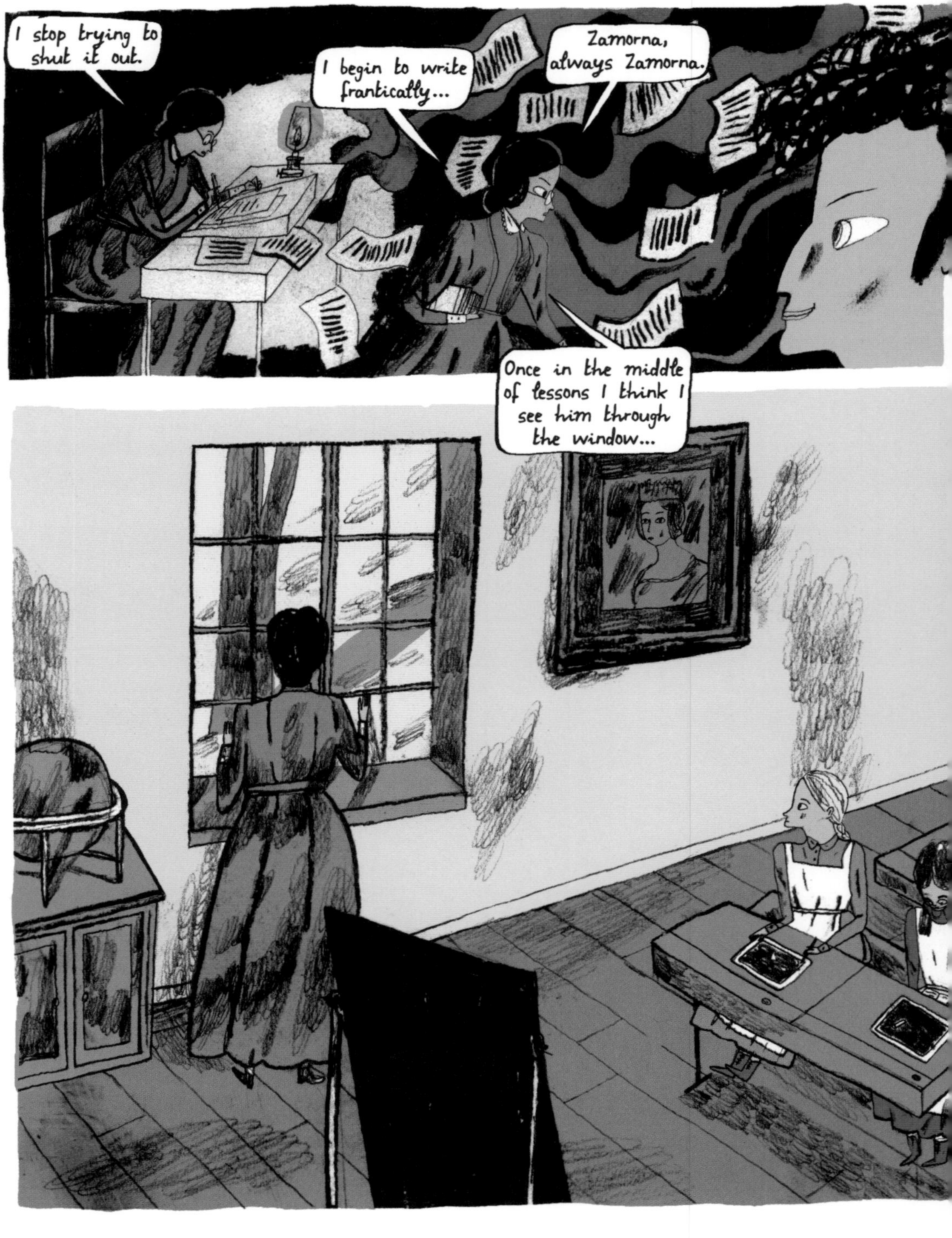
I stop trying to shut it out.
I begin to write frantically...
Zamorna, always Zamorna.
Once in the middle of lessons I think I see him through the window...

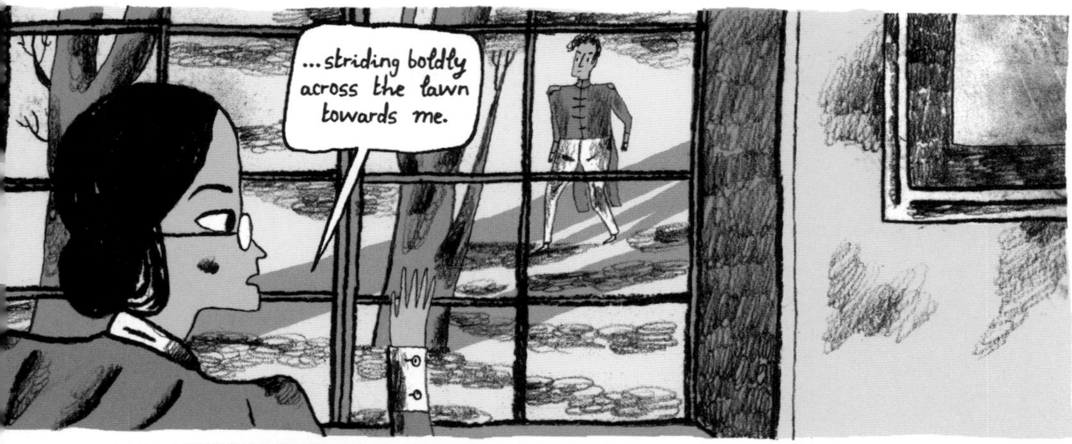
...striding boldly across the lawn towards me.

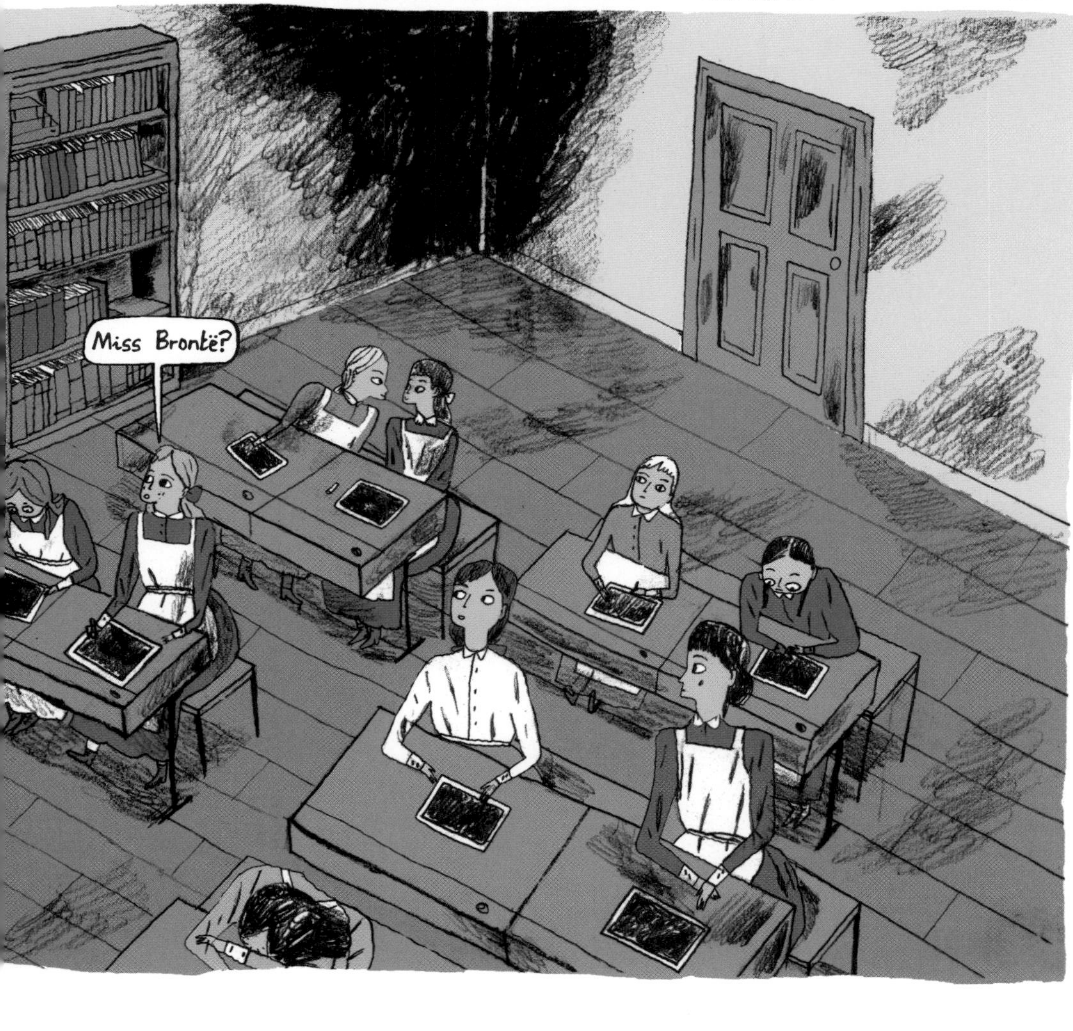
Miss Brontë?

Behind him the grey Yorkshire hills fade away. And there is Glass Town: golden towers and crystal windows, the tropical sky burning a merciless, fierce blue and the palm trees still in the breezeless air.

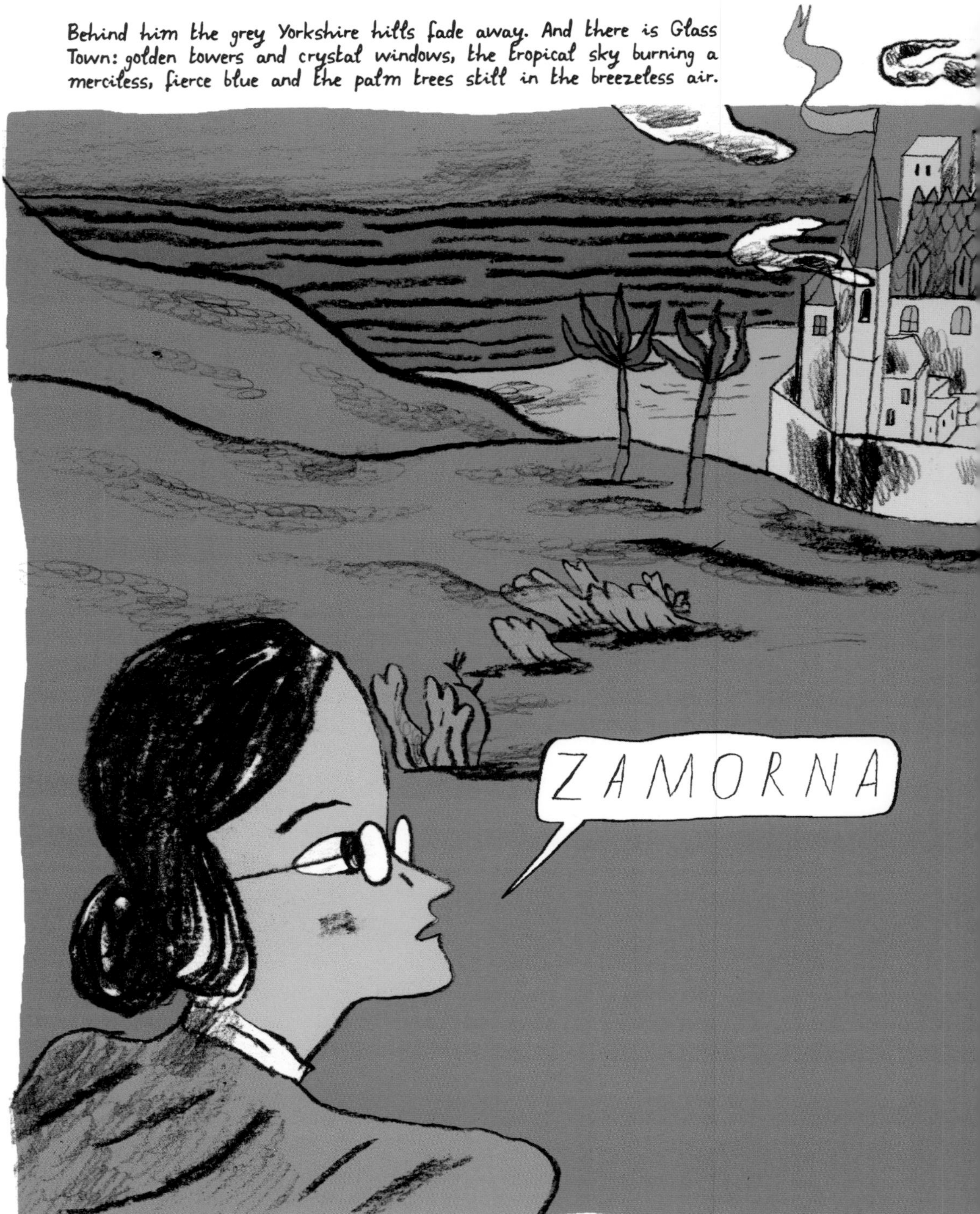
ZAMORNA

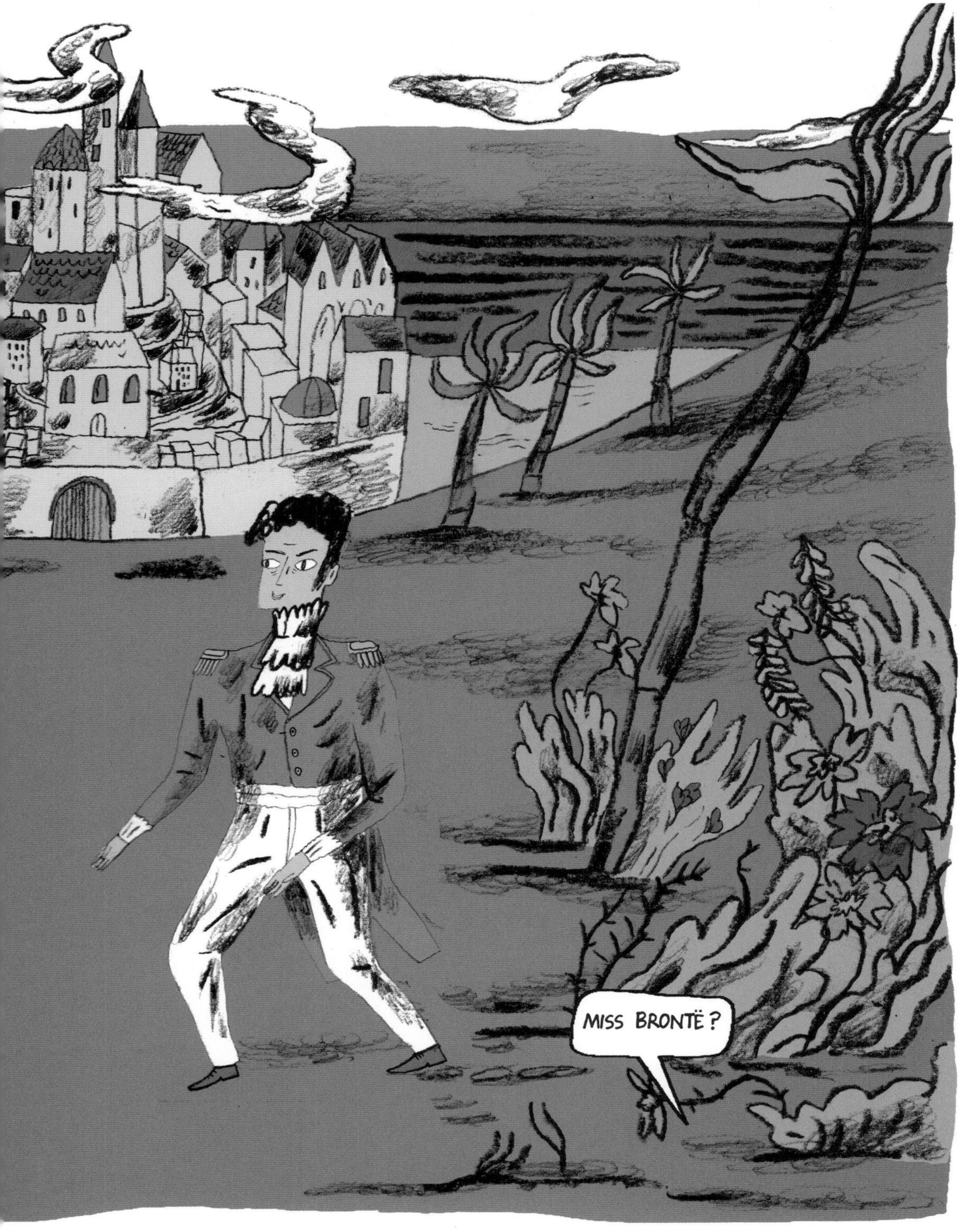
MISS BRONTË?

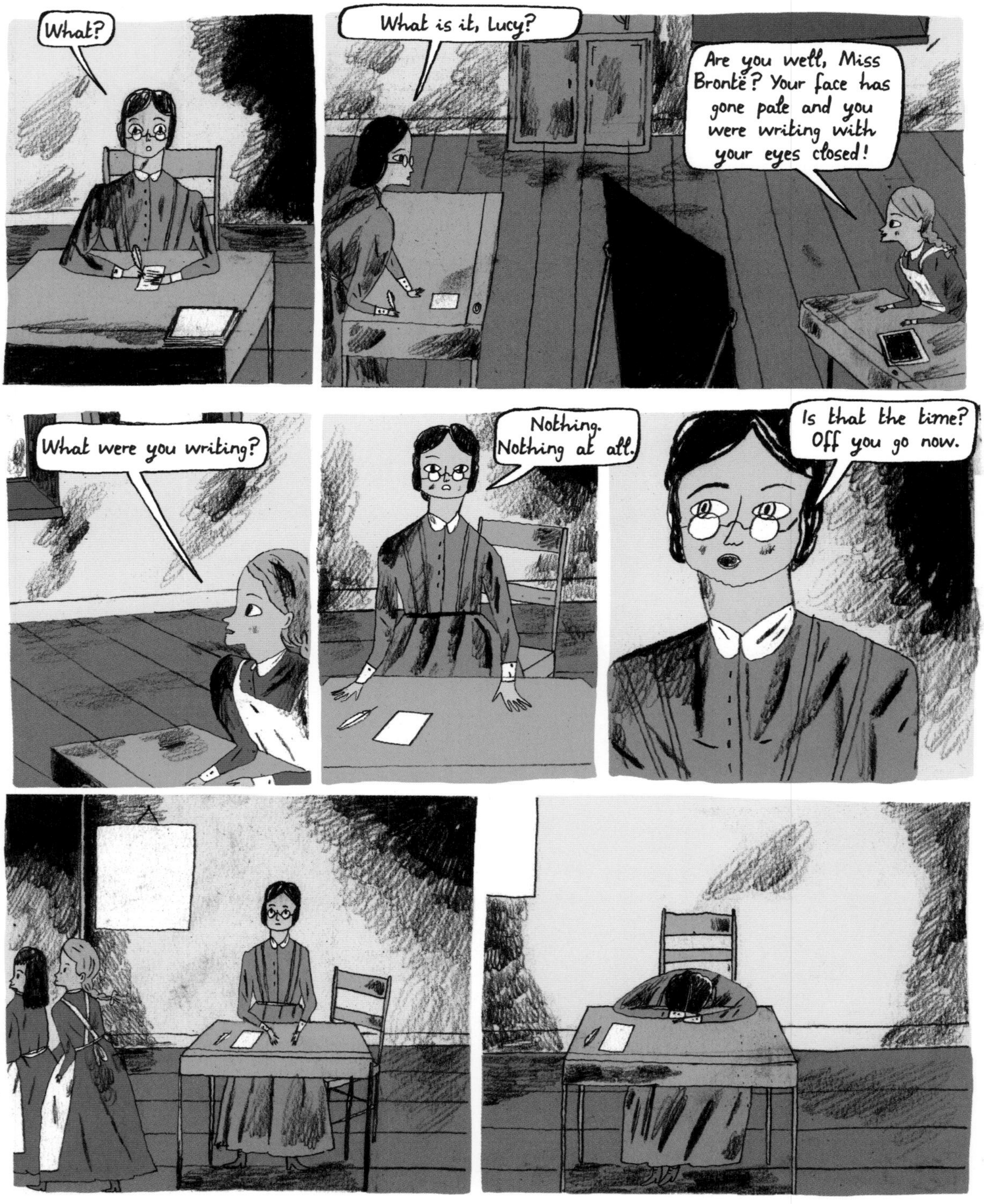
What?
What is it, Lucy?
Are you well, Miss Brontë? Your face has gone pale and you were writing with your eyes closed!
What were you writing?
Nothing. Nothing at all.
Is that the time? Off you go now.

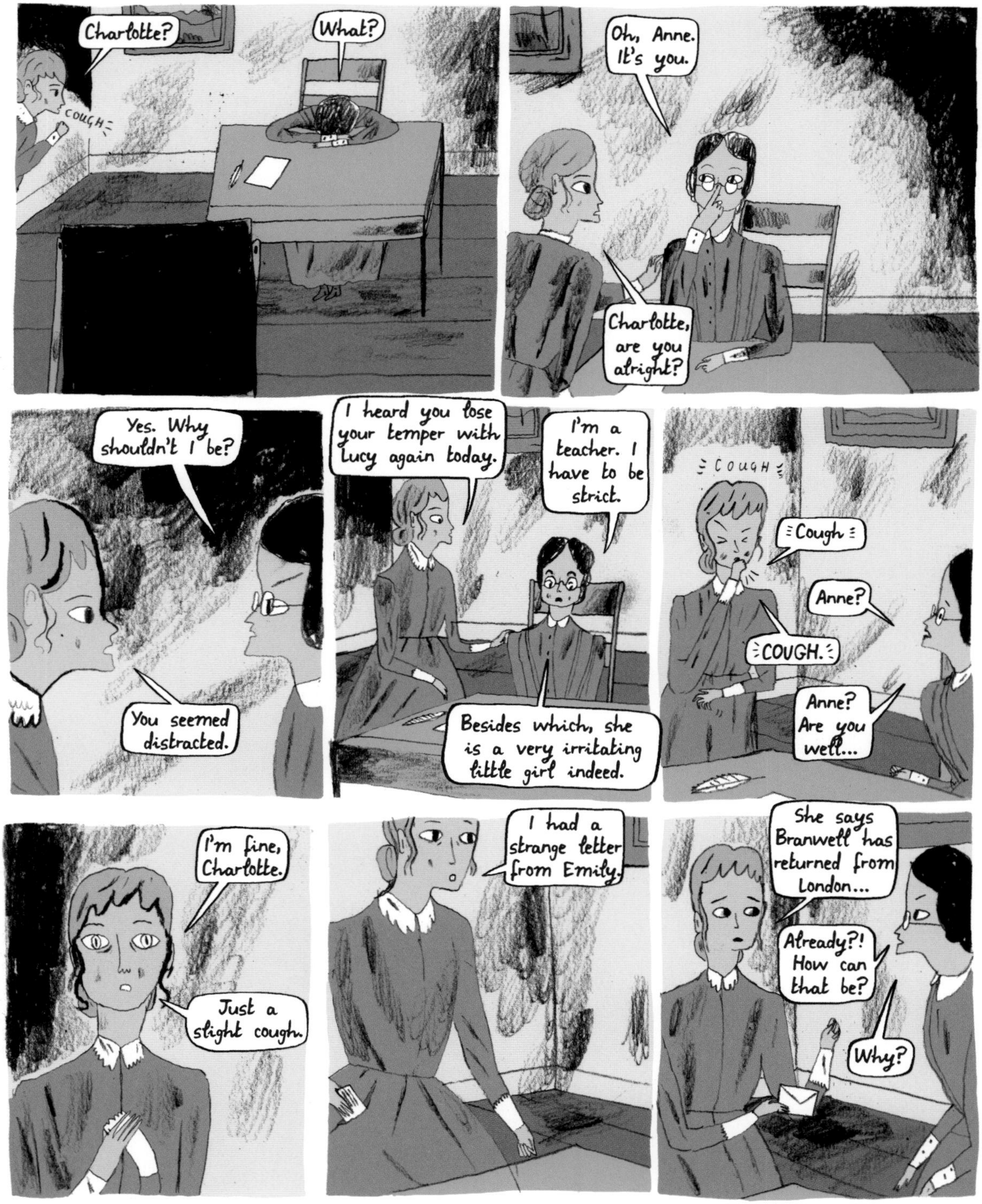
Charlotte?
COUGH
What?
Oh, Anne. It's you.
Charlotte, are you alright?
Yes. Why shouldn't I be?
You seemed distracted.
I heard you lose your temper with Lucy again today.
I'm a teacher. I have to be strict.
Besides which, she is a very irritating little girl indeed.
COUGH
Cough
Anne?
COUGH.
Anne? Are you well...
I'm fine, Charlotte.
Just a slight cough.
I had a strange letter from Emily.
She says Branwell has returned from London...
Already?! How can that be?
Why?

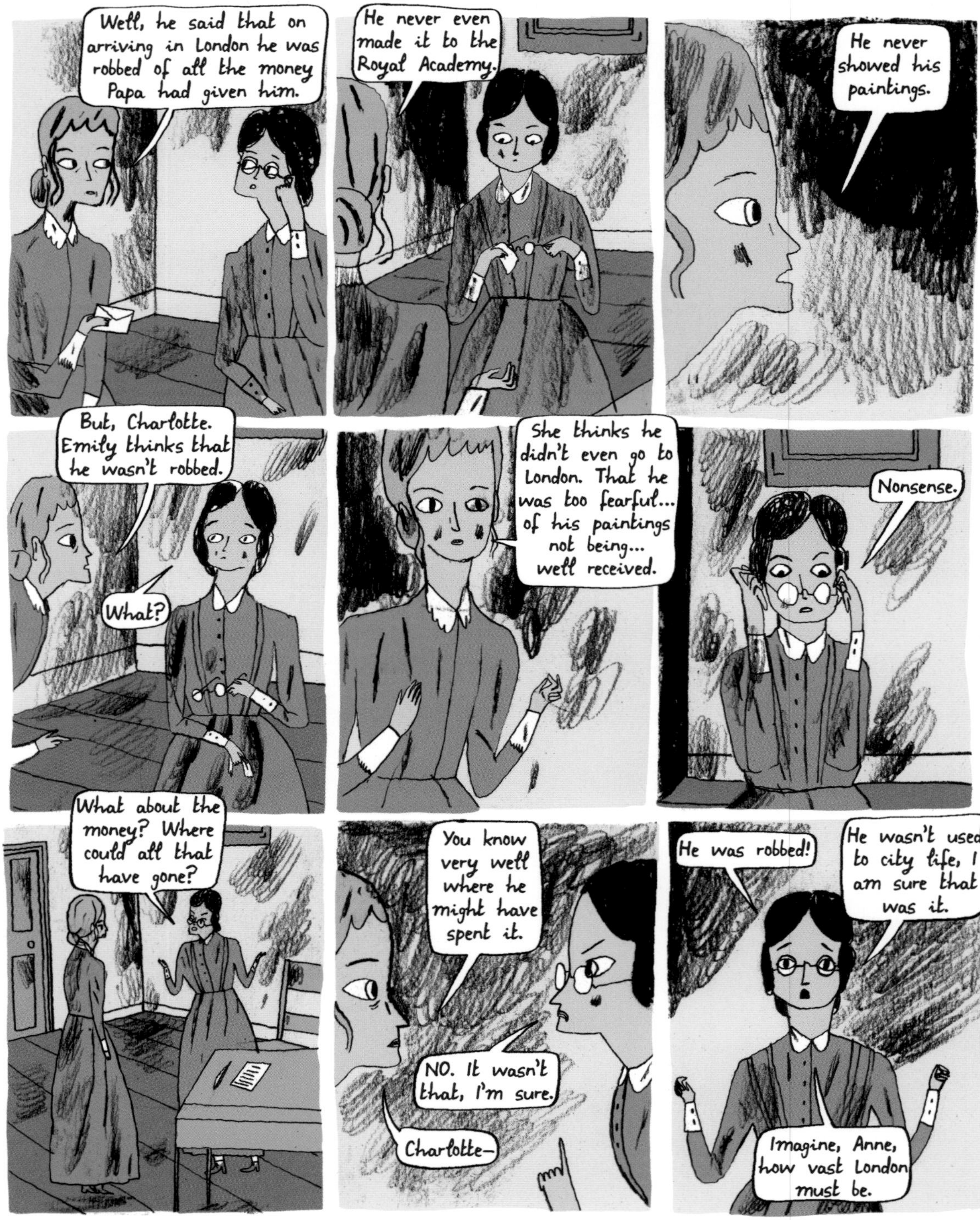
Well, he said that on arriving in London he was robbed of all the money Papa had given him.
He never even made it to the Royal Academy.
He never showed his paintings.
But, Charlotte. Emily thinks that he wasn't robbed.
What?
She thinks he didn't even go to London. That he was too fearful... of his paintings not being... well received.
Nonsense.
What about the money? Where could all that have gone?
You know very well where he might have spent it.
NO. It wasn't that, I'm sure.
Charlotte-
He was robbed!
He wasn't used to city life, I am sure that was it.
Imagine, Anne, how vast London must be.

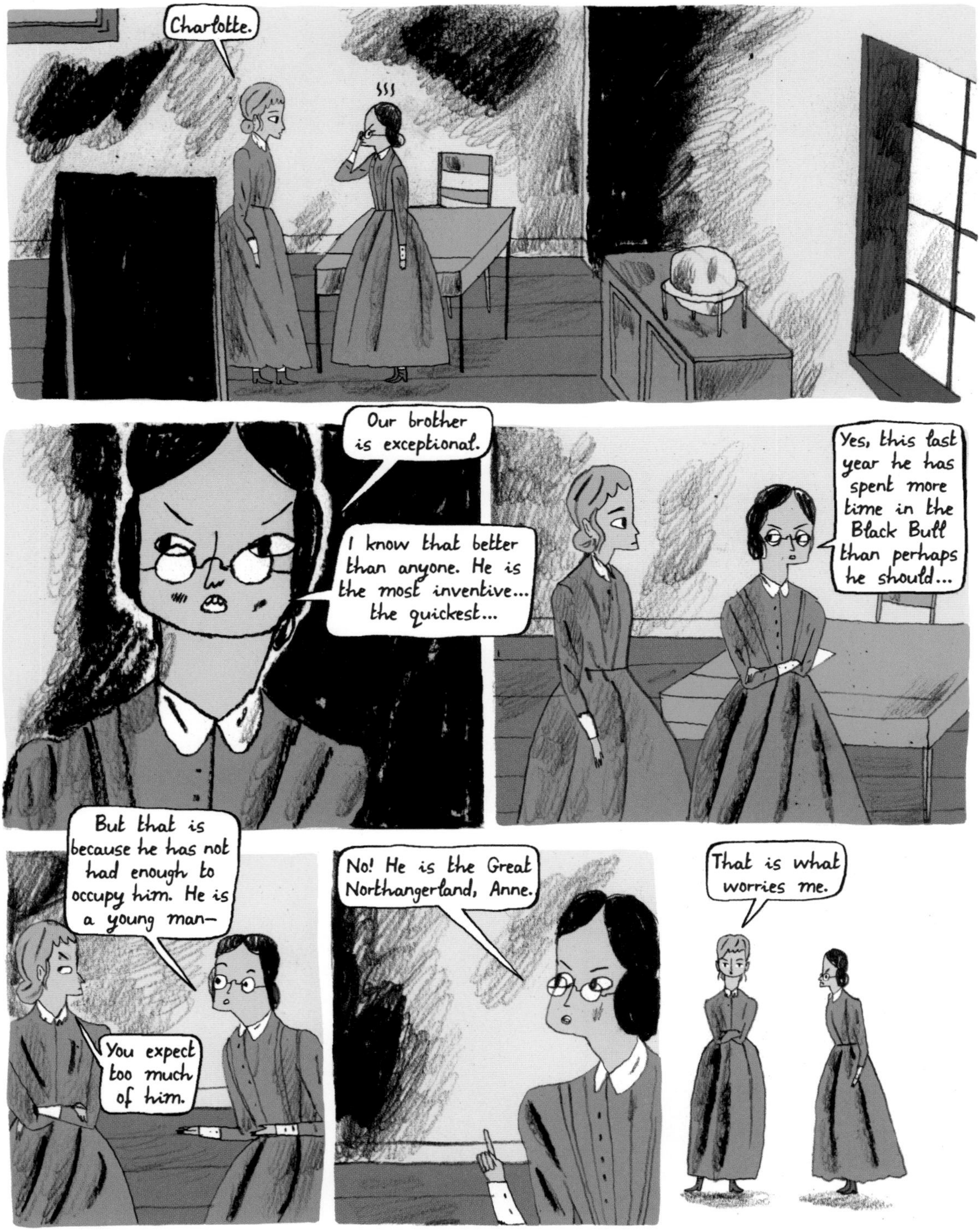
Charlotte.
Our brother is exceptional.
I know that better than anyone. He is the most inventive... the quickest...
Yes, this last year he has spent more time in the Black Bull than perhaps he should...
But that is because he has not had enough to occupy him. He is a young man—
You expect too much of him.
No! He is the Great Northangerland, Anne.
That is what worries me.

Northangerland

With his daughter married to Zamorna, and a temporary truce called between himself and the latter, Northangerland found he had nothing to occupy himself with. And so he started to fall back into hobbies he had abandoned when Mary had lived with him: drinking, gambling and carousing.

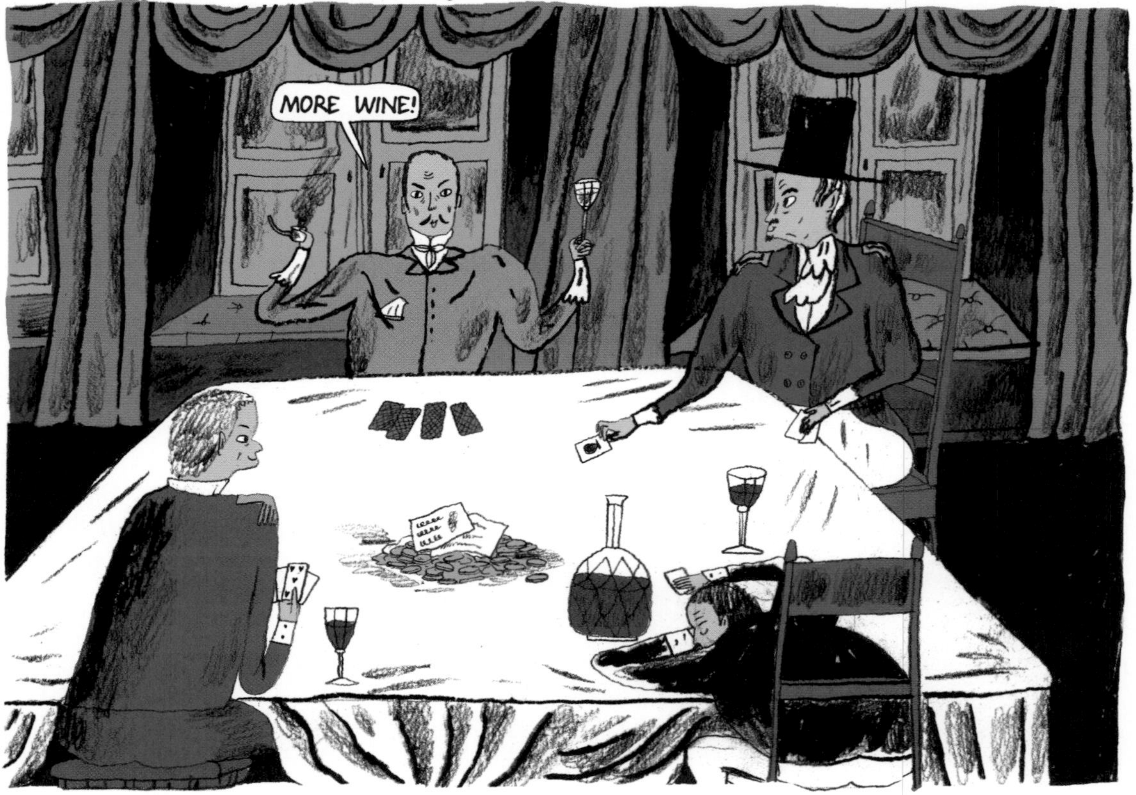
MORE WINE!

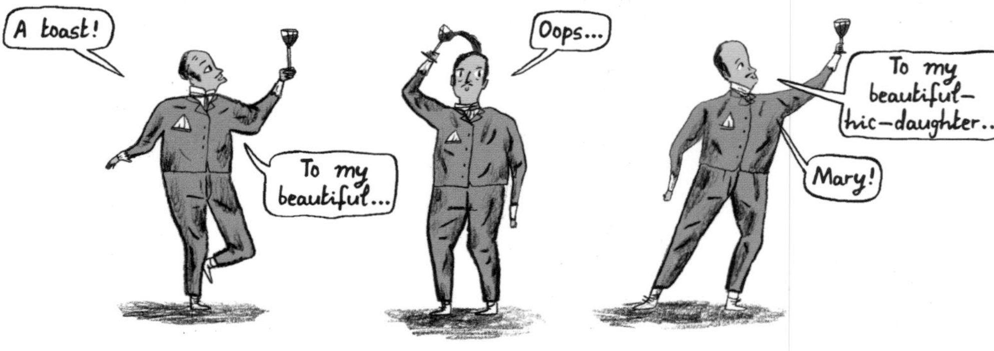
A toast!
To my beautiful...
Oops...
To my beautiful—hic—daughter...
Mary!

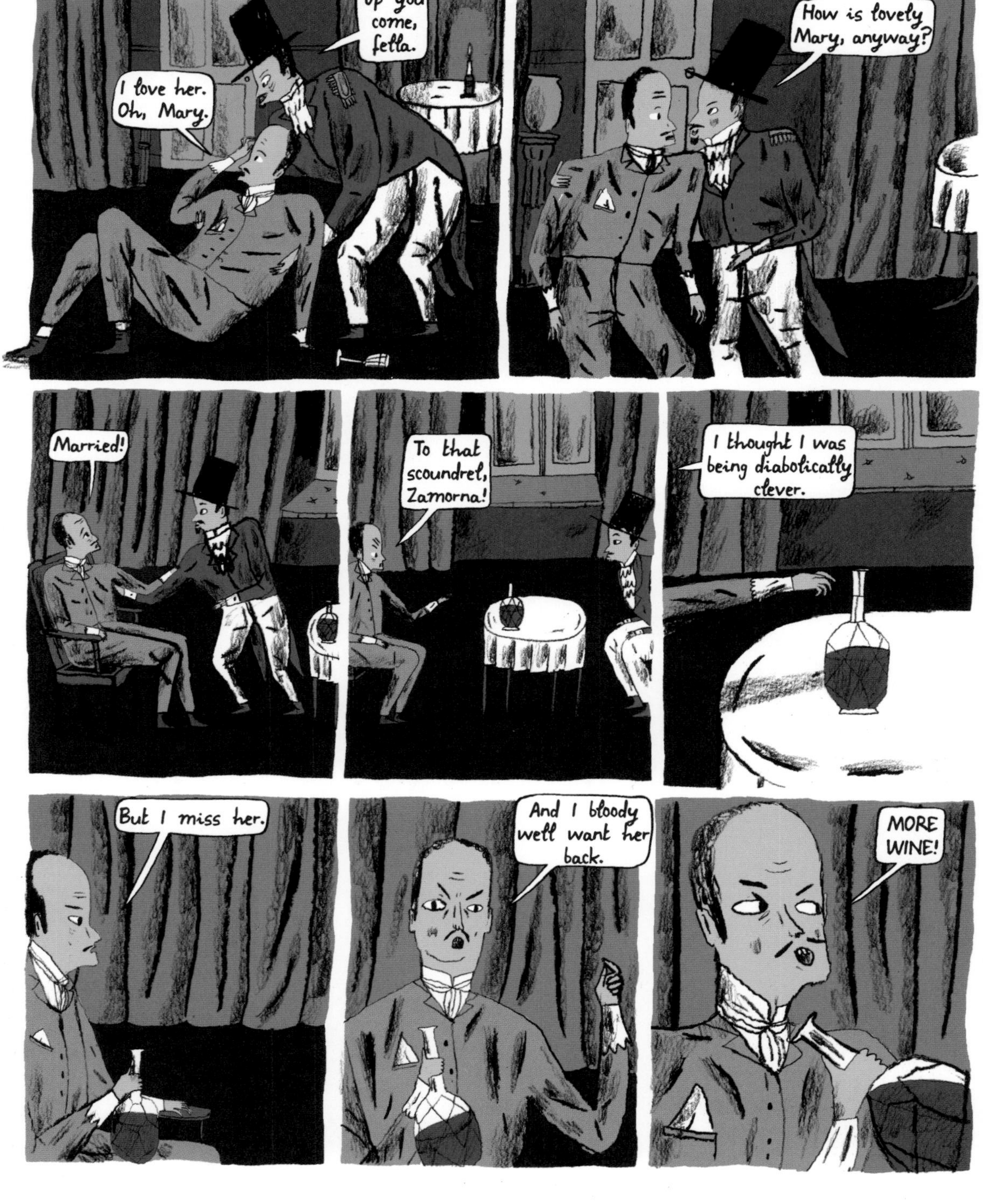
Up you come, fella.
I love her. Oh, Mary.
How is lovely Mary, anyway?
Married!
To that scoundrel, Zamorna!
I thought I was being diabolically clever.
But I miss her.
And I bloody well want her back.
MORE WINE!

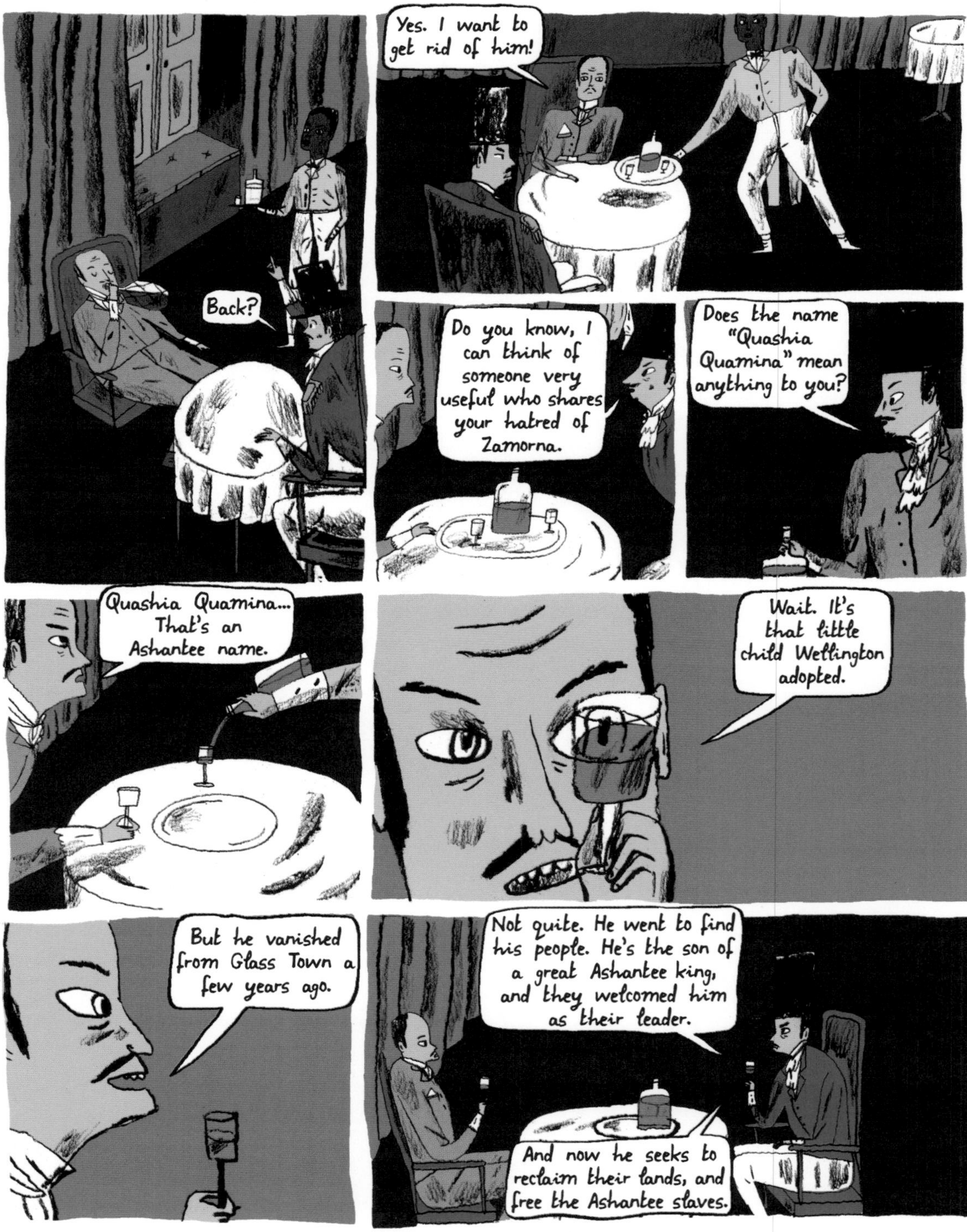
Back?
Yes. I want to get rid of him!
Do you know, I can think of someone very useful who shares your hatred of Zamorna.
Does the name "Quashia Quamina" mean anything to you?
Quashia Quamina... That's an Ashantee name.
Wait. It's that little child Wellington adopted.
But he vanished from Glass Town a few years ago.
Not quite. He went to find his people. He's the son of a great Ashantee king, and they welcomed him as their leader.
And now he seeks to reclaim their lands, and free the Ashantee slaves.

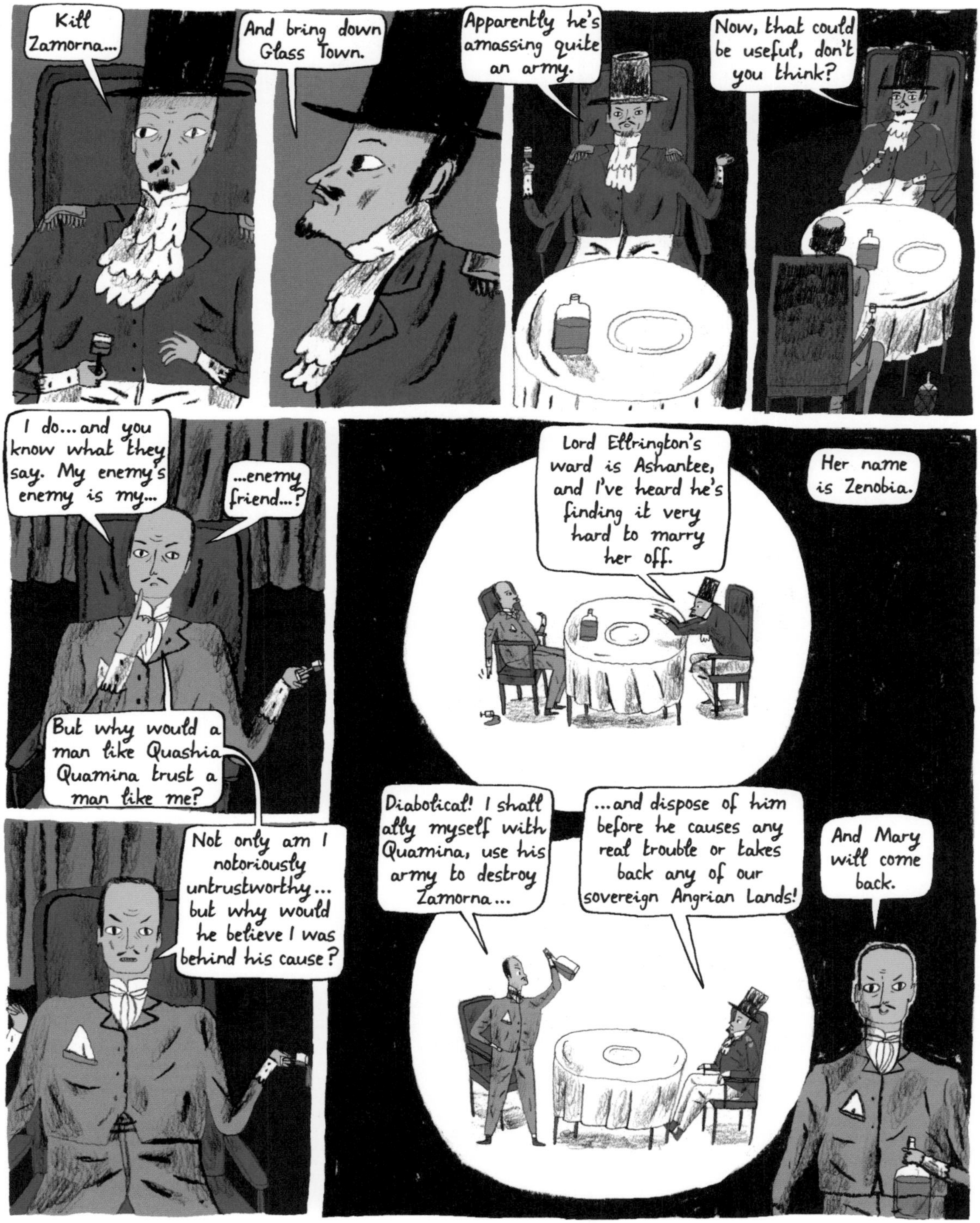
Kill Zamorna...
And bring down Glass Town.
Apparently he's amassing quite an army.
Now, that could be useful, don't you think?
I do...and you know what they say. My enemy's enemy is my...
...enemy friend...?
But why would a man like Quashia Quamina trust a man like me?
Not only am I notoriously untrustworthy... but why would he believe I was behind his cause?
Lord Ellrington's ward is Ashantee, and I've heard he's finding it very hard to marry her off.
Her name is Zenobia.
Diabolical! I shall ally myself with Quamina, use his army to destroy Zamorna...
...and dispose of him before he causes any real trouble or takes back any of our sovereign Angrian Lands!
And Mary will come back.

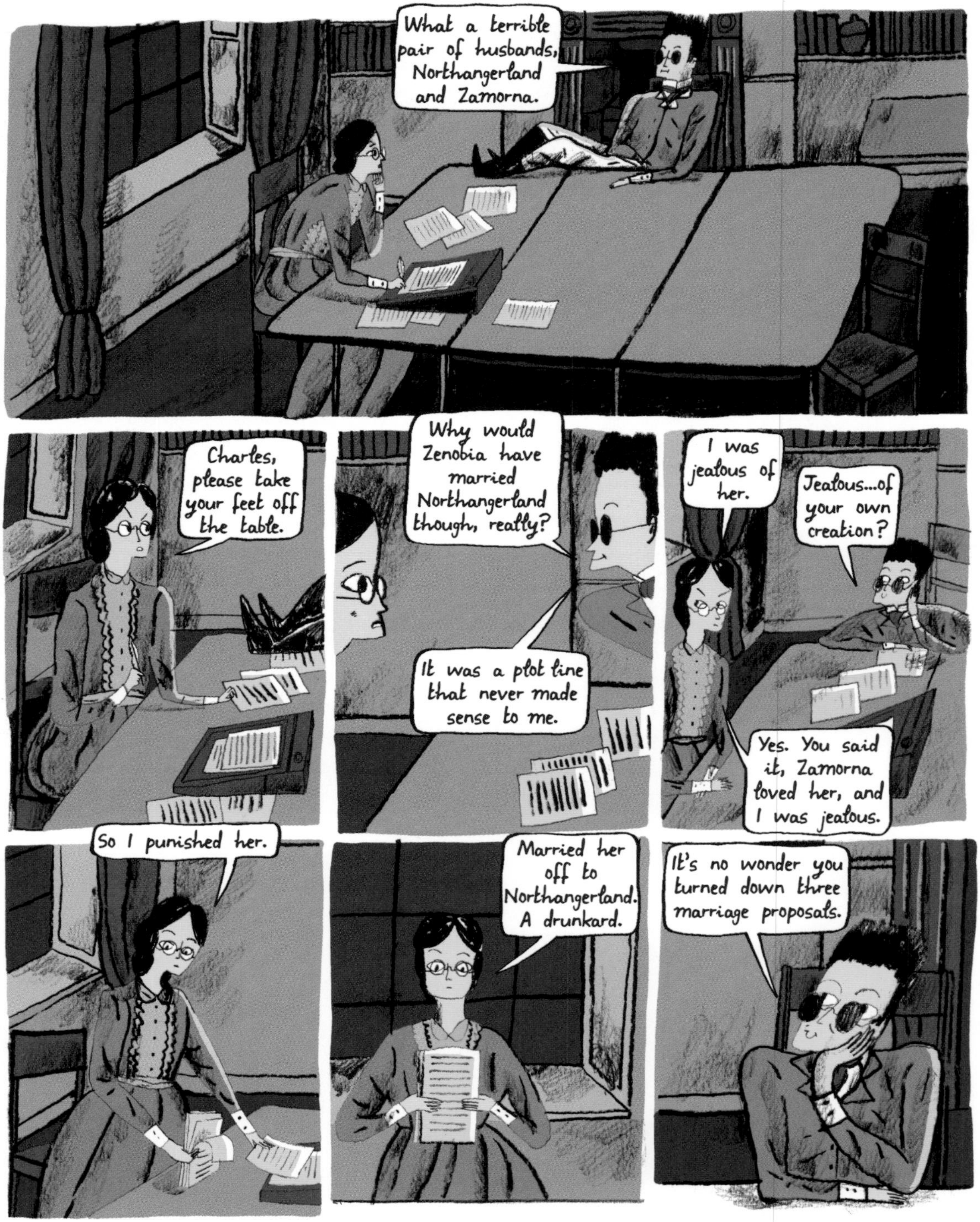

What a terrible pair of husbands, Northangerland and Zamorna.
Charles, please take your feet off the table.
Why would Zenobia have married Northangerland though, really?
It was a plot line that never made sense to me.
I was jealous of her.
Jealous...of your own creation?
Yes. You said it, Zamorna loved her, and I was jealous.
So I punished her.
Married her off to Northangerland. A drunkard.
It's no wonder you turned down three marriage proposals.

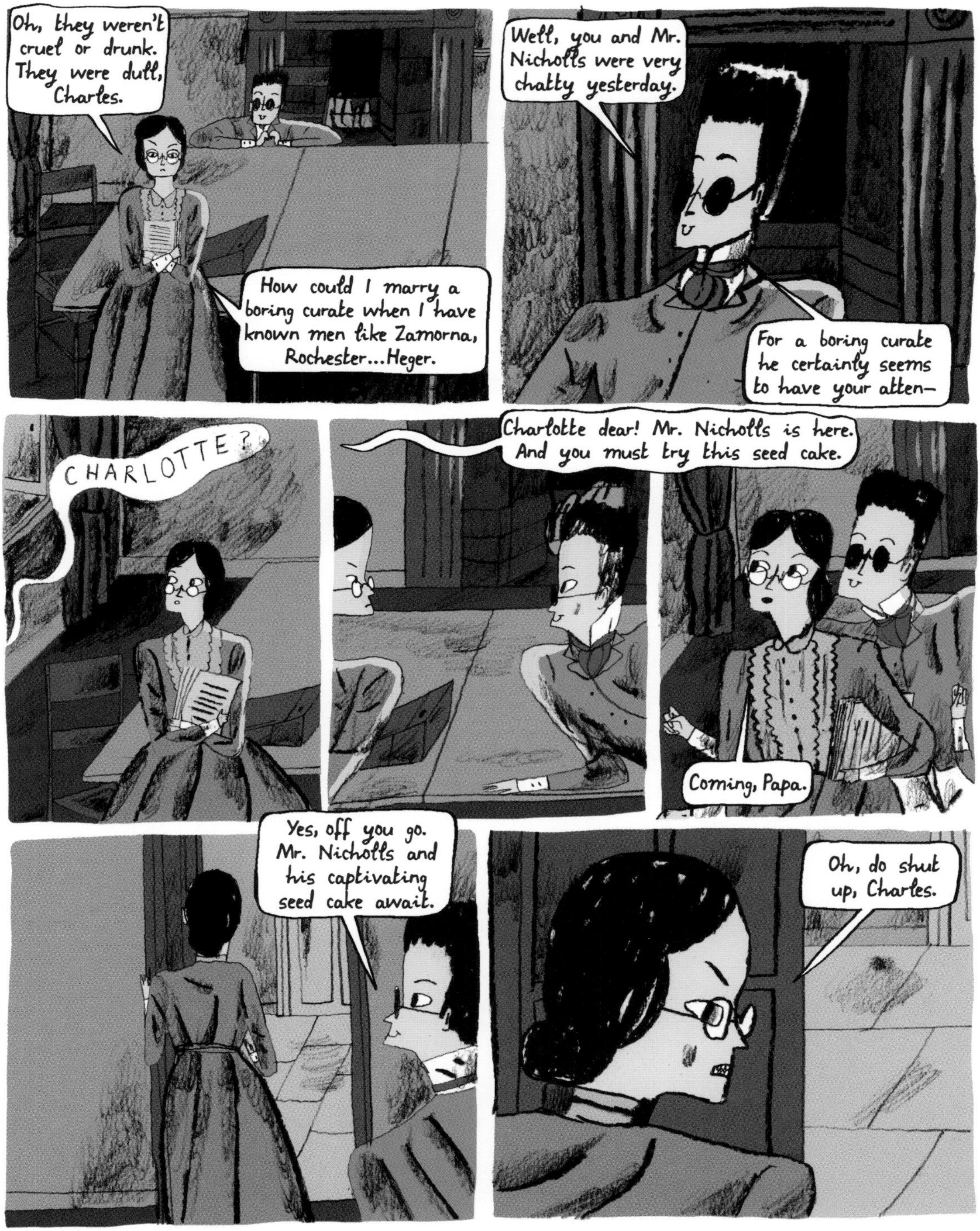
Oh, they weren't cruel or drunk. They were dull, Charles.
How could I marry a boring curate when I have known men like Zamorna, Rochester...Heger.
Well, you and Mr. Nicholls were very chatty yesterday.
For a boring curate he certainly seems to have your atten—
CHARLOTTE?
Charlotte dear! Mr. Nicholls is here. And you must try this seed cake.
Coming, Papa.
Yes, off you go. Mr. Nicholls and his captivating seed cake await.
Oh, do shut up, Charles.

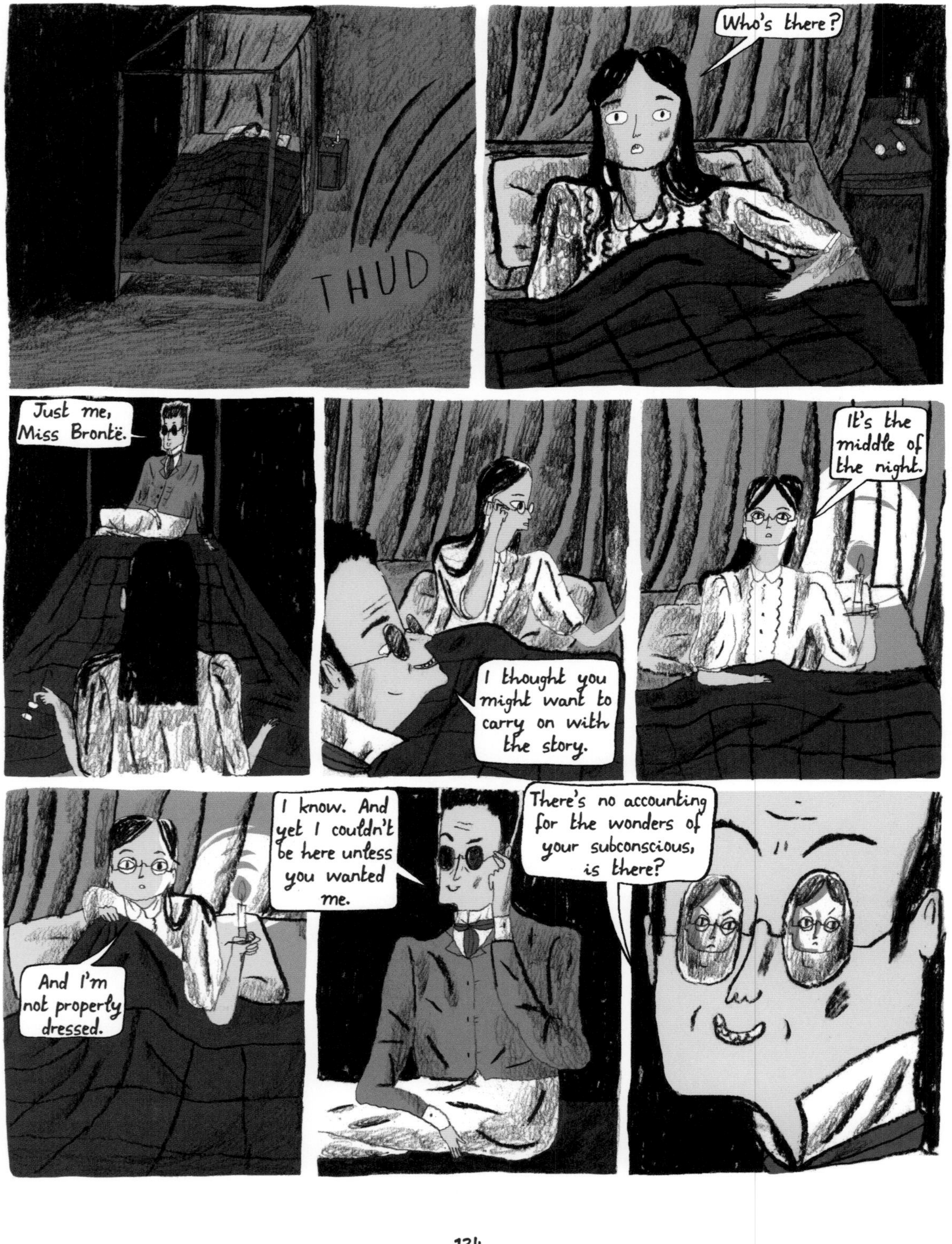
THUD
Who's there?
Just me, Miss Brontë.
I thought you might want to carry on with the story.
It's the middle of the night.
And I'm not properly dressed.
I know. And yet I couldn't be here unless you wanted me.
There's no accounting for the wonders of your subconscious, is there?

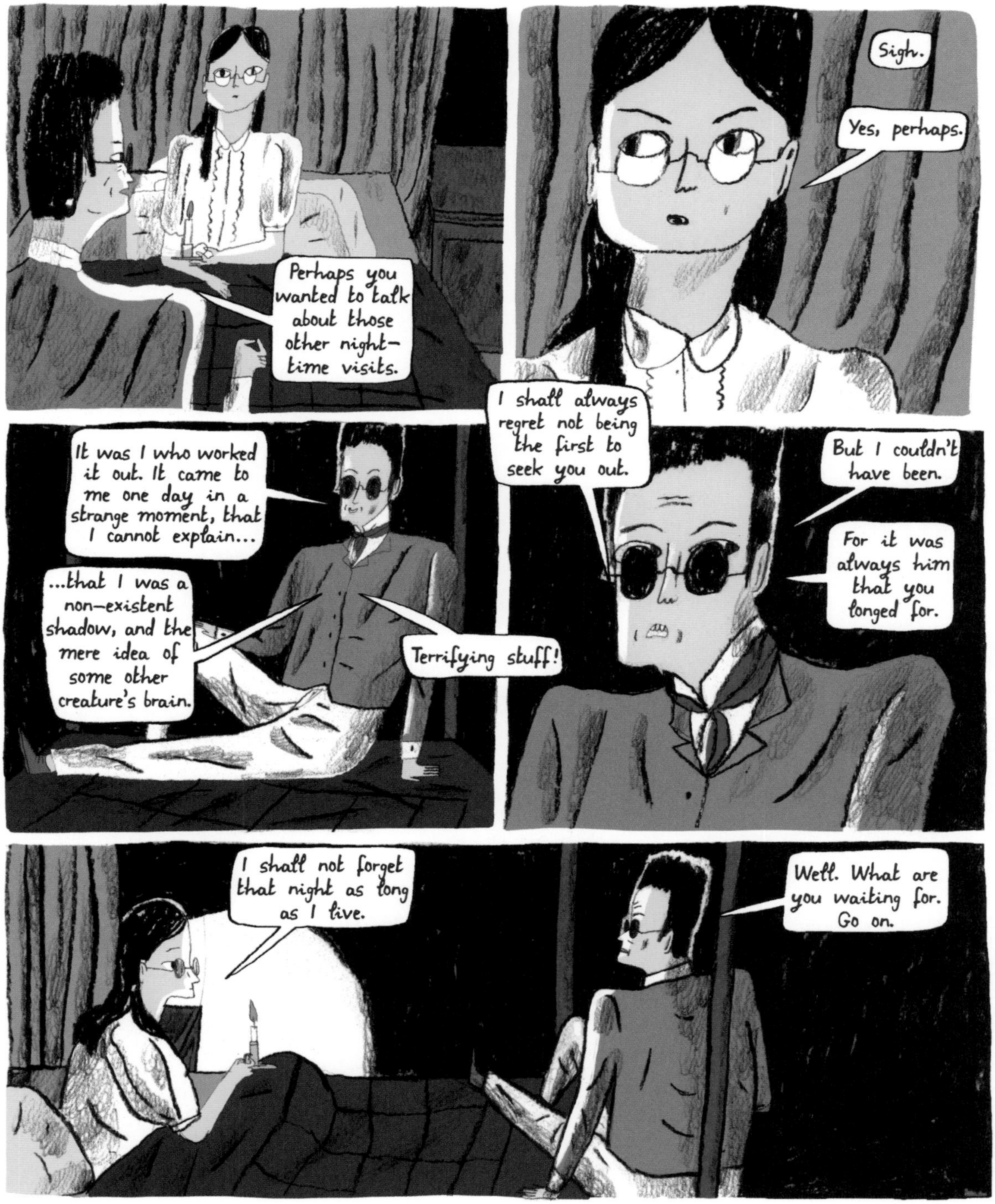
Perhaps you wanted to talk about those other night-time visits.
Sigh.
Yes, perhaps.
It was I who worked it out. It came to me one day in a strange moment, that I cannot explain...
...that I was a non-existent shadow, and the mere idea of some other creature's brain.
Terrifying stuff!
I shall always regret not being the first to seek you out.
But I couldn't have been.
For it was always him that you longed for.
I shall not forget that night as long as I live.
Well. What are you waiting for. Go on.

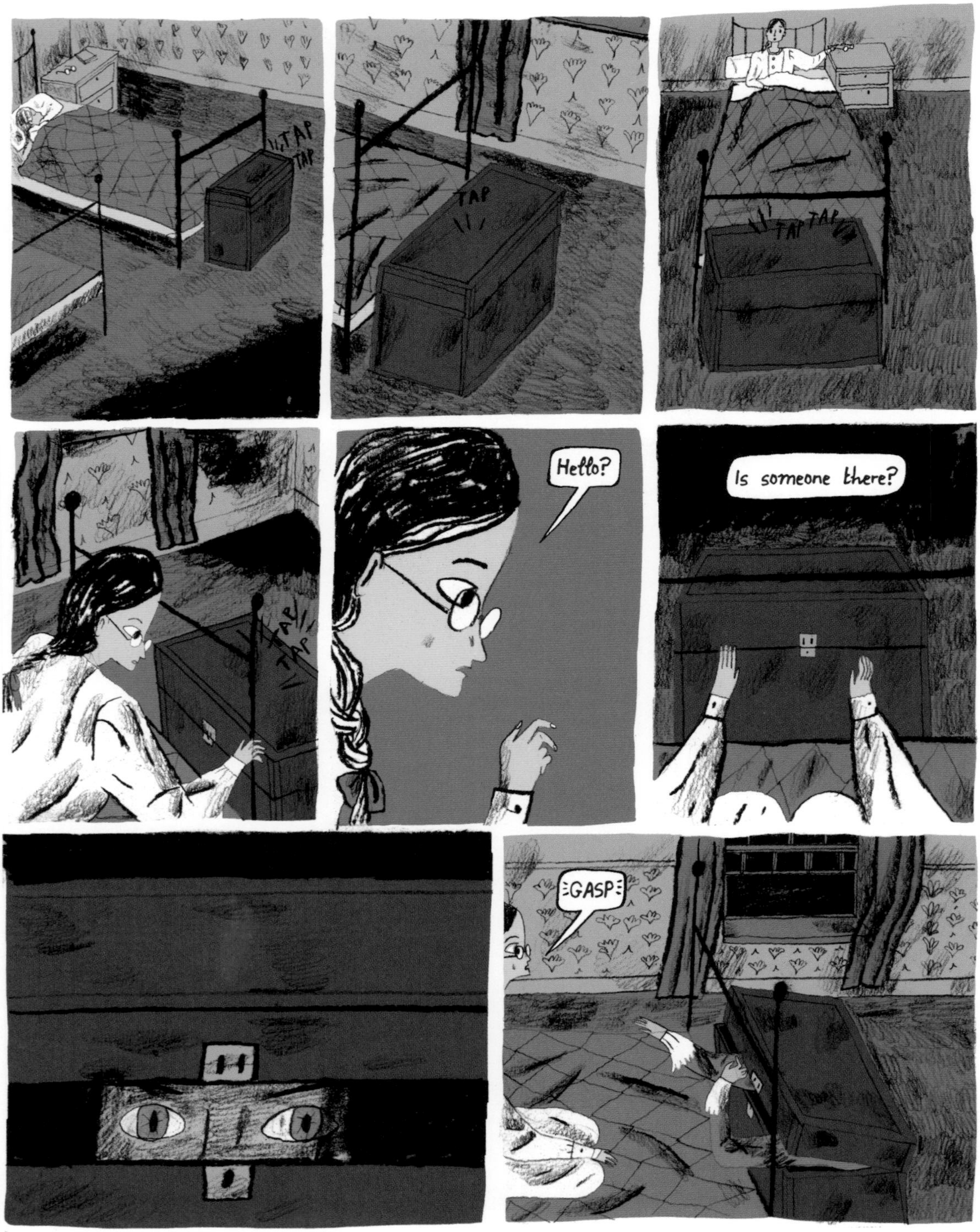
TAP
TAP
TAP
TAP TAP
TAP TAP
Hello?
Is someone there?
GASP

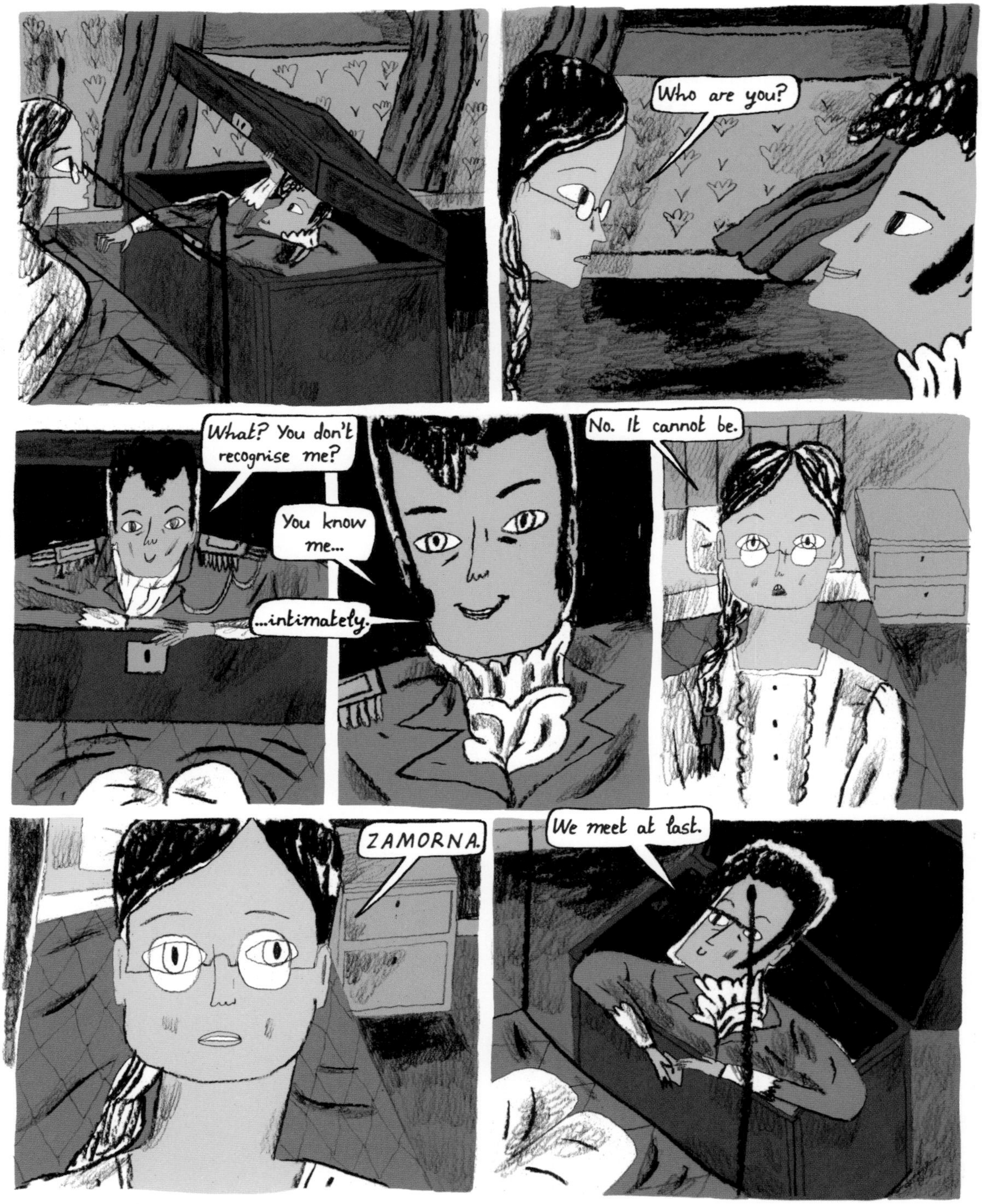
Who are you?
What? You don't recognise me?
You know me...
...intimately.
No. It cannot be.
ZAMORNA.
We meet at last.

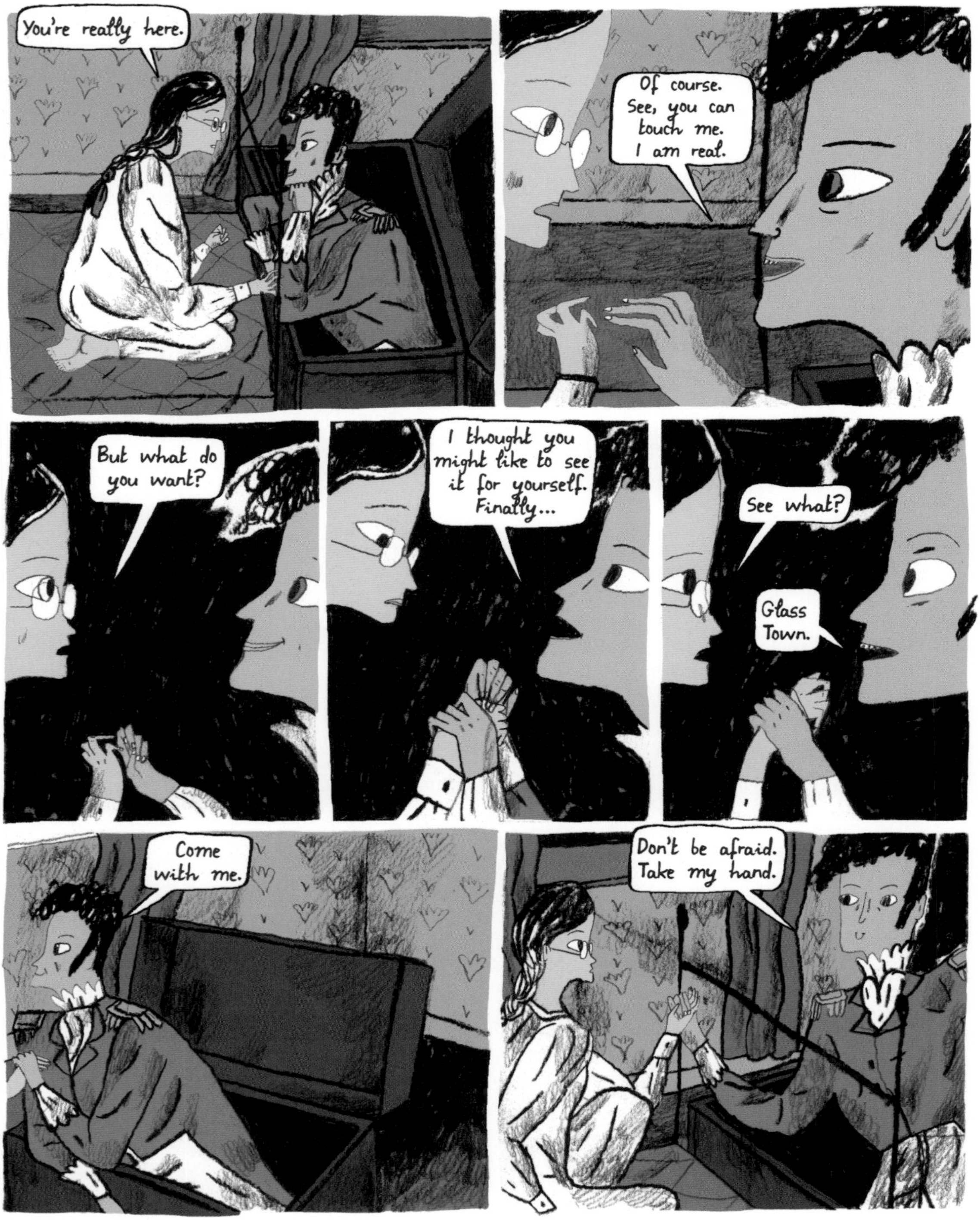
You're really here.
Of course. See, you can touch me. I am real.
But what do you want?
I thought you might like to see it for yourself. Finally...
See what?
Glass Town.
Come with me.
Don't be afraid. Take my hand.

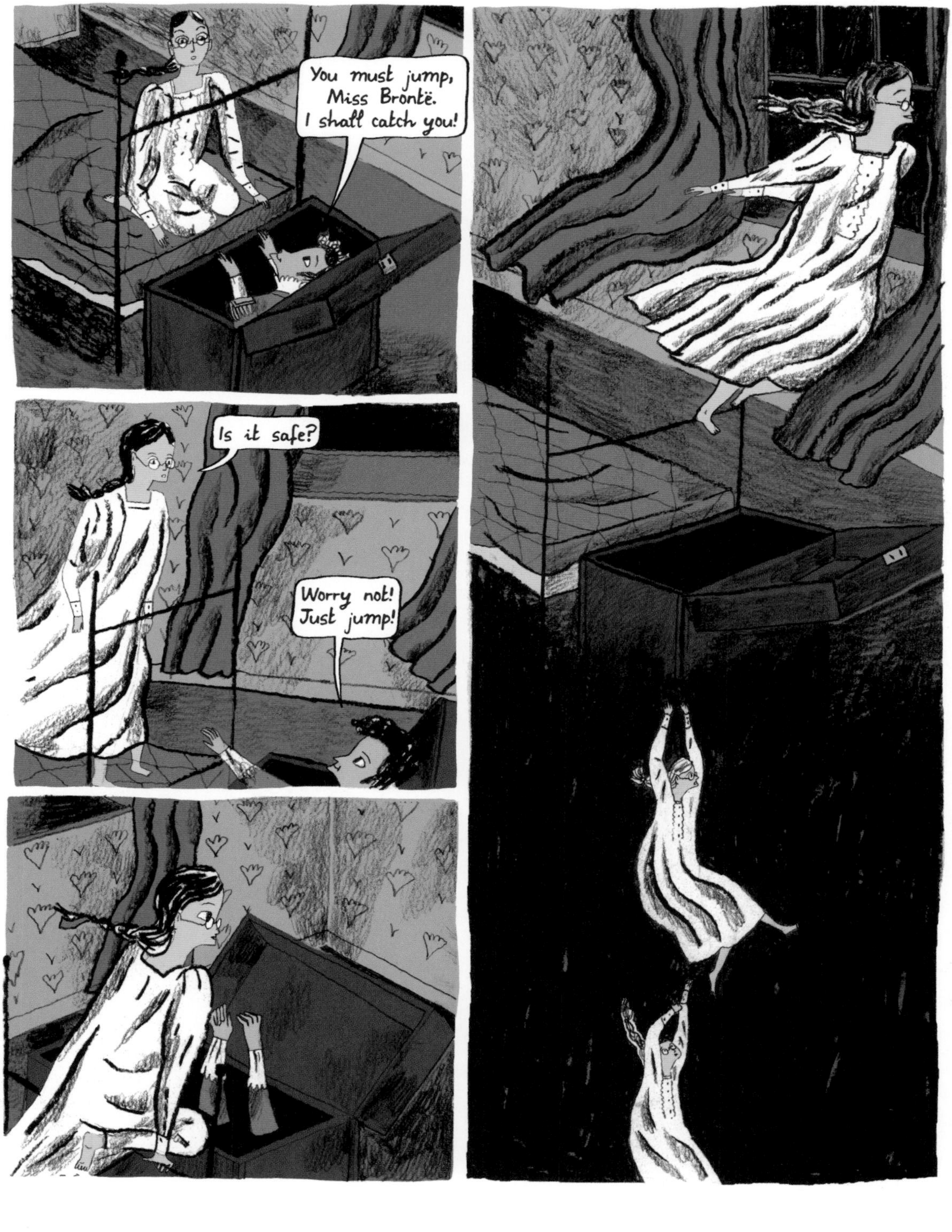
You must jump, Miss Brontë. I shall catch you!
Is it safe?
Worry not! Just jump!

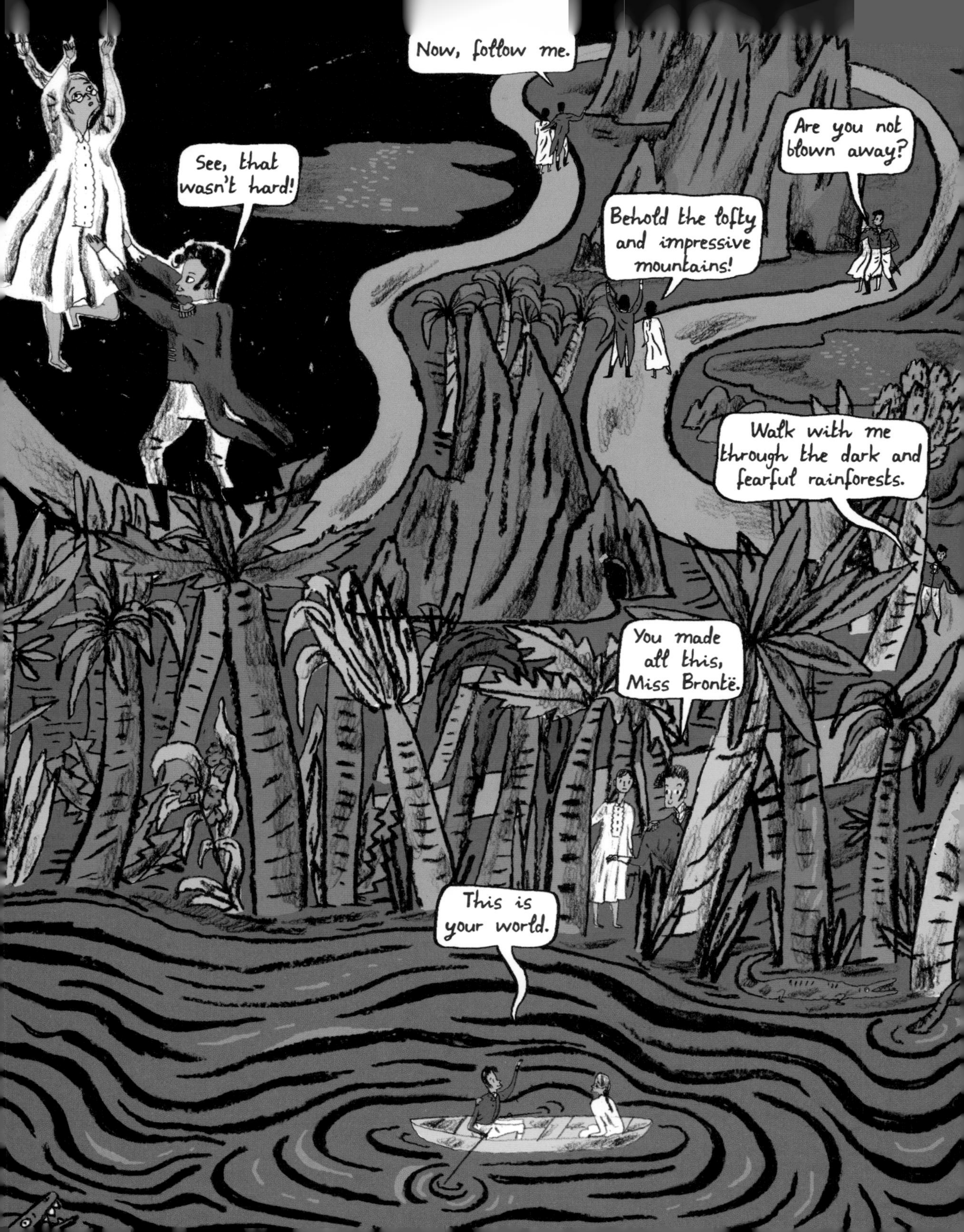
See, that wasn't hard!
Now, follow me.
Are you not blown away?
Behold the lofty and impressive mountains!
Walk with me through the dark and fearful rainforests.
You made all this, Miss Brontë.
This is your world.

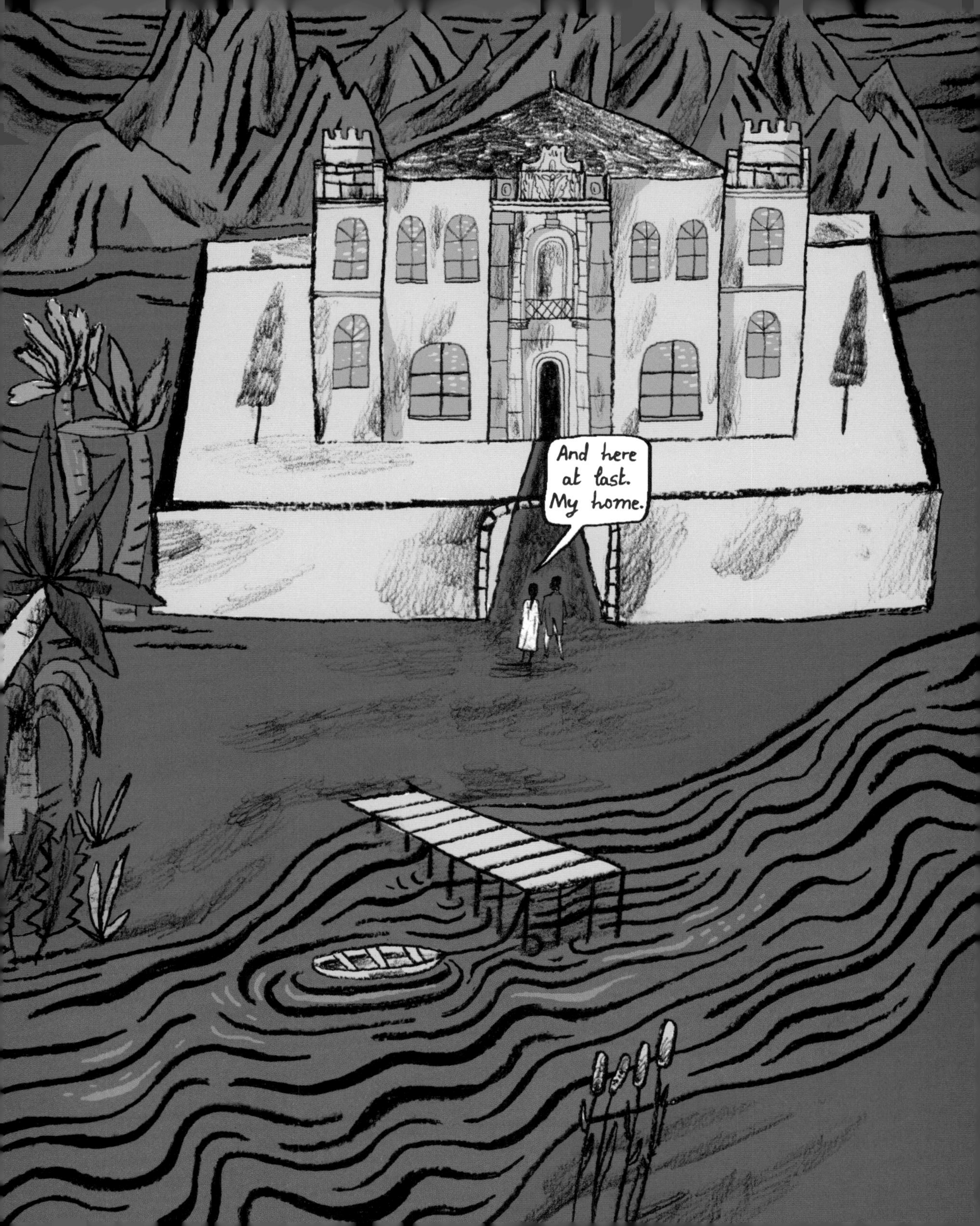
And here at last. My home.

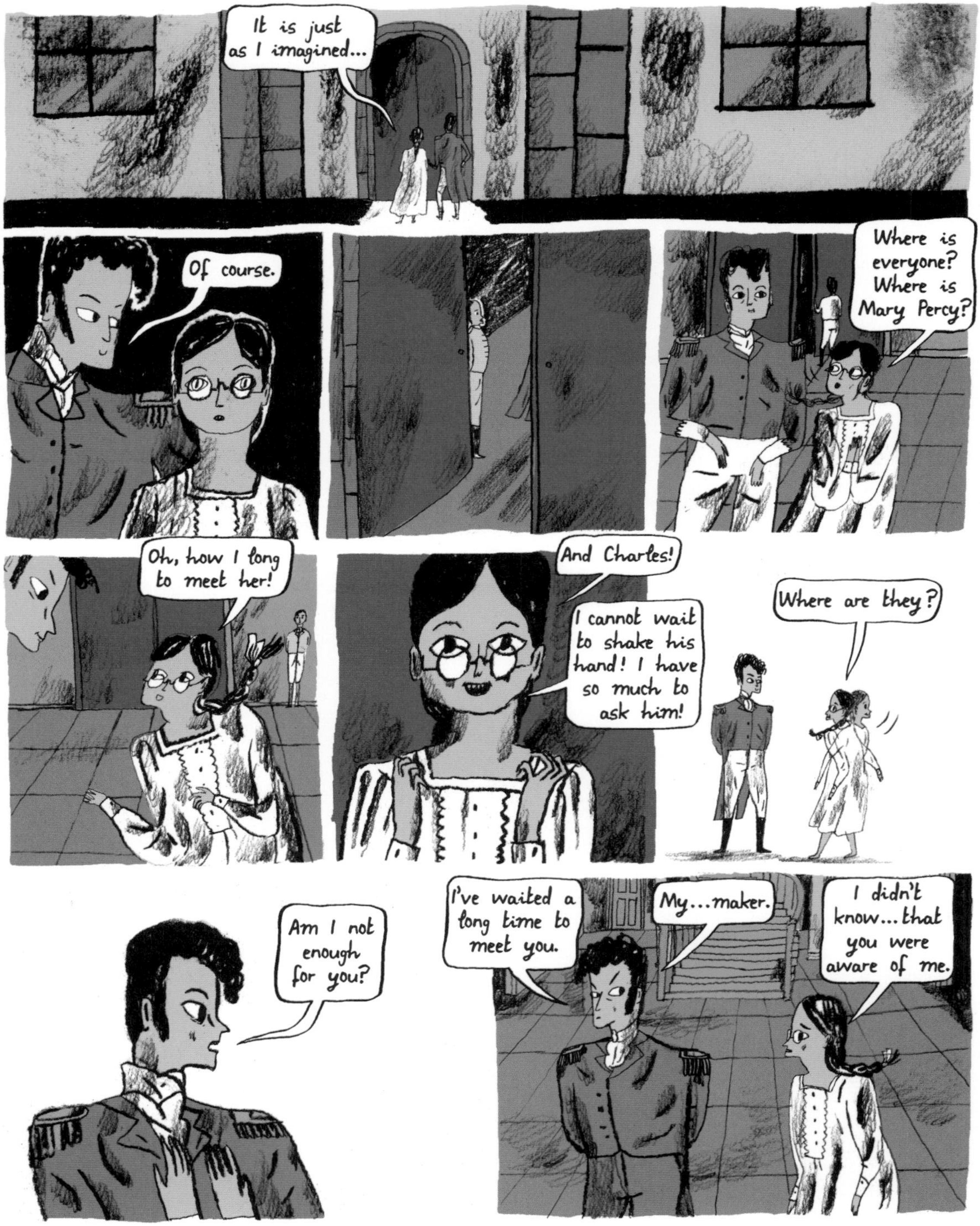
It is just as I imagined...
Of course.
Where is everyone? Where is Mary Percy?
Oh, how I long to meet her!
And Charles!
I cannot wait to shake his hand! I have so much to ask him!
Where are they?
Am I not enough for you?
I've waited a long time to meet you.
My...maker.
I didn't know...that you were aware of me.

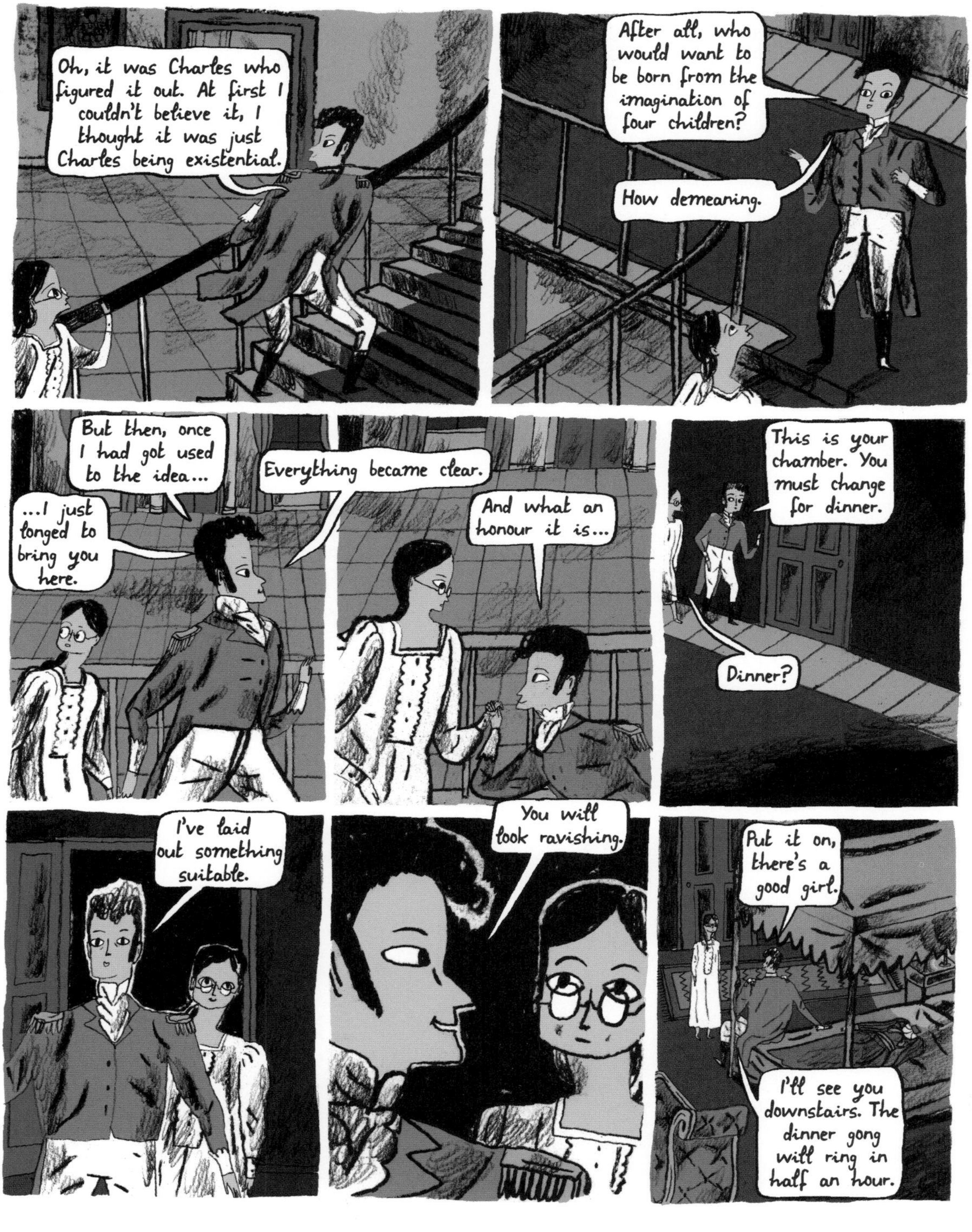
Oh, it was Charles who figured it out. At first I couldn't believe it, I thought it was just Charles being existential.
After all, who would want to be born from the imagination of four children?
How demeaning.
But then, once I had got used to the idea...
...I just longed to bring you here.
Everything became clear.
And what an honour it is...
This is your chamber. You must change for dinner.
Dinner?
I've laid out something suitable.
You will look ravishing.
Put it on, there's a good girl.
I'll see you downstairs. The dinner gong will ring in half an hour.

SLAM

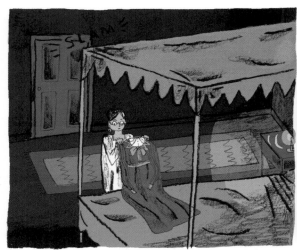

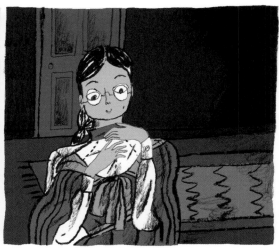

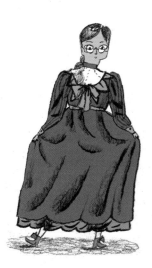

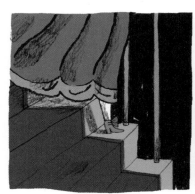

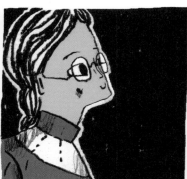

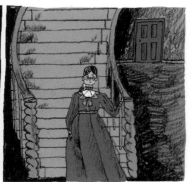

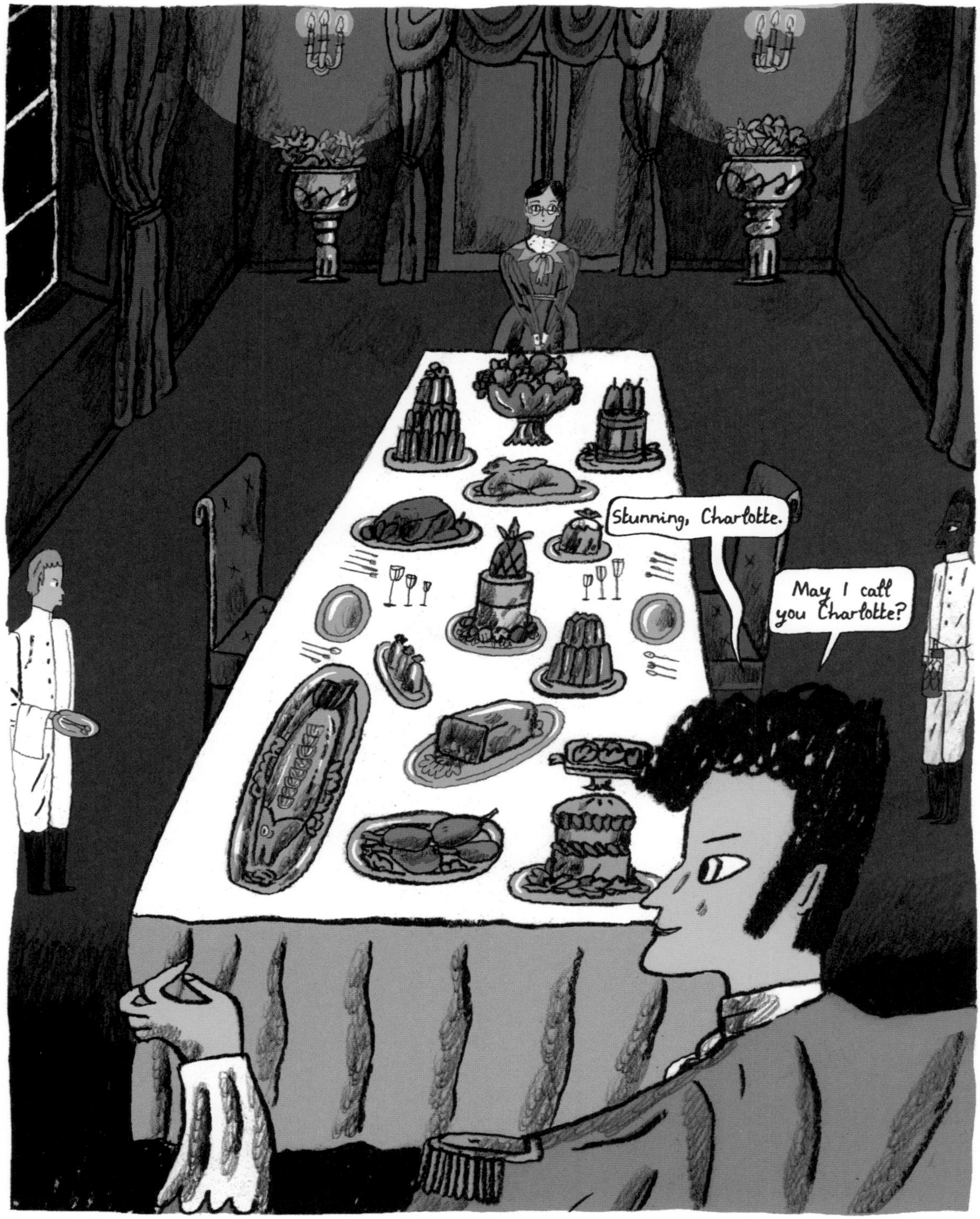
Stunning, Charlotte.
May I call you Charlotte?

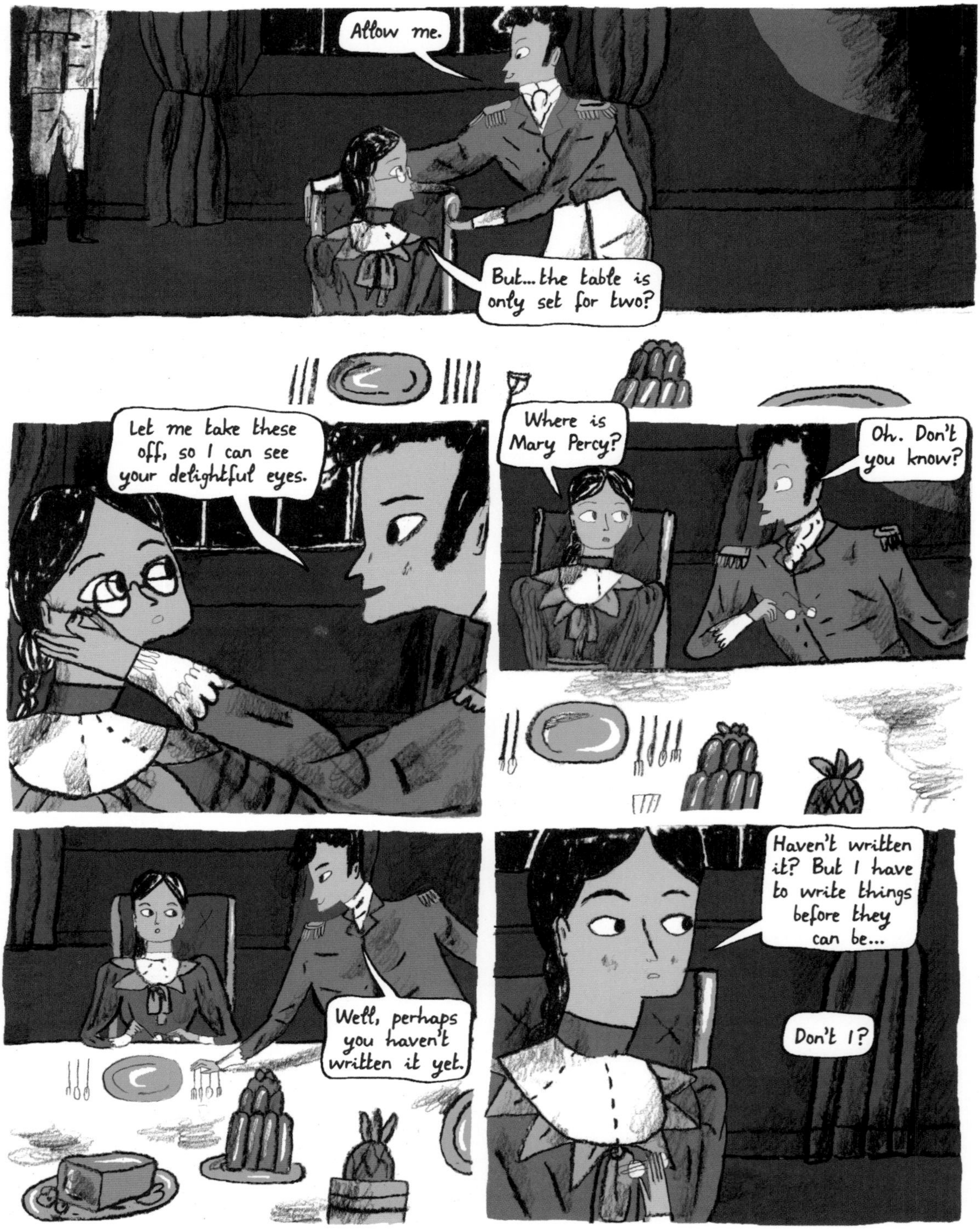
Allow me.
But... the table is only set for two?
Let me take these off, so I can see your delightful eyes.
Where is Mary Percy?
Oh. Don't you know?
Well, perhaps you haven't written it yet.
Haven't written it? But I have to write things before they can be...
Don't I?

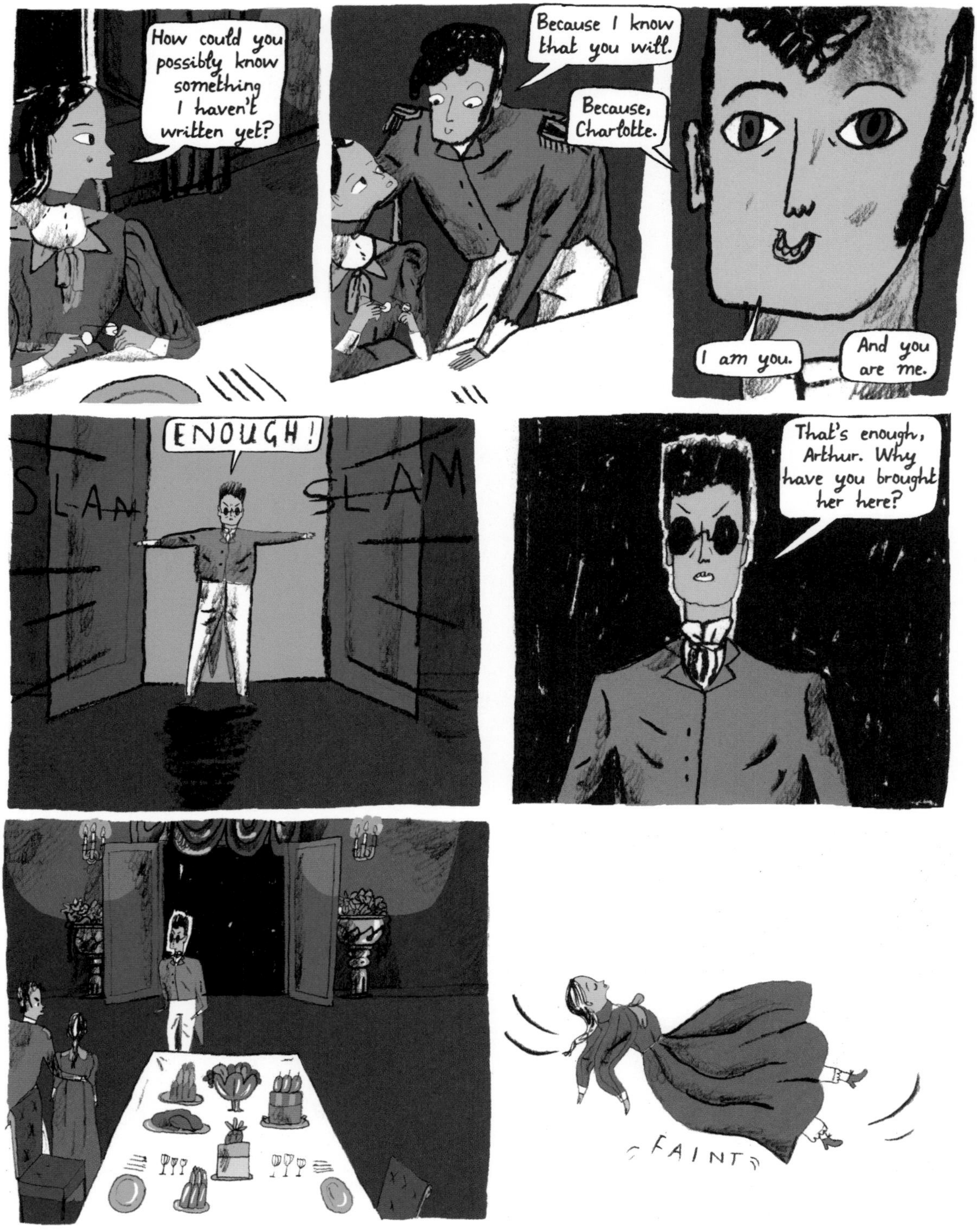
How could you possibly know something I haven't written yet?
Because I know that you will.
Because, Charlotte.
I am you.
And you are me.
ENOUGH!
SLAM
SLAM
That's enough, Arthur. Why have you brought her here?
FAINT

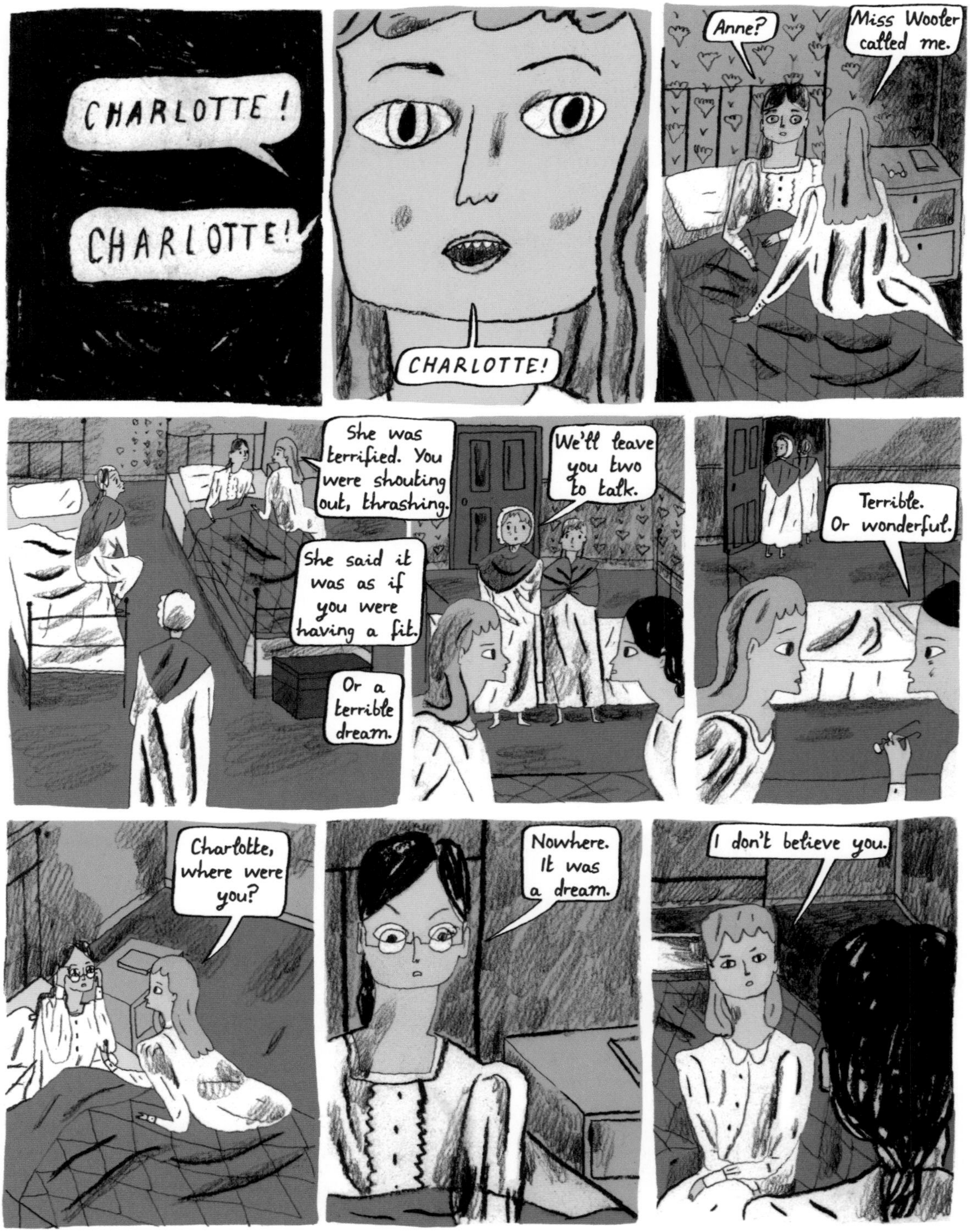
CHARLOTTE!
CHARLOTTE!
CHARLOTTE!
Anne?
Miss Wooler called me.
She was terrified. You were shouting out, thrashing.
She said it was as if you were having a fit.
Or a terrible dream.
We'll leave you two to talk.
Terrible. Or wonderful.
Charlotte, where were you?
Nowhere. It was a dream.
I don't believe you.

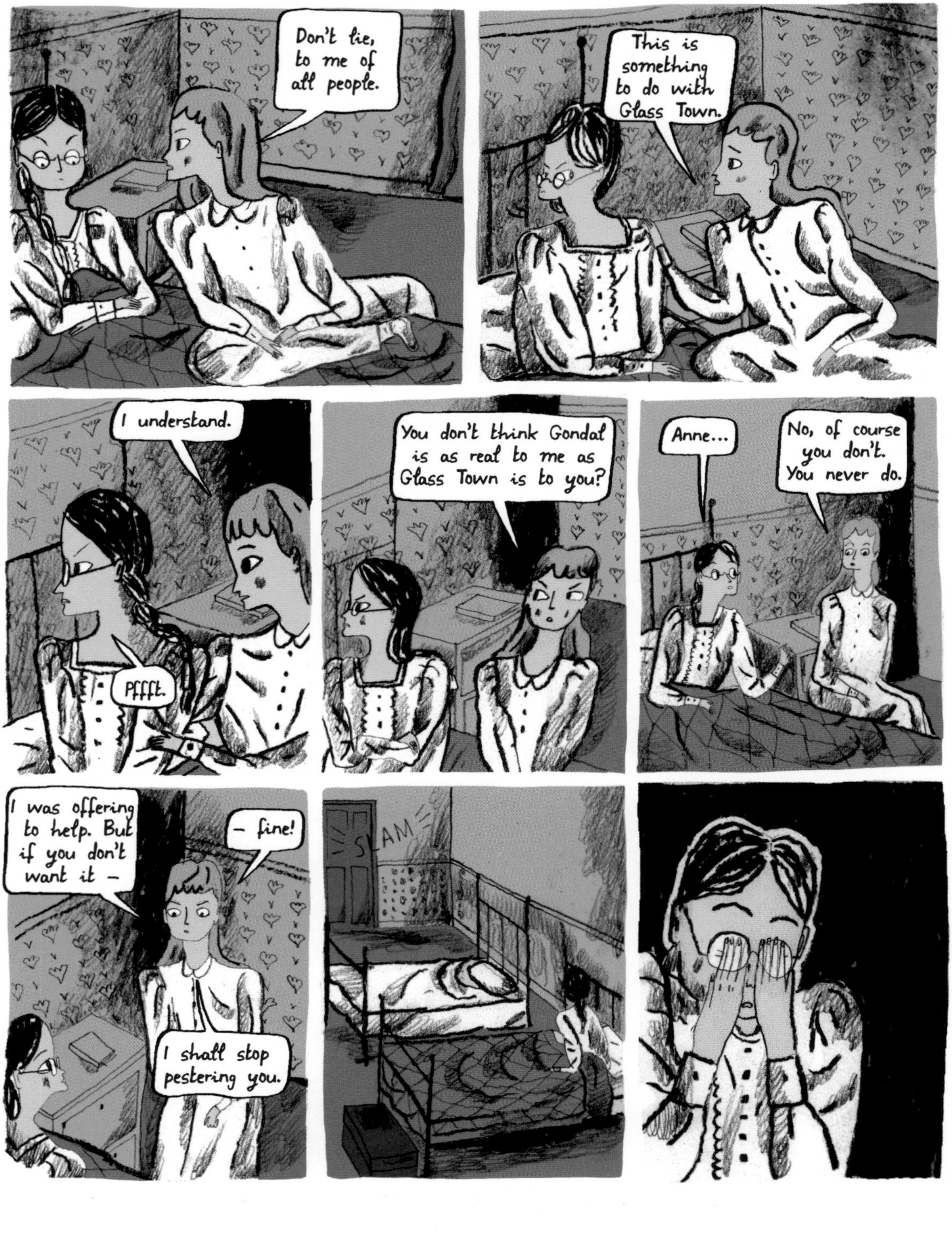
Don't lie, to me of all people.
This is something to do with Glass Town.
I understand.
Pffft.
You don't think Gondal is as real to me as Glass Town is to you?
Anne...
No, of course you don't. You never do.
I was offering to help. But if you don't want it –
– fine!
I shall stop pestering you.
SLAM

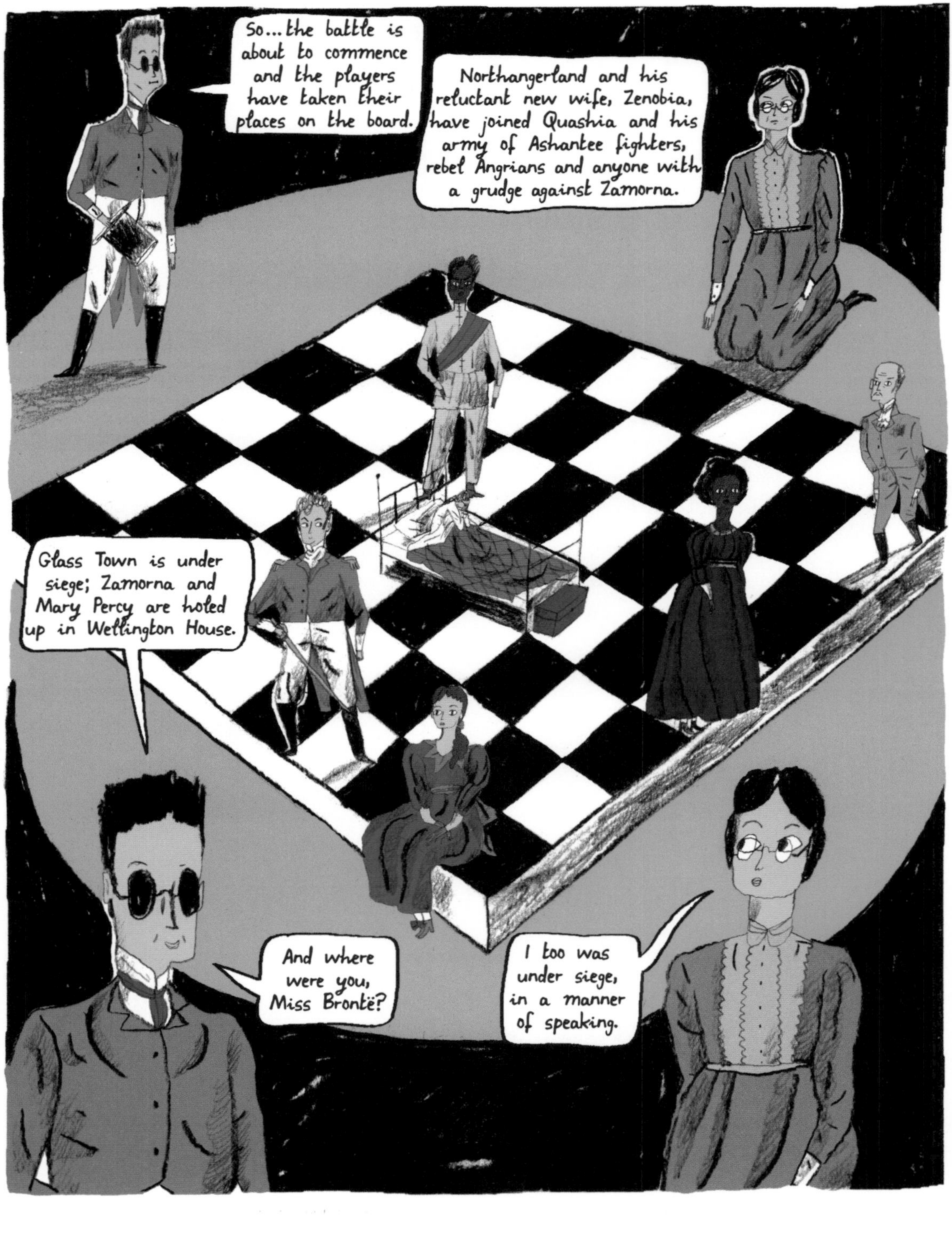
So... the battle is about to commence and the players have taken their places on the board.
Northangerland and his reluctant new wife, Zenobia, have joined Quashia and his army of Ashantee fighters, rebel Angrians and anyone with a grudge against Zamorna.
Glass Town is under siege; Zamorna and Mary Percy are holed up in Wellington House.
And where were you, Miss Brontë?
I too was under siege, in a manner of speaking.

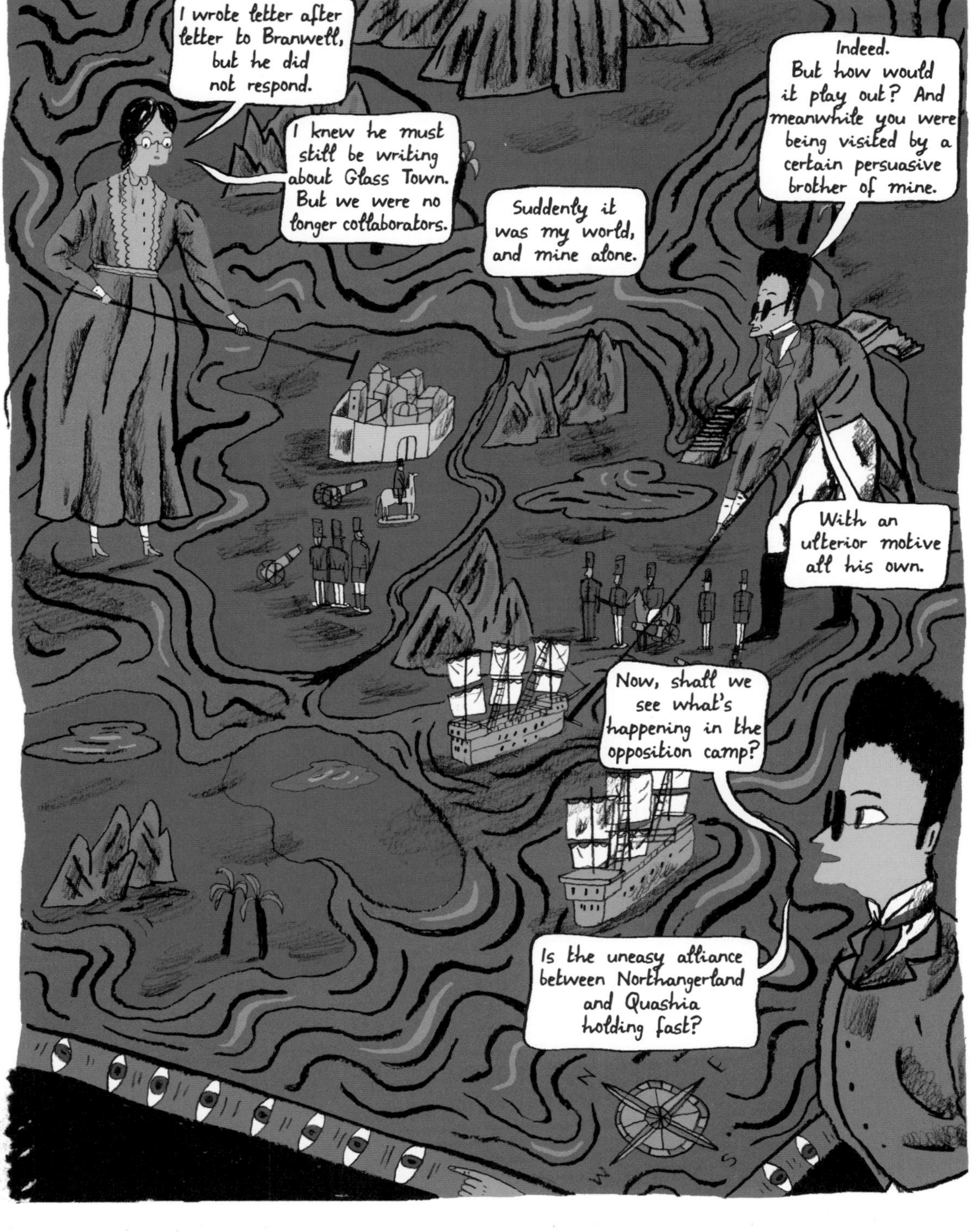

I wrote letter after letter to Branwell, but he did not respond.
I knew he must still be writing about Glass Town. But we were no longer collaborators.
Suddenly it was my world, and mine alone.
Indeed. But how would it play out? And meanwhile you were being visited by a certain persuasive brother of mine.
With an ulterior motive all his own.
Now, shall we see what's happening in the opposition camp?
Is the uneasy alliance between Northangerland and Quashia holding fast?

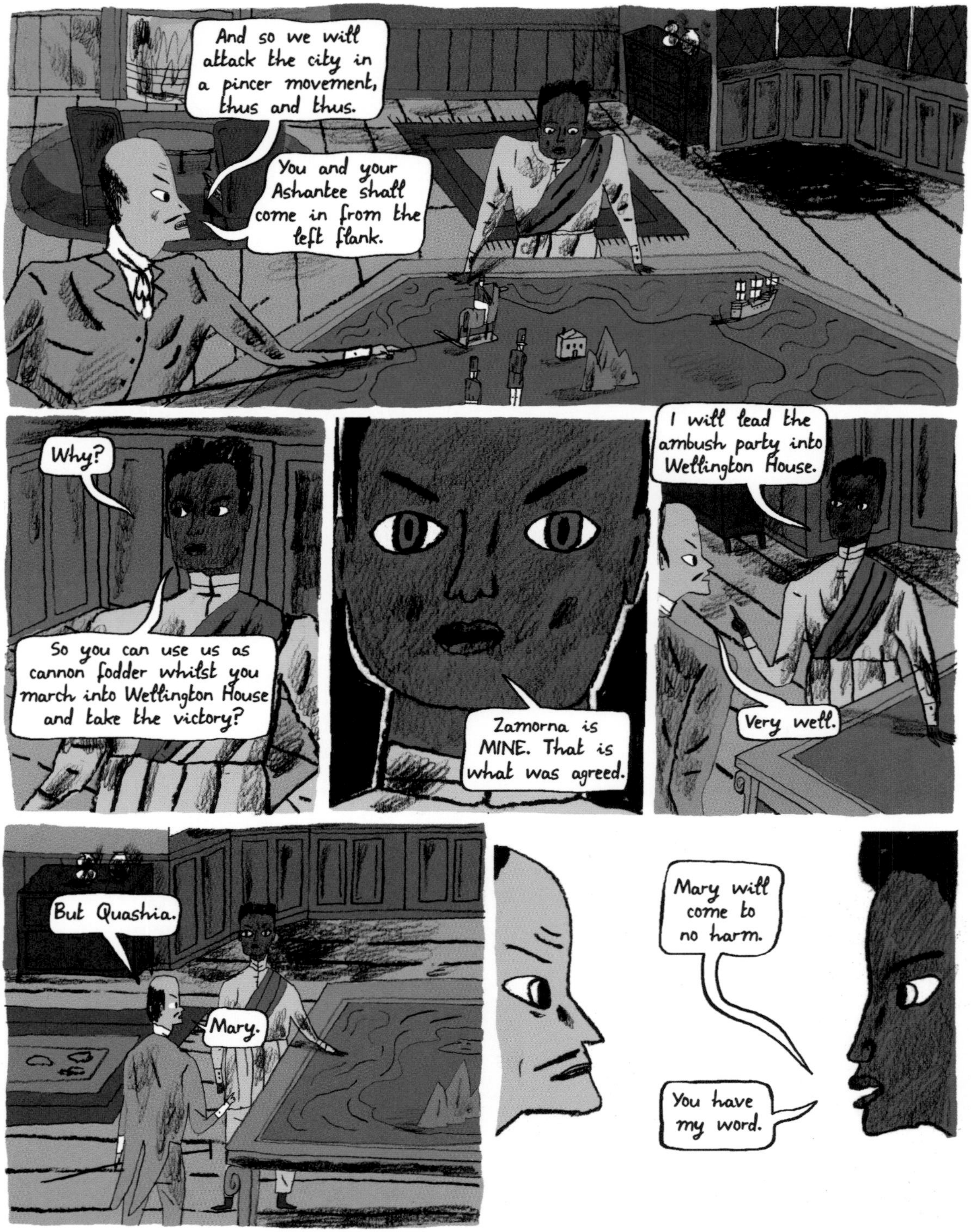
And so we will attack the city in a pincer movement, thus and thus.
You and your Ashantee shall come in from the left flank.
Why?
So you can use us as cannon fodder whilst you march into Wellington House and take the victory?
Zamorna is MINE. That is what was agreed.
I will lead the ambush party into Wellington House.
Very well.
But Quashia.
Mary.
Mary will come to no harm.
You have my word.

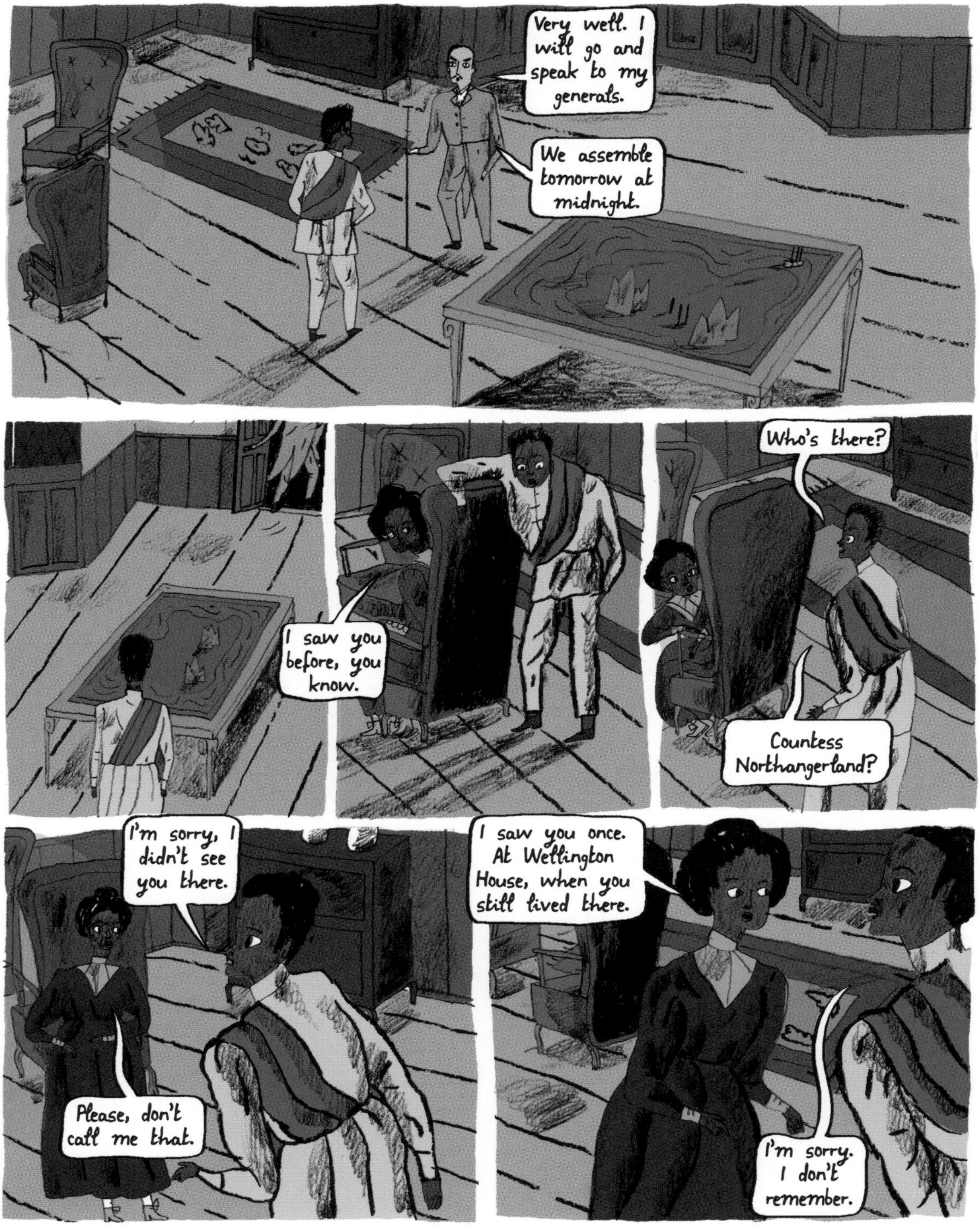
Very well. I will go and speak to my generals.
We assemble tomorrow at midnight.
I saw you before, you know.
Who's there?
Countess Northangerland?
I'm sorry, I didn't see you there.
Please, don't call me that.
I saw you once. At Wellington House, when you still lived there.
I'm sorry. I don't remember.

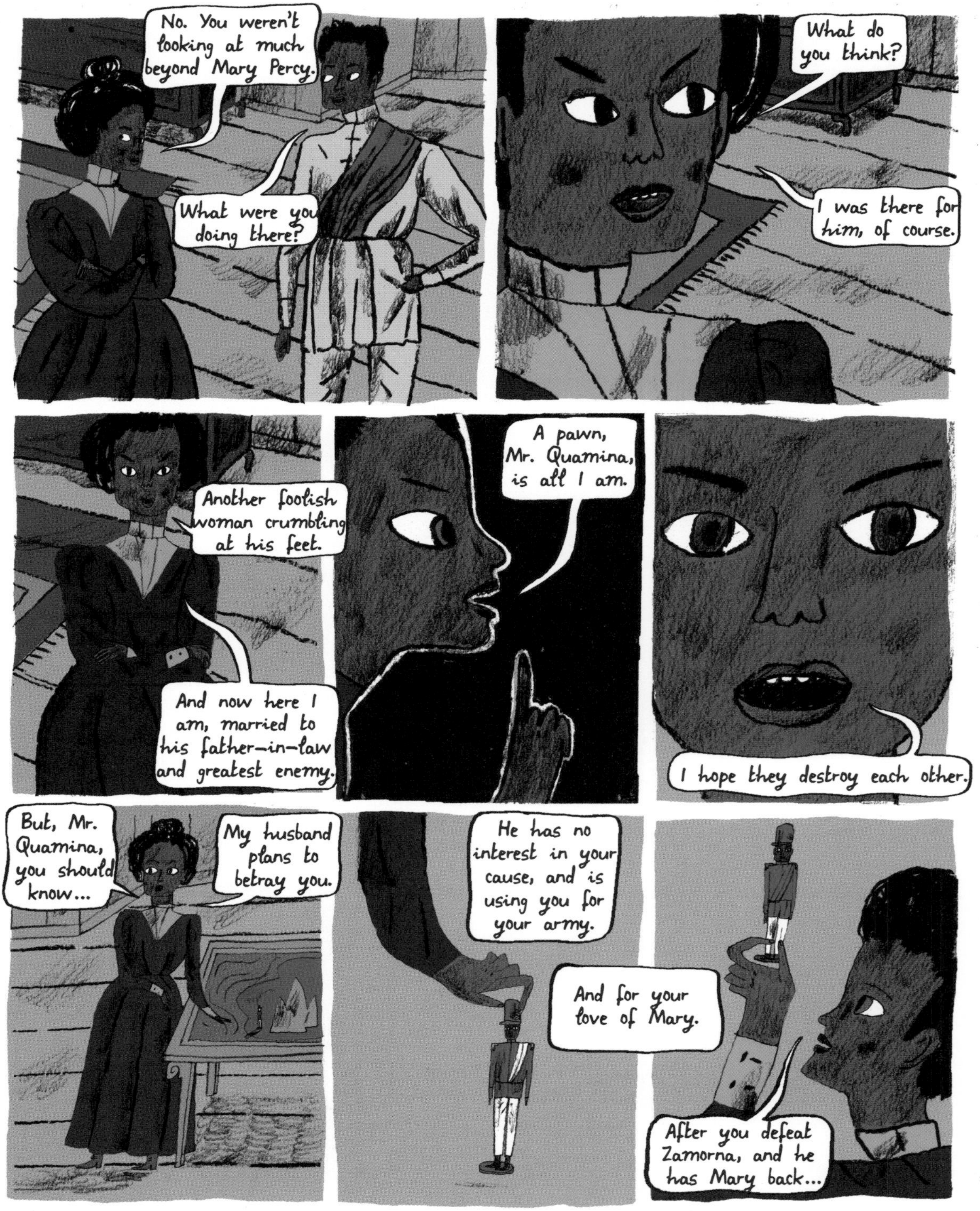
No. You weren't looking at much beyond Mary Percy.
What were you doing there?
What do you think?
I was there for him, of course.
Another foolish woman crumbling at his feet.
And now here I am, married to his father-in-law and greatest enemy.
A pawn, Mr. Quamina, is all I am.
I hope they destroy each other.
But, Mr. Quamina, you should know...
My husband plans to betray you.
He has no interest in your cause, and is using you for your army.
And for your love of Mary.
After you defeat Zamorna, and he has Mary back...

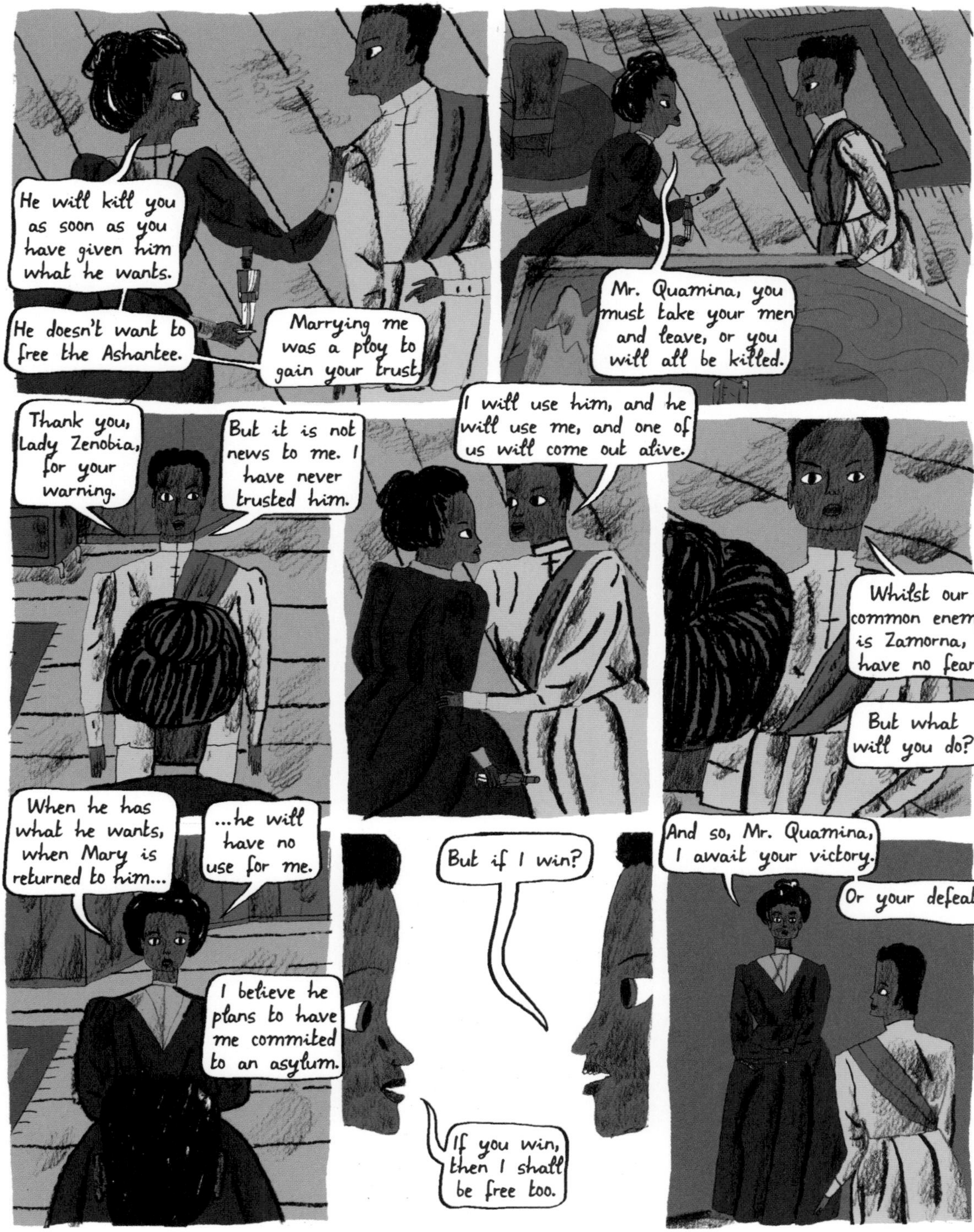

He will kill you as soon as you have given him what he wants.
He doesn't want to free the Ashantee.
Marrying me was a ploy to gain your trust.
Mr. Quamina, you must take your men and leave, or you will all be killed.
Thank you, Lady Zenobia, for your warning.
But it is not news to me. I have never trusted him.
I will use him, and he will use me, and one of us will come out alive.
Whilst our common enemy is Zamorna, I have no fear.
But what will you do?
When he has what he wants, when Mary is returned to him...
...he will have no use for me.
I believe he plans to have me commited to an asylum.
But if I win?
If you win, then I shall be free too.
And so, Mr. Quamina, I await your victory.
Or your defeat.

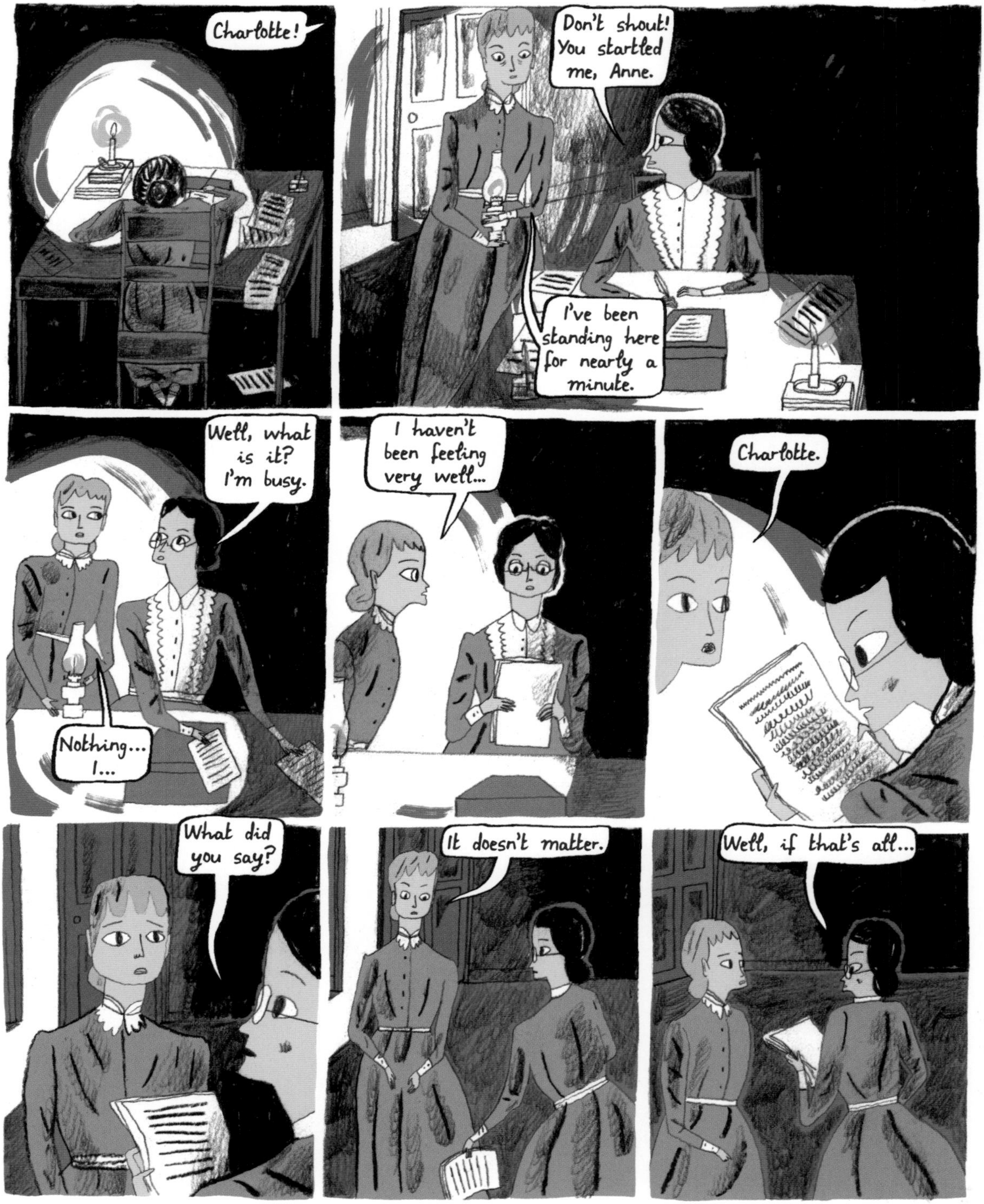
Charlotte!
Don't shout! You startled me, Anne.
I've been standing here for nearly a minute.
Well, what is it? I'm busy.
Nothing... I...
I haven't been feeling very well...
Charlotte.
What did you say?
It doesn't matter.
Well, if that's all...

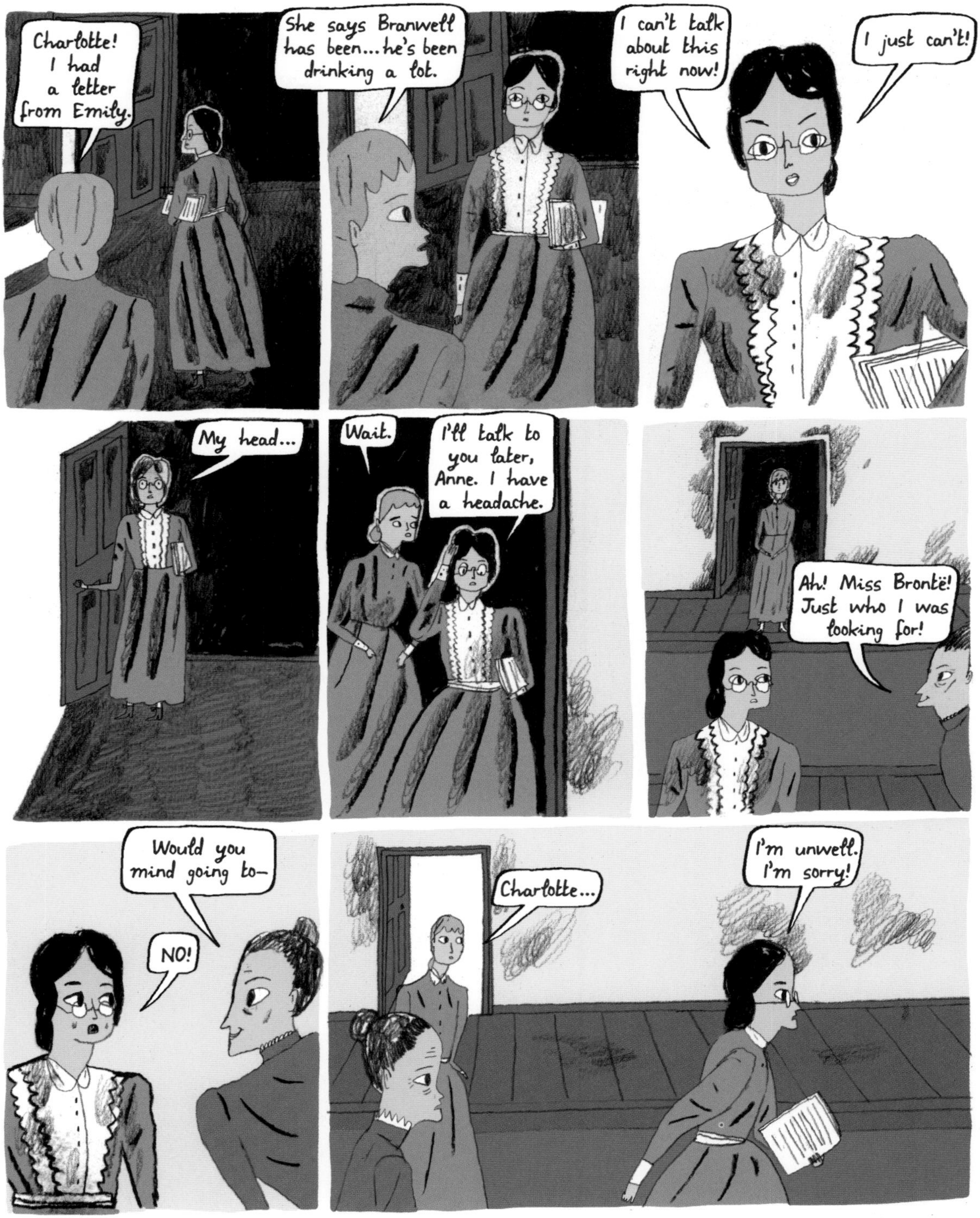
Charlotte! I had a letter from Emily.
She says Branwell has been...he's been drinking a lot.
I can't talk about this right now!
I just can't!
My head...
Wait.
I'll talk to you later, Anne. I have a headache.
Ah! Miss Brontë! Just who I was looking for!
Would you mind going to–
NO!
Charlotte...
I'm unwell. I'm sorry!

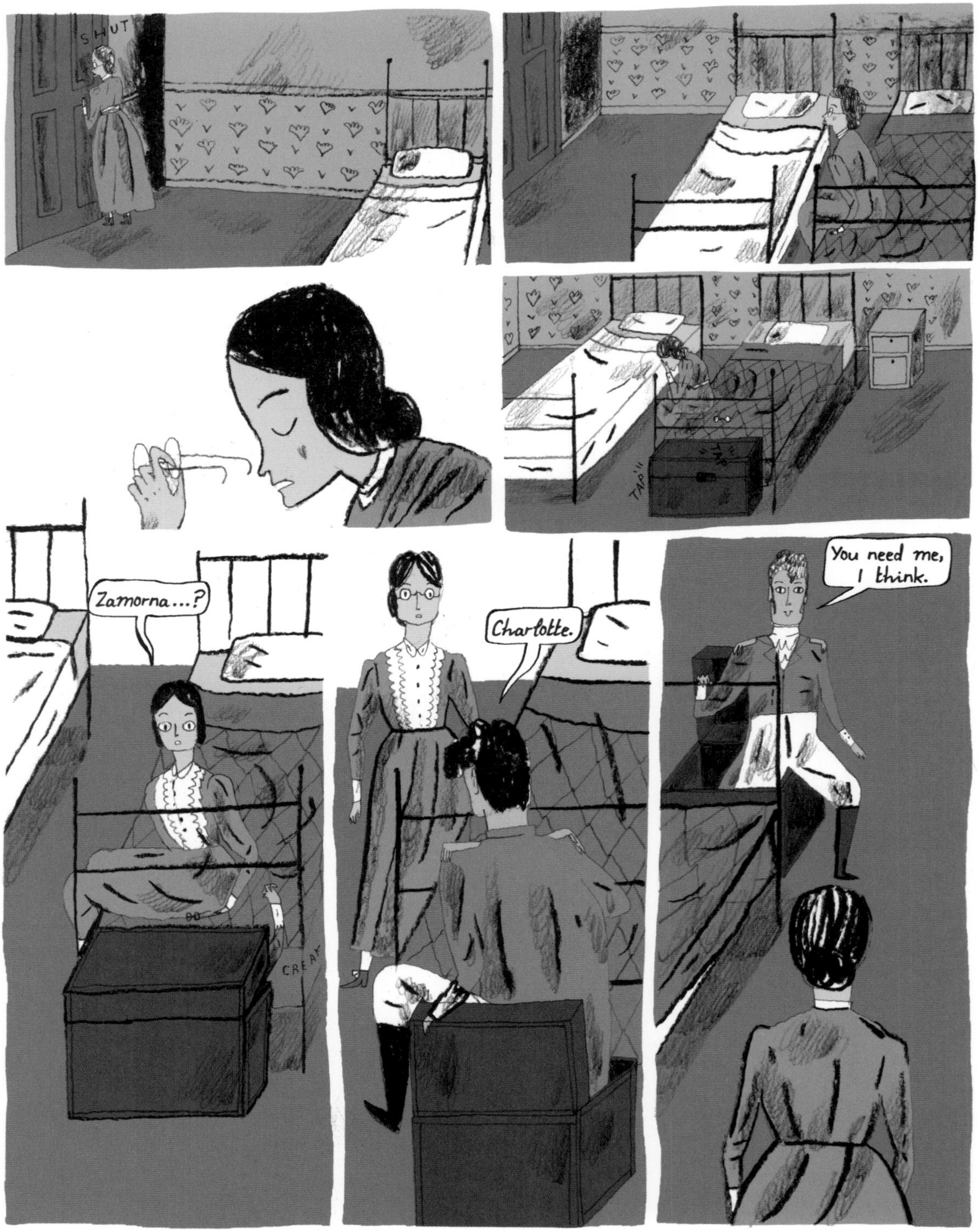
SHUT
TAP
TAP
Zamorna...?
CREAK
Charlotte.
You need me, I think.

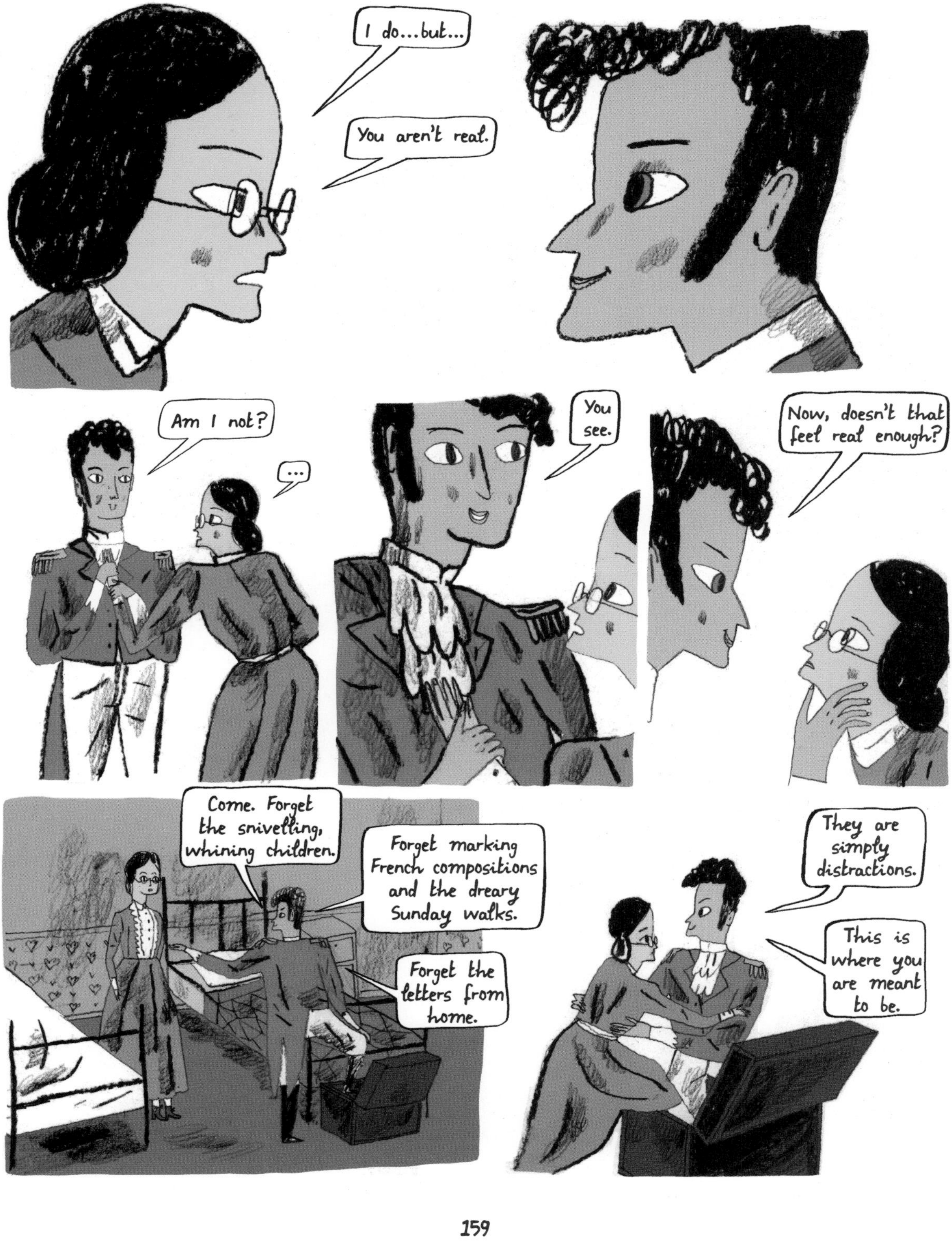

I do...but...
You aren't real.
Am I not?
...
You see.
Now, doesn't that feel real enough?
Come. Forget the snivelling, whining children.
Forget marking French compositions and the dreary Sunday walks.
Forget the letters from home.
They are simply distractions.
This is where you are meant to be.

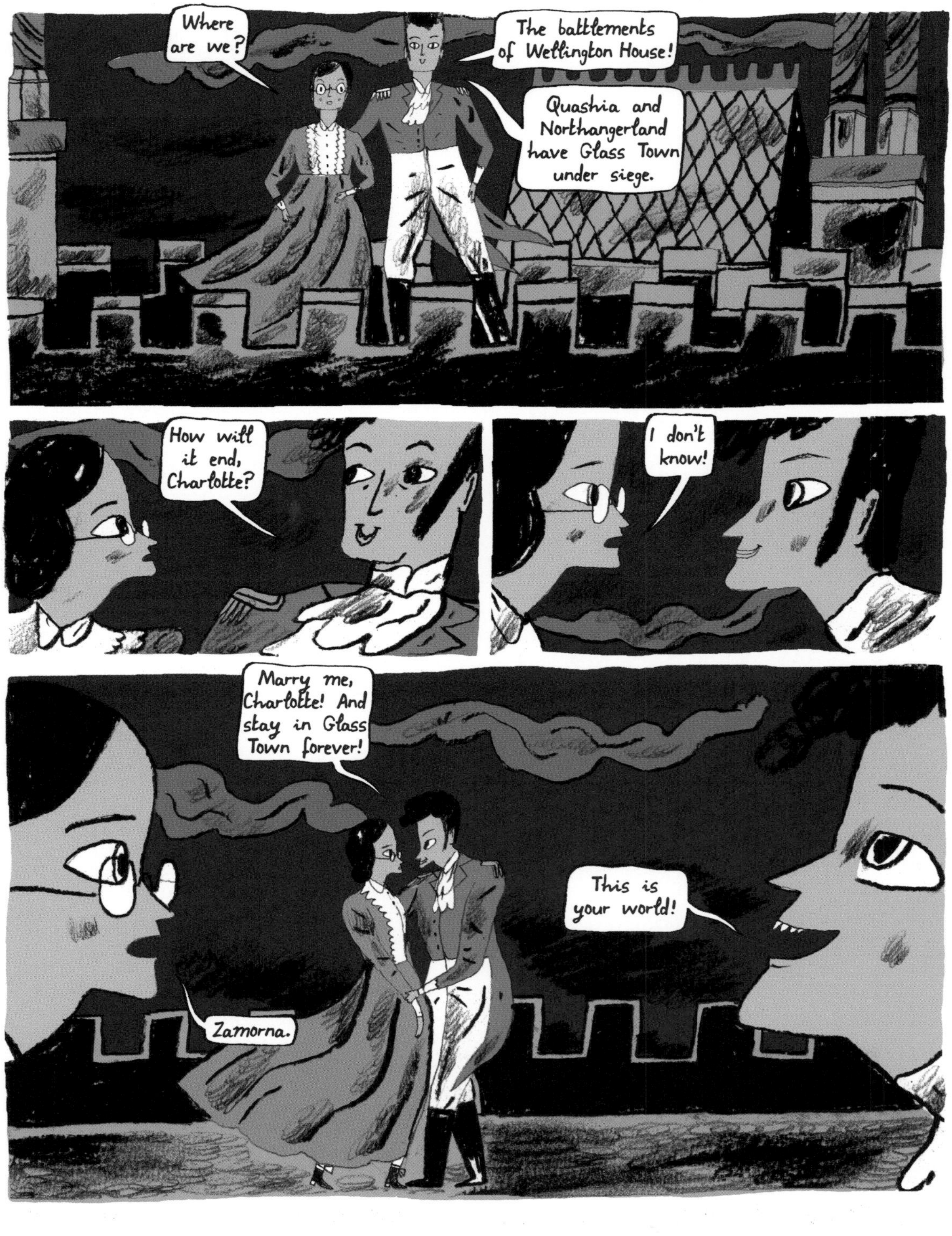
Where are we?
The battlements of Wellington House!
Quashia and Northangerland have Glass Town under siege.
How will it end, Charlotte?
I don't know!
Marry me, Charlotte! And stay in Glass Town forever!
This is your world!
Zamorna.

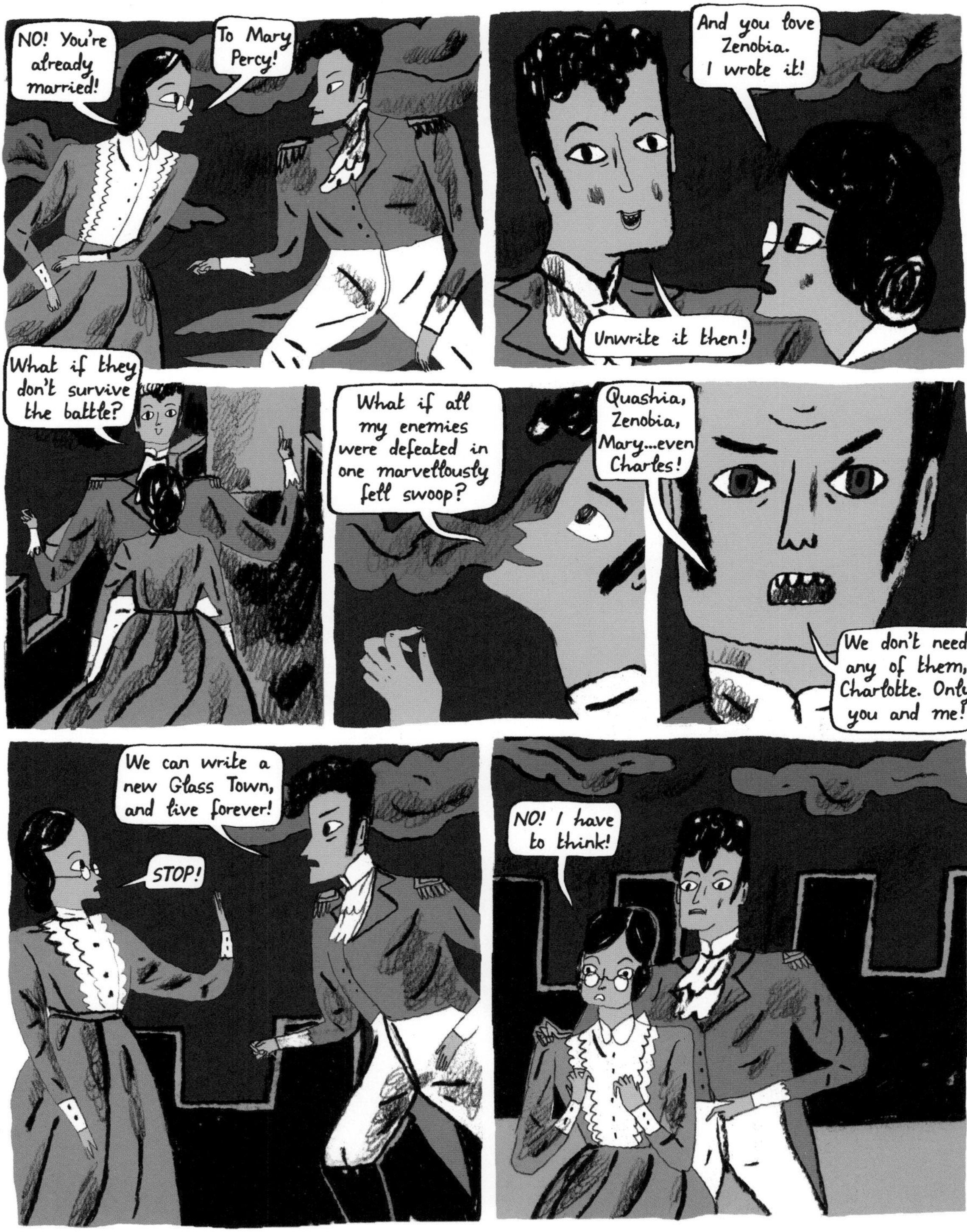
NO! You're already married!
To Mary Percy!
And you love Zenobia. I wrote it!
Unwrite it then!
What if they don't survive the battle?
What if all my enemies were defeated in one marvellously fell swoop?
Quashia, Zenobia, Mary...even Charles!
We don't need any of them, Charlotte. Only you and me!
We can write a new Glass Town, and live forever!
STOP!
NO! I have to think!

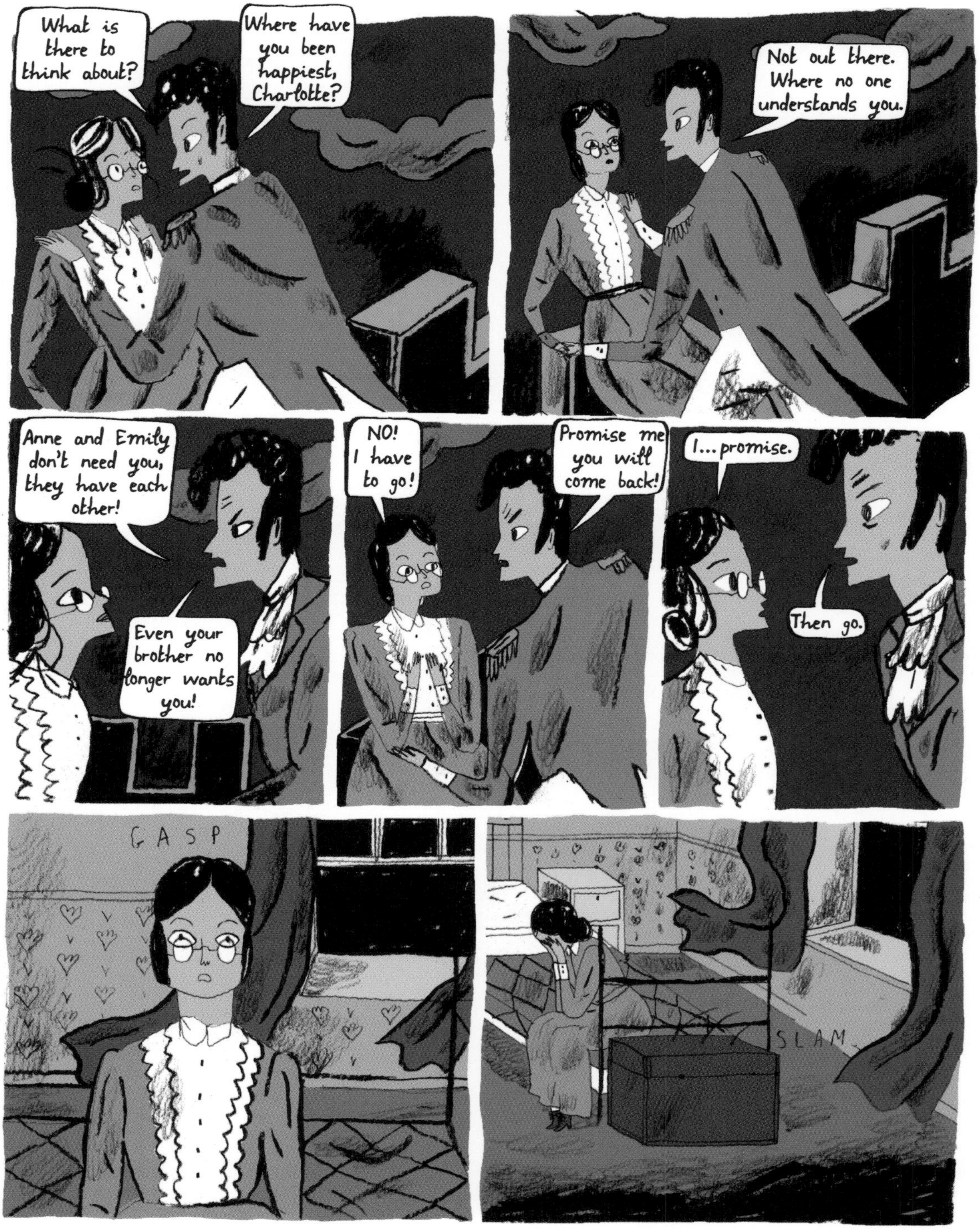
What is there to think about?
Where have you been happiest, Charlotte?
Not out there. Where no one understands you.
Anne and Emily don't need you, they have each other!
Even your brother no longer wants you!
NO! I have to go!
Promise me you will come back!
I... promise.
Then go.
GASP
SLAM

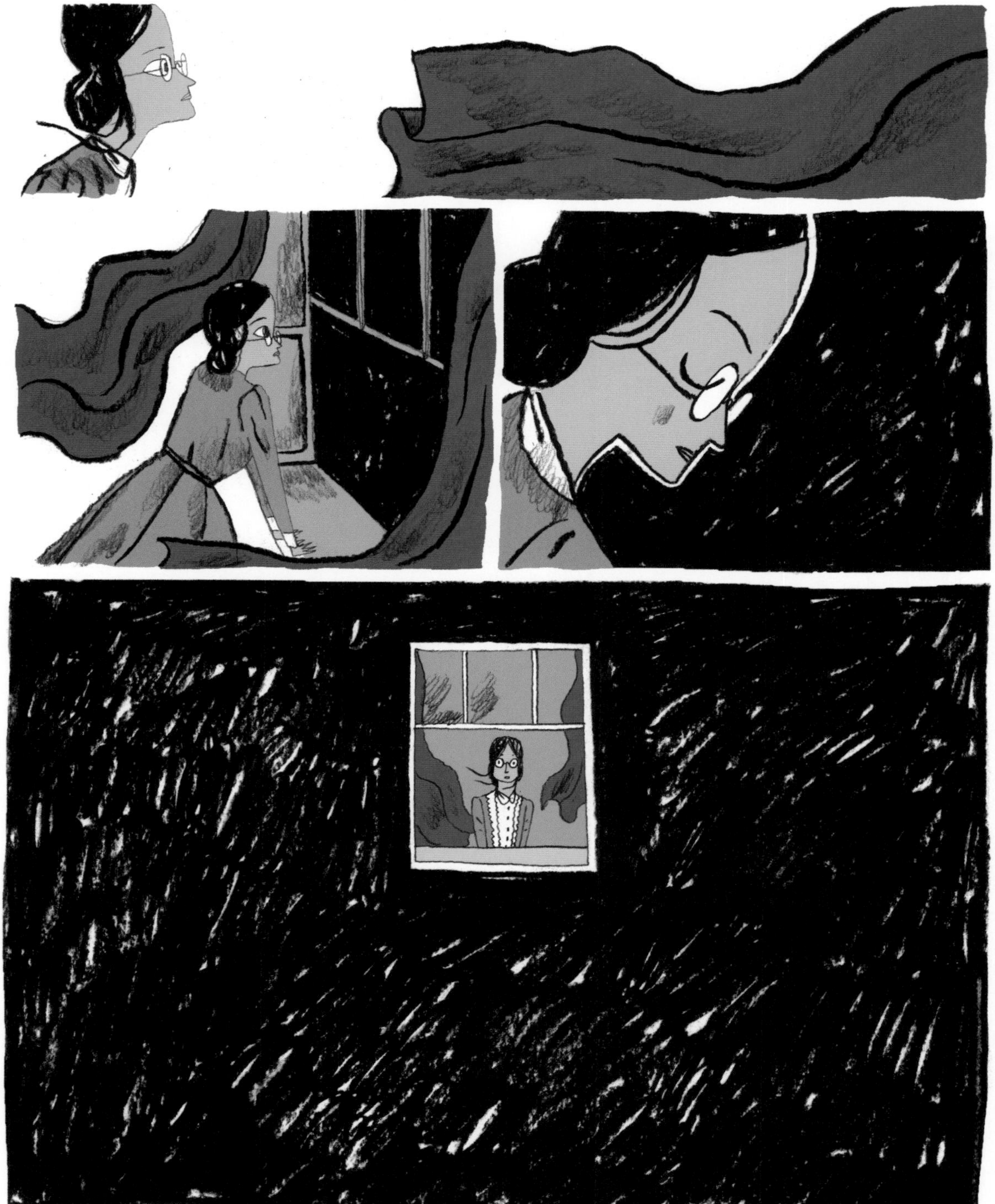

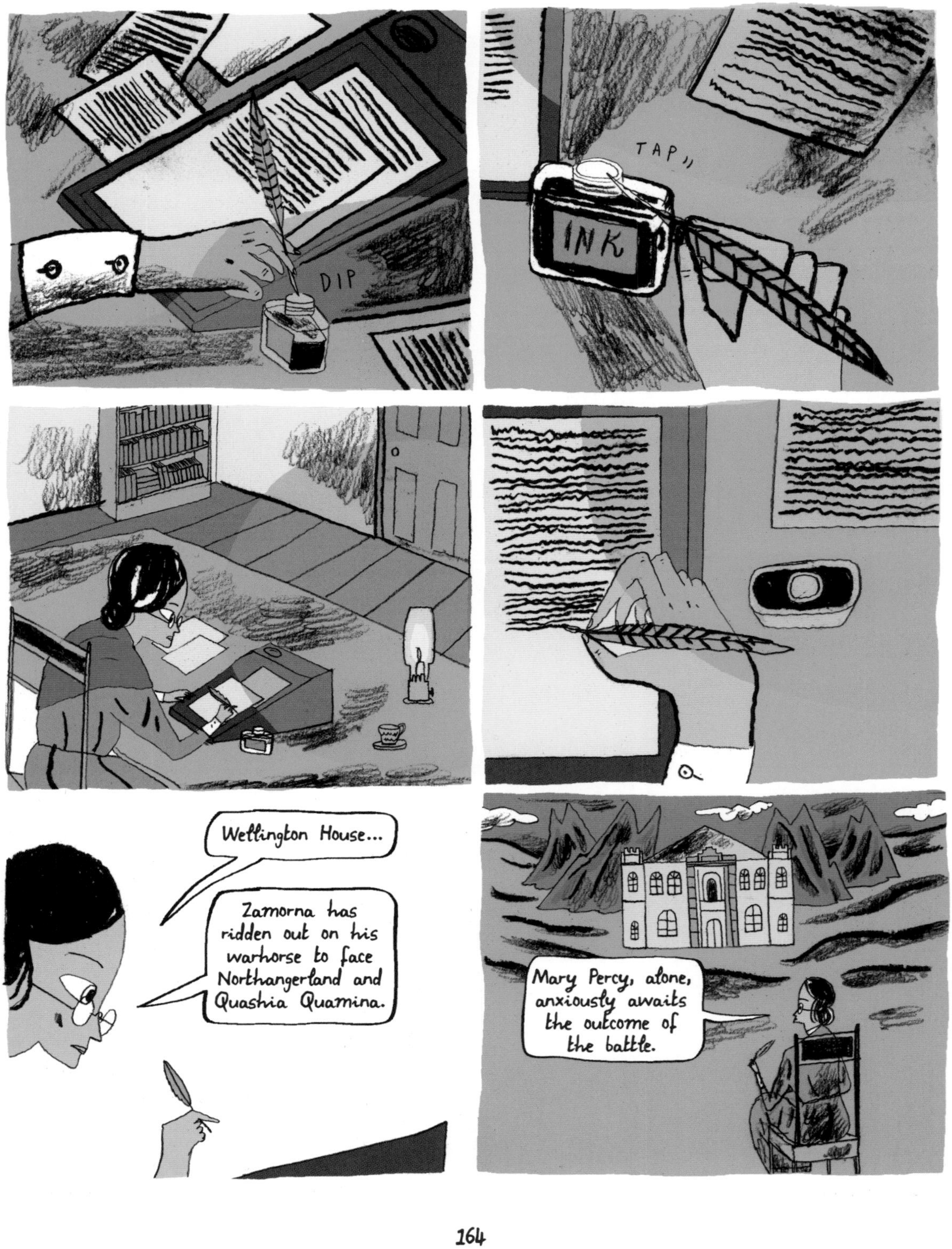
DIP
TAP
INK
Wellington House...
Zamorna has ridden out on his warhorse to face Northangerland and Quashia Quamina.
Mary Percy, alone, anxiously awaits the outcome of the battle.

Will she lose her husband, her father, or Quashia?

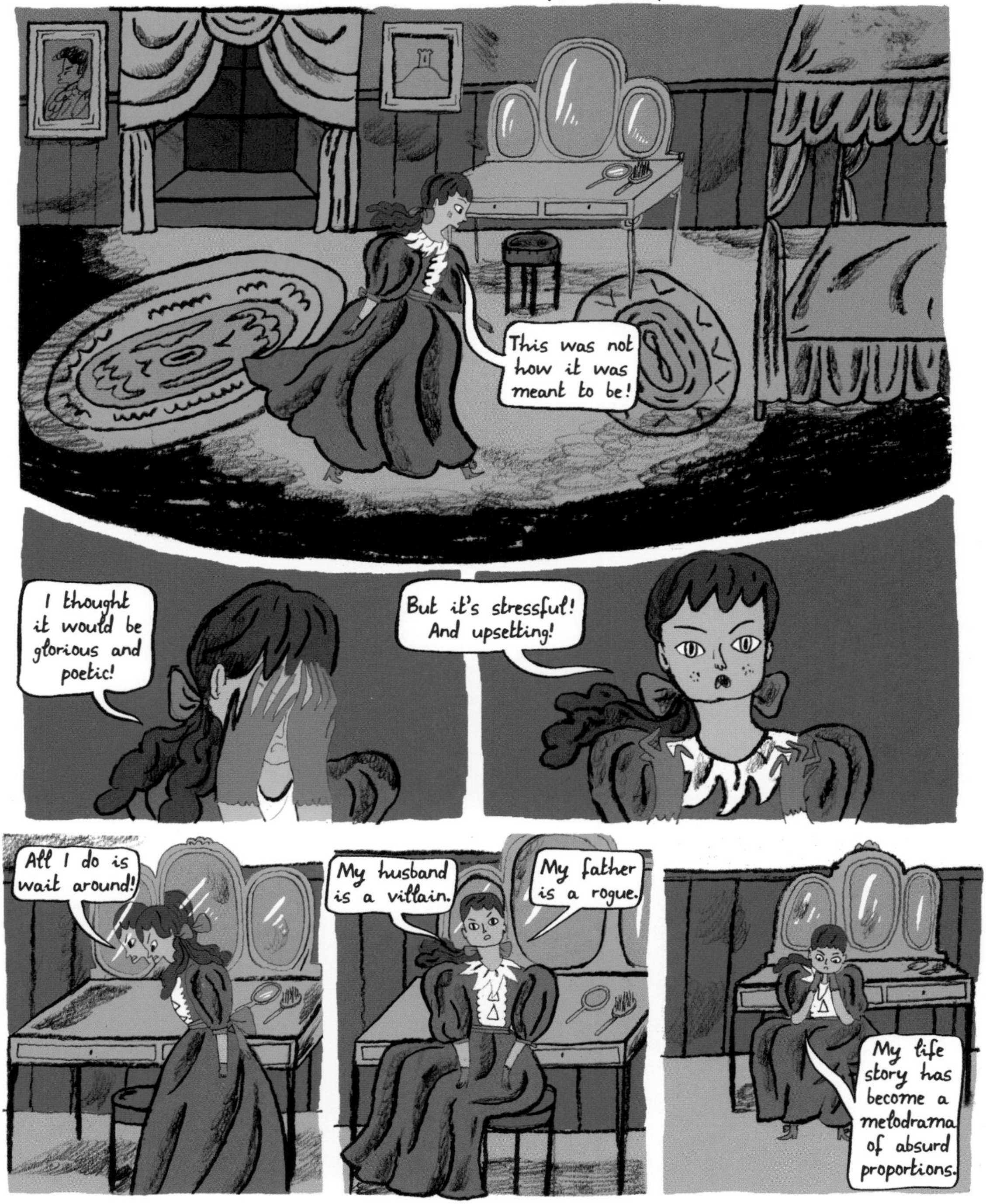
This was not how it was meant to be!
I thought it would be glorious and poetic!
But it's stressful! And upsetting!
All I do is wait around!
My husband is a villain.
My father is a rogue.
My life story has become a melodrama of absurd proportions.

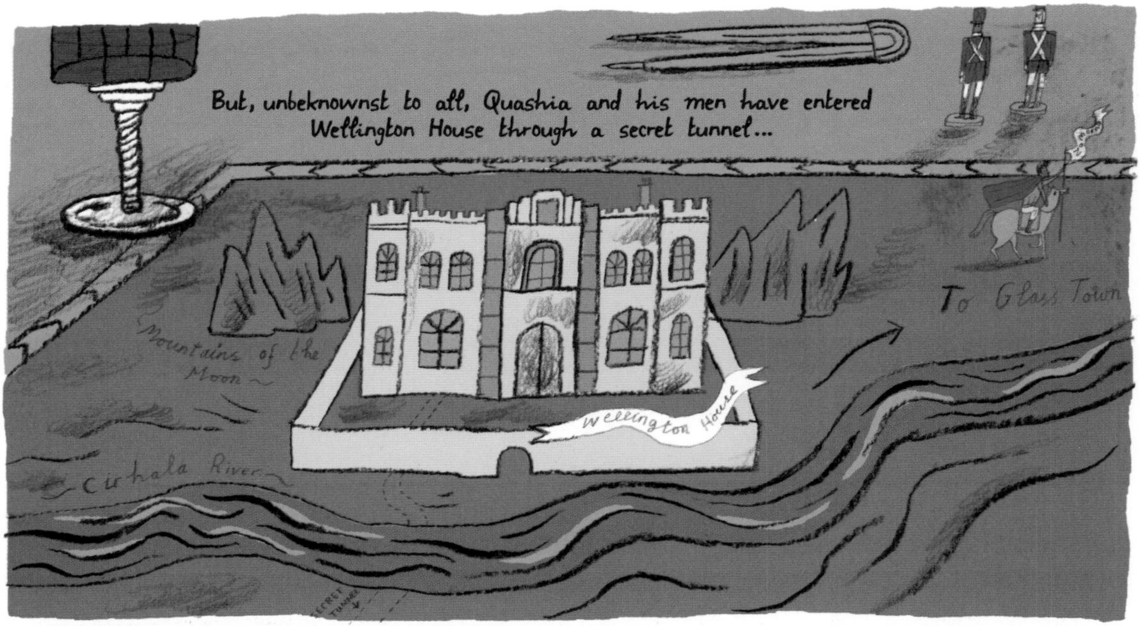
But, unbeknownst to all, Quashia and his men have entered Wellington House through a secret tunnel...
Mountains of the Moon
Wellington House
To Glass Town
Cirhala River

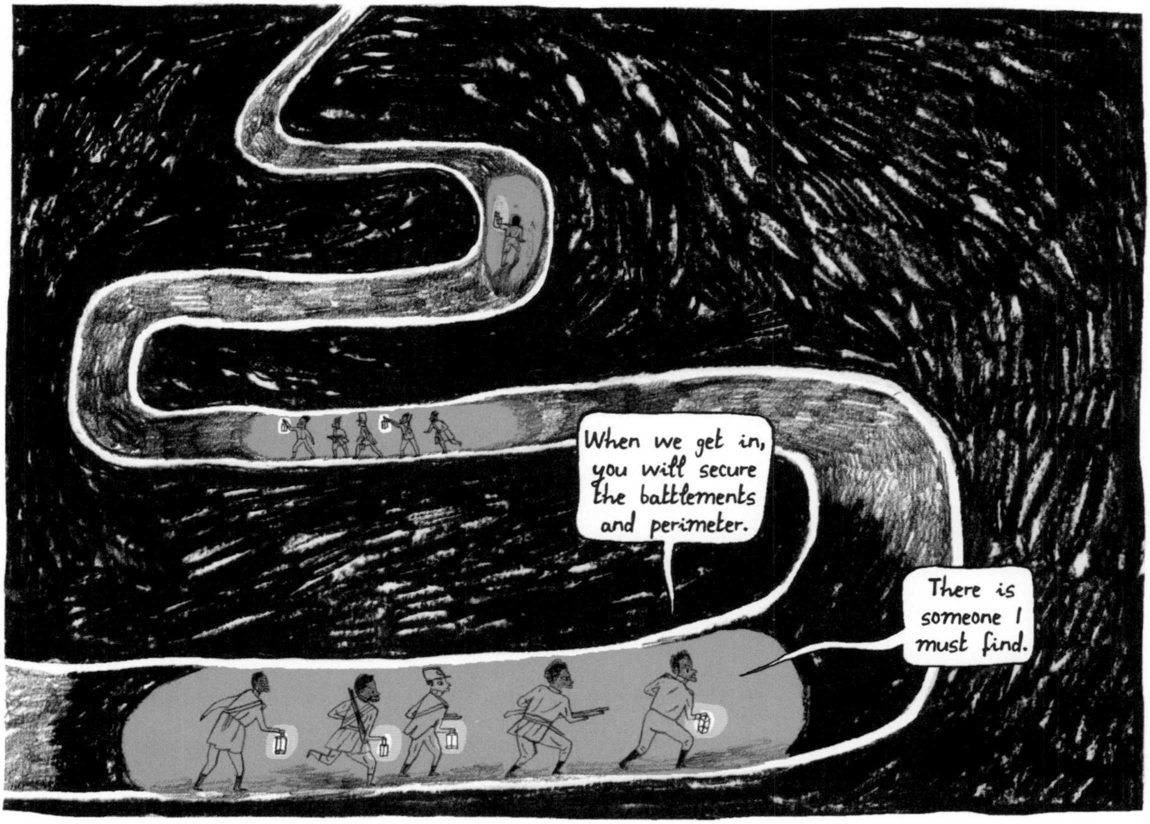
When we get in, you will secure the battlements and perimeter.
There is someone I must find.

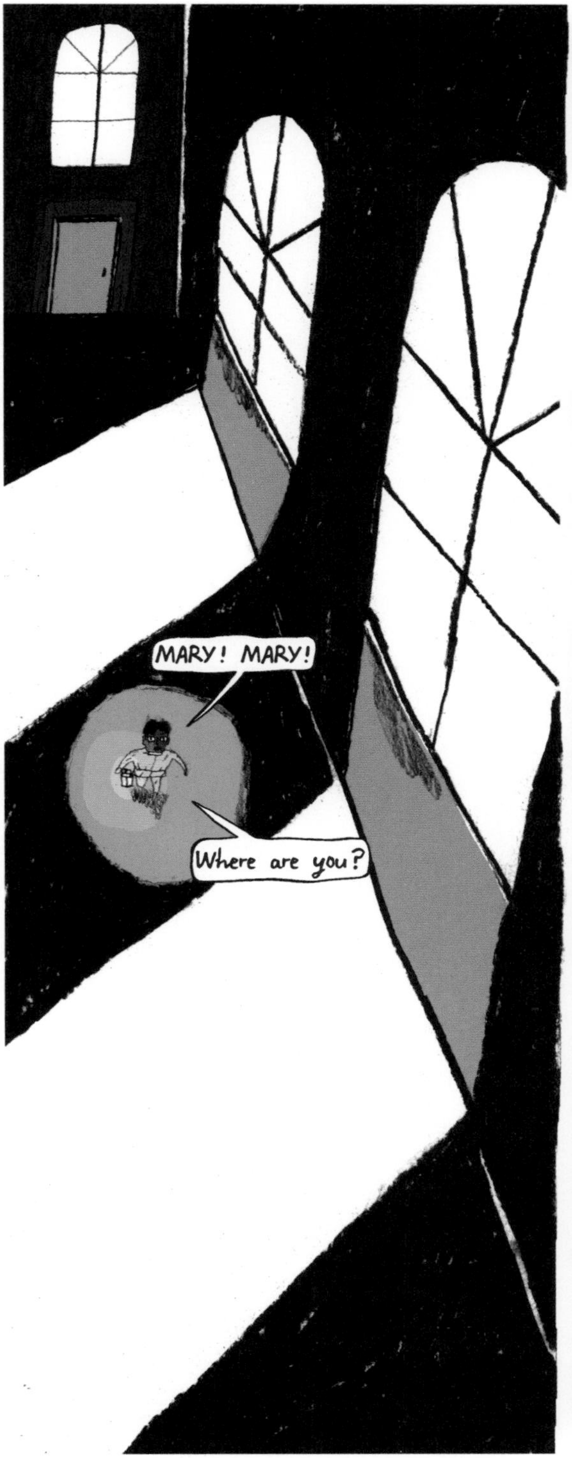
MARY! MARY!
Where are you?

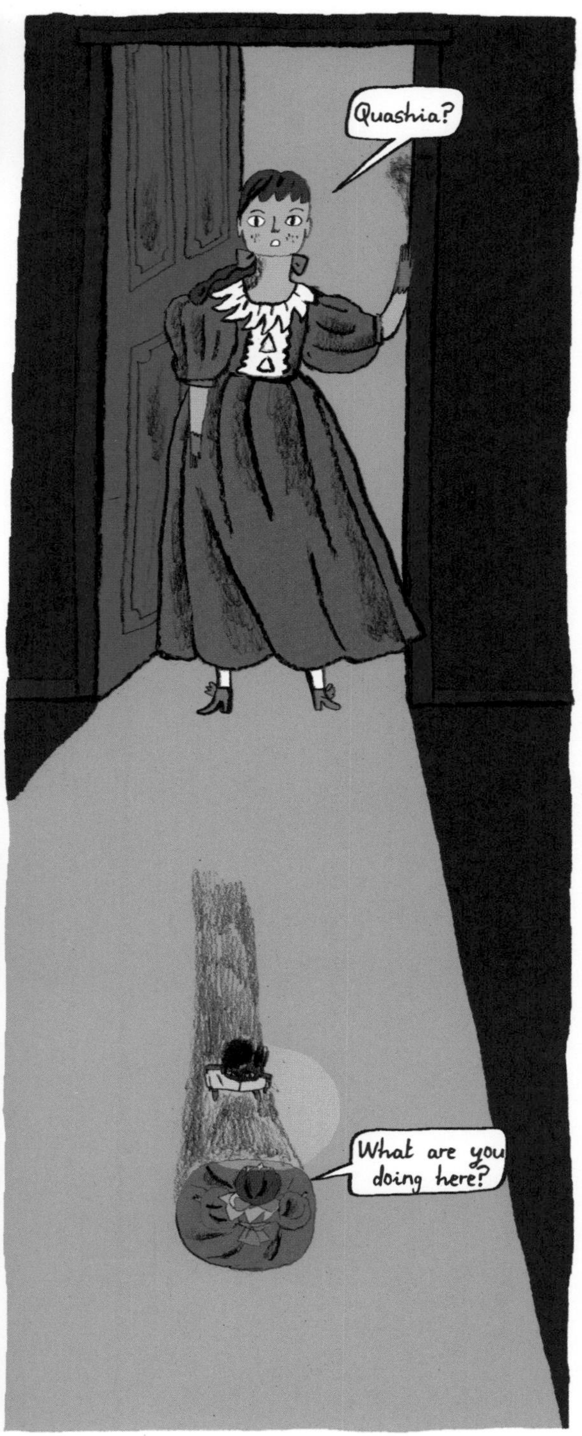
Quashia?
What are you doing here?

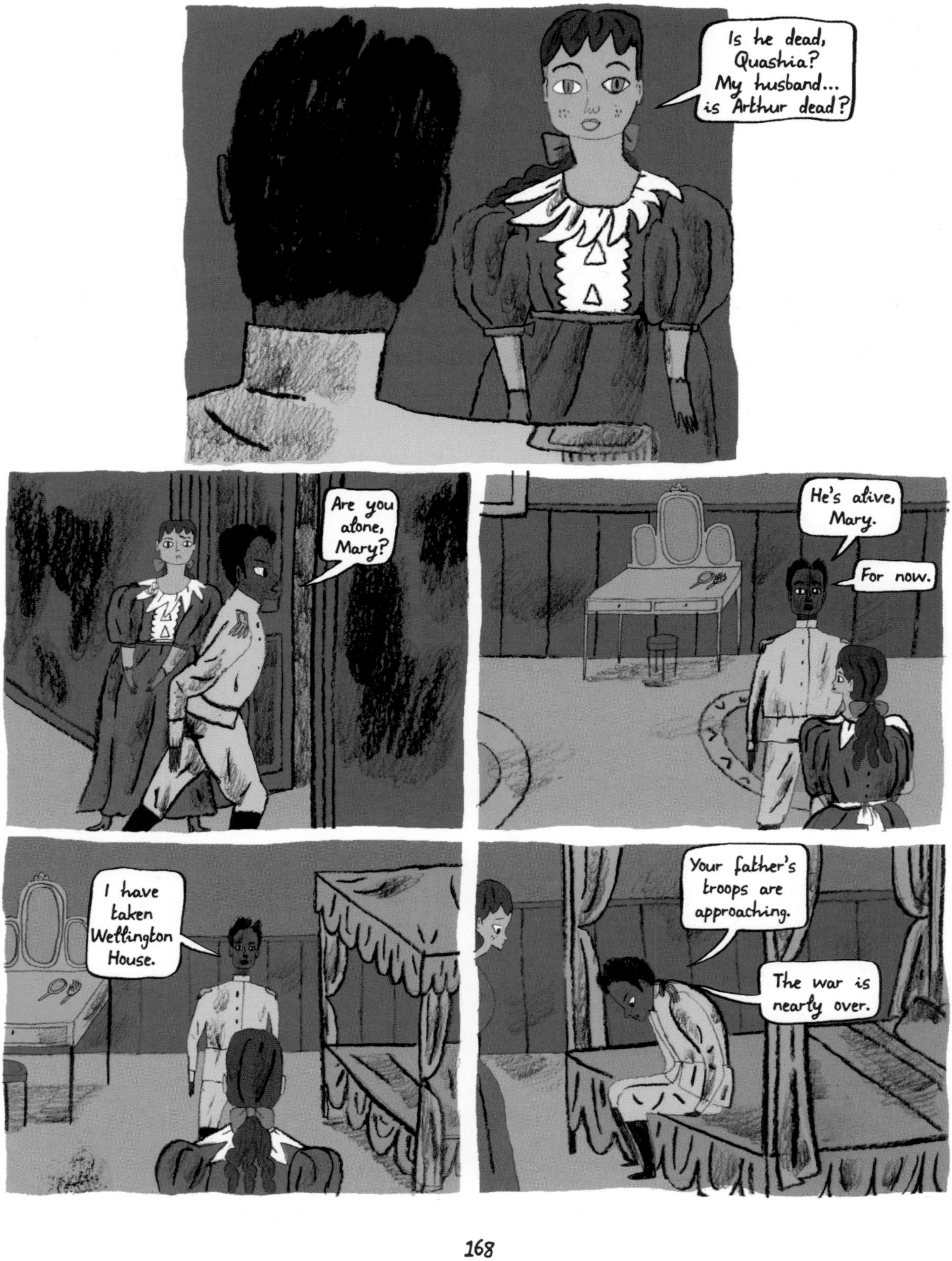
Is he dead, Quashia? My husband... is Arthur dead?
Are you alone, Mary?
He's alive, Mary.
For now.
I have taken Wellington House.
Your father's troops are approaching.
The war is nearly over.

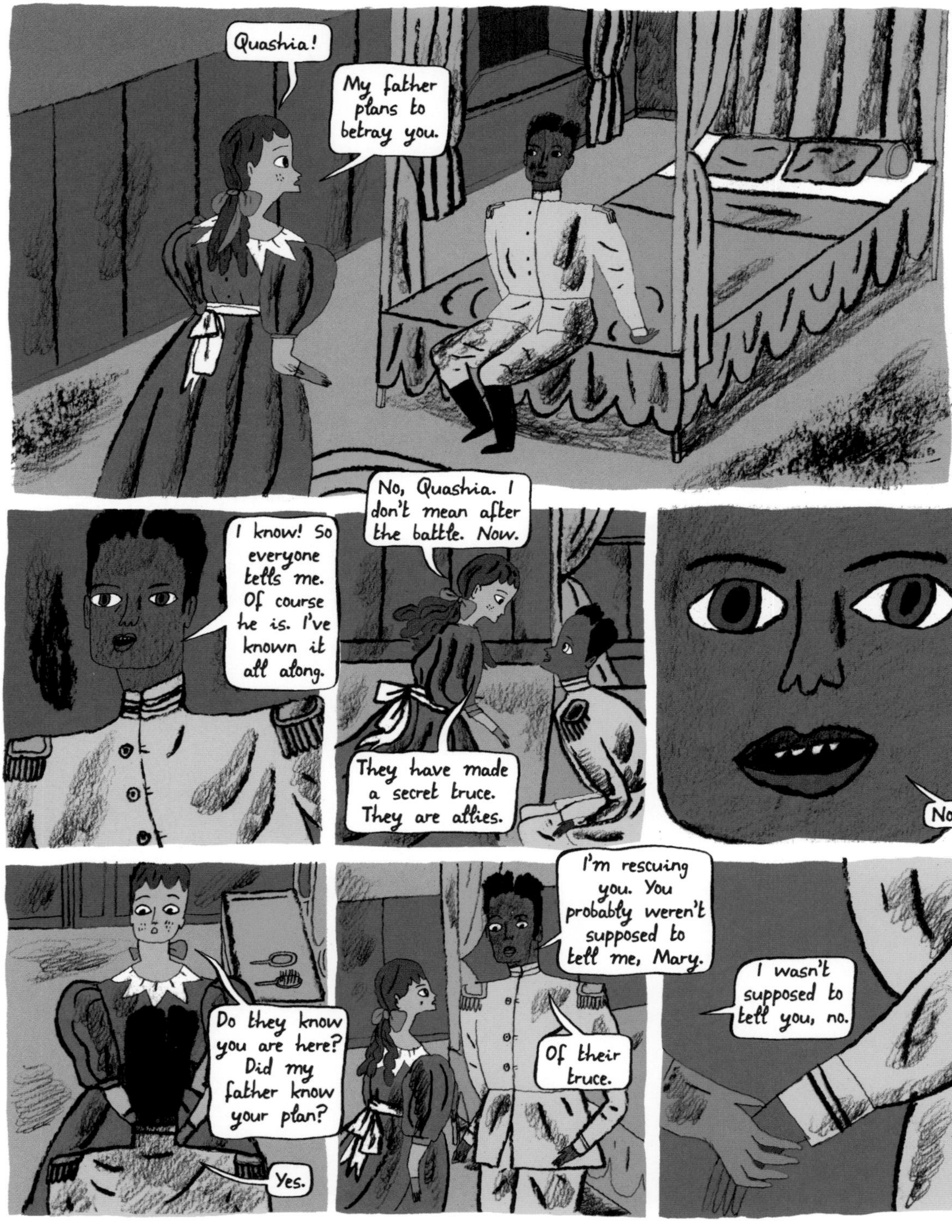
Quashia!
My father plans to betray you.
I know! So everyone tells me. Of course he is. I've known it all along.
No, Quashia. I don't mean after the battle. Now.
They have made a secret truce. They are allies.
No.
Do they know you are here? Did my father know your plan?
Yes.
I'm rescuing you. You probably weren't supposed to tell me, Mary.
Of their truce.
I wasn't supposed to tell you, no.

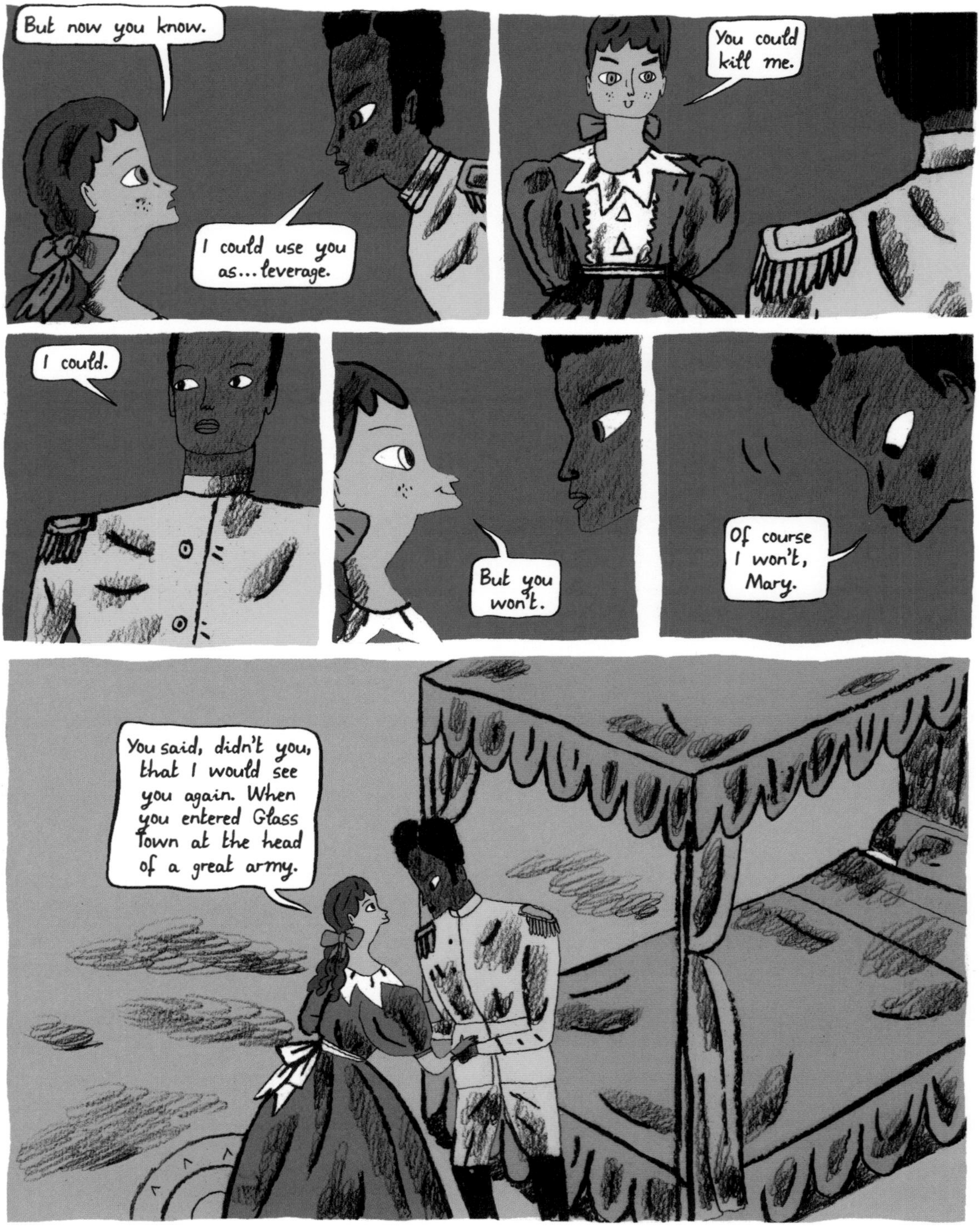
But now you know.
I could use you as... leverage.
You could kill me.
I could.
But you won't.
Of course I won't, Mary.
You said, didn't you, that I would see you again. When you entered Glass Town at the head of a great army.

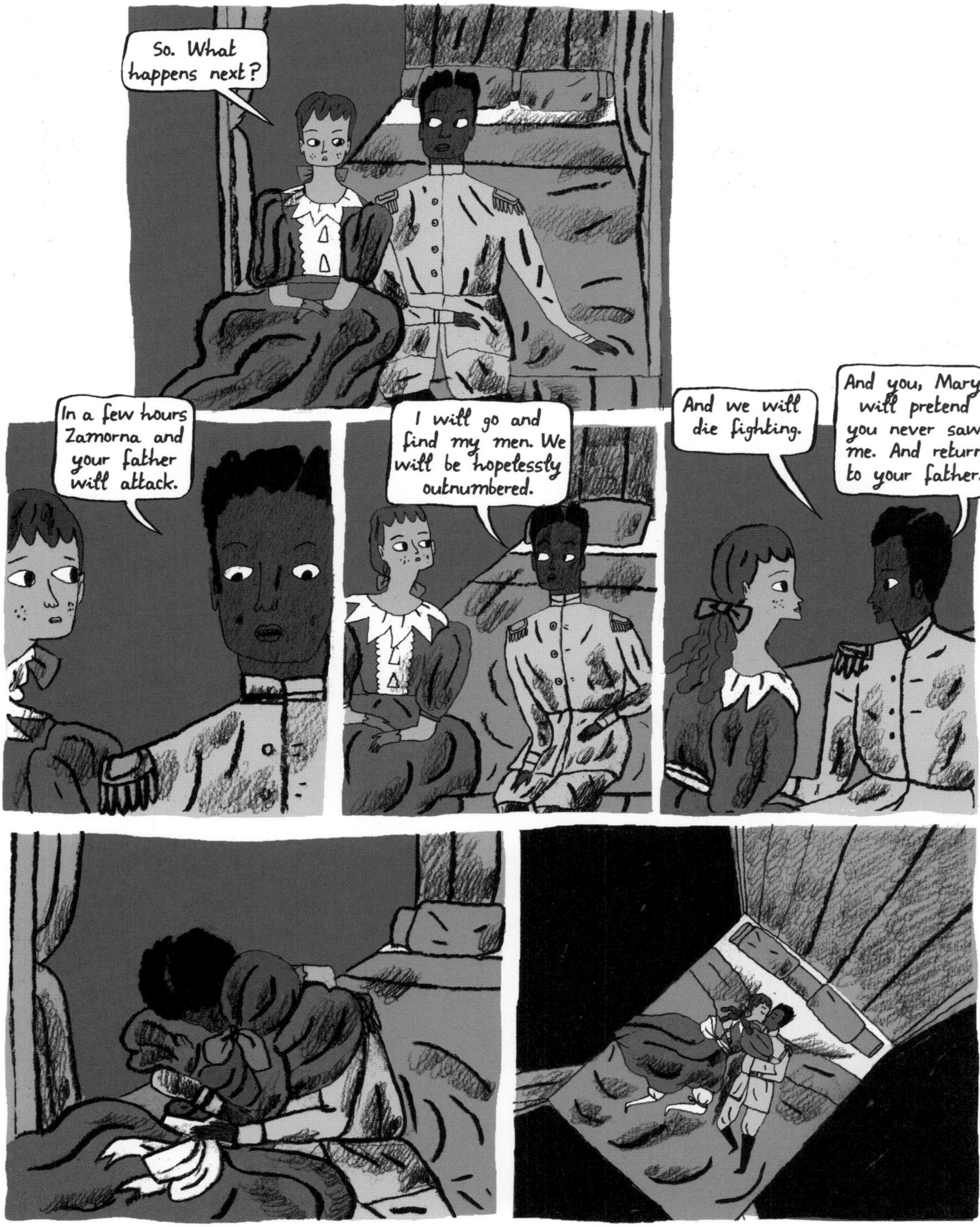
So. What happens next?
In a few hours Zamorna and your father will attack.
I will go and find my men. We will be hopelessly outnumbered.
And we will die fighting.
And you, Mary, will pretend you never saw me. And return to your father.

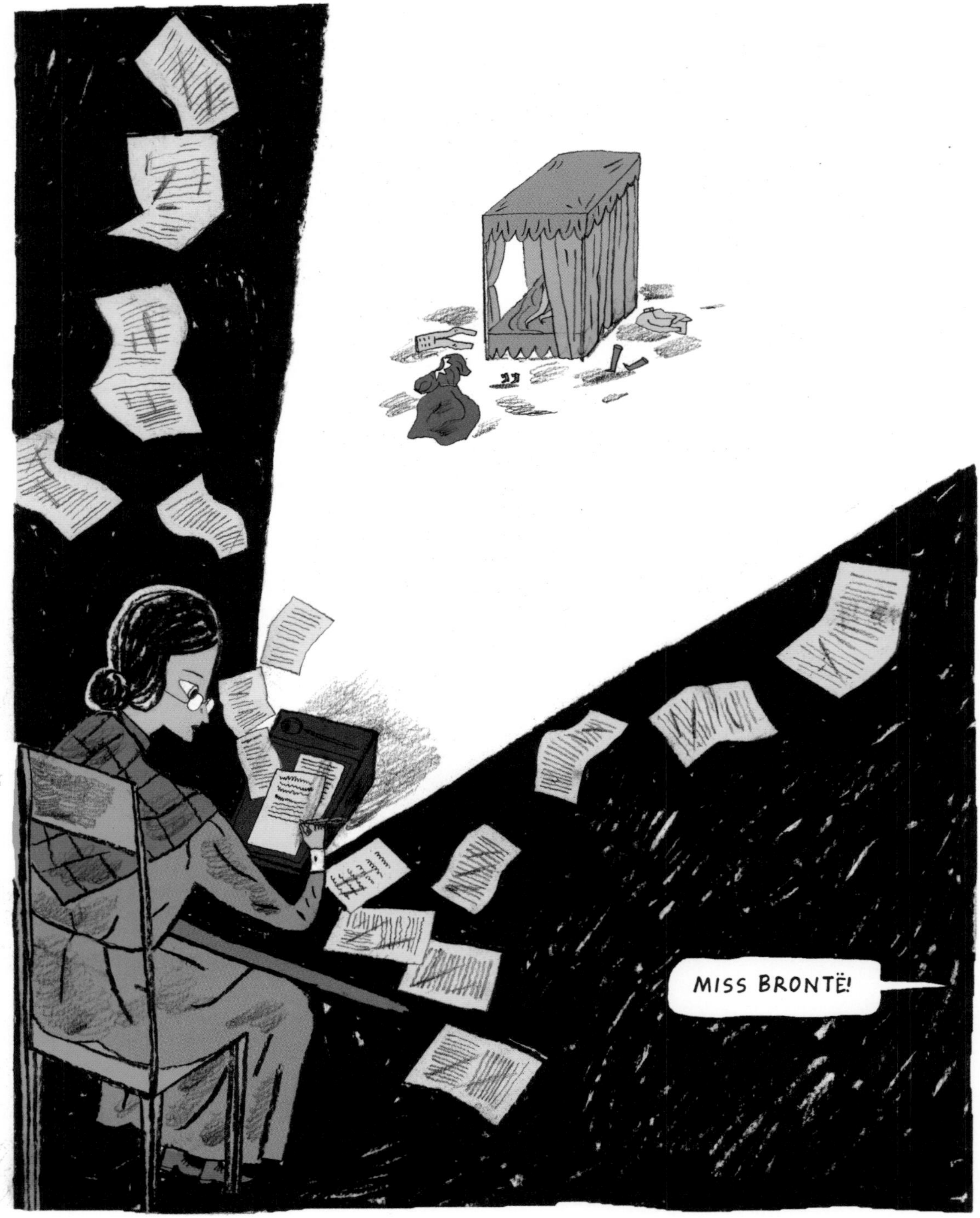
MISS BRONTË!

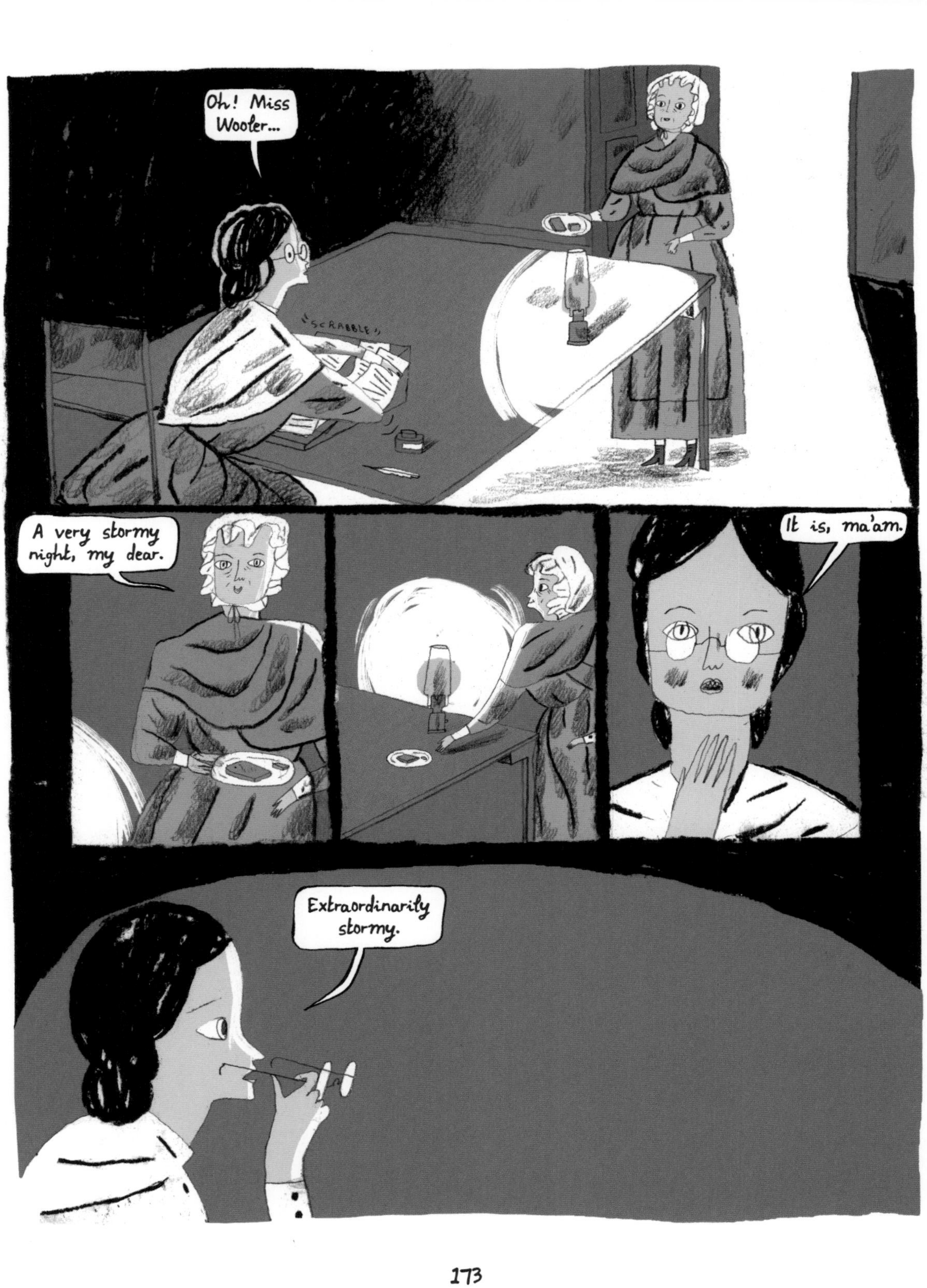
Oh! Miss Wooler...
SCRABBLE
A very stormy night, my dear.
It is, ma'am.
Extraordinarily stormy.

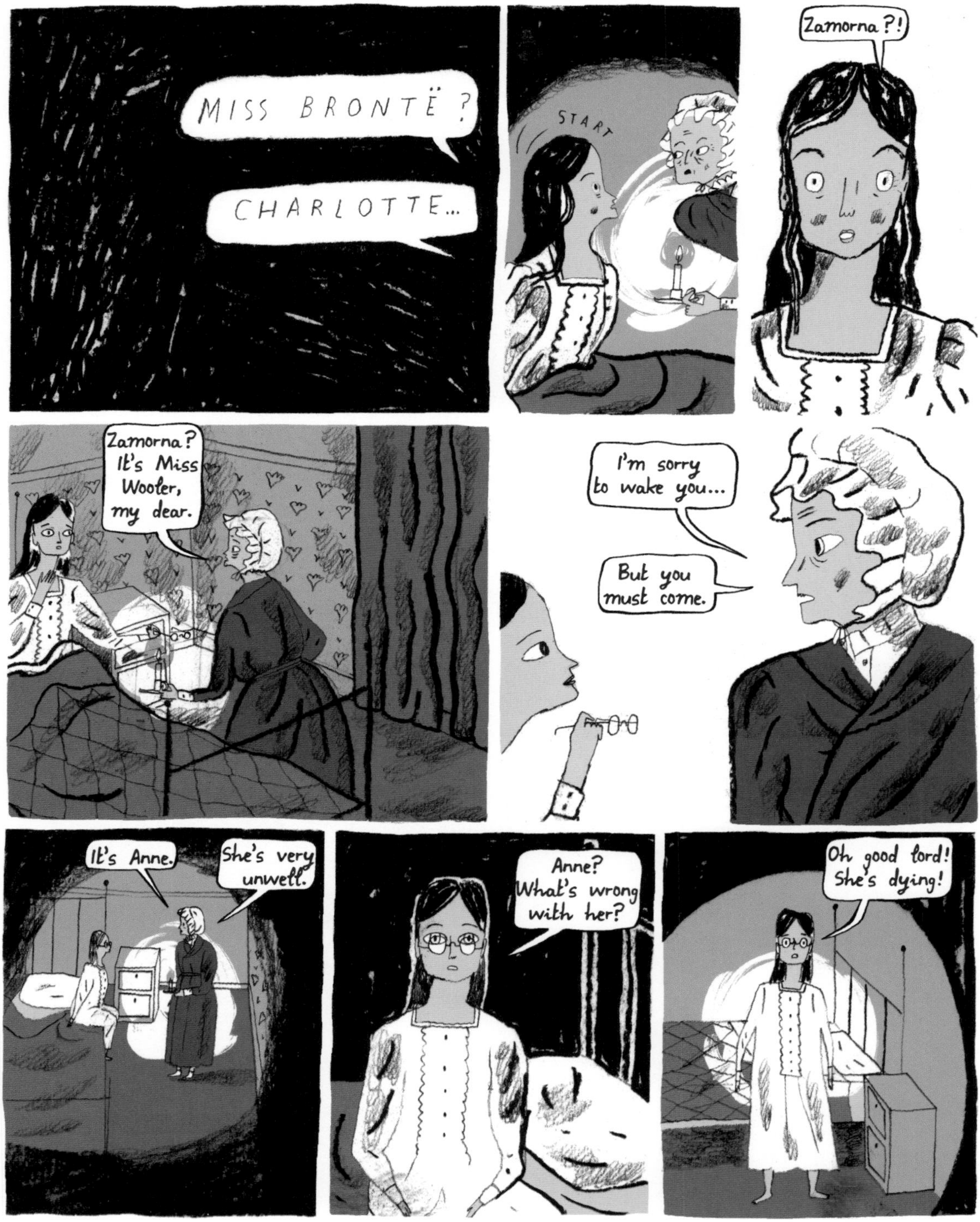
MISS BRONTË ?
CHARLOTTE...
START
Zamorna ?!
Zamorna? It's Miss Wooler, my dear.
I'm sorry to wake you...
But you must come.
It's Anne.
She's very unwell.
Anne? What's wrong with her?
Oh good lord! She's dying!

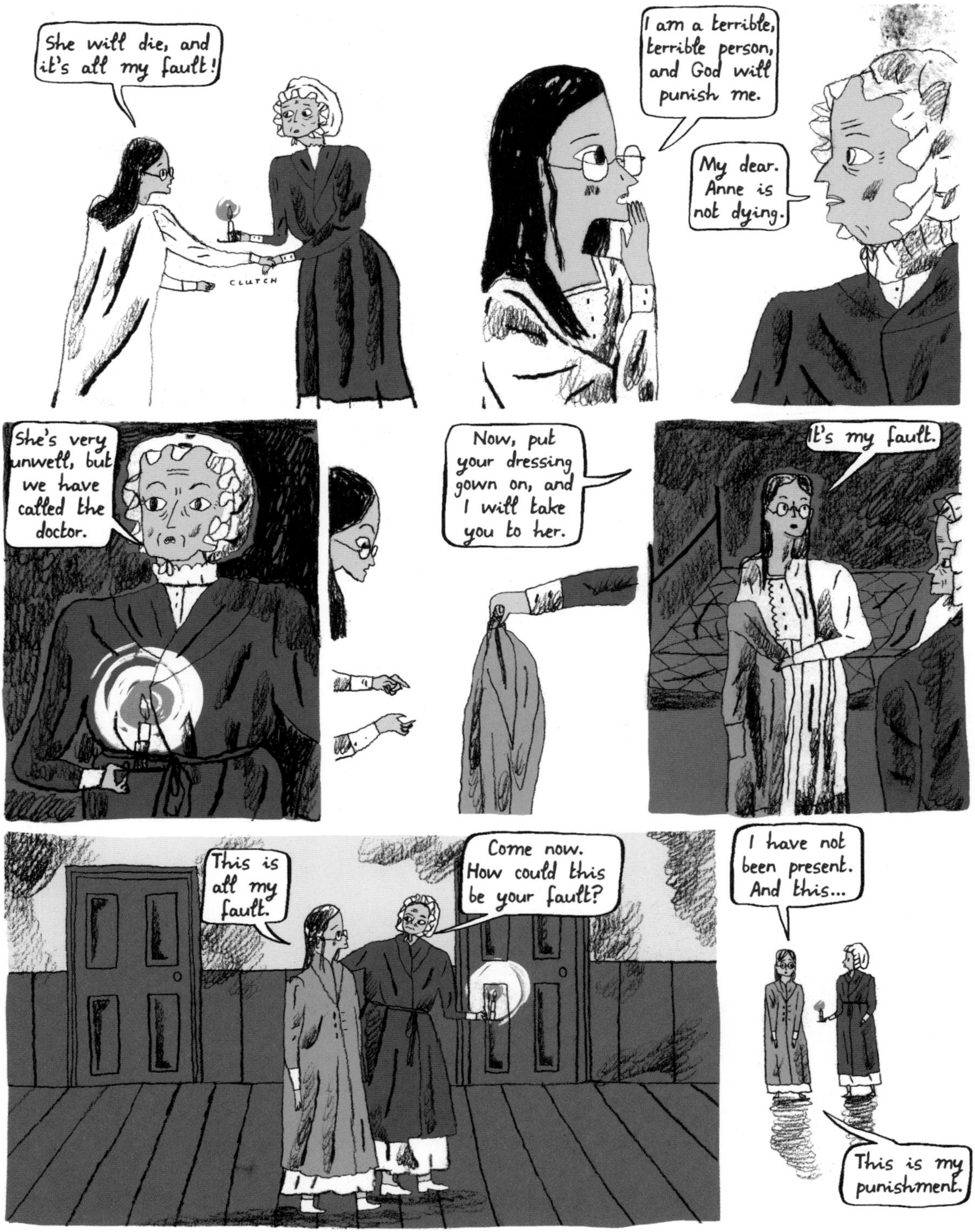
She will die, and it's all my fault!
CLUTCH
I am a terrible, terrible person, and God will punish me.
My dear. Anne is not dying.
She's very unwell, but we have called the doctor.
Now, put your dressing gown on, and I will take you to her.
It's my fault.
This is all my fault.
Come now. How could this be your fault?
I have not been present. And this...
This is my punishment.

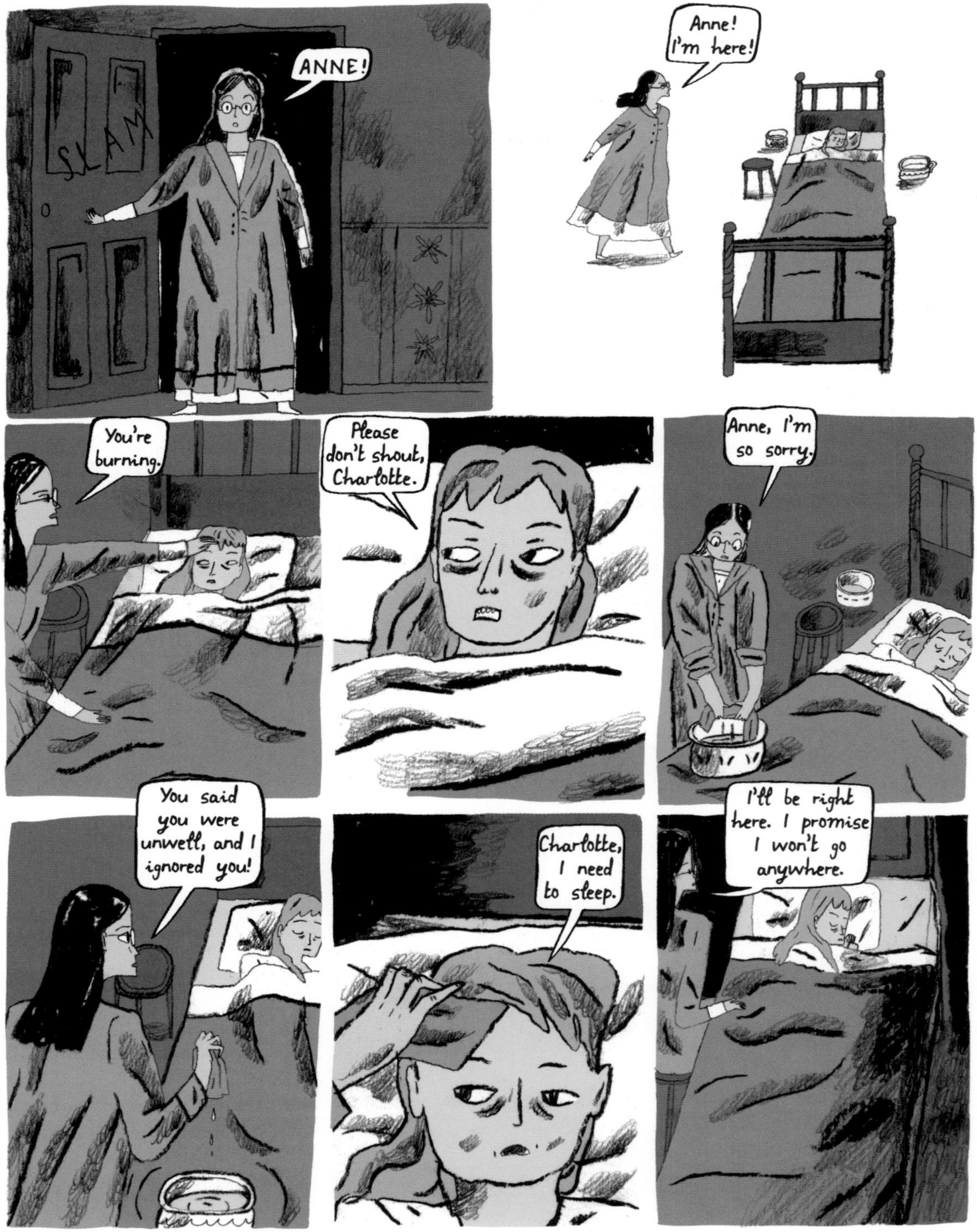
ANNE!
SLAM
Anne! I'm here!
You're burning.
Please don't shout, Charlotte.
Anne, I'm so sorry.
You said you were unwell, and I ignored you!
Charlotte, I need to sleep.
I'll be right here. I promise I won't go anywhere.

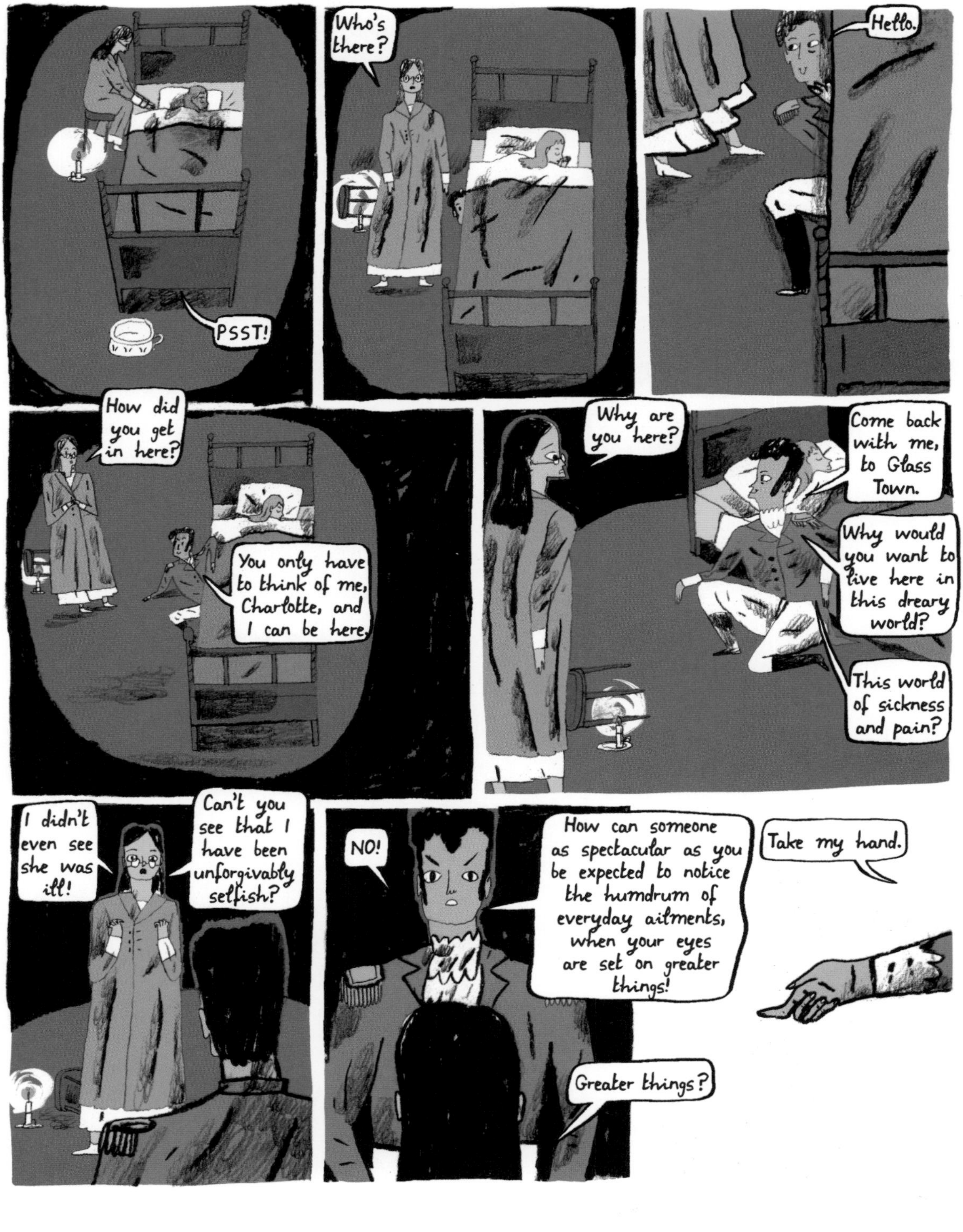
PSST!
Who's there?
Hello.
How did you get in here?
You only have to think of me, Charlotte, and I can be here.
Why are you here?
Come back with me, to Glass Town.
Why would you want to live here in this dreary world?
This world of sickness and pain?
I didn't even see she was ill!
Can't you see that I have been unforgivably selfish?
NO!
How can someone as spectacular as you be expected to notice the humdrum of everyday ailments, when your eyes are set on greater things!
Greater things?
Take my hand.

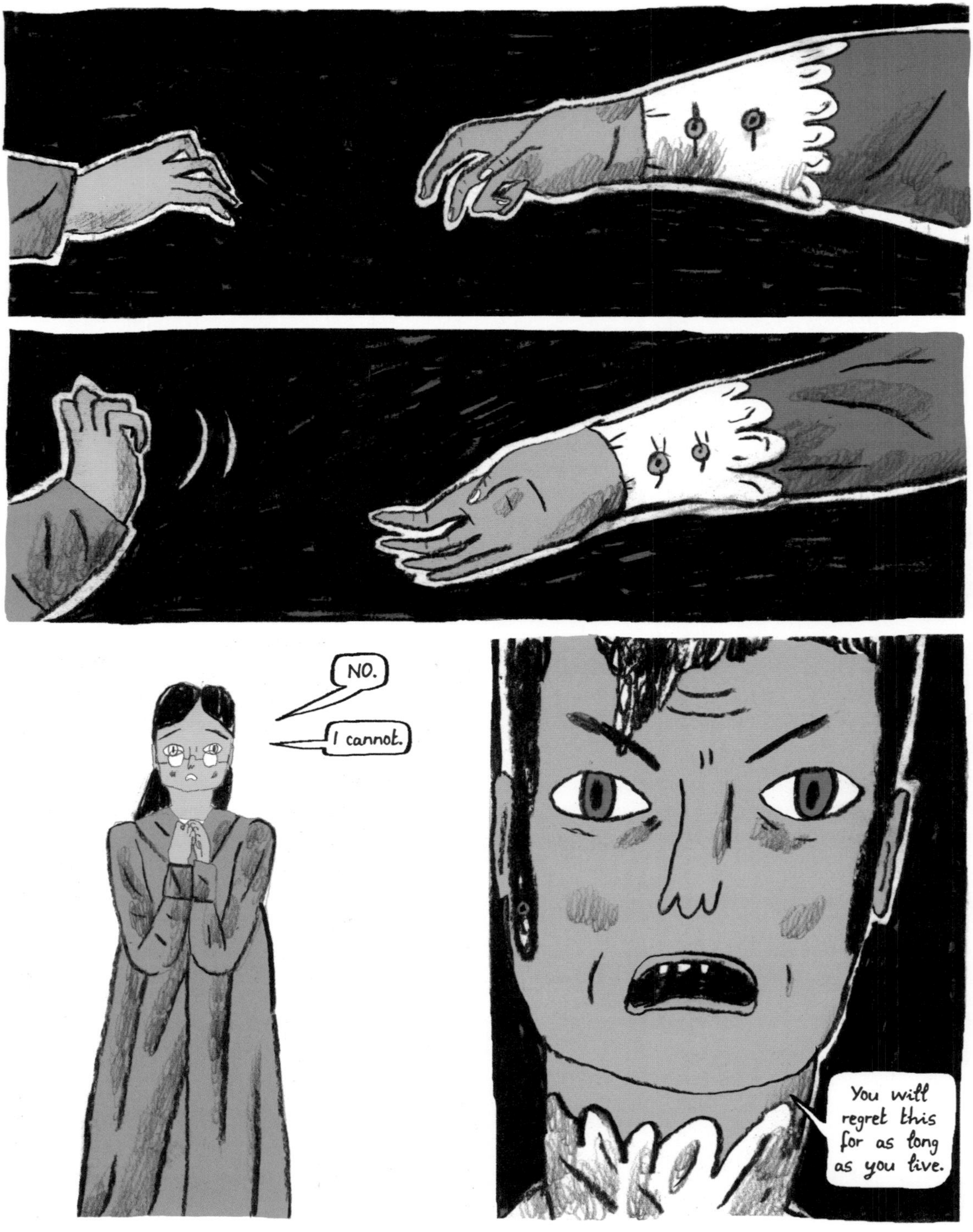
NO.
I cannot.
You will regret this for as long as you live.

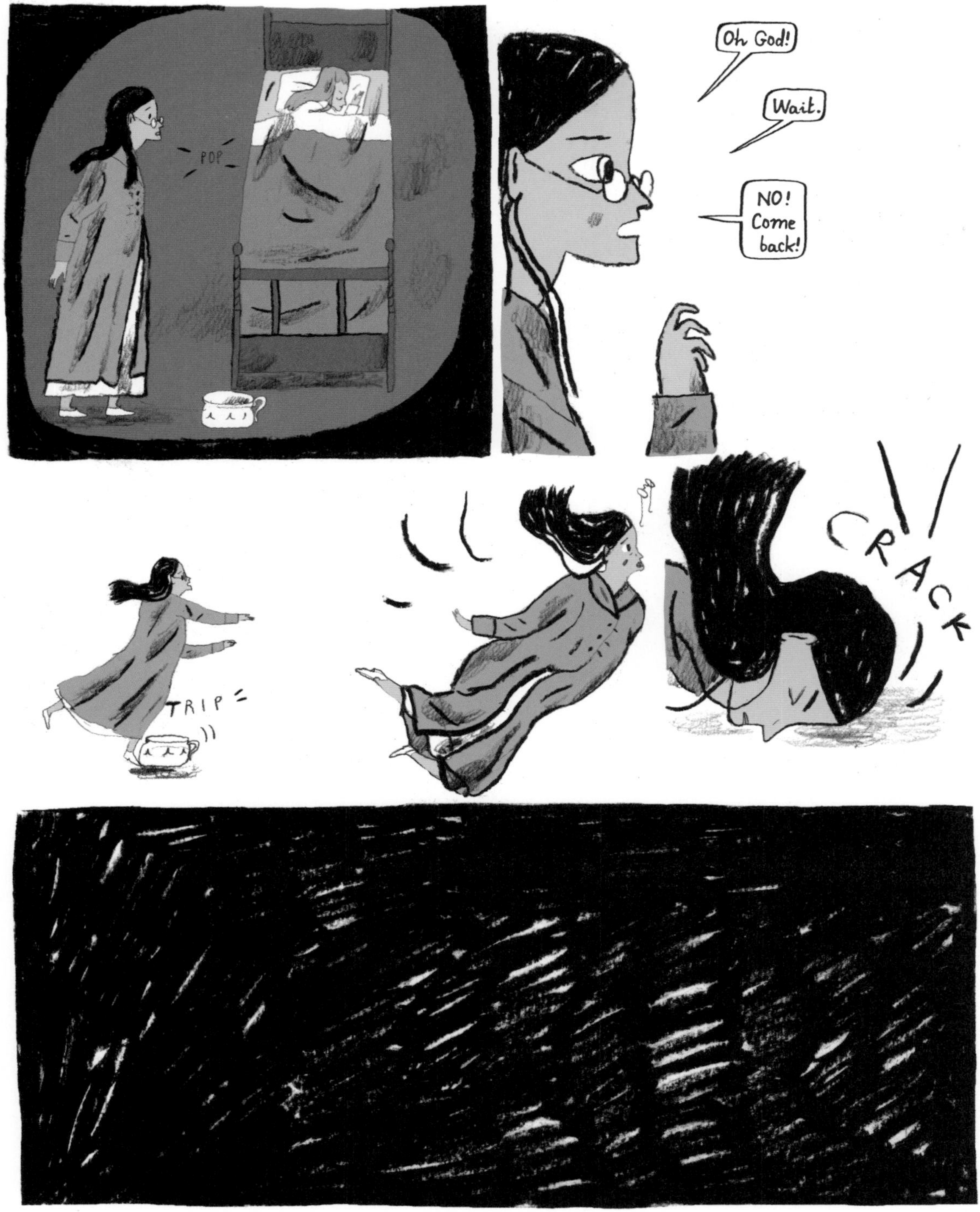
POP
Oh God!
Wait.
NO! Come back!
TRIP
CRACK

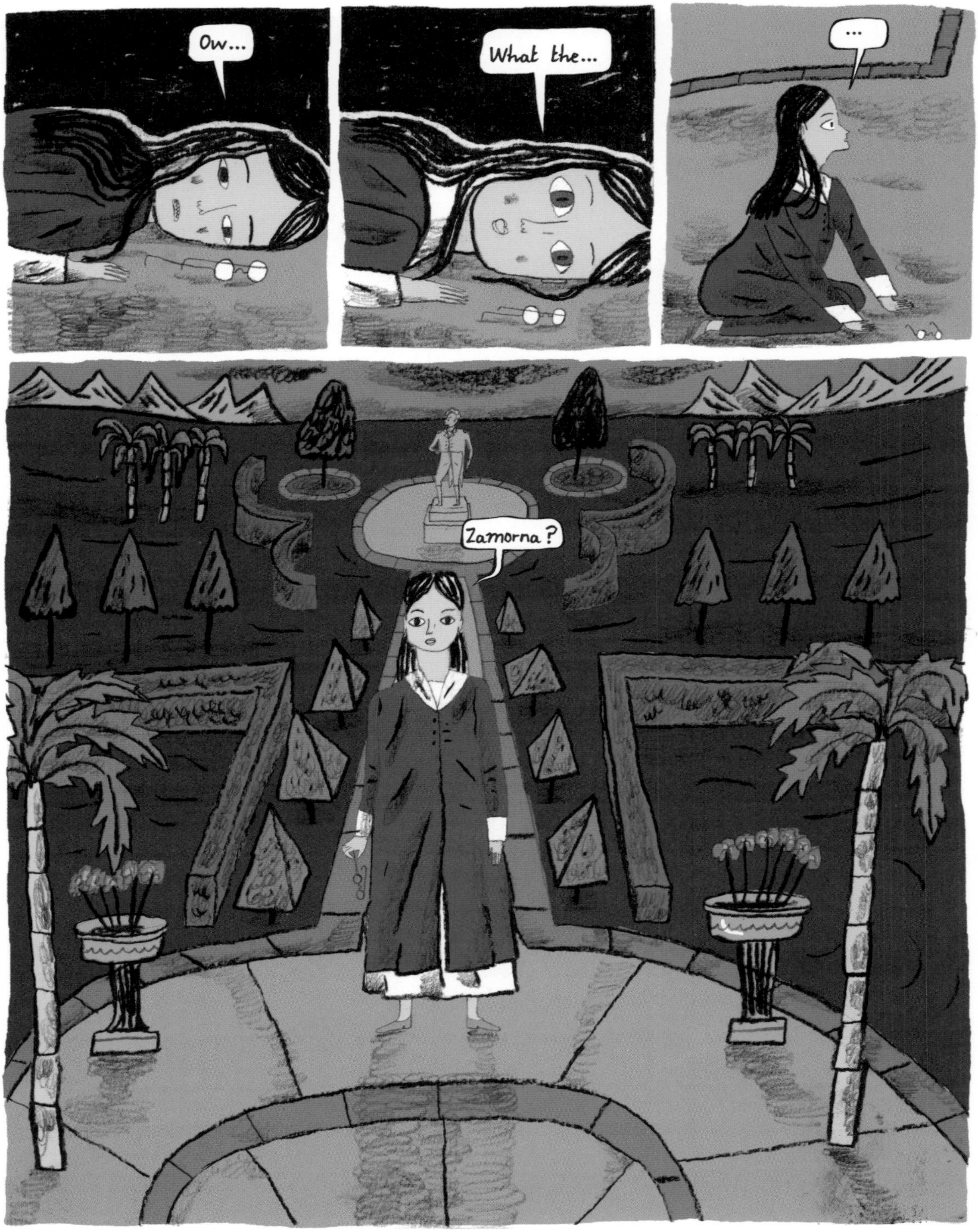
Ow...
What the...
...
Zamorna?

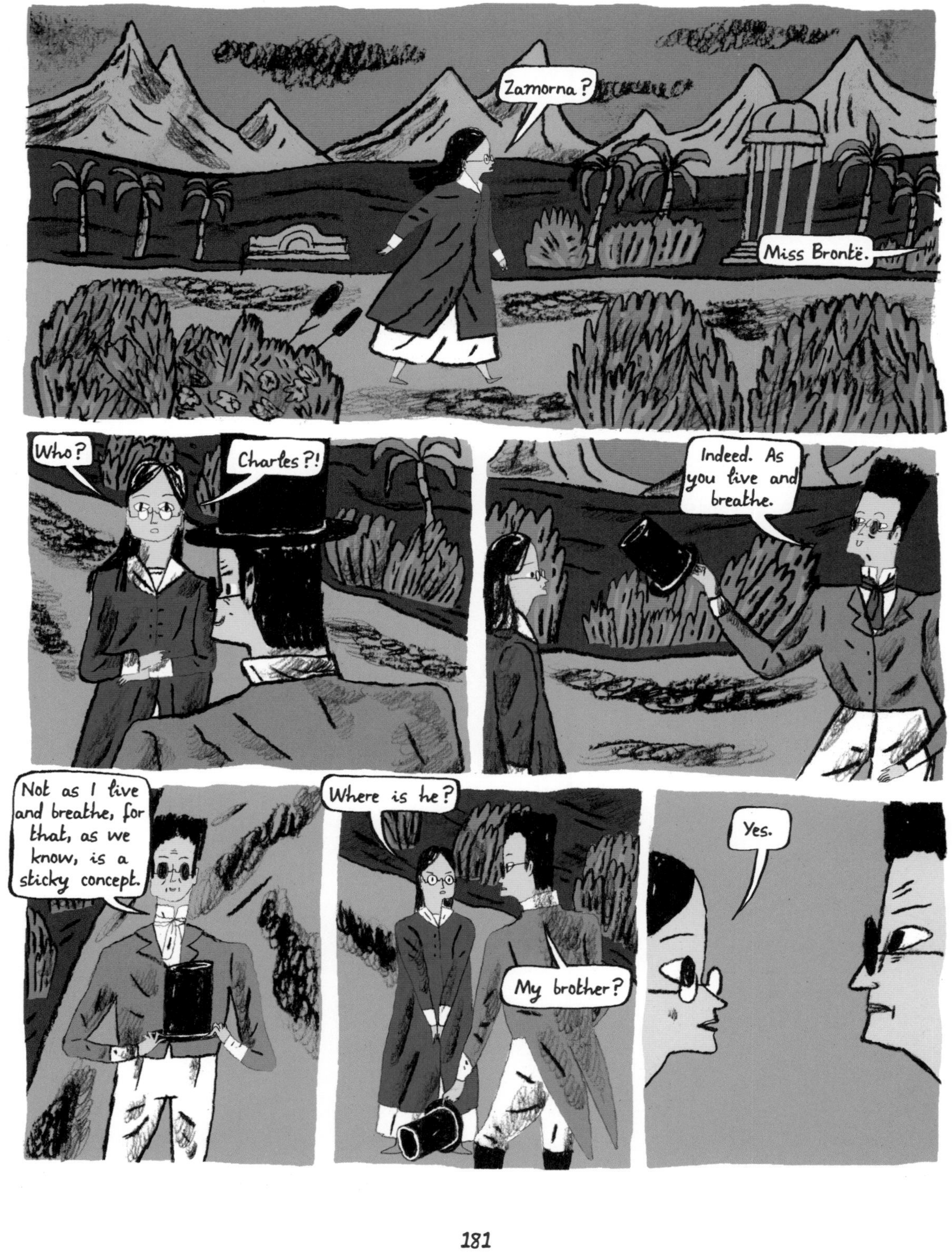
Zamorna?
Miss Brontë.
Who?
Charles?!
Indeed. As you live and breathe.
Not as I live and breathe, for that, as we know, is a sticky concept.
Where is he?
My brother?
Yes.

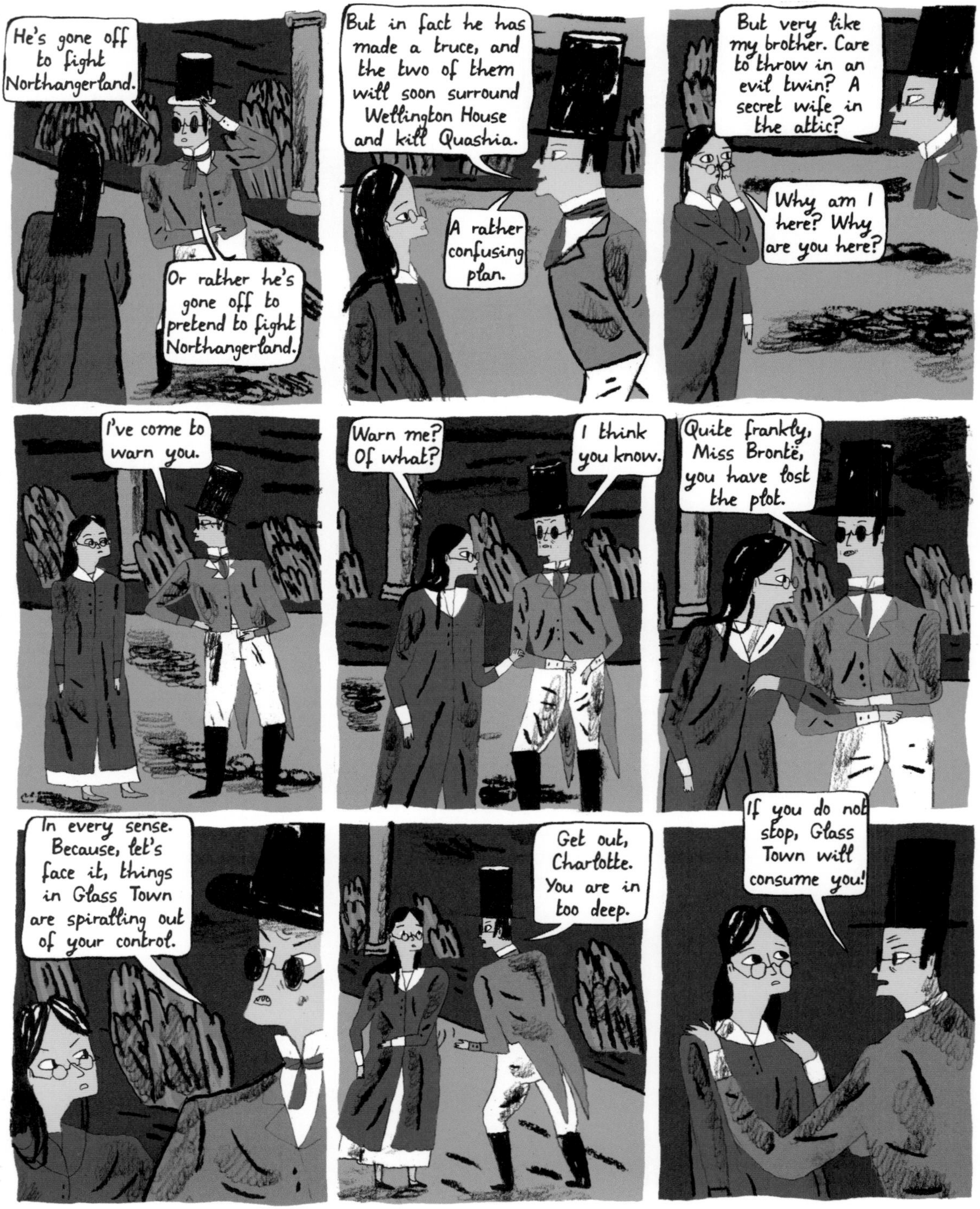
He's gone off to fight Northangerland.
Or rather he's gone off to pretend to fight Northangerland.
But in fact he has made a truce, and the two of them will soon surround Wellington House and kill Quashia.
A rather confusing plan.
But very like my brother. Care to throw in an evil twin? A secret wife in the attic?
Why am I here? Why are you here?
I've come to warn you.
Warn me? Of what?
I think you know.
Quite frankly, Miss Brontë, you have lost the plot.
In every sense. Because, let's face it, things in Glass Town are spiralling out of your control.
Get out, Charlotte. You are in too deep.
If you do not stop, Glass Town will consume you!

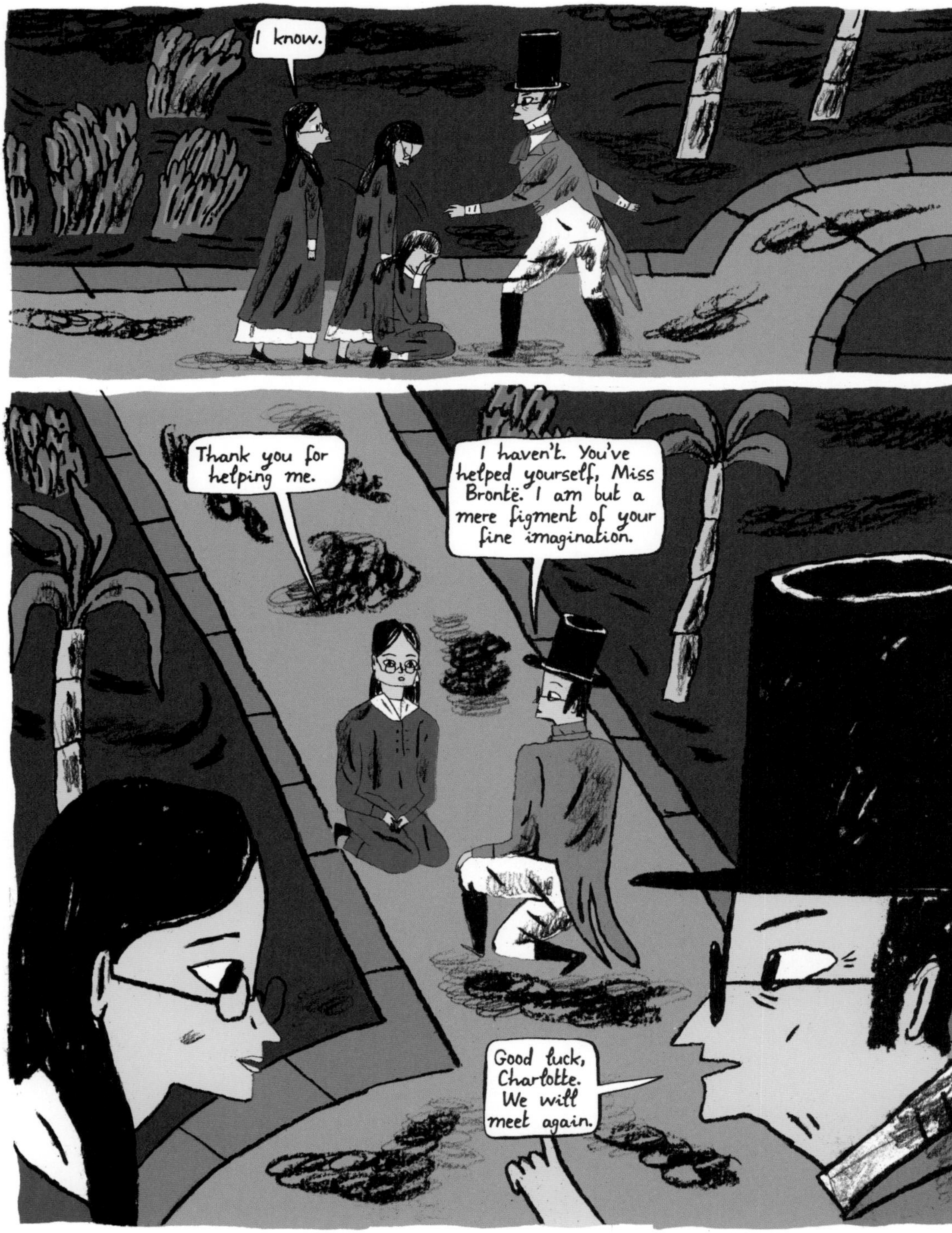
I know.
Thank you for helping me.
I haven't. You've helped yourself, Miss Brontë. I am but a mere figment of your fine imagination.
Good luck, Charlotte. We will meet again.

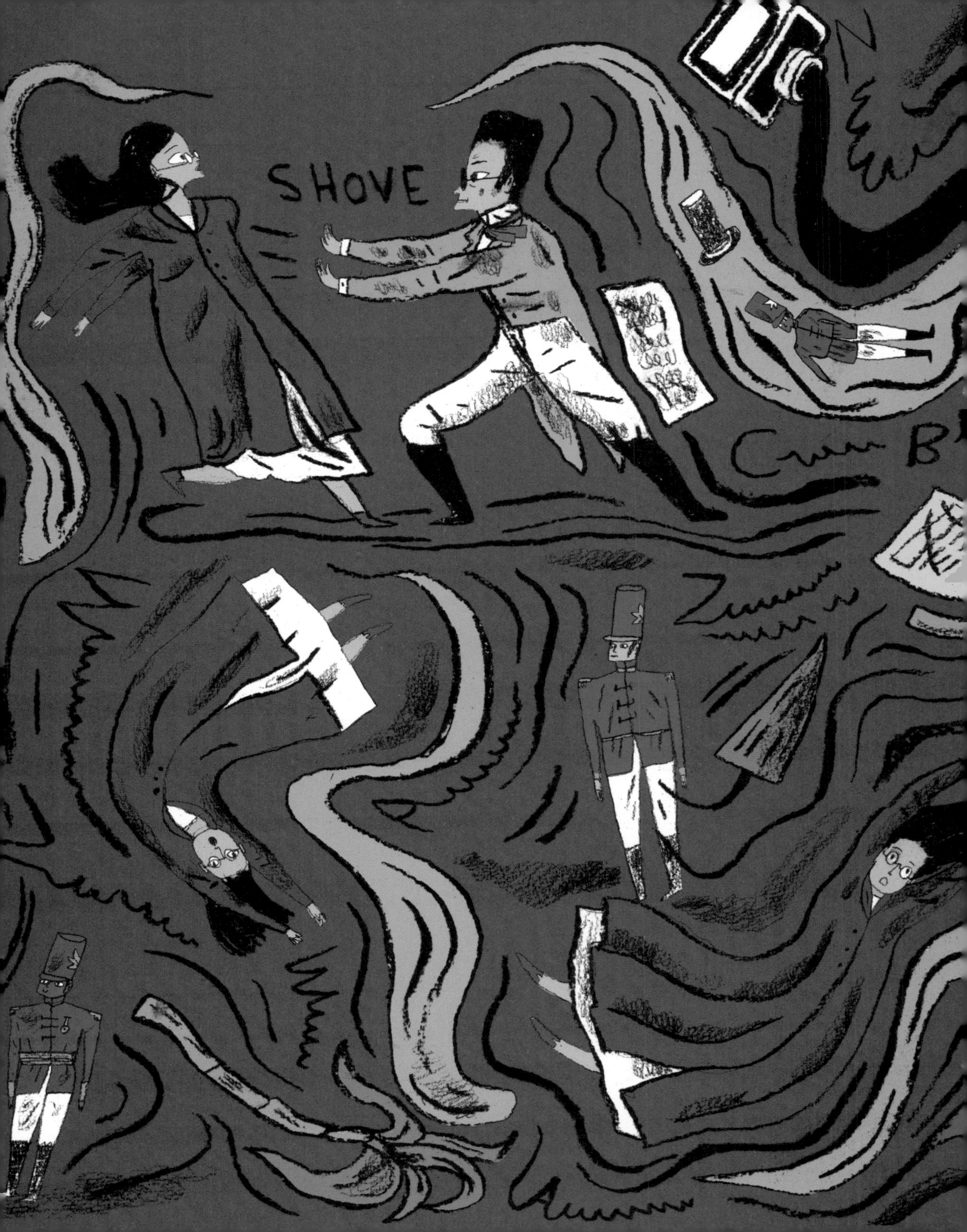
SHOVE

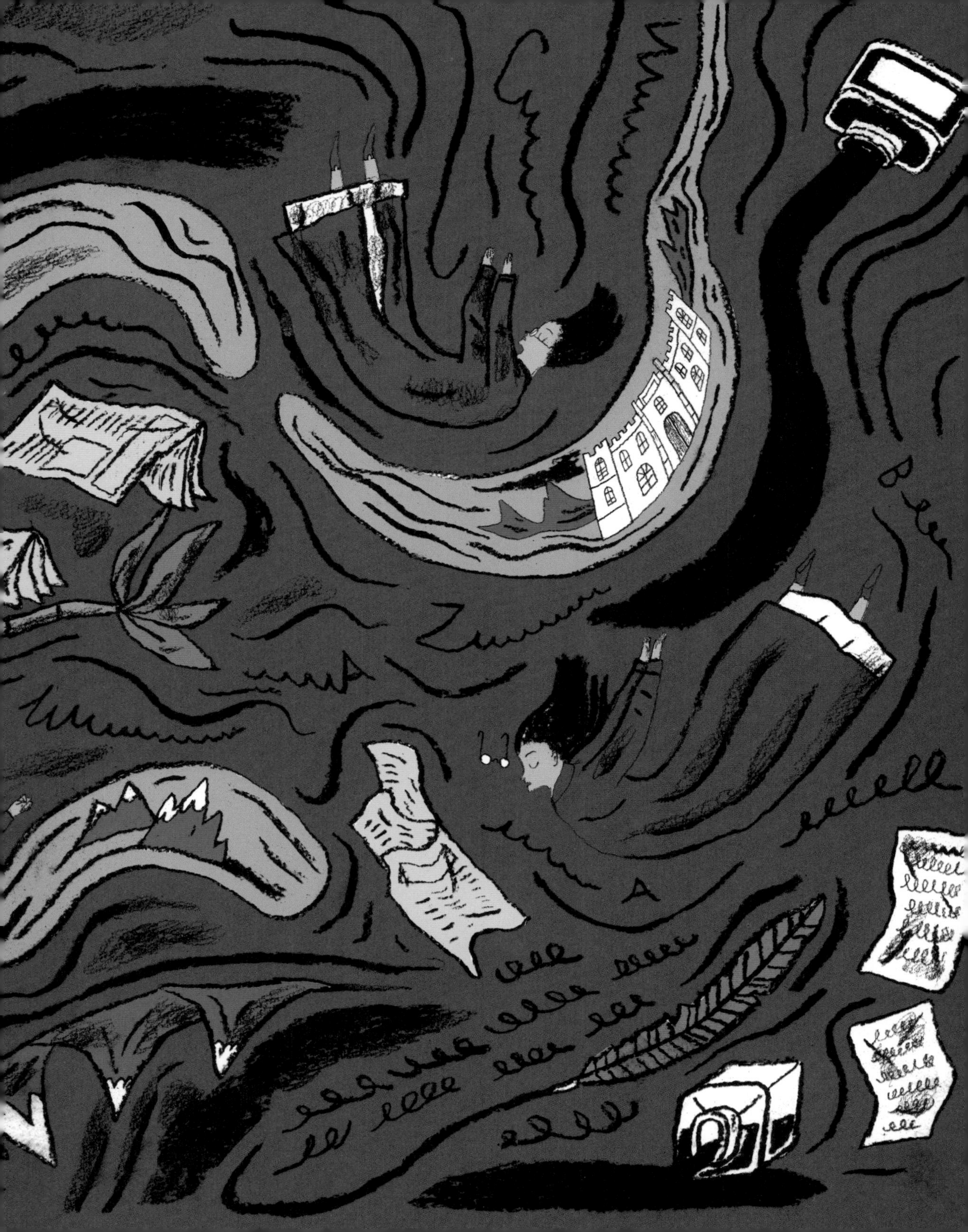

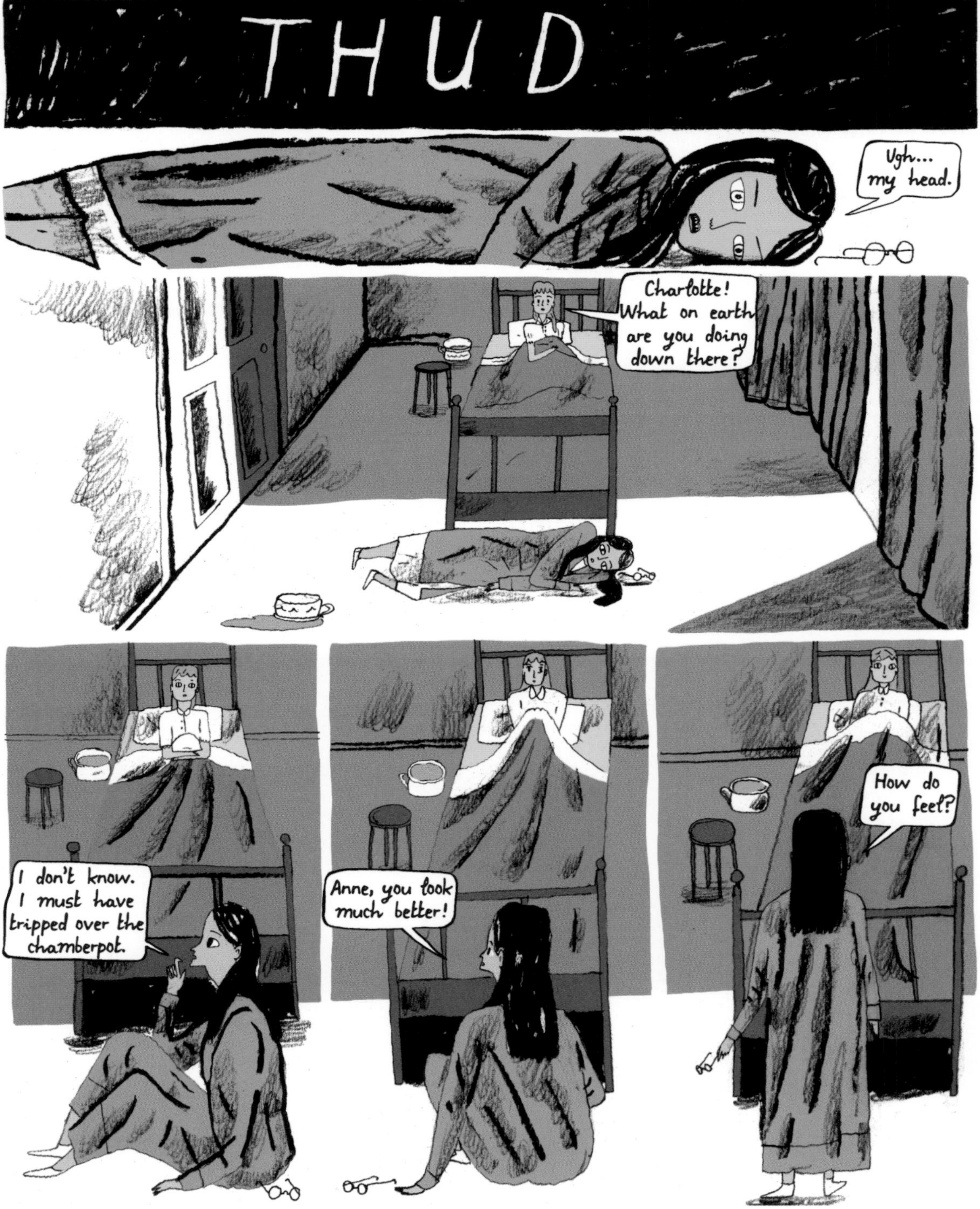
THUD
Ugh... my head.
Charlotte! What on earth are you doing down there?
I don't know. I must have tripped over the chamberpot.
Anne, you look much better!
How do you feel?

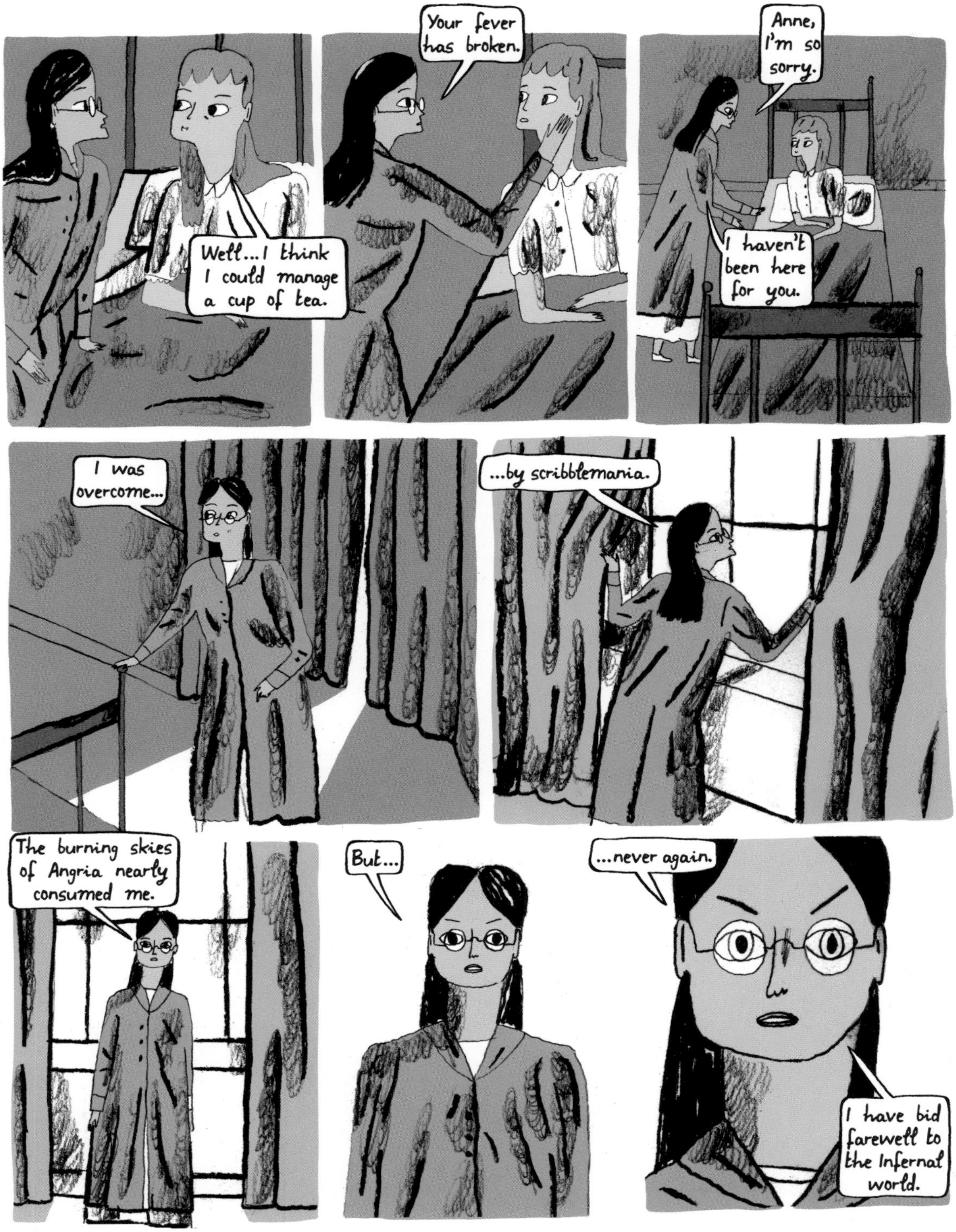
Well...I think I could manage a cup of tea.
Your fever has broken.
Anne, I'm so sorry.
I haven't been here for you.
I was overcome...
...by scribblemania.
The burning skies of Angria nearly consumed me.
But...
...never again.
I have bid farewell to the Infernal world.

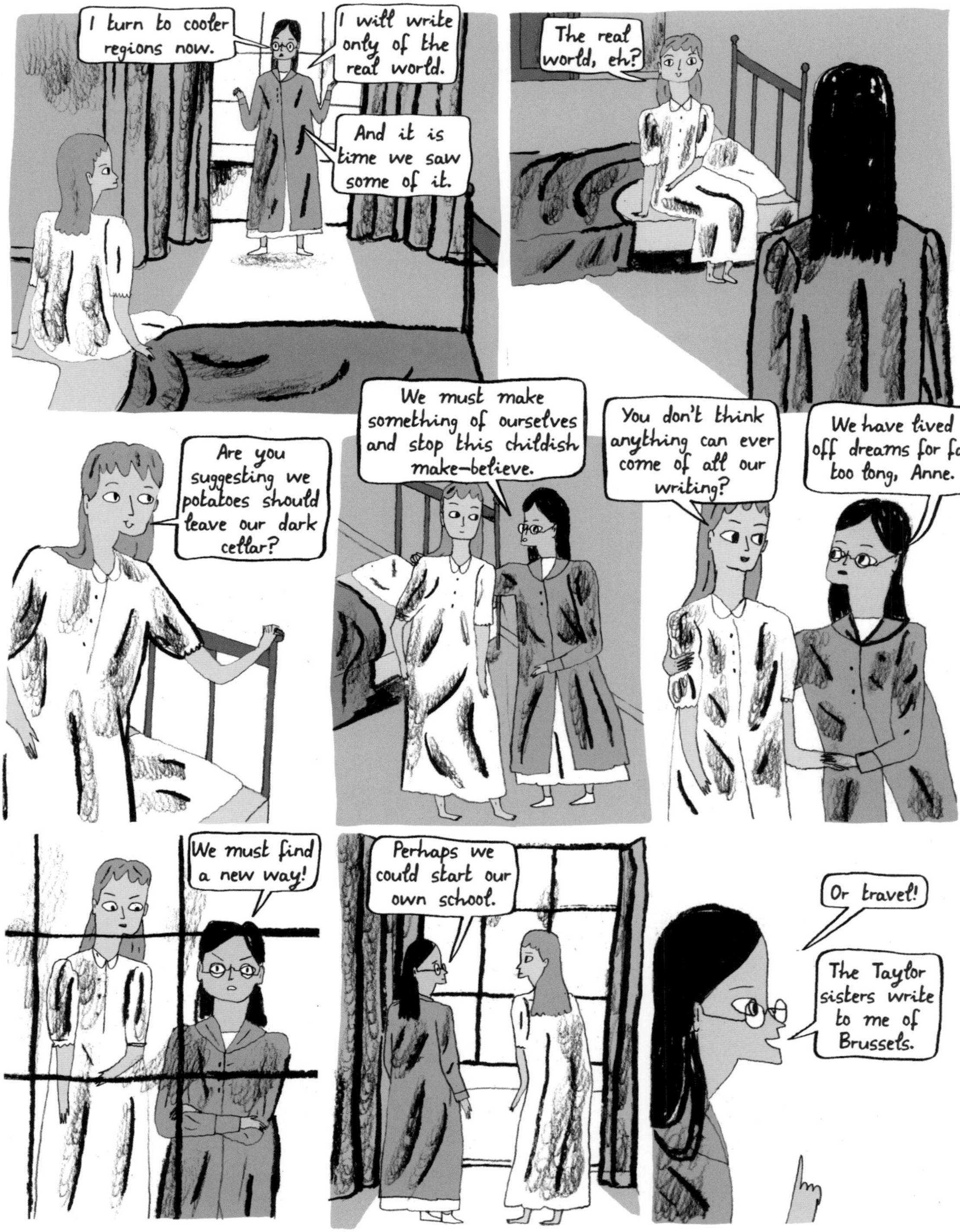
I turn to cooler regions now.
I will write only of the real world.
And it is time we saw some of it.
The real world, eh?
Are you suggesting we potatoes should leave our dark cellar?
We must make something of ourselves and stop this childish make-believe.
You don't think anything can ever come of all our writing?
We have lived off dreams for far too long, Anne.
We must find a new way!
Perhaps we could start our own school.
Or travel!
The Taylor sisters write to me of Brussels.

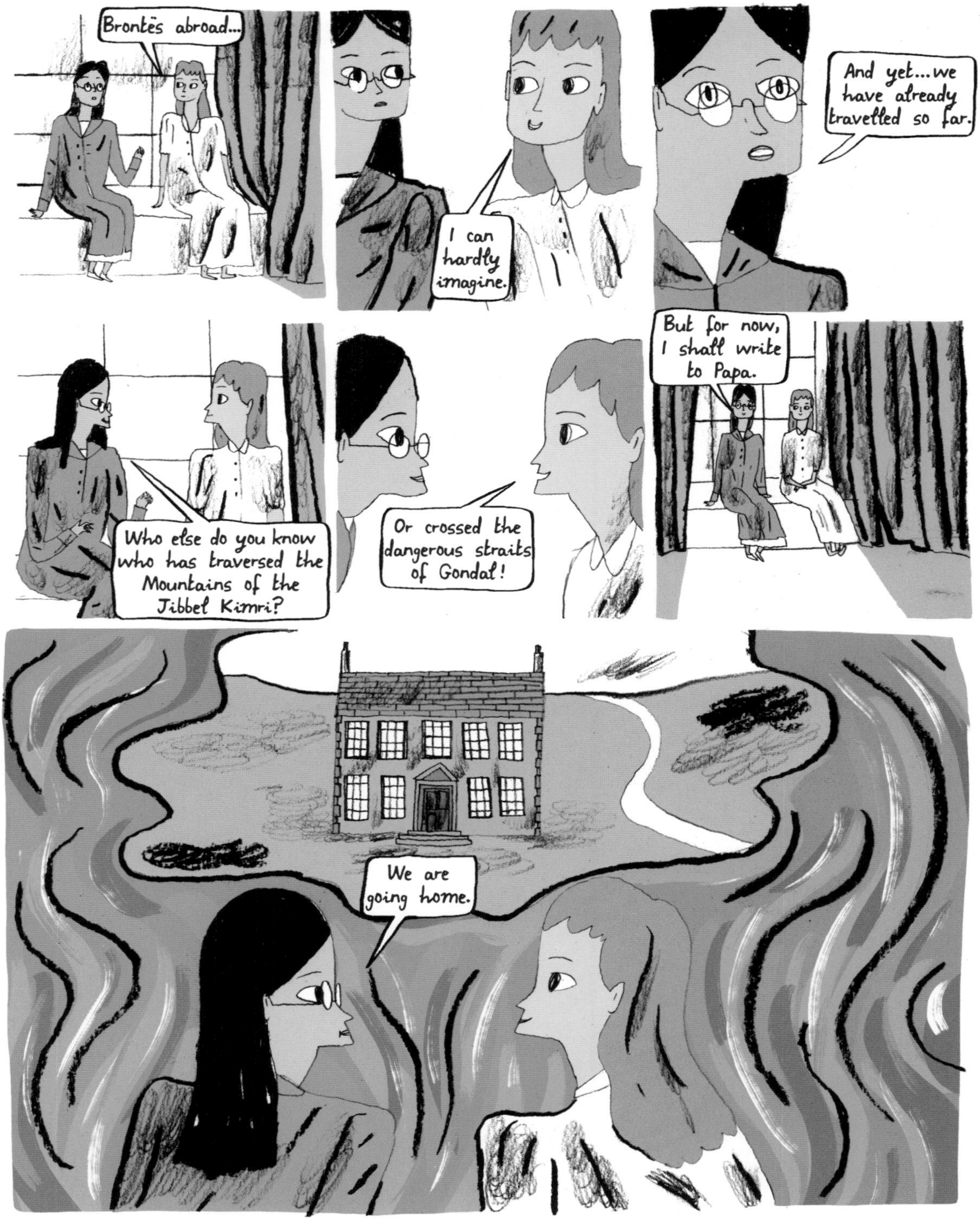
Brontës abroad...
I can hardly imagine.
And yet...we have already travelled so far.
Who else do you know who has traversed the Mountains of the Jibbel Kimri?
Or crossed the dangerous straits of Gondal!
But for now, I shall write to Papa.
We are going home.

CHAPTER
FOUR

1847

Farewell to Glass Town

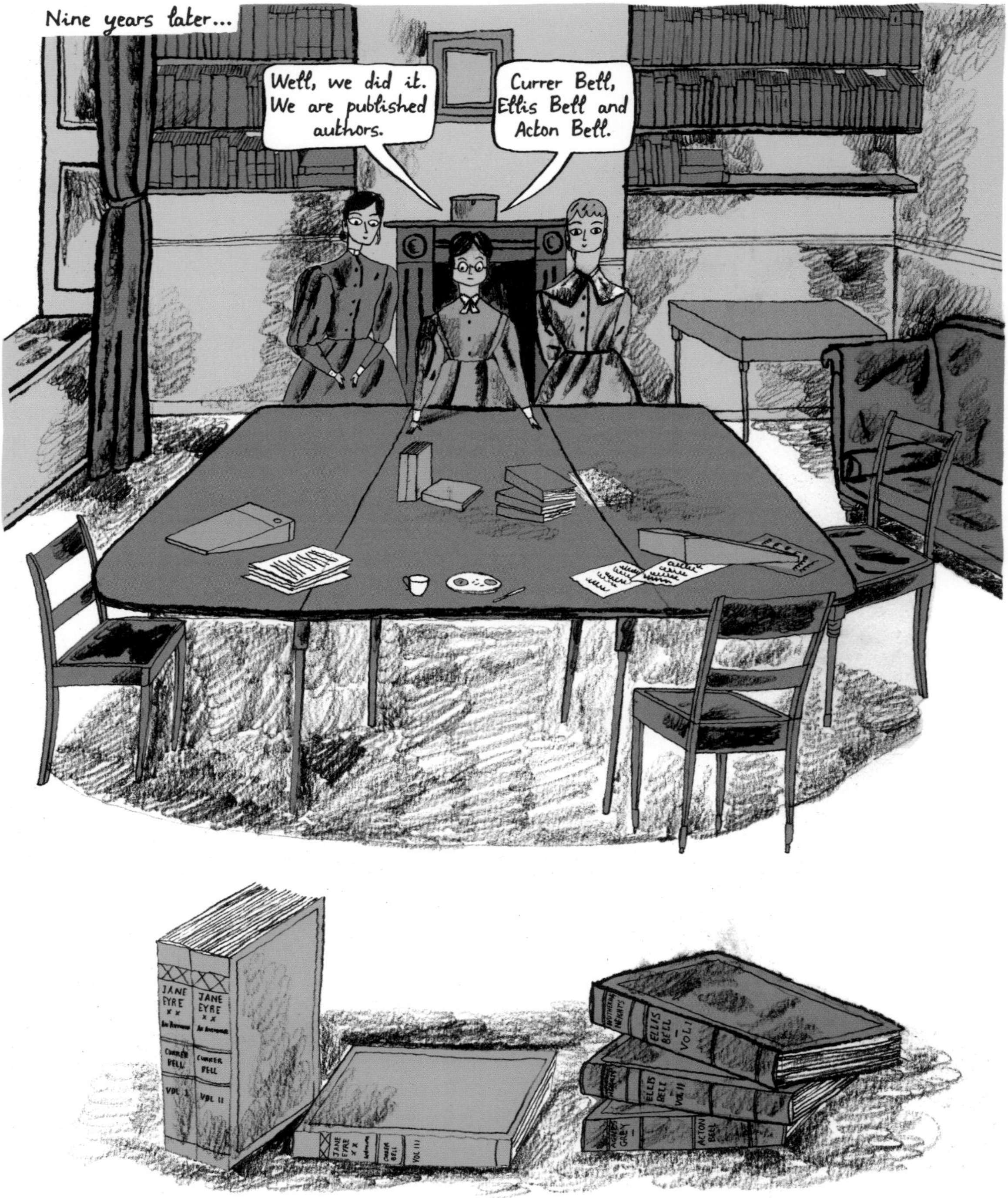
Nine years later...
Well, we did it. We are published authors.
Currer Bell, Ellis Bell and Acton Bell.
JANE EYRE
CURRER BELL
VOL II
ELLIS BELL VOL I
ELLIS BELL VOL II
ACTON BELL

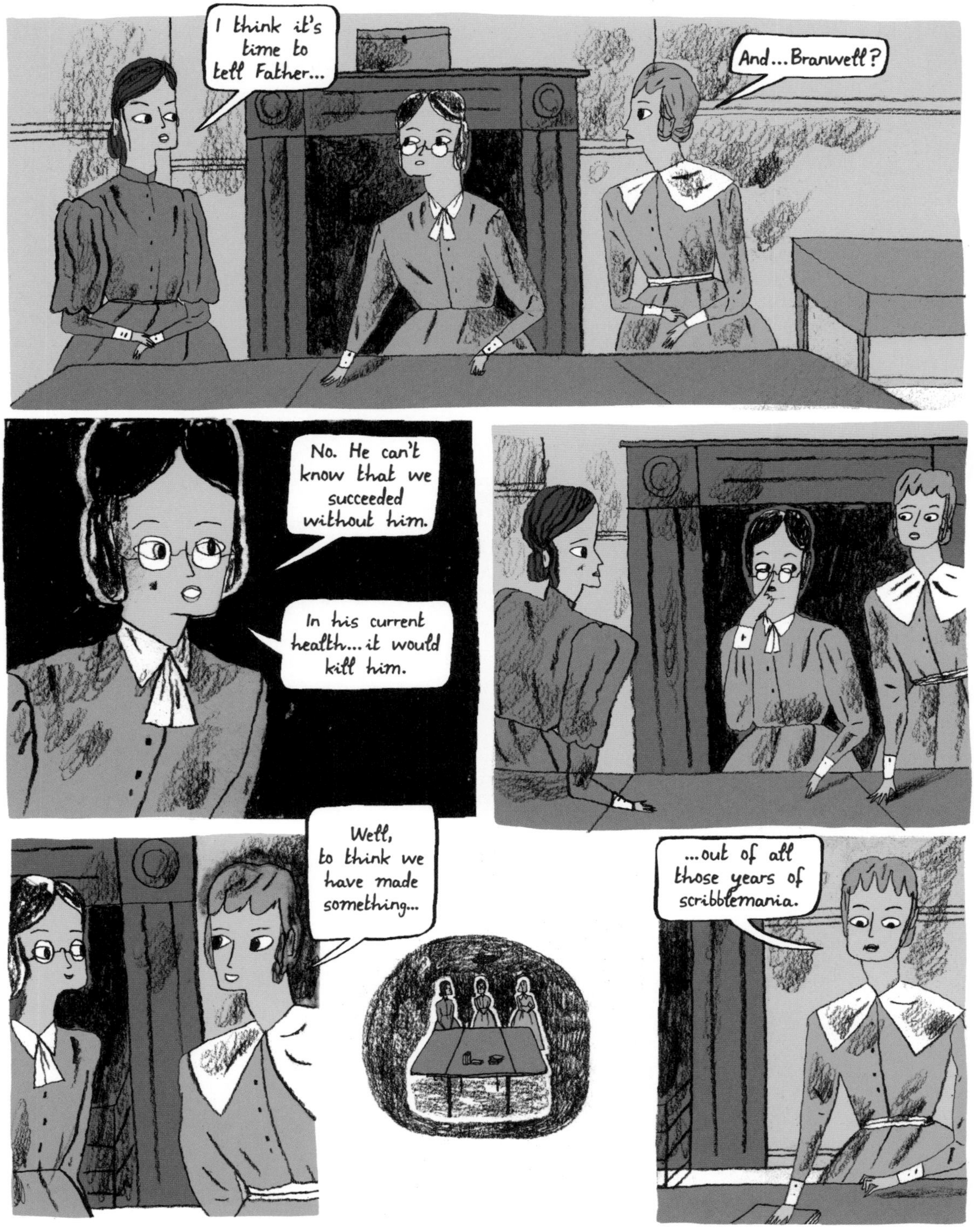
I think it's time to tell Father...
And...Branwell?
No. He can't know that we succeeded without him.
In his current health... it would kill him.
Well, to think we have made something...
...out of all those years of scribblemania.

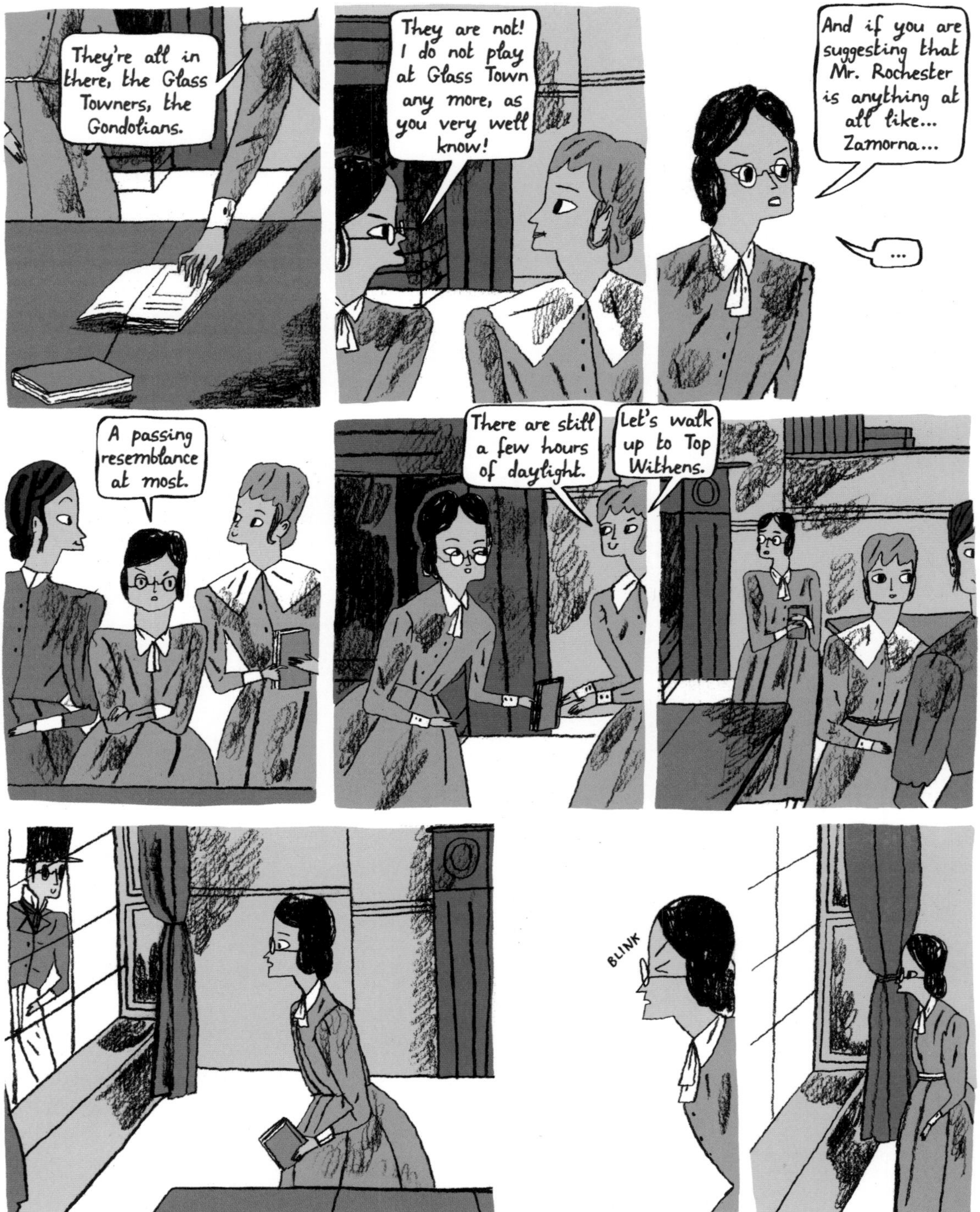
They're all in there, the Glass Towners, the Gondolians.
They are not! I do not play at Glass Town any more, as you very well know!
And if you are suggesting that Mr. Rochester is anything at all like... Zamorna...
...
A passing resemblance at most.
There are still a few hours of daylight.
Let's walk up to Top Withens.
BLINK

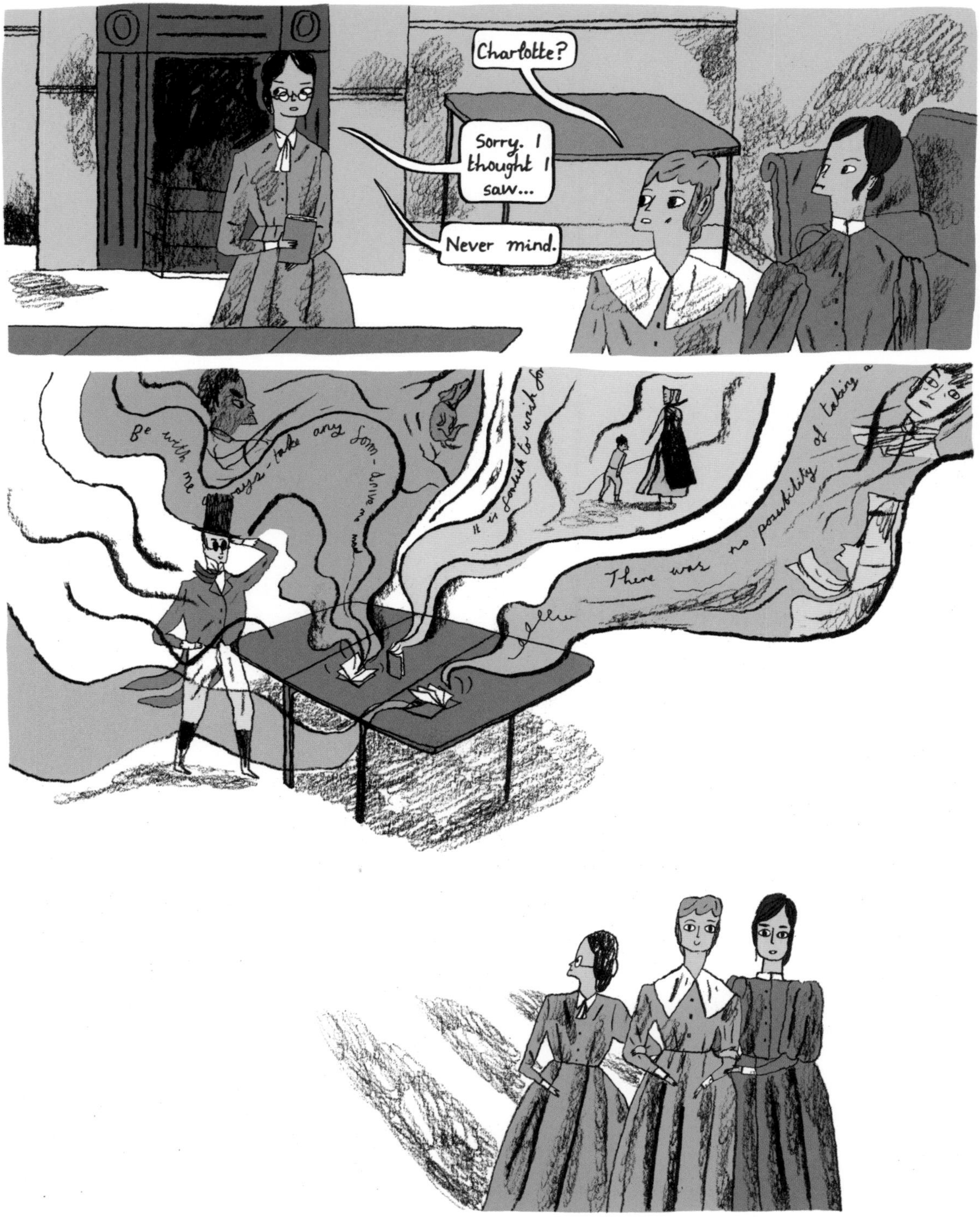
Charlotte?
Sorry. I thought I saw...
Never mind.
Be with me
take any form - drive me mad
It is foolish to wish
There was no possibility of taking

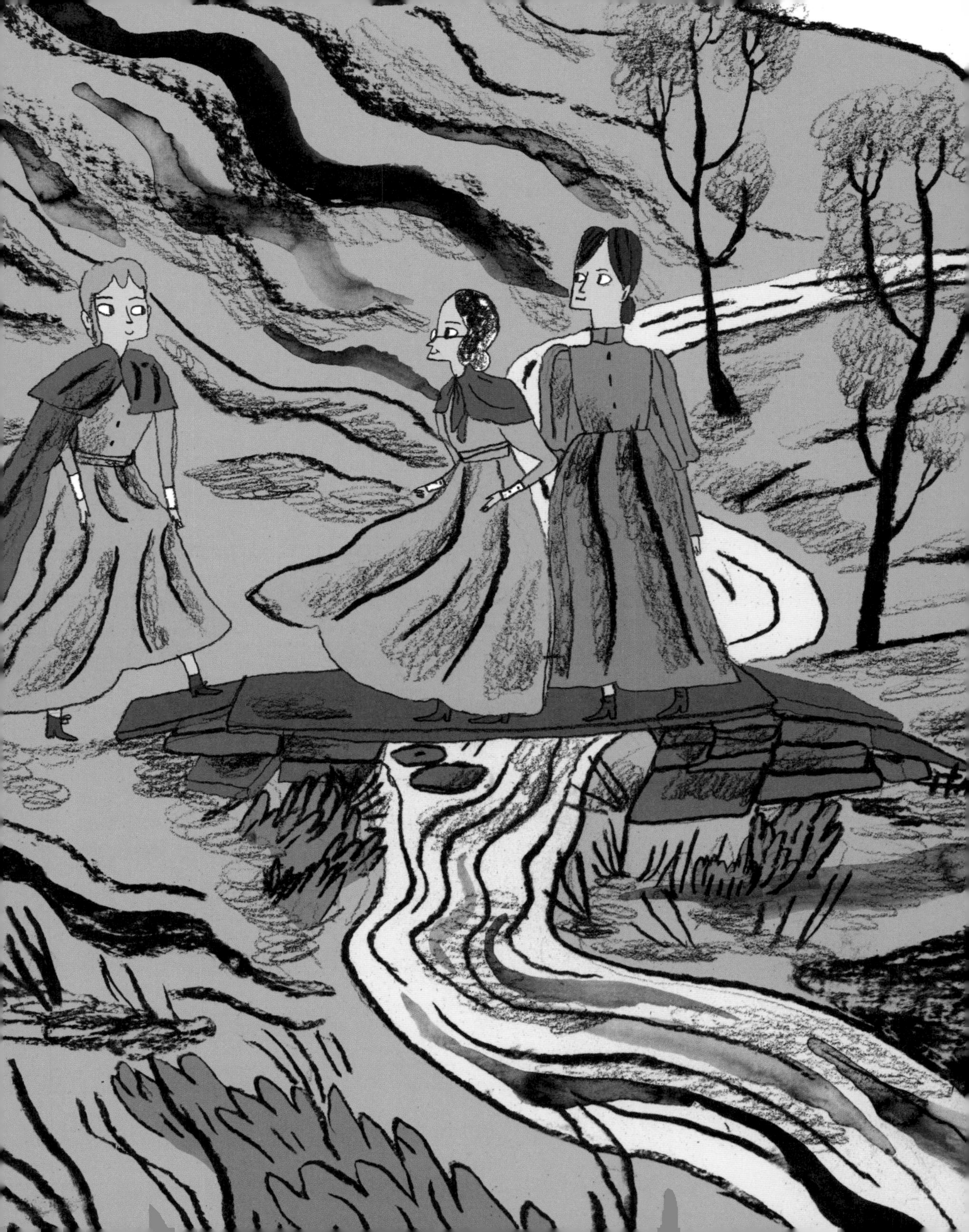

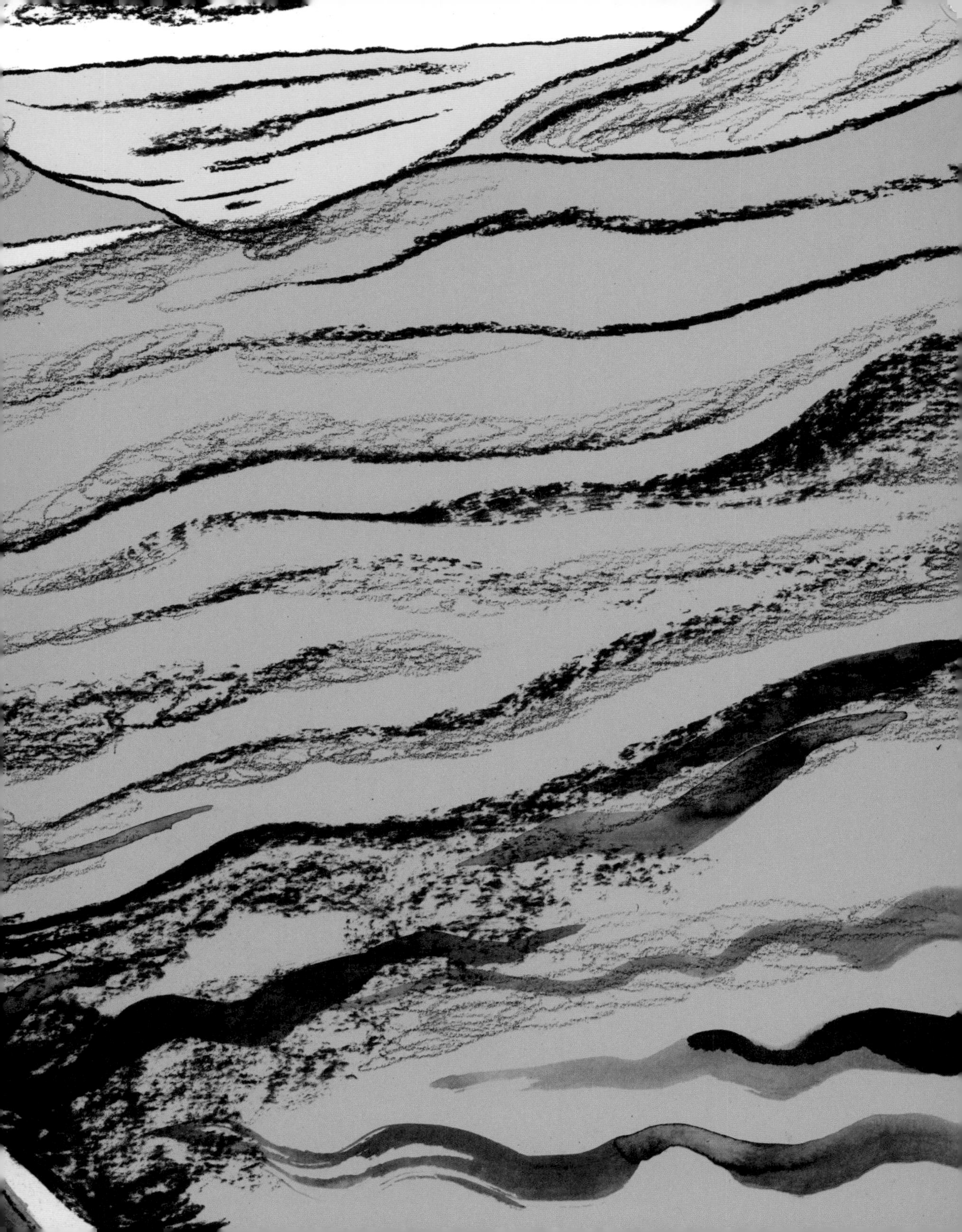

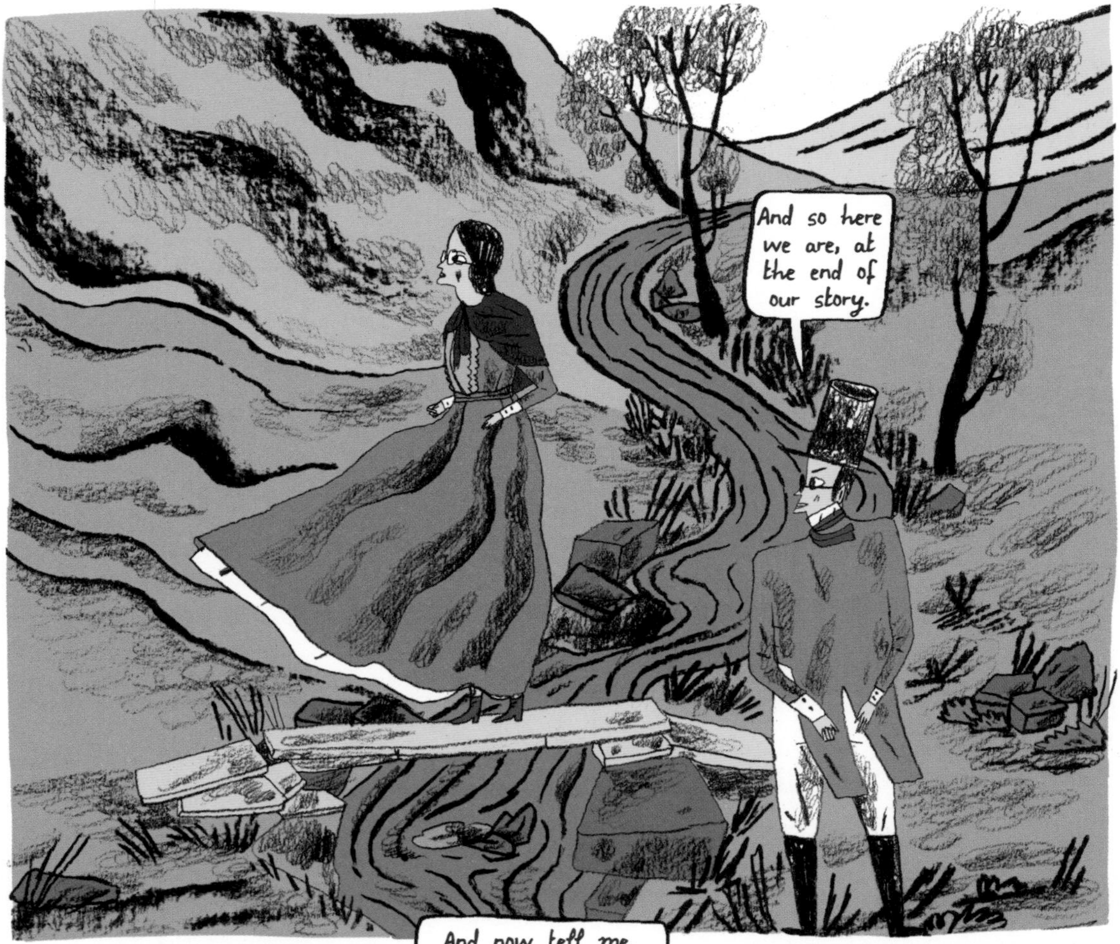
And so here we are, at the end of our story.

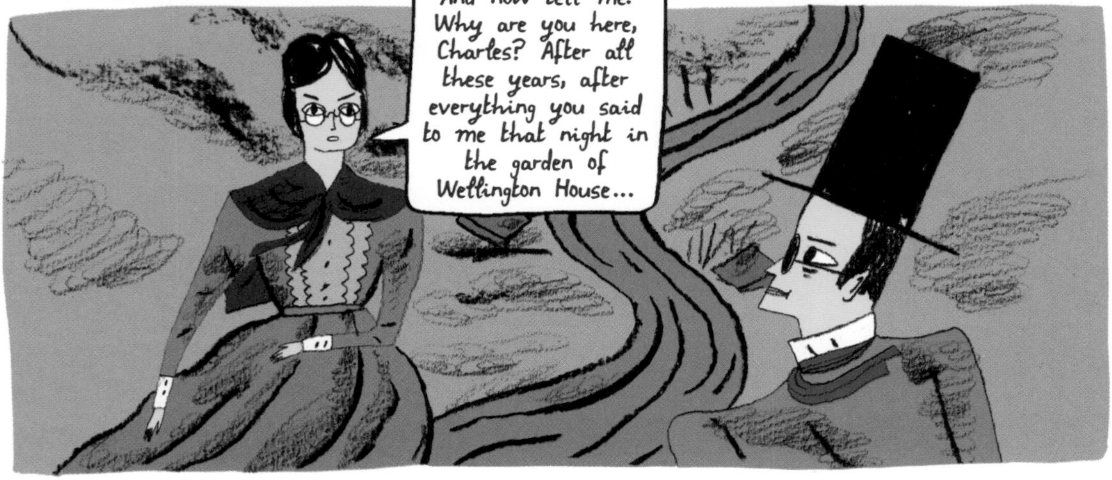
And now tell me. Why are you here, Charles? After all these years, after everything you said to me that night in the garden of Wellington House...

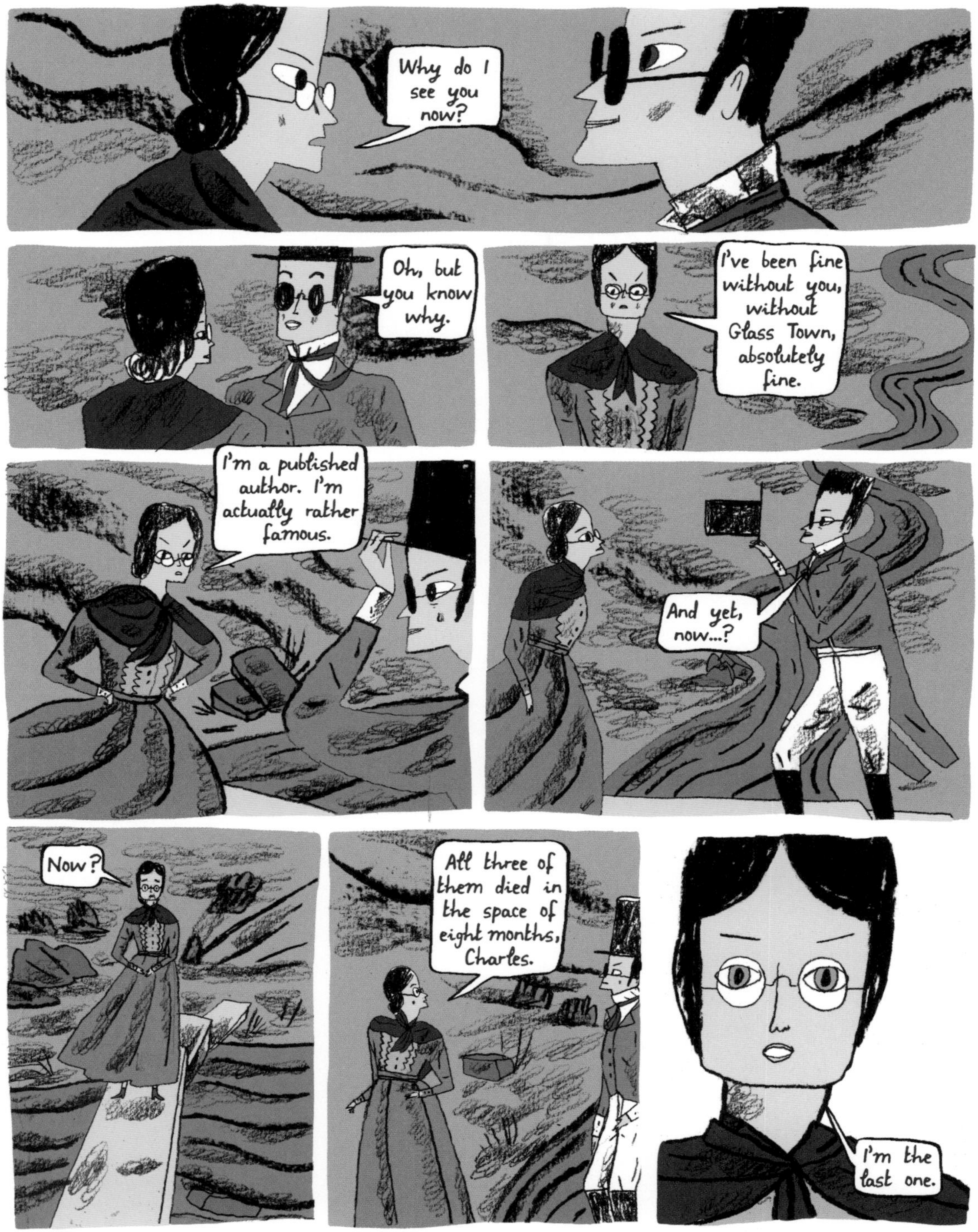
Why do I see you now?
Oh, but you know why.
I've been fine without you, without Glass Town, absolutely fine.
I'm a published author. I'm actually rather famous.
And yet, now...?
Now?
All three of them died in the space of eight months, Charles.
I'm the last one.

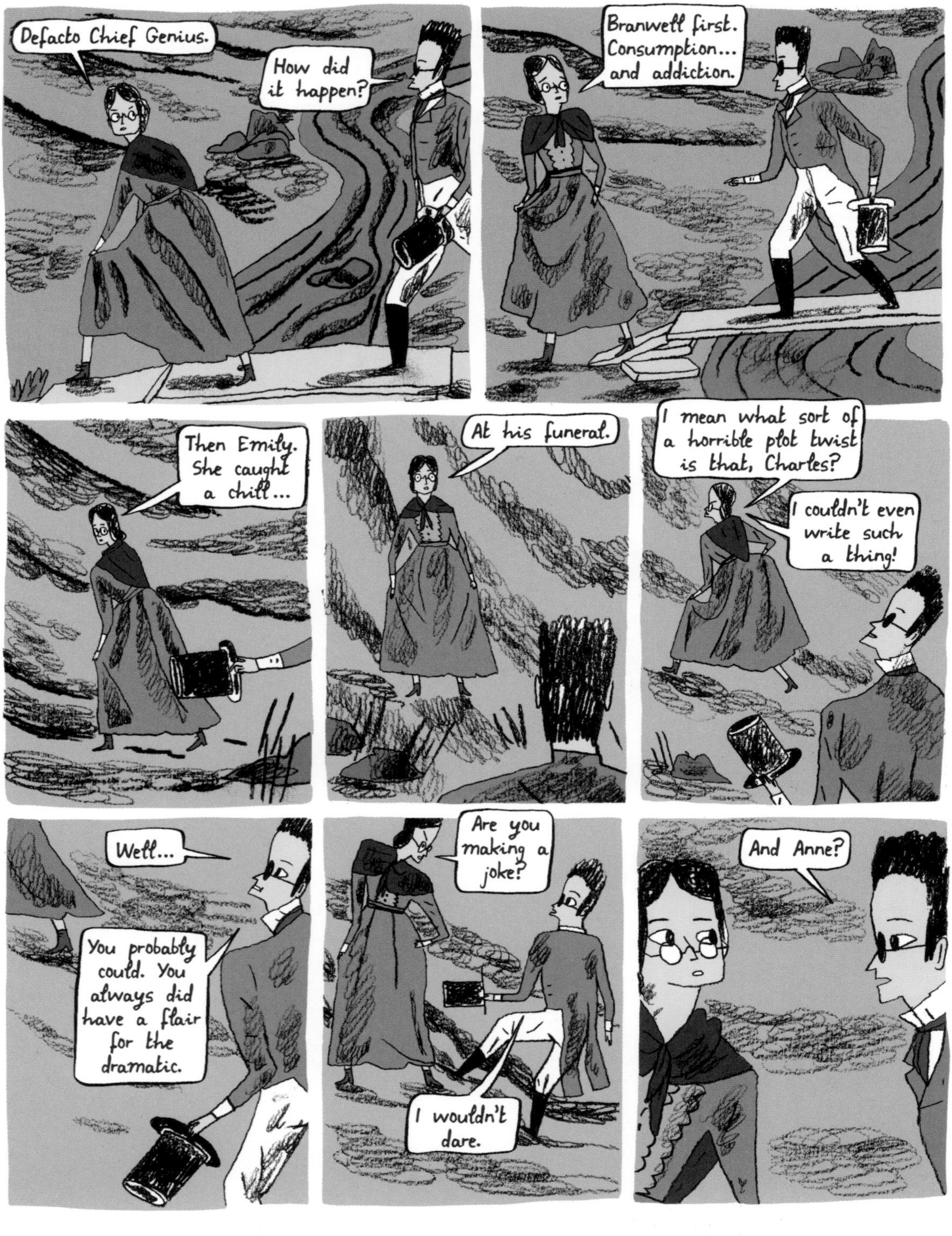
Defacto Chief Genius.
How did it happen?
Branwell first. Consumption... and addiction.
Then Emily. She caught a chill...
At his funeral.
I mean what sort of a horrible plot twist is that, Charles?
I couldn't even write such a thing!
Well...
You probably could. You always did have a flair for the dramatic.
Are you making a joke?
I wouldn't dare.
And Anne?

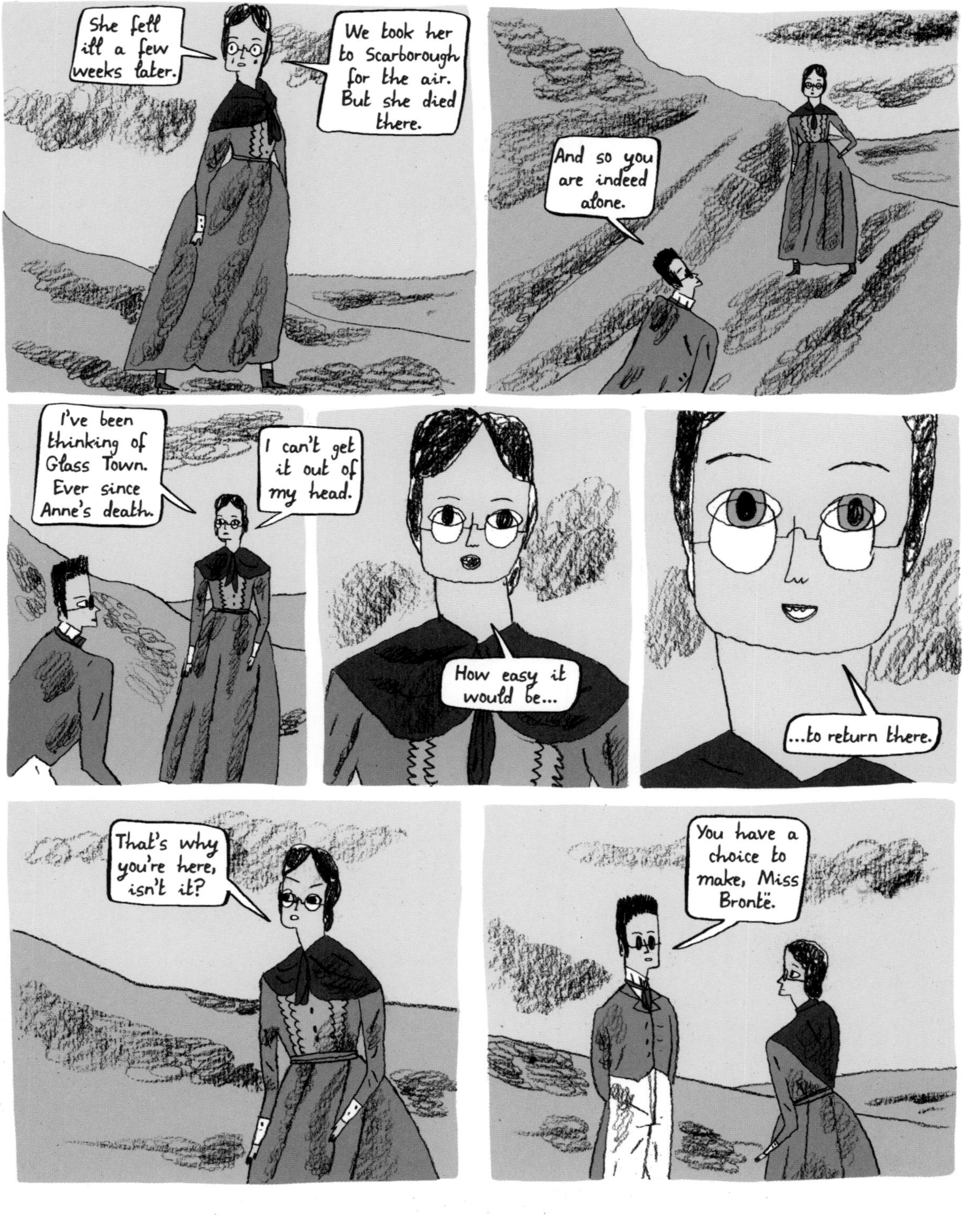
She fell ill a few weeks later.
We took her to Scarborough for the air. But she died there.
And so you are indeed alone.
I've been thinking of Glass Town. Ever since Anne's death.
I can't get it out of my head.
How easy it would be...
...to return there.
That's why you're here, isn't it?
You have a choice to make, Miss Brontë.

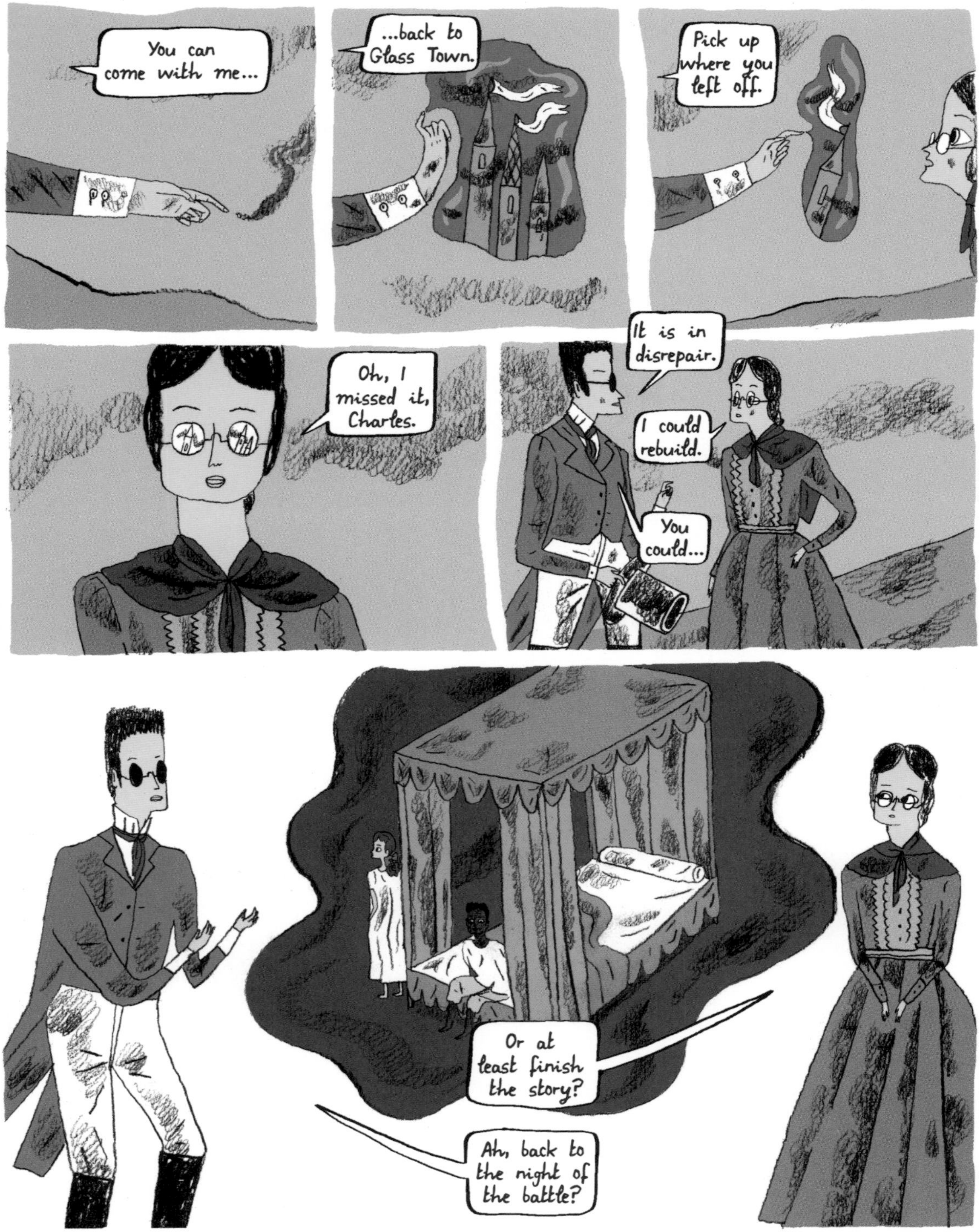
You can come with me...
...back to Glass Town.
Pick up where you left off.
Oh, I missed it, Charles.
It is in disrepair.
I could rebuild.
You could...
Or at least finish the story?
Ah, back to the night of the battle?

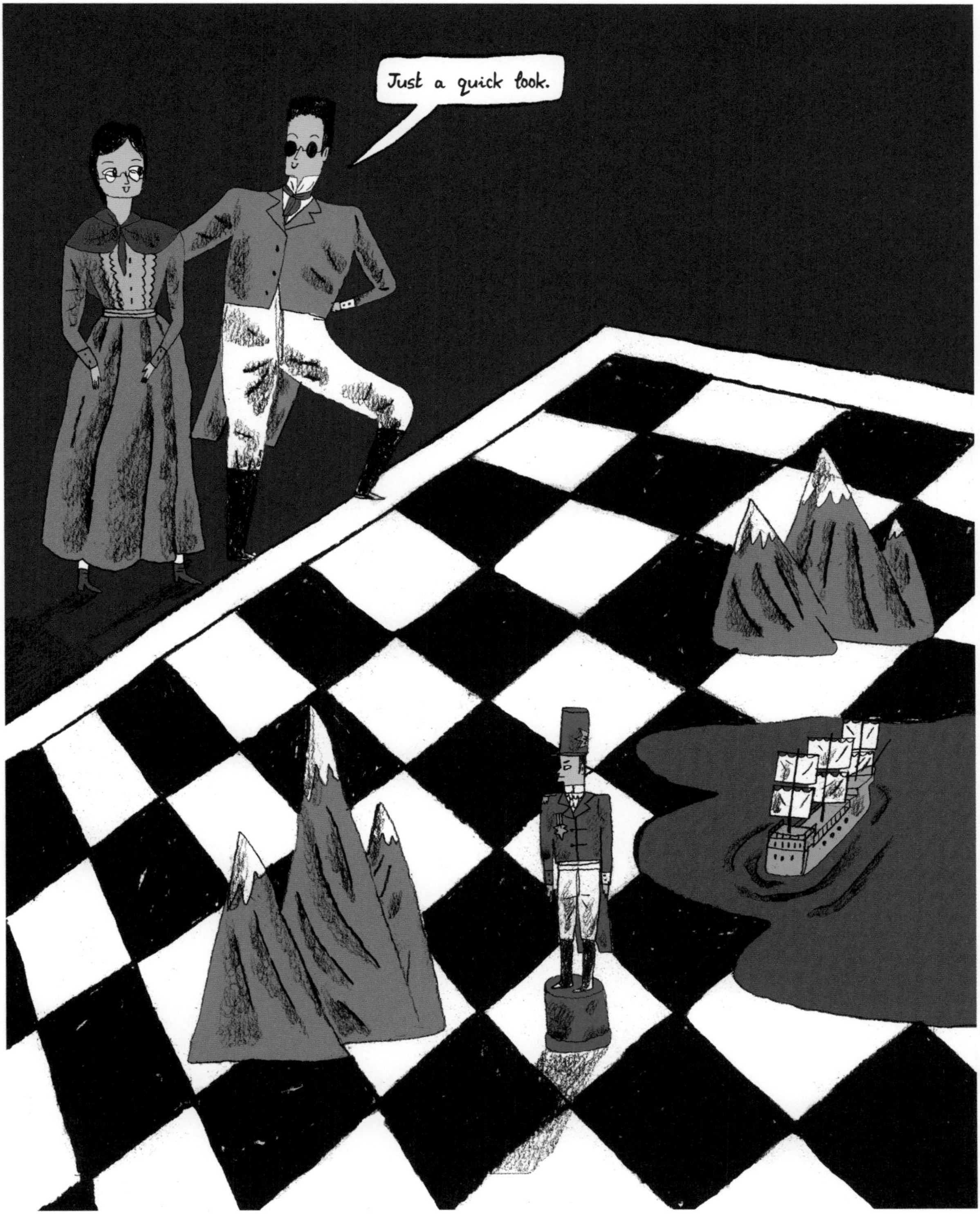
Just a quick look.

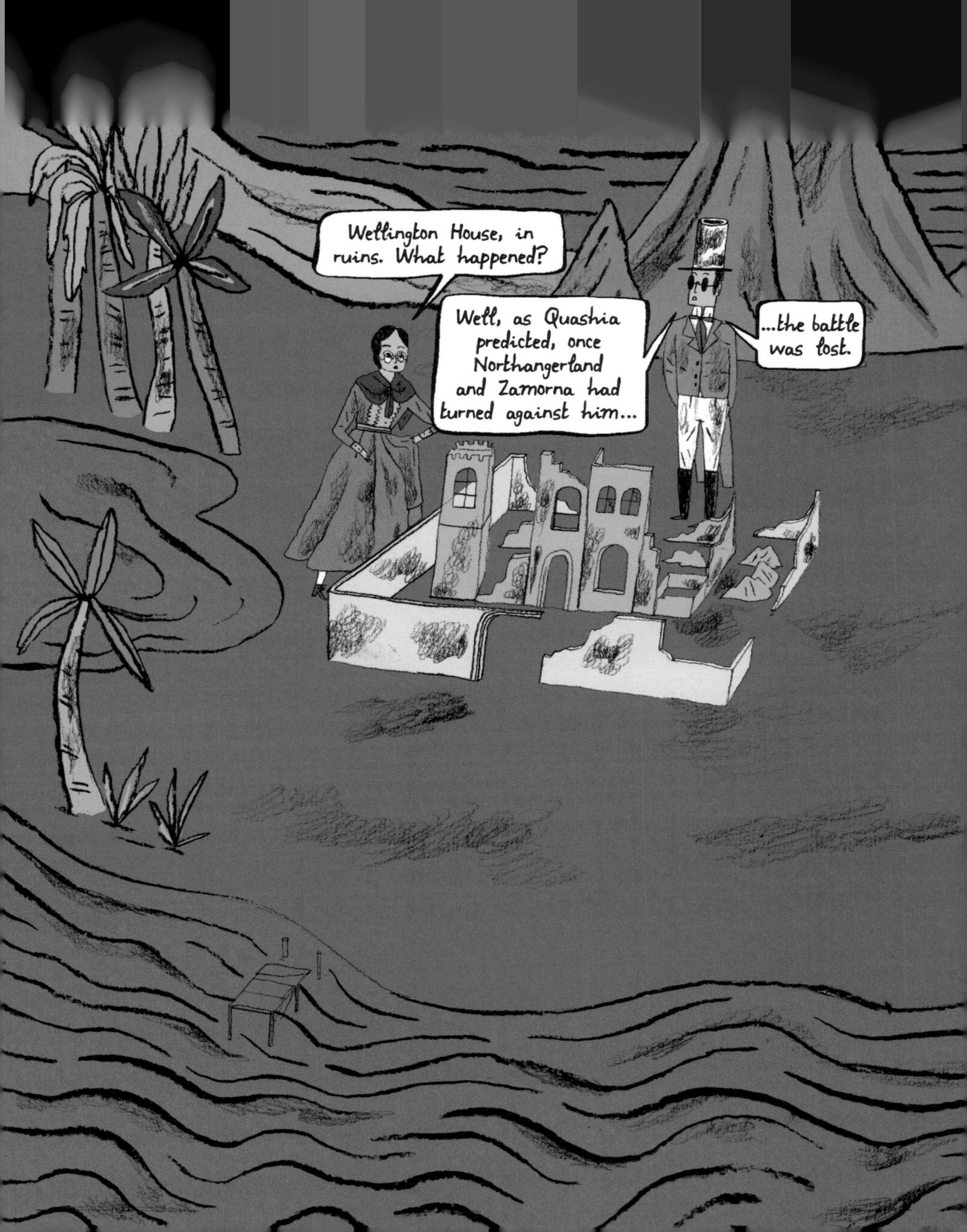
Wellington House, in ruins. What happened?
Well, as Quashia predicted, once Northangerland and Zamorna had turned against him...
...the battle was lost.

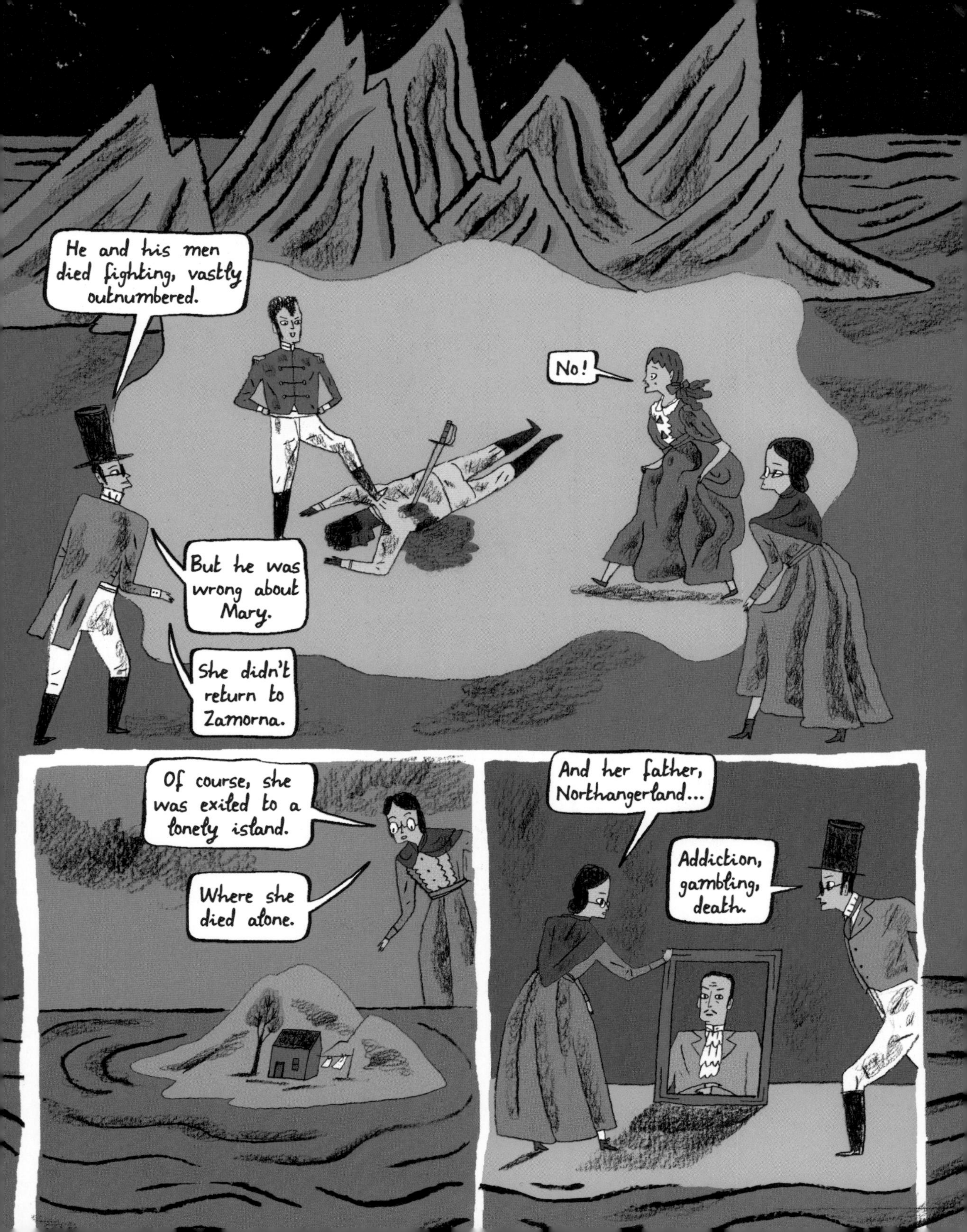
He and his men died fighting, vastly outnumbered.
No!
But he was wrong about Mary.
She didn't return to Zamorna.
Of course, she was exiled to a lonely island.
Where she died alone.
And her father, Northangerland...
Addiction, gambling, death.

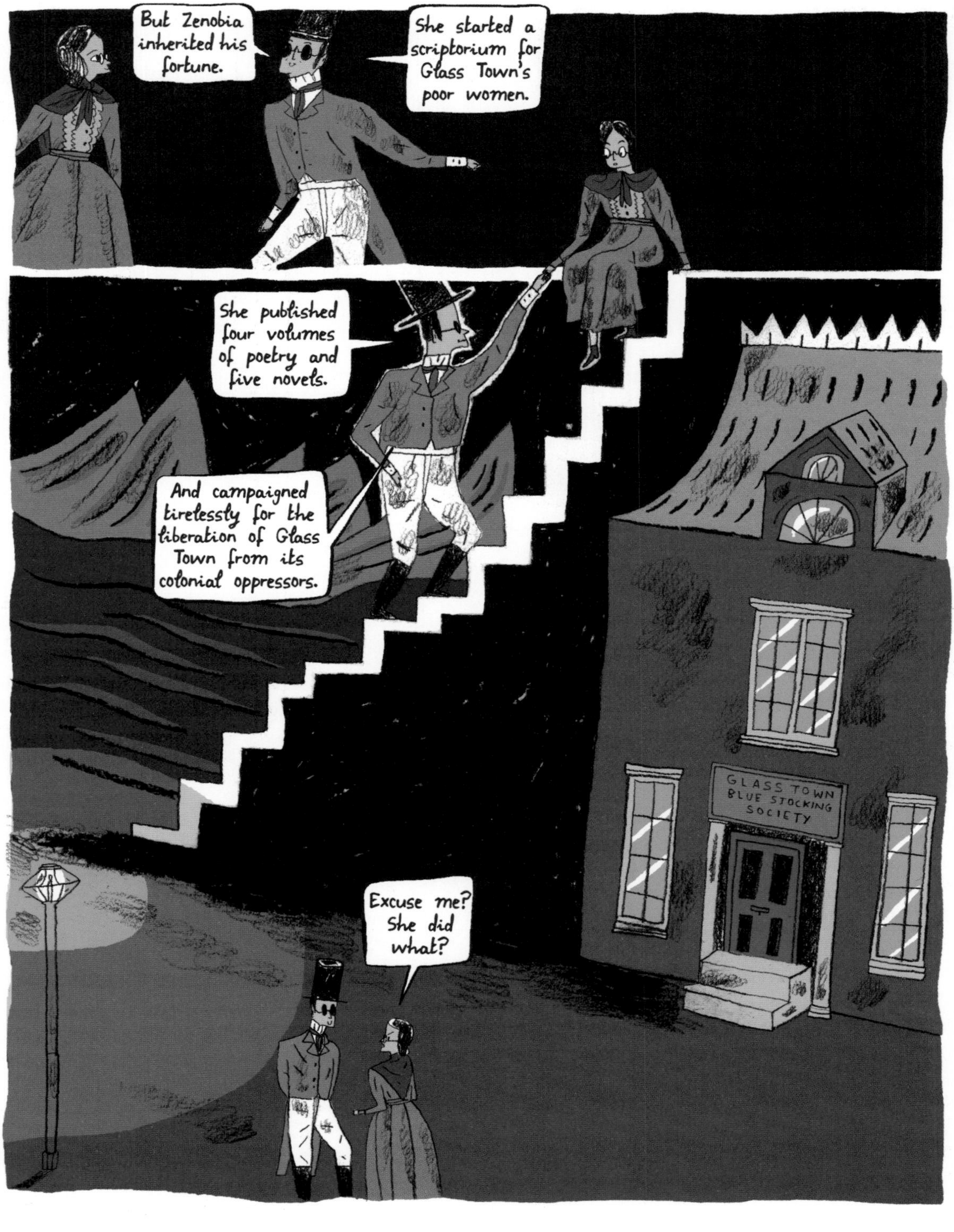
But Zenobia inherited his fortune.
She started a scriptorium for Glass Town's poor women.
She published four volumes of poetry and five novels.
And campaigned tirelessly for the liberation of Glass Town from its colonial oppressors.
GLASS TOWN BLUE STOCKING SOCIETY
Excuse me? She did what?

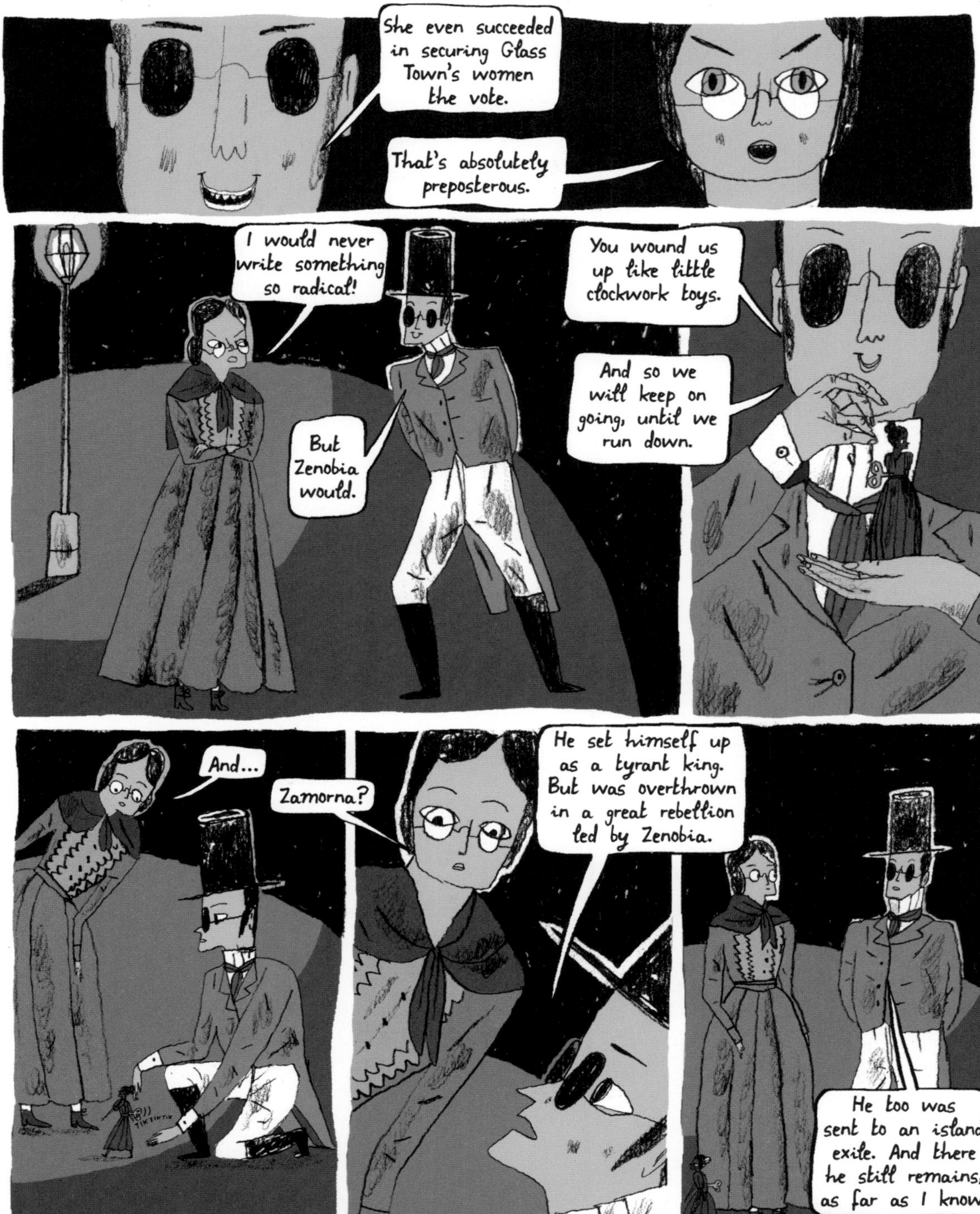
She even succeeded in securing Glass Town's women the vote.
That's absolutely preposterous.
I would never write something so radical!
But Zenobia would.
You wound us up like little clockwork toys.
And so we will keep on going, until we run down.
And...
Zamorna?
He set himself up as a tyrant king. But was overthrown in a great rebellion led by Zenobia.
He too was sent to an island exile. And there he still remains, as far as I know.

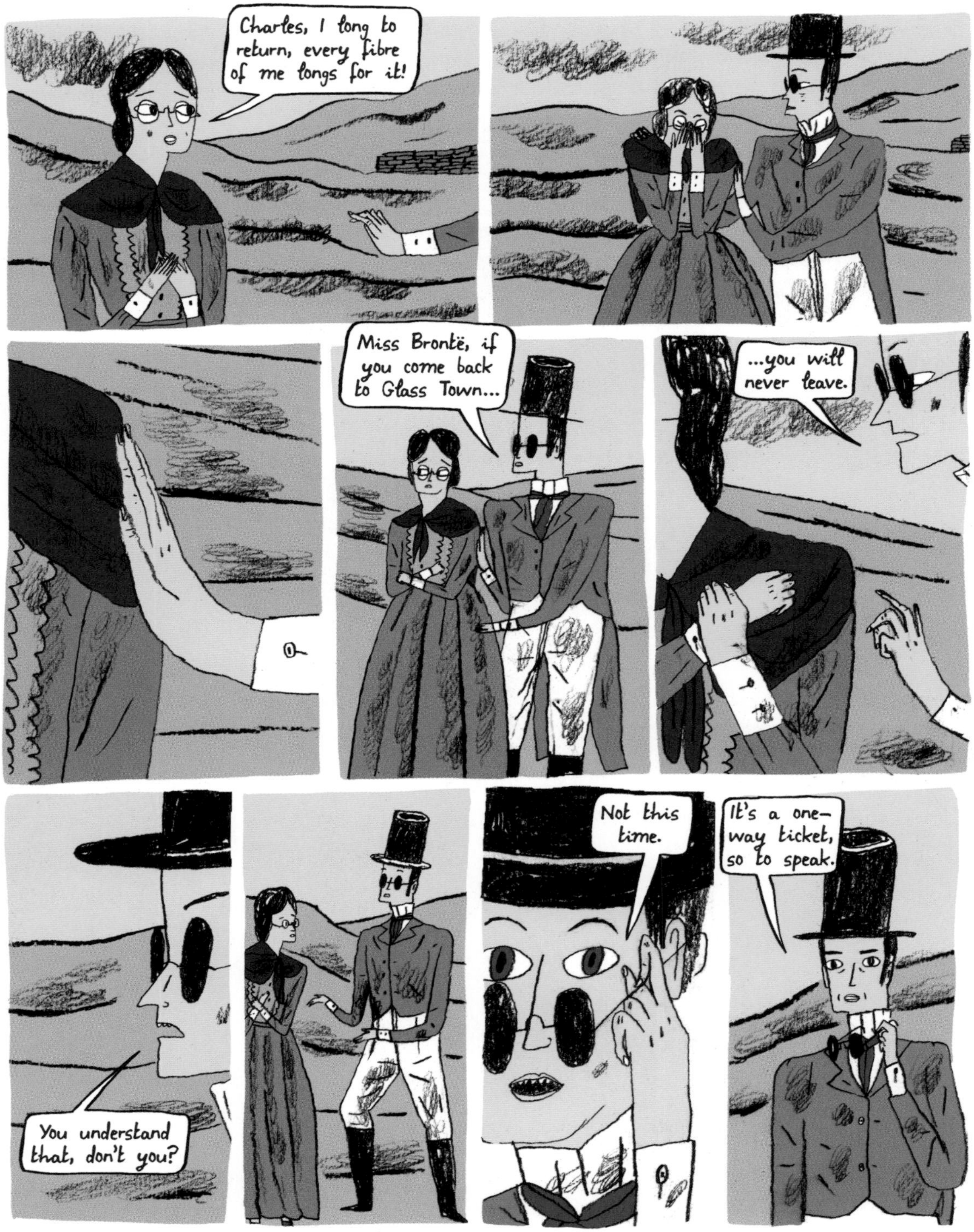
Charles, I long to return, every fibre of me longs for it!
Miss Brontë, if you come back to Glass Town...
...you will never leave.
You understand that, don't you?
Not this time.
It's a one-way ticket, so to speak.

What will happen to Glass Town, if I abandon it now?

The players will wind down.

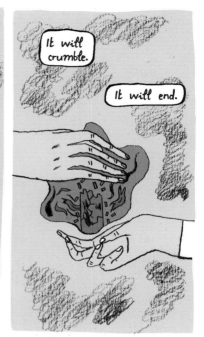

It will crumble.

It will end.

But some things cannot be made alive again.

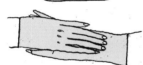

And nor should they be.

I know.

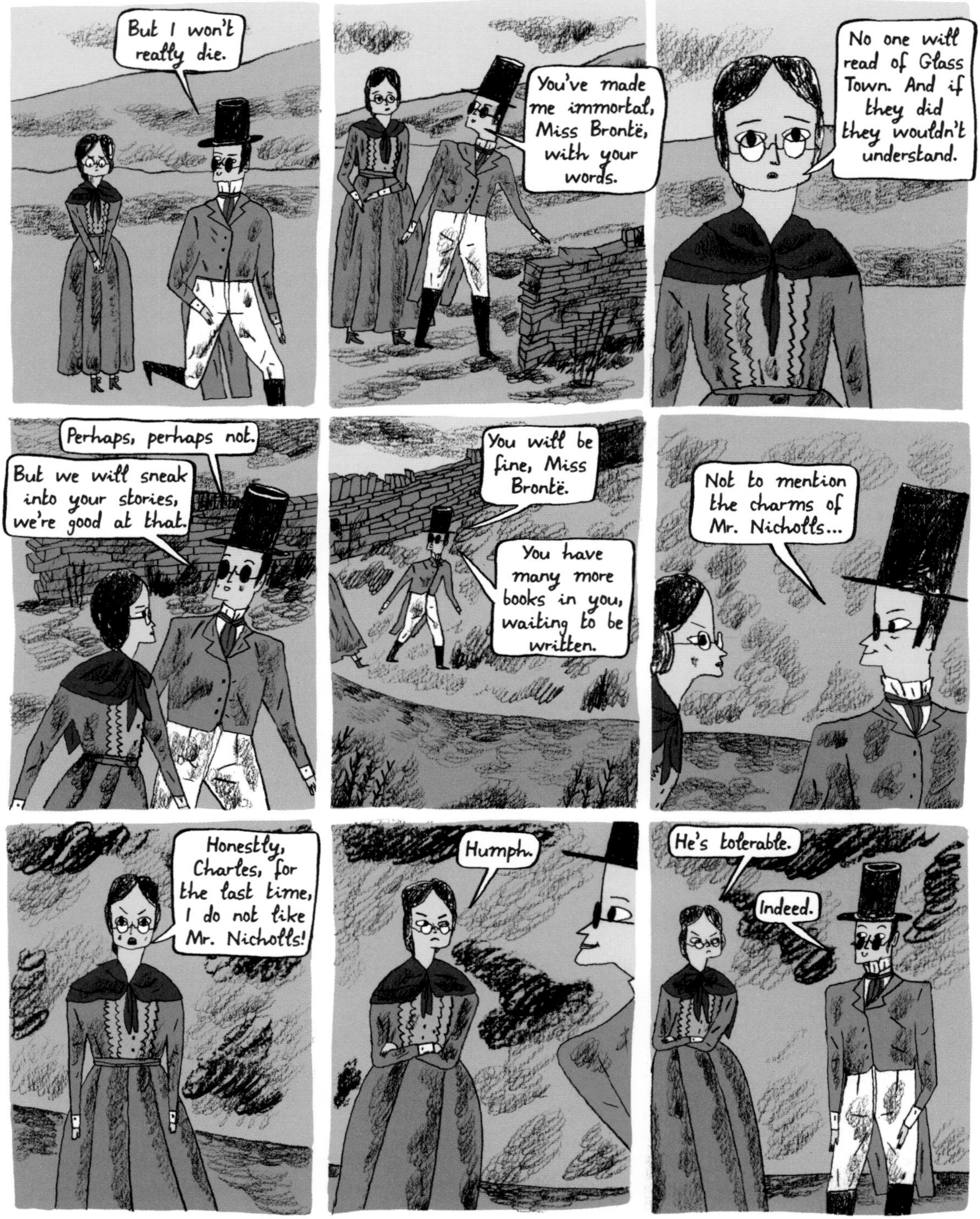
But I won't really die.
You've made me immortal, Miss Brontë, with your words.
No one will read of Glass Town. And if they did they wouldn't understand.
Perhaps, perhaps not.
But we will sneak into your stories, we're good at that.
You will be fine, Miss Brontë.
You have many more books in you, waiting to be written.
Not to mention the charms of Mr. Nicholls...
Honestly, Charles, for the last time, I do not like Mr. Nicholls!
Humph.
He's tolerable.
Indeed.

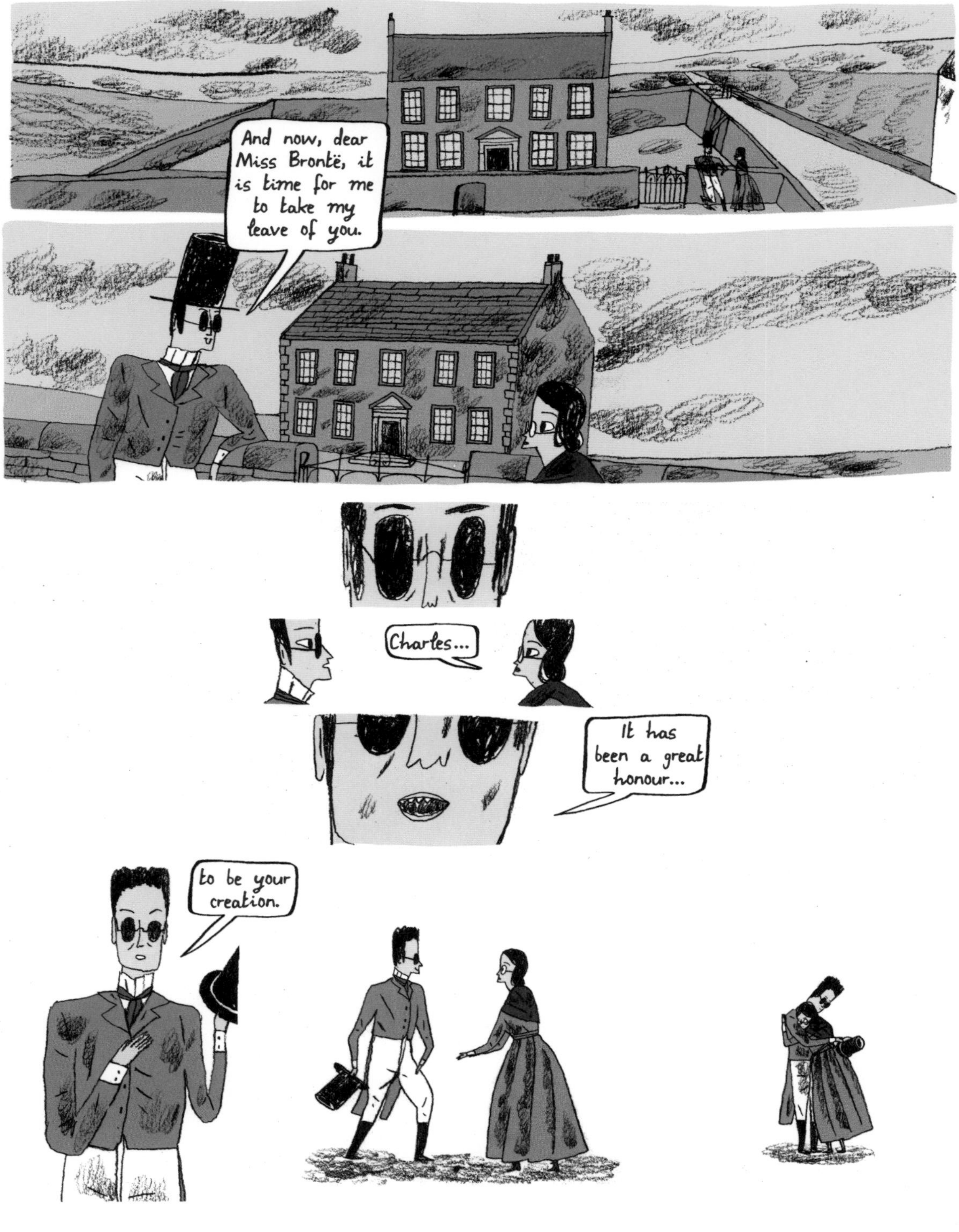
And now, dear Miss Brontë, it is time for me to take my leave of you.
Charles...
It has been a great honour...
to be your creation.

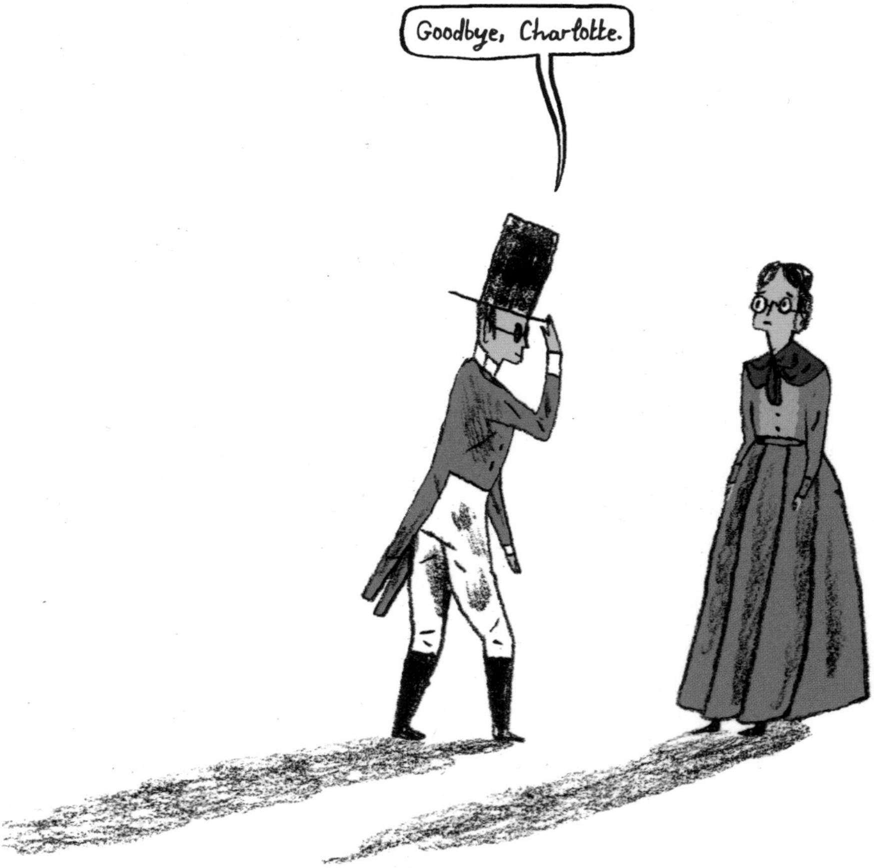
Goodbye, Charlotte.

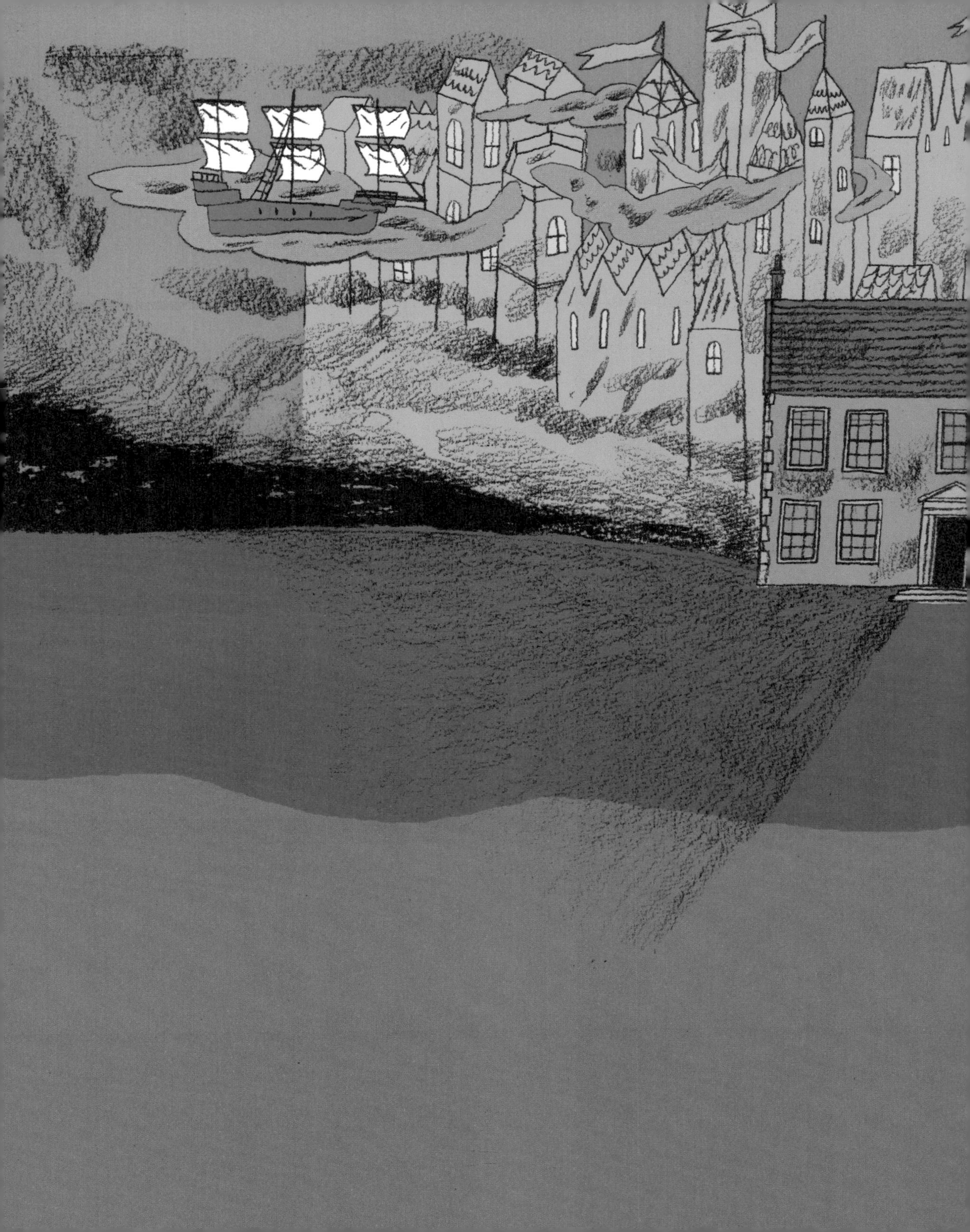

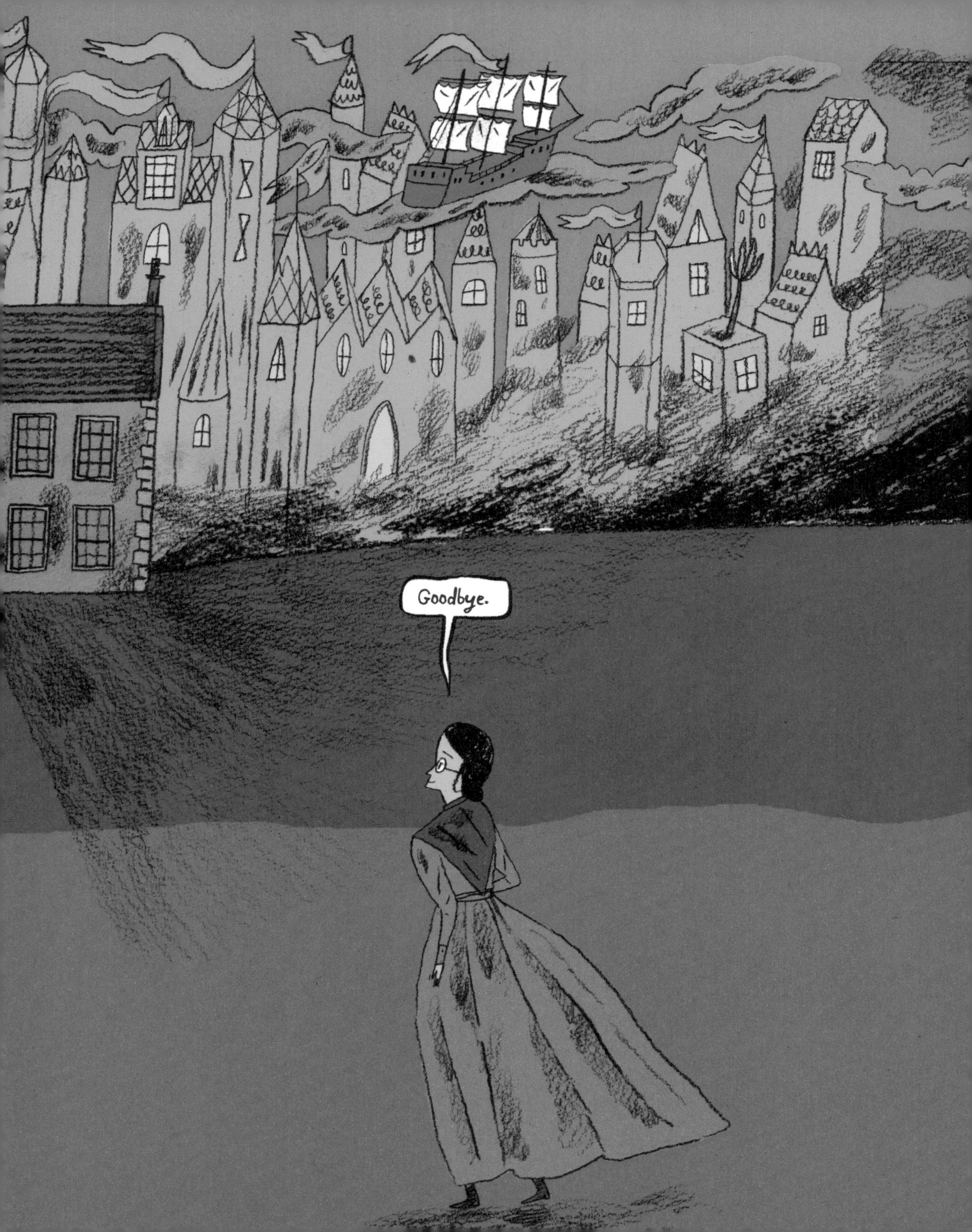
Goodbye.

Afterword

The Brontë sisters—Charlotte, Emily, and Anne—between them wrote some of the most famous works of fiction in the English language: Jane Eyre, Villette, Shirley, Wuthering Heights, The Tenent of Wildfell Hall, and Agnes Grey.

Charlotte outlived her sisters and brother, and went on to publish a further two novels. She married Arthur Bell Nicholls, but died from complications of pregnancy at age 38.

If you have enjoyed this book, I would encourage you to read the actual work of the Brontës (if you haven't already), and to seek out the works of the juvenilia for yourself. Although much of Charlotte's and Branwell's early writing remains, Emily's and Anne's, but for poetry, is all but lost. So we may never really know the mysteries of Gondal. Perhaps that's how they would have liked it, though.

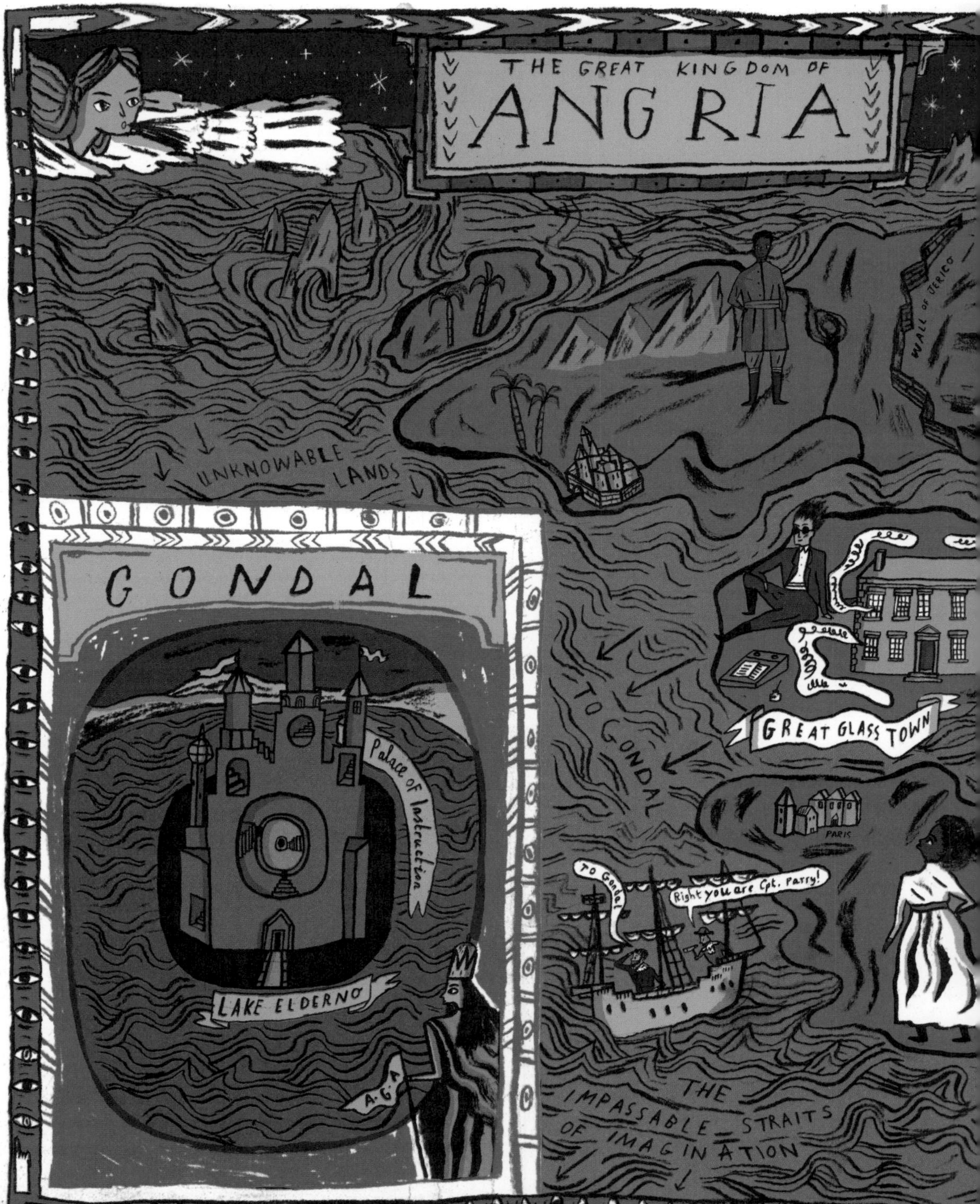
THE GREAT KINGDOM OF
ANGRIA
WALL OF JERICO
UNKNOWABLE LANDS
GONDAL
Palace of Instruction
LAKE ELDERNO
A.G.A
TO GONDAL
GREAT GLASS TOWN
PARIS
To Gondal
Right you are Cpt. Parry!
THE IMPASSABLE STRAITS OF IMAGINATION

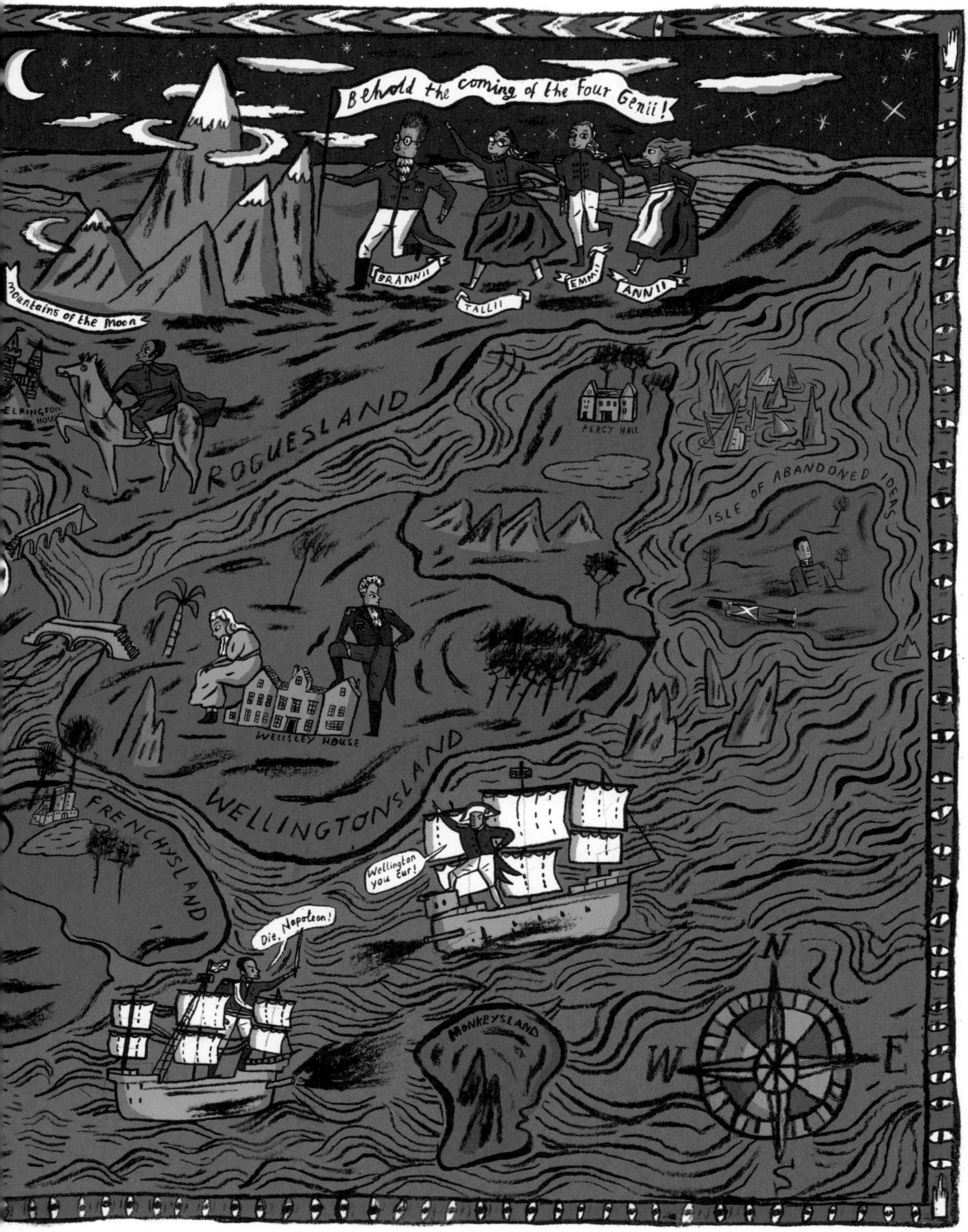
Behold the coming of the Four Genii!
BRANNII
TALLII
EMMII
ANNII
mountains of the moon
ROGUESLAND
PERCY HALL
ISLE OF ABANDONED IDEAS
WELLESLEY HOUSE
WELLINGTONSLAND
FRENCHYSLAND
Wellington you cur!
Die, Napoleon!
MONKEYSLAND
N
W
E
S

ALSO BY ISABEL GREENBERG

The Encyclopedia of Early Earth
The One Hundred Nights of Hero

Huge thank-yous to everyone at Abrams, especially Sam and Pam.
Thank you to my agent, Seth Fishman, and to Caspian Denis.
Thank you to Imogen Greenberg, Alexis Deacon, Rosa Campbell and Gordon Wallace for reading this book in its various stages of completion.
And to parents, friends, family, et cetera.

Editor: Samantha Weiner
Designer: Pamela Notarantonio
Managing Editor: Lisa Silverman
Production Manager: Erin Vandeveer

Cataloging-in-Publication Data has been applied for and may be obtained from the Library of Congress.

ISBN: 978-1-4197-3268-3

Published in 2020 by Abrams ComicArts®, an imprint of ABRAMS.

Printed and bound in China
10 9 8 7 6 5 4 3 2 1

Abrams ComicArts books are available at special discounts when purchased in quantity for premiums and promotions as well as fundraising or educational use. Special editions can also be created to specification. For details, contact specialsales@abramsbooks.com or the address below.

Abrams ComicArts® is a registered trademark of Harry N. Abrams, Inc.

ABRAMS The Art of Books
195 Broadway, New York, NY 10007
abramsbooks.com

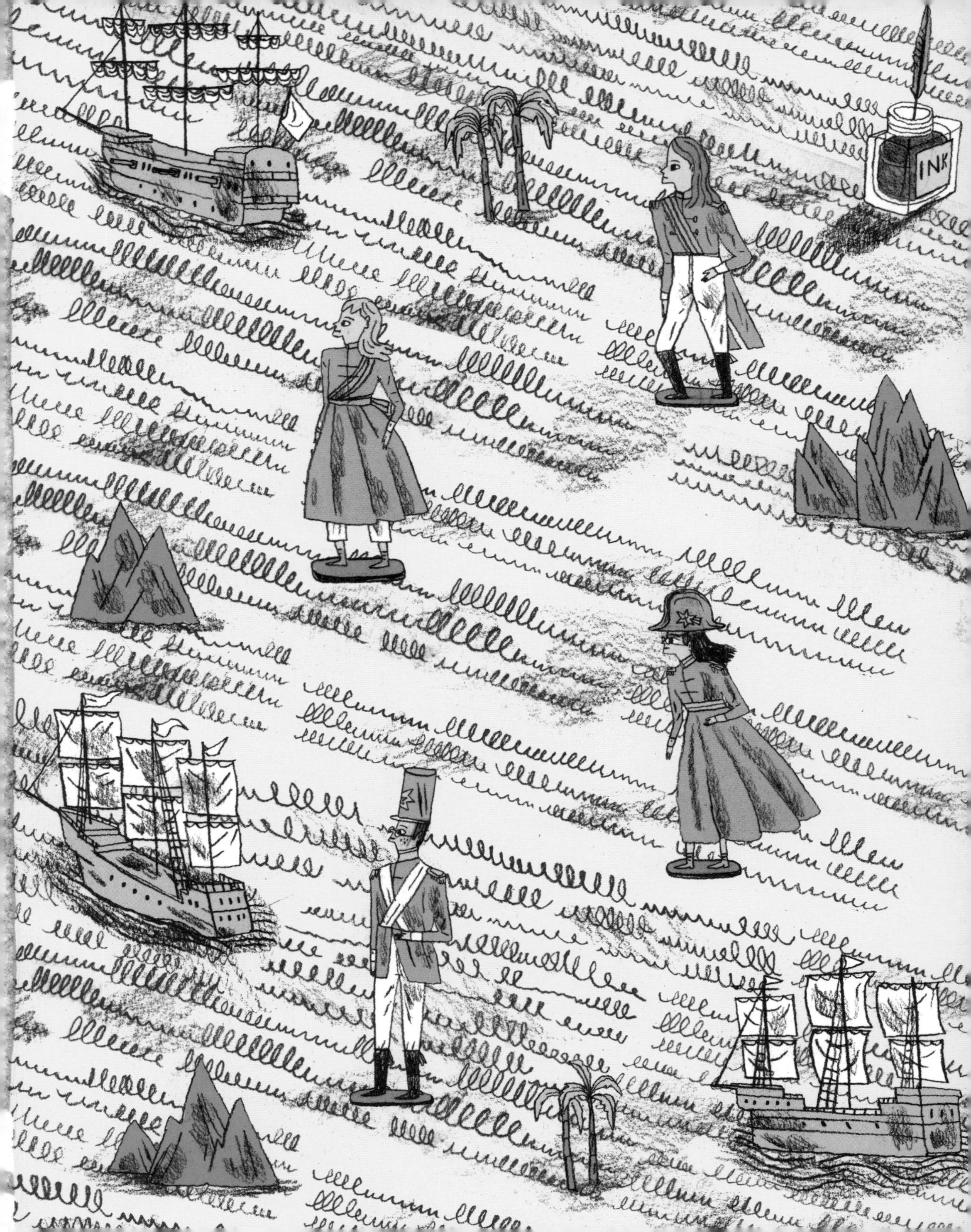
INK

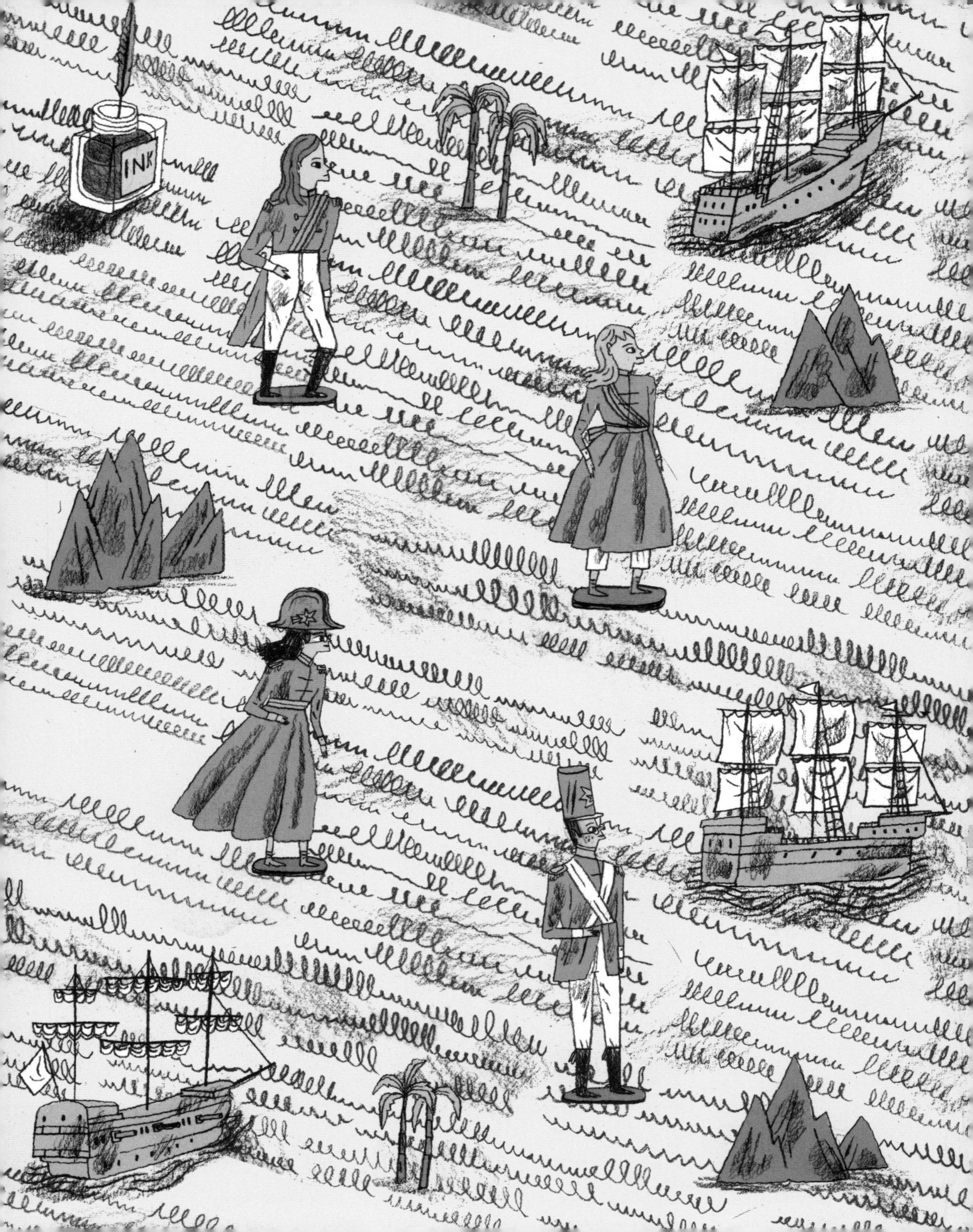
INK